HELPING YOU[R CHILD]

WHEN MEALTIMES ARE HARD

LOVING SUPPORT FOR ANXIOUS EATING, WEIGHT AND NUTRITION WORRIES,
and
EVERYTHING IN BETWEEN

KATJA ROWELL, MD
THE FEEDING DOCTOR

ISBN-13: 979-8320315188

First Edition

Published by Family Feeding Dynamics, LLC Wenatchee, WA

Book Design: Stephanie Larson

Disclaimers and Terms of Use

Privacy

To protect the privacy of the children and their families who have generously consented to share their experiences for this book, I have changed identifying details. To illustrate a point or further protect a family's identity, an anecdote or quote may be a composite of one or more family's experiences. Direct quotes from identified individuals, online, or comments on my social media are shared with permission.

Financial and Conflict of Interest

I receive royalties for *Helping Your Child with Extreme Picky Eating* (Rowell and McGlothlin, New Harbinger Publications) as well as for *Conquer Picky Eating*, a workbook for teens and adults (McGlothlin and Rowell) and *Love Me, Feed Me: the Foster and Adoptive Parent's Guide to Responsive Feeding.* (**THIS BOOK IS ADAPTED FROM** *LOVE ME, FEED ME* FOR THE GENERAL POPULATION, WITH SUBSTANTIAL IDENTICAL CONTENT.) Otherwise, I receive no financial reward from any books or products mentioned in this text.

Medical Disclaimer

This book and the information it contains are provided for educational purposes only. This book is not intended to replace careful observation, evaluation, diagnosis, or ongoing medical or nutritional care for a child or youth, and the text of this book should not be used in place of such. I have provided general information and cannot make any assurances regarding the applicability of any information to any particular person in any particular set of circumstances. The reader assumes all risk of taking any action based on the information contained in this book. I shall have no liability or responsibility for any such action taken or decision made by any reader of this book, and no liability for any loss, injury, damage, or impairment allegedly arising from the information provided in this book.

Responsive Support for All

This book strives to present weight-neutral and body-affirming support; and seeks to offer neurodiversity-affirming information.

Health Is Not an Obligation

While we want our children to be as healthy and happy as they can be, and this book supports that goal, the idea of "health" is complicated. As speaker, writer, and activist Ragen Chastain wrote, "Health is not an obligation, barometer of worthiness, completely within our control, or guaranteed under any circumstance."[1]

Care for the Reader

This book covers challenging topics including bullying, eating disorders, and weight. It might bring up painful or triggering memories. If there are topics that are difficult, therapy with a professional could help to process your experiences in a safe and supportive way. Additionally, there are online peer and lived-experience support communities. This book may also offer you some understanding and healing of your own journey with food and your relationship with your body.

Language

I try to approach my work from what author, scholar, and activist bell hooks called an "ethic of love." I strive to use inclusive and respectful language, listening to individuals with lived experience, and recognizing that language and meaning evolve. I use neutral descriptors such as "fat," "bigger body," or "smaller-than-average" to describe bodies when necessary. "Obese" or "underweight" appear in quotations when it is a direct quote. You will see o*erweight and o*ese with an * as a reminder that these terms harm. (Chapter 7 has more on weight bias.) It's jarring visually, but weight bias causes too much harm to do things the usual way.

Table of Contents

Introduction:
A New Path Begins Here

Worry and conflict about food, nutrition, and growth are common. You are not alone. Parents and caregivers put in time and energy trying to raise healthy and happy kids, but much of the advice out there when it comes to feeding your child backfires.

This book will offer practical support and reassurance whether you're hoping to set a healthy foundation with eating, dealing with typical challenges, or struggling with complex concerns.

The approach you'll learn about responds to you and your children's needs, with special attention to supporting children with sensory differences, children who are neurodivergent, may have a history of medical trauma, brain-based differences, or have other challenges that impact eating.

The Focus Is *How* to Feed

The focus of this book is on *how* you can support a healthy feeding relationship, which is essential regardless of *what* you feed your family. As one parent said, *"I was dreading another lecture about vegetables. What a relief!"* You won't find calorie or portion recommendations; plenty of other resources provide those, and in my opinion, most are not helpful.

I aim to relieve the confusion, worry, and sense of failure about what your kids are (or aren't) eating. *How* you feed matters as much as, or more than, the what.

> **The terms "feeding" and "feeding relationship" cover everything that happens between parents and children around food and mealtimes.**

I'm not saying that nutrition doesn't matter. It is important. *What* you put on the table is personal—with cultural and financial factors in the mix. A responsive approach helps children feel calm and connected, and better able to experience joy and curiosity at eating times—which supports improved nutrition over time. Responsive feeding helps you enjoy your children more, and dread mealtimes less.

Responsive Feeding

Responsive feeding (RF) is increasingly supported by research and promoted by the American Academy of Pediatrics and the World Health Organization (WHO).[1,2]

"Responsive" feeding focuses on a caring adult observing, adjusting, and accommodating based on the child's needs (could think of this as attunement). Researcher Maureen Black wrote, "Responsive feeding promotes children's attentiveness and interest in feeding, attention to their internal cues of hunger and satiety. . . "[3]

It's not your job to get your child to eat more, less, or different foods. One mom at a workshop said, *"This is my ah-ha moment. You're saying I don't have to control how much he eats; that it's his job. This feels so good."* While you might still worry about it for a while, how much they eat is not up to you. You can't control it. The more you try to make kids eat a certain way, the worse things usually get.

I'm part of a responsive feeding therapy (RFT) "movement" along with dietitians, speech pathologists, occupational therapists, eating disorder specialists, psychotherapists, PhDs, and feeding researchers. Here is part of the working definition: Responsive feeding therapy facilitates the (re)discovery of internal cues, curiosity, and motivation, while building skills and confidence. It is flexible, prioritizes the feeding relationship, and respects and develops autonomy.[4]

I Know How Feeding Struggles Feel

As a family doctor, I saw the physical and emotional burden patients dealt with due to struggling with food and their bodies. I counseled parents and children when the child was o*erweight, and nagged and cheered adults. But that weight-centered approach—based on the idea that higher weight is always harmful, and that losing weight always helps—was wrong. And it felt awful.

I didn't know then that trying to lose weight and keep it off fails about 95 percent of the time. (The evidence for diets failing is as strong as the link between smoking and lung cancer.)[5] I thought my patients just weren't doing what I recommended. Ack!

When my daughter was born, a dose of humility came home with us from the hospital. It shook my identity as a mother and doctor. I'd been giving feeding advice but *wasn't trained to do so*. I knew roughly *what* I was supposed to feed her, but not *how*. By 14 or so months, with us following standard guidance, my daughter was food-preoccupied—therefore, so was I. My anxiety spoiled our time together. *I* needed to learn how to raise a healthy, happy child.

Then I stumbled on the work of childhood feeding expert Ellyn Satter. Within a few weeks of letting my daughter decide how much to eat at predictable meal and snack times, her inborn capabilities with eating began emerging: She enjoyed meals, wasn't constantly seeking food, and was happier. I left most of the worry behind, stopped trying to control her weight, and felt more confident. My daughter and I enjoyed each other more fully.

I *had* to learn more. I read widely about weight, growth, and feeding. I attended conferences on feeding therapies for children with sensory-motor challenges; read books and papers about child development, intuitive eating, eating disorders, trauma, and binge eating; and I learned from and collaborated with colleagues from different specialties. Since then my work has been devoted to helping parents struggling with feeding and weight concerns, and eventually, training other professionals.

It is gratifying to see children and parents get on a better path with food, and able to relax and enjoy each another more fully. **Helping a child grow up to have as healthy a relationship with food and their body as possible is powerful medicine.**

More than one parent has told me along the lines of, *"If our story can help someone, it will mean so much."* Parents say that support from other parents is powerful, so I've included their words in italics throughout. By sharing their experiences, I hope to inspire you and help you gain confidence that responsive feeding can help your family too.

How to Use This Book

You don't have to read the whole book (it's big!). I've tried to touch on most of the topics that have come up with clients over the years. If you're experiencing typical food battles, I suggest you read from beginning to end; **skim headings to guide you.** General ideas such as serving family style and "modified" meals will appear in the chapters on responsive feeding (3 and 4), while Chapters 5, 6, and 7 focus on selective eating and food preoccupation.

With responsive feeding, you can feed children who are big or small, anxious eaters, food-preoccupied, or with sensory differences with the same underlying framework. You don't have to worry that something you learn to support an avoidant eater will hurt a food-preoccupied child.

If you're in crisis, start with Chapters 1 through 3, then use the table of contents or the index to find relevant information; skim headings, and learn as much as you can. Come back later and fill in the pieces. You may also want to share this book with family and childcare providers.

Start a simple journal now. It will help you look for patterns and track progress. Use a notebook/tablet to keep your thoughts and observations accessible. Pay attention to *your* worries and emotional triggers, as well as how mealtimes are going. Look for patterns if you've had a particularly challenging episode or a good day with food.

Much of this book is adapted from my book *Love Me, Feed Me: the Foster and Adoptive Parent's Guide to Responsive Feeding*. This book contains additional interviews and removes content specific to fostering and adoption.

What You Will Learn

Part I, "What Are You Worried About? Dealing with the Big Challenges," will help you understand the *why* and what to *do*.

This foundation of understanding (though tempting to skip) will help you handle day-to-day challenges. You'll be less likely to fall back on temporary, but counterproductive patterns.

You'll start with:

- An introduction to the Worry Cycle, common worries and misperceptions, and how families get stuck. (Chapter 1)
- Why felt safety matters for nutrition and health. (Chapter 2)
- Implementing responsive feeding. (Chapters 3 and 4)

Part I then takes a deeper dive into the main areas of concern, including:

- Typical picky eating and power struggles. (Chapter 5)
- Low weight worries, avoidant/anxious eating, including oral-motor and sensory concerns. (Chapter 6)
- Food seeking and preoccupation, concerns about weight gain, and caring for higher-weight kids. (Chapter 7)

Part II, "Filling in the Gaps: Common Pitfalls and Navigating Healing" (Chapters 8–12), covers topics ranging from eating disorders to how our thin-obsessed culture makes it all harder, and how to help children access hunger and fullness cues (interoception). Chapter 11, "Nutrition Worries and What to Serve" considers special diets and allergies, and aims to reassure and educate about common nutrition worries including protein and sugar. Chapter 12, "Your Role and Wrapping Things Up," examines how you were fed as a child and how it impacts how you feed your children, as well as a check-in on what you've learned.

There is some repetition of ideas. For example, if you're struggling with picky/avoidant eating, the sections on power struggles, sensory-motor, and "underweight" may all be relevant.

Take notes in the margins, observe what feels good—and what doesn't— for *your* family. Reflect:

- Does a story remind you of your child or another child you know? *"My niece begs for food all day, my sister is constantly trying to get her to eat less."*
- What resonates? *"I was forced to eat yams, and I still won't touch them."*
- Are there stories or tips from parents that give you hope?
- Note what make you skeptical or uncomfortable. *"If we serve dessert with the meal, he'll never eat a vegetable."*
- Anything that makes you say, "Yes!" or "Aha!"

What's Important Now (WIN)

We want children to enjoy good nutrition, and the concept of WIN may help you decide what to attend to first. The answer to *What's Important Now* will almost always be *to prioritize helping children feel calm and safe, and their connection with caring adults.*

During a workshop Q and A, a dietitian shared that the idea of What's Important Now particularly resonated for fathers, military, and first-responders, whom she observed wanted to jump in and fix things fast.

Considering your goals and what to prioritize (WIN) will guide feeding choices. You may be thinking something like: *"I want Sam to eat more vegetables,"* or *"Lilly needs to learn portion control so she'll lose weight,"* or *"Tanya is so small. I have to get her to eat more protein."* And you probably also want to stop worrying and fighting about food and enjoy a deeper connection with your child.

That goal of feeling more connected to your child isn't secondary. As I wrote with my coauthors in the *Journal for Nutrition Education and Behavior,* ". . . harmony, love, and connection are more important than vegetables and are likely to help with the long-term goal of raising a child who enjoys eating them."[6]

It's Not Your Fault

This book isn't about pointing fingers. I've been there with feeding and nutrition worries, and made feeding "mistakes." Most families I've worked with have struggled for months or years. Well-meaning (and untrained) professionals may offer unhelpful advice. (I'm sorry to admit I was one them.)

Trying to get kids to eat more or less makes their eating worse and makes them less calm, more dysregulated, and even ashamed. Non-responsive feeding is a barrier to connection. This understanding is foundational as you transition to responsive feeding.

And while feeding children well is a lot of effort, and may feel revolutionary (hello, dessert *with* dinner), the payoff is worth it. Adina's mom Rebecca said, *"That burden of having to constantly try to get her to eat less is lifted. It's such a relief, I can't even describe it."* Lean into that relief.

While it's not your fault that you're struggling, you'll see that you are key to helping transform mealtimes and shape your child's relationship to food and their bodies.

Part 1:

What Are You Worried About? Dealing with the Big Challenges

Chapter 1
Feeding Struggles and the Worries That Fuel Them

Parents are frustrated, battling over bites, confused, trying tips from social media, and buying fancy plates, but things aren't getting better. Understanding where you are now, and *why*, is critical.

> A major goal of this chapter is to reassure you about things you don't need to worry about. Letting go of worries means trusting your child and the process, and fewer battles to control outcomes you can't (and don't need to try to) control.

Most of us were raised by adults who dieted or struggled with body image, and we are raising children in a culture that is messed up around food and bodies. Consider:

- Parents ask their child's physician for help with feeding, but many if not most doctors aren't adequately trained.
- Up to 80 percent of kids with developmental differences will have trouble with eating.[1]
- Early feeding problems correlate with accelerated adolescent weight gain[2] and an increased risk of eating disorders.[3,4]
- Parental worry about o*esity, even in a "normal" weight child, correlates with accelerated adolescent weight gain.[2]
- Parents who pressure or restrict—and the majority of American parents do—tend to have kids who are more picky and more likely to have weight diverge higher or lower.[5,6,7,8]
- Eating disorder diagnoses are on the rise, and in ever-younger children.[9,10,11]
- One in three preschoolers eats no vegetables, and one in four eats no fruit on any given day.[12]
- In one study, two-thirds of teens diet, with half using extreme measures such as vomiting, fasting, and laxatives.[13]
- Roughly half of nine-year-olds wish they were thinner, and about half of the nine-year-old girls in one study said they felt better about themselves when they dieted.[14]
- Roughly one in five children in America is food insecure.

The Worry Cycle Illustrates Counterproductive Feeding

The parents I've worked with generally care a lot about nutrition, shop for and provide nutritious food, and try to eat with their kids. But mealtimes are battles and children are struggling. Parents have compared this to "circling the drain," or a "black hole"—the more effort they put into getting their child to eat "right," the worse things get.

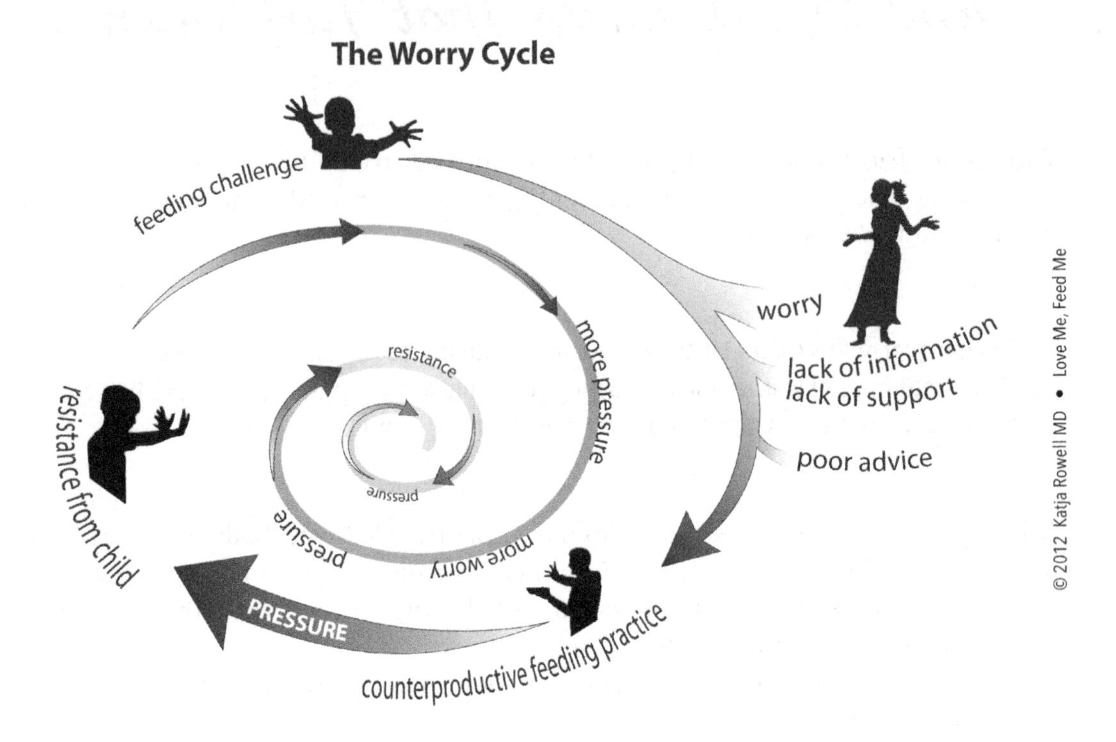

Figure 1.1: The Worry Cycle.

This cycle illustrates this dynamic: The child presents with feeding differences or challenges, and worried, under-supported parents try to get kids to eat more, less, or different foods. Pressure and restriction predictably backfire.

Generally, the harder parents work to get children to eat more, less, or different foods, the worse children eat. Research on this is clear.

I call it the Worry Cycle because worry fuels counterproductive practices. Many parents shared how validating this visual is; how they felt understood. We will briefly tour the cycle, illustrating principles that are expanded on in later chapters.

Importantly, we'll look at worries that fuel the cycle. As you read, consider *your* worries. What do you wish your child did differently with their eating? Would you worry about their eating if they were bigger or smaller? The tour ends with an introduction to counterproductive feeding practices, and why children resist.

I want to be clear that I don't judge the worry, and my goal isn't to stop worry completely (that's not going to happen). My goal is to help you discern where you can let worry go, how worry gets in the way, and later in the book, if there is a cause for concern, what you can do about it.

Challenges a Child Might Bring to the Table

Children may experience a variety of feeding differences or struggles. **Anything that makes (or made early) eating or feeding painful, difficult, scary, or challenging can make a child anxious around food. It makes sense; if something doesn't feel good, humans try to avoid it.** This will be explored more in Chapters 5 and 6, but briefly, it may look like:

- Having a medical or anatomical reason why eating is or was difficult or painful (such as reflux or motor differences).
- Sensory differences.
- A scary episode such as choking, or frequent gagging or vomiting.

What Parents Bring to the Feeding Relationship

You likely have your own goals, and worries if expectations aren't met. You probably get little support, and even unhelpful advice, which can make matters worse (more worry!). The worry prompts unhelpful feeding practices. Here are some reasons why parents try to get kids to eat more, less, or different foods:

- Worry that the child is too big or too small, or will become so. (Weight)
- Worry that the child eats too much or too little. (Appetite)
- Wanting the child to eat more of something specific, such as protein or vegetables. (Nutrition)

These are additional reasons why parents may fall into pressuring and restricting:

- It works in the short term to get in a few more bites.
- To try to support sleep. Parents may encourage the child to finish a bottle or eat more at the last meal of the day so "they don't wake up hungry."
- To save money and try to reduce food or formula waste.
- It's how the parents were fed, so it's what they know.
- It's how others around them feed their children.
- Using food routinely to manage behavior.
- It's recommended by professionals, which includes tactics such as making children eat nonpreferred foods before they can have a preferred food (i.e., "growing food" first) or the ominous, "Do whatever you have to, just get food in."

Take some time to work through the Feeding Legacy exercise on page 308 to bring some clarity to how your childhood plays a role in how you feed your children.

Media Is Designed to Make You Worry

Social media, articles, and podcasts amplify worries. A scary headline hooks you: "Fussy Eater Goes Blind!" Many articles written about eating and weight, even in reputable newspapers and journals, are full of inaccuracies and bias.

Good studies are difficult, and take time and money. Friends or family members will forward articles or videos that warn of the horrors of sugar, or with a new trick to get your child to eat, bumping you into that Worry Cycle. One mom shared that an article about eating more fish threw her off track. *"Fish? He won't even eat chicken. I tried pushing fish sticks. I knew it was wrong, and I knew how much progress we were making, but it just brought up that old anxiety."*

Tune out. Turn it off. Don't click the link or swipe to the story. When you get sucked in, talk yourself down, read the "serenity prayer for feeding" (page 68), or look back at your journals to remind you of where you've been.

Responsive feeding is not the cultural norm for most of us. Be prepared to tune out voices of doubt. Observe your child and family, celebrate successes, and let them give you strength.

Misperceptions Fuel Worry

We'll take a significant pitstop on the Worry Cycle tour to explore misperceptions. **A misperceived problem means seeing a problem where there isn't one; or missing it when there is.** A misperception around growth, for example, can kick families into the Worry Cycle, as in *"They're too small so I have to get them to eat."*

This section will help you decide 1) if you need to worry; and 2) if you can let go of the worry and break free from the cycle. There are major opportunities to reassure and access healing when misperceptions are at play. But your worries need to be addressed first.

The Canadian Pediatric Society (among others) identifies misperceptions as a factor in food refusal (which could look like low appetite, avoidant, or picky eating): "Unrealistic parental expectations may result in unnecessary concern, and inappropriate threats or punishments may aggravate a child's refusal to eat."[15]

Commons misperceptions that fuel counterproductive feeding include:

- Misunderstanding appetite and self-regulation of intake (how much kids eat).
- Misunderstanding the process of learning to eat more variety (related to picky eating).
- Misperceptions and harmful myths around weight and growth.
- Misperceptions around nutrition.

Misperceptions About How Much Kids Eat

Virtually all humans are born with the capacity to self-regulate intake: to eat the amount of food needed to grow in a healthy way. This capacity is reinforced through reliable access to food and responsive feeding, and sabotaged by pressure and restriction.[16] (Other factors impact self-regulation of intake, such as food insecurity, dieting, and poor body image. Look for sections on *interoception.*)

Misunderstandings about self-regulation abound. Standard nutrition education, maybe even the handout from your pediatrician, implies that a child of a certain age or weight should eat certain portion sizes or calories every day. That's not how young children eat (or almost anyone, for that matter).

I worked with the parents of a three year-old first (mis)labeled as "obese" at four months old when she was exclusively breast fed. The pediatrician recommended stopping night-time feeds and making mom wait thirty minutes to breast feed when the child indicated she was hungry. The baby soon became frantic with feeds and seemed to prove that she wasn't able to stop eating. After almost two years where the parents spent most of each day fending off whining, begging, and tantrums for food, it resolved within weeks when the little girl was able to eat as much as she wanted at meals and snacks.

I've seen an "underweight" child who was healthy and growing steadily following a dietitian's plan that only allowed drinks with cream added, and fats and oils added to all foods to try to get the child to the 50th percentile. The child fought every bite, and the first food she happily ate was plain spinach.

These all-too-common examples indicate a lack of understanding about how kids eat and grow.

Self-Regulation of Energy Intake Looks Erratic

The amounts and types of food young children eat vary greatly on any given day or week. A self-regulating child might eat half a cracker and a bite of banana for lunch one day, and two bananas and a piece of bread with three slices of lunchmeat the next. One child may eat far more than another, and both can thrive. We all know adults who eat large amounts and are thin, and fatter adults who eat relatively little.

"My children have different body types—Fannah's more 'solid' than her brother, who's like a bird—and she has more of a need to burn off energy. Clearly their bodies ask for different things. They are both growing steadily, though she's on the high end of the curve and he's on the low end."

— Elsa, mother of Fannah, age six, and Beckett, age eight

"Breakfast was one Greek yogurt, a big bowl of raisin bran, a whole banana, and half a grilled cheese sandwich. Lunch was less impressive, but he can put away a surprising amount of food."

— Molly, mother of Colin, age 18 months, growing steadily around the 50th percentile

"I see patterns with my six-year-old; there still is the occasional day where he eats very little and then he eats a lot on a different day, like when he was younger."

— Chloe, mother of a six-year-old boy

"One day my daughter ate four slices of toast for breakfast. At lunch I made her a quesadilla (a usual favorite) and she had two bites, but ate about a cup and a half of cottage cheese. I trust her now to take in what she needs."

— Meghan, mother of an 18-month-old

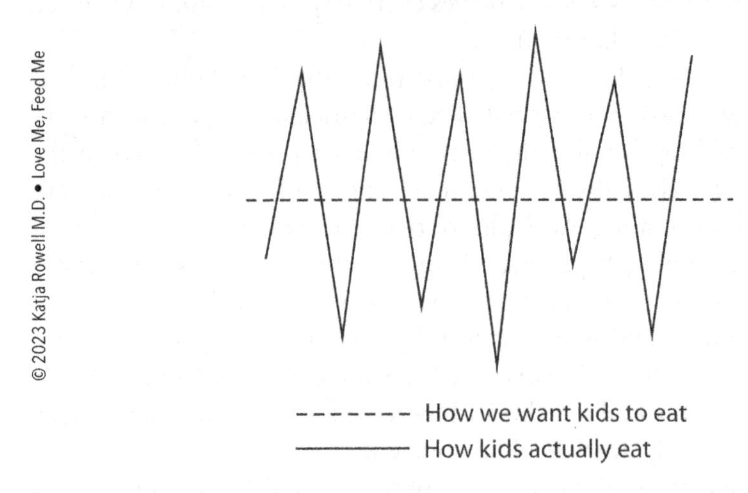

Figure 1.2: Schematic of how we want kids to eat, and how they actually eat.

These erratic, but self-regulated (child decides how much), eating patterns can worry parents, especially if they fret over a child's size. The parent of a small child tends to try to get the child to eat more, while the parent of a large child may feel alarmed by a hearty appetite and try to get the child to eat less.

Knowing that typical patterns of eating can mean a lot of food one meal or one day, and less the next, will help you trust this process. Children self-regulate intake over a day or days, and trying to make each meal or snack even out will backfire.

"Portion Control" or Trying to Get Kids to Eat Less Is Not Responsive

Increasingly, pediatricians and feeding specialists endorse "responsive" feeding. If at the same time portion control or certain amounts are recommended, that is the adult, not the child-deciding how much the child eats, and it is not responsive.

No wonder parents have questions; you may have been told to trust your child to know how much to eat, but only if they are in the range on the growth curve labeled as "normal." Bigger children are routinely advised to eat less, and smaller children to eat more. And, I've noticed that RF seems more trusted for children in smaller, rather than bigger bodies. RF plus portion control, or attempts to get children to eat less, is not RF.

How Kids Learn to Eat Variety

A second common misperception revolves around how kids learn to eat different foods. This relates to picky eating. You've probably heard, "It takes 10 times of trying a new food for a child to like it." If only it were that simple! Children who are more cautious, have a challenging feeding past, or have developmental, neuromuscular, or sensory differences may need dozens to hundreds of opportunities. Ideally, those experiences are pleasant and free of pressure. And of course, easier-to-like foods usually take one try before they are accepted.

Parents try to do the right thing and get those ten tries in, but how children experience opportunities to try new foods matters a lot! As one team of researchers wrote, "Physical and emotional reactions and associations to the consumption of a novel [new] food are crucial . . . if the experience is negative or coercive in any way, this will be associated with the food item and rejection will inevitably follow. The related research bestows a significant message that children like and benefit from a degree of autonomy."[17]

Focusing on connection and avoiding battles is so important to helping children enjoy new foods. We will get to the importance of autonomy soon!

Children can take a long time to learn to like new foods. Hydee Becker, RD, a pediatric dietitian, served chicken in every imaginable preparation to her son for more than two years before he tried a drumstick. At age four he enjoyed chicken prepared many ways.

Children do not follow the old U.S. Department of Agriculture's (USDA) Food Guide Pyramid or the newer "MyPlate," or eat from every food group at each meal or snack. **Children mostly pick and choose one or two things from what is served. At the end of the day—or week—it tends to even out.**

Humans generally want to grow up to eat a variety of foods, but trying to predict what (or how much) a child will eat invites disappointment. Even if they make a special request, they are likely to reject it. If you like bananas and you would like your little one to have the opportunity to learn to like them, keep serving them and enjoy them with your child. One day out of the blue, they will probably enjoy bananas for the first time (or again if they've been passed on for a while).

"This last week Cori started eating cucumbers, and just tonight, finally tried eggs! Two years of waiting patiently, not forcing, just offering . . . and we still see it pay off!"

— Alicia, mother of Cori, age four

"Since he's developed an opinion about what he eats, green foods are out. It's so curious to me. He calls broccoli 'trees' and puts them in his mouth, but promptly spits them out. Until two days ago he was a huge fan of broccoli. He's hated hummus—until today. I fear the diaper after all those heaping spoonfuls."

— Molly, mom to Colin, age 18 months

"One day my toddler ate apples for breakfast, sour cream and chives for lunch, brown rice with tamari for snack, and chicken for dinner. It was wild. But after three years of this, I know I can relax because she knows what she needs. Her preschool teacher tells me she's the best example of mindful eating she's ever seen. Take that, USDA food pyramid or plate or whatever you are these days!"

— Hillary, mother of a three-and-a-half-year-old

Misunderstandings that Impact Picky Eating

Advice from professionals to "not raise a picky eater" makes the process sound logical and more under your control than it is. Let's learn about selective eating:

Learning to like new foods is not a logical process. It looks random. And research gives us clues as to what helps children learn to enjoy more variety, including: 1) seeing caring adults they trust enjoy food; 2) neutral opportunities to explore a food, over and over again so they can smell it, look at it for a while, touch it, put it in their mouths and spit it out, and eventually swallow it; and 3) offering context or neutral descriptors (more on this to come).

Learning to like new foods can look like rejection. Many infants display serious-looking expressions or frown when trying new foods. This look of perhaps concentration or curiosity may be mistaken as a sign that the child doesn't like the food. But with repeated opportunities, most will learn to like them. In one study, although the infants ate more and more green beans after eight times being served, the mothers decided that the children didn't like them.[18] This matters because once parents decide a child doesn't like something, I've observed they are less likely to serve it again. (Been there, done that too.)

You may believe you have to work hard to get your child to try new foods. We don't need to (and can't) control the process of learning to like new foods; we provide opportunities. Making fancy faces or art projects with food, or using charts or rewards is generally not only not necessary, but children may feel it as pressure.

As Skye Van Zetten wrote about her son when he began to branch out to new foods, *"TJ does a better job managing his own eating than I could ever encourage him to do."*

The less pressure, focus, and attention we put on the process of learning to like new foods the better; children then don't have to fail, try to please, or push back. There is space for curiosity and exploration. **We want to raise humans who eat for pleasure and fuel, connection, and satisfaction (to the best of their capabilities), not as a reaction to something adults say or do.**

But there is effort in feeding children well. If children are only served their accepted foods, they have fewer opportunities to learn to like new foods. I've seen intake journals (page 347) for children with avoidant eating where the only foods served were their handful of accepted foods, meal after meal, month after month. (If you're stuck in this relatable pattern because "putting anything other than Dino nuggets on his plate sends him into a major meltdown," Chapters 5 and 6 will help.) One of the best predictors of whether or not your child will enjoy a certain food is whether or not you enjoy and serve it.

Early progress is not about what they put in their mouths. One of my first clients was a dietitian whose toddler, Chelsea, only ate plain pasta, rice, and a few other foods. Chelsea cried for pasta first thing every morning. On our second call, Mom was discouraged because Chelsea had chewed a blueberry but spit it out. I, on the other hand, was thrilled. Chelsea had never put a blueberry in her mouth before! And, the crying for pasta had stopped. Once mom realized how much progress Chelsea was making, it helped her not slip back into trying to make Chelsea eat.

Underestimating children can limit opportunities. At Target one day, I was behind a man and his daughter in the frozen fruit section. As she wandered along, pointing to and reaching for various bags, he scolded, "No Sophie, you don't like raspberries, no Sophie, you don't like blueberries, you don't like mangos . . ." Dad was doing two things that will make it harder for Sophie to expand her tastes. First, he was missing opportunities to expose her to different foods; and second, he reinforced the message that she can't learn to like new foods.

Similarly, another mom—this time heading into an Indian restaurant—said to her daughter, "Well, you probably won't like anything, but they do have rice." Even if all she eats is rice, that's okay, but setting up the negative expectation in advance can undermine a child's confidence and make them feel less capable. (For an anxious eater, it's okay to let her know there is rice, just hold off on the negative predictions.)

Yiseth's family offered another example of limiting opportunities. 16-year-old Yiseth had parents who were working on offering more variety and ending food battles. She said, *"A food would come up, and I'd say, 'Oh my gosh, I love that,' and my parents would say, 'Really? You do?' It might be something we hadn't had for years because they thought I didn't like it."* (To be fair to Yiseth's parents, she probably emphatically said "yuck" the last time those foods were served.)

Another client with three boys worried about protein. I asked if her selective four-year-old had tried shrimp. Mom answered, *"He doesn't like shrimp."* Dad looked at her and said, *"We haven't had shrimp since we moved into this house—five years ago."* Her son had never had the opportunity to try shrimp, partly because she believed he didn't like it.

Learning to like new foods goes quickly for some children and more slowly for others. It's easy to get stuck with lists of what we think children will or won't eat. But they can surprise you, as one parent discovered: *"You mentioned to serve fruit frozen. We did and she tried a chunk of mango! Not sure why I never thought of that!"* If they never have the opportunity, they can't try anything new. Remind yourself: *"They may not eat it yet, or like it right now . . ."* and keep serving the foods you enjoy.

"You Don't Like It *Yet*," Can Help or Harm

"Yet" is a popular idea you'll come across in the kid-feeding world. When your child says, "I don't like peas!" You're instructed to reply, "You don't like peas, *yet*," or, "You're learning to like peas." While I get that the idea is to teach children that learning to like new foods is a process, to a child, frequent reminders can feel like a challenge or that you discount their preferences.

Imagine if you were eating out and a waiter recommends the salmon mousse, and you say, "No thank you, I don't really like fish." The waiter replies, "You mean, you don't like it *yet*..." You might understandably think, "Who are you to tell me what I don't like!?"

If you try, "You don't like it yet; I didn't like asparagus until I was a teenager, but now I love it!" and your child is fine with that, no worries. If your child argues back or seems annoyed, then it's not for you! And generally, the less said the better, especially if the motive is to get your child to eat something.

Misperceptions About Weight

The third category of misperception concerns weight and growth. We'll examine this in some detail because **worry about weight is the main reason why I see parents pressure and restrict with feeding.** Many parents (like me), and even healthcare professionals (like me), have misperceptions around weight and growth—with harmful consequences. Understanding some basics about weight and tracking growth will help you trust a responsive approach.

Bodies Come in a Range of Sizes

Children come in all shapes, sizes, and builds. To illustrate: When my young teen daughter received a bracelet from an older relative, it wouldn't fit. While this bracelet slipped easily on and off the adult's wrist, it wasn't even close to large enough for my daughter. The relative was petite and "small boned" while my daughter was five feet 10 inches tall, and broad. The fact that weight charts and BMI do not take build into account (and apply labels that imply risk) is one problem with BMI.

Dr. Lesley Williams, adoptive mother, family doctor, author, and eating disorder specialist explains, "Even if children eat the same things and have the same activity levels, they will look different. The most powerful thing foster and adoptive parents can do for the health of their children is to raise them in a loving and accepting environment that makes them feel brave enough to love their body just the way it is." This is true for *all* children. And notice she stressed that this is for the child's *health*, not just self-esteem, but we'll get to that later.

Let's look at a "bell curve" (shaped like a bell) pattern for populations that we observe in nature. Weight in populations roughly follows this curve. It shows that while most people are around the middle or average weight, there will always be those who are smaller and those who are bigger. They are not automatically *abnormal.*

The standard weight-focused medical advice of the last handful of decades has encouraged individuals to fit into the "normal" weight range, currently defined in adults as a BMI of 18.5–24.9 (narrowed from 18.5–28 in 1998) which is one standard deviation from the mean. This ignores the reality that healthy bodies come in a wider range of sizes than reflected by the "normal" cutoffs.

Katherine Zavodni RD, MPH, eating disorder and feeding specialist warns, **"Not all bodies are meant to be thin bodies. This is true for kids and true for adults. Believing all bodies should be thin makes us sick."**

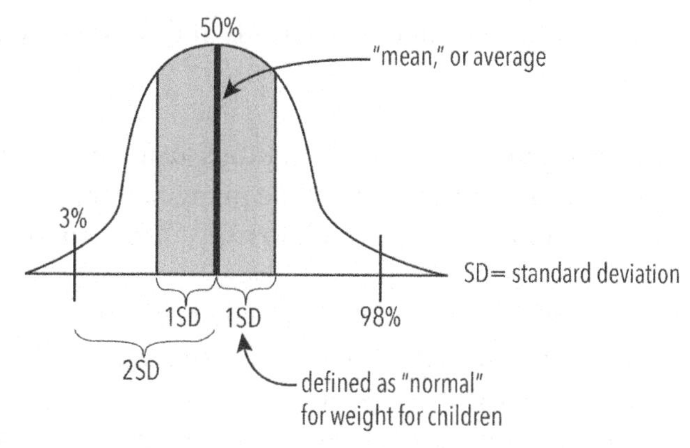

Figure 1.3: Bell Curve

Many Factors Play a Role in Weight

There are hundreds of interrelated factors that influence weight. Potentially unhealthy weight patterns usually have multiple contributors.

While we have seen the curve shift to the right for both height and weight (getting taller and heavier) in many human populations, we don't know definitively why (and we can't make the leap that calorie restriction is helpful). Animals in the wild are also larger than they were a few decades ago, as well as lab animals fed constant diets. Many factors, from genes, to pollution, food systems, dieting, weight stigma, and toxic stress impact weight. Higher weight in and of itself isn't necessarily problematic. (More about higher weight in Chapter 7; Chapter 6 goes into more detail on lower weight.)

Some factors in weight dysregulation are modifiable. We need to think about *how* the child is fed and what messages they learn around food—not just what or how much they eat. Restricting (calories, portions, kinds of foods), pressure with feeding, and having a parent who diets and binges are factors associated with problematic eating and weight patterns in children.[19,20,21] Other factors that are linked to concerning growth include:

- Stress or chaos in the home: complex trauma impacts stress hormones, cortisol, thyroid hormones, insulin, and digestion.
- Anxiety or depression that can impact appetite and eating.
- Food insecurity and/or malnutrition (not enough food, inadequate nutrition, diluting formula, etc.).
- History of dieting and/or restricting children.
- Not enough restful sleep.[22,23]
- Excessive time in front of screens.
- Medical conditions such as thyroid problems, frequent infections, or cystic fibrosis, to name a few.
- Medications that influence appetite (steroids and ADHD medications such as stimulants).

Dramatic yet unproblematic, growth deviations can occur with puberty and catch-up growth which we will cover later. While many factors contribute to growth and weight changes, most clinicians only think to ask, "What and how much are you feeding them?"

It's important to note that the Academy of Pediatrics 2023 guidelines on childhood o*esity highlighted the impact of social determinants on population trends around weight, yet the proposed "treatment" was to try to get fewer calories into children; achieved via restriction, or medications and surgery that interfere with appetite and the functioning of the healthy digestive tract. Myself and many other clinicians believe that these guidelines are misguided and dangerous.

Labels Increase Worry and Non-Responsive Feeding

It can feel like you've failed if your child is deemed "too big" or "too small." Labels lead to worry, which leads to pressure. The charts were created as a way to compare an individual's growth to a comparison population. Data was collected over decades from thousands of (mostly white) children at various ages measured at one point in time.[24]

The current standard in children arbitrarily chooses the 85th percentile or above as o*erweight. I say arbitrary because the cutoff was lowered from 95 percent in 2010, cutoffs differ in other countries, and they are not meaningfully linked with clinical outcomes. An eighth of an inch or a few ounces may push a child out of the "normal" range; yet those changes do not indicate the risk that the label implies.

Any label other than "normal" turns the child's body into a problem to solve. Trying to force the broad range of human bodies into the middle part of the curve drives more people to the extremes on the curve through dieting, disordered eating, and other practices that fight physiology and psychology.

BMI Mislabels and Misses Opportunities to Help

BMI has been misused for a few decades in medical care as a way to try to quickly and cheaply identify fatness (it doesn't) and health risk (it doesn't) for individuals. *It was not designed for nor intended to be used for this purpose.* The BMI is a statistical equation developed by an 18th-century Belgian mathematician to describe the "ideal" human body based on data from military recruits (white adult men).

On the growth charts used in the United Kingdom (UK), the Department of Health describes the BMI as "a simple and reliable indicator of thinness and fatness in childhood." In reality, it is far from reliable. In one study of nine-year-old boys, BMI mischaracterized fatness (and the assumed associated health risk) in a quarter of the boys.[25] Another study indicated that about six of ten children labeled o*erweight or o*ese did not have higher fat mass.[26] Similar estimates of BMI failing to reliably predict health risk exist in adults.[27]

Relying on weight or BMI as an indicator of health falsely flags many larger or smaller-than-average children as higher risk, and misses opportunities to help "normal" weight children.

Consider a typical pediatric office visit. A nine-year-old boy who is "normal" weight but plays video games for hours a day, is socially isolated, misses meals, sleeps poorly, and drinks several sodas a day may not have their health habits explored. The very next nine year-old, who happens to be in a bigger body, gets lectured about eating more vegetables and getting more exercise—even though he is on the swim team, gets the recommended amount of sleep, has a broad social network, and eats a variety of foods.

This happened to nine-year-old Hugh. Hugh's mom, Meghan shared her frustration, "*They don't even ask; we just get the handout and lecture about not drinking soda or juice, and to get 60 minutes of exercise a day. It's infuriating and confuses my son. I guess they get to bill for 'prevention.' It's a joke.*"

The BMI is a terrible screening test that should not be used with children.

Body Type, Ethnicity, and BMI

Another problem with BMI or weight cutoffs is that they more often harm people of color. Individuals from certain ethnic groups tend to have more dense body types; therefore, these children are mislabeled as "over" weight more often when plotted on standard charts, when in fact their weight may be healthy—for them. (See page 170 for more.) Your child's growth should be interpreted based on their own curve.

Follow Growth Over Time

What matters is your child's growth over time. If a child has always been big or small and the relative percentile is tracking about the same, that is reassuring.

If the rate of weight or height gain increases or decreases more than two lines on the chart, for example from 10th to 50th percentile or 85th to 50th, that should be looked into. (A clear example is Greta's chart on page 22, where early deviation was unproblematic growth variation, but the later rapid acceleration resulted from restrictive feeding.) When growth curves deviate up (rate of gain is increasing) or down (gain is slowing or stopped but not necessarily weight loss), a thorough history and physical exam with lab testing if indicated, should happen (but often doesn't). **Weight loss always warrants evaluation.**

Parents' worries over the amount or variety a child eats, or the way they relate to food are often dismissed if growth is "normal." If you have concerns, try to clearly convey your observations to the child's provider. Feeding challenges can lead to growth deviation.

Interpreting Growth

Growth curves are not report cards, but it can feel like it. They are a screening tool, a potential warning sign for further evaluation and a basic measure of overall wellness (is a child getting enough to feed a growing brain and body). It helps to have some understanding of the uses and limitations of growth charts. (I follow weight-for-length, height-for-age, and weight-for-age charts.)

Many children who are smaller or larger than average, or experiencing normal growth variation, are mislabeled and subject to inappropriate and often harmful intervention. The CDC warned in 2011 "... overdiagnosis of underweight might damage the parent-child interaction, subjecting families to unnecessary interventions and possibly unintentionally creating an eating disorder."[24] That they didn't offer the same warning for mislabeling higher-weight kids is an example of weight bias in healthcare. I believe that mislabeling higher-weight children carries the same risk and is more harmful in a culture with so much anti-fat bias.

Inaccurate Measurements Can Harm

Advocate for accurate measurements, using the same scale, clothing, and experienced staff. One mother told me about how her daughter (being considered for a feeding tube for slow weight gain so the stakes were high) was weighed one week wearing shoes, jeans, and a shirt, and the next visit in just her underpants. The team was concerned that she had "lost weight!" I've also seen charts where children appeared to shrink inches, resulting in falsely worrying "weight-for-height" trends.

Kids Don't Need to Know How Much They Weigh

Take the focus off weight. Poor body image leads to less healthful behaviors. If you have a scale at home, consider getting rid of it. Eating disorder specialist Lesley Williams, MD, shared, "Kids, siblings especially, are always looking for a reason to compete and compare. When children know their weight, they often see it as one more point that reflects their inadequacy. I have a smaller-than-average child and a larger-than-average child—both are teased around their weight."

Williams recommends having children weighed at health care visits with their backs to the scale and not telling them the weight (known currently as "blind" weights). This is common in eating disorder treatment. "I have all my children weighed 'blind,' and think it's a great strategy," Lesley explained.

You may ask the medical assistant ahead of time (or ask for a note to go in the chart for future visits as well), "Our child does better not knowing how much they weigh. Would it be okay to just turn them around for weights and you can write it in the chart?" (See more on navigating the medical system on page 341.)

And don't forget about schools. Unless school is the only place a child receives healthcare, there is no good reason to weigh a child at school. You may need to reach out to your child's teacher and principal that you do not consent to have your child weighed, including as part of a phys-ed. assessment, data collection, or science activities. For example, a graphing exercise comparing students' weight is not appropriate. I've worked with families where small and large children were bullied around weight in school. And the argument for school weights falls apart as data from a decade of weight "report cards" indicates they don't help and may harm.[25]

Movement Around the Curve May Be Completely Healthy

I used to think—and many clinicians still believe—that "steady growth is healthy growth"[26] even if larger or smaller than average. While true, *I was surprised to learn that more than half of infants under 6 months will move across two lines or more on the curve,* say from 10th to 50th percentile or 85th to 20th. *Even up to age two, almost one in four will continue to shift on the curve.*[27,28]

The statistics used on tens of thousands of data points resulted in smooth lines on the growth charts, creating the impression that growth is continuous. Growth, especially for young children, is in fact highly discontinuous (meaning growth happens in "spurts").

"Steady" growth doesn't mean your child's growth must plot exactly along a percentile line. There is usually some variation around a general area on the curve.

This is important to know, since diagnostic criteria for things like "failure to thrive" or avoidant restricting food intake disorder (ARFID) include, "falling off the growth curve" or not "maintaining" expected growth. I've also had parents of breastfed infants who crossed lines upward told to cut back on feeding!

As children grow, weight often increases first, followed by height, which results in a wavy pattern on the weight-for-height chart. Discontinuous growth is one example where the alarm bell is rung around changes that are perfectly normal and not problematic.

Author Virginia Sole-Smith, wrote in her newsletter,[29] "Kids' bodies are growing, and this means they are constantly changing. And it's normal to have phases of growth where kids look rounder or bigger. Sometimes they lean out a few months or years later. Sometimes they don't. Some of us are going to be fat, and that has to be okay with the people who love us." Hang tight if you're having an intense reaction to this statement. I would have had trouble accepting this had I read it 20 years ago. We will delve into worries around higher weight in Chapter 7.

Look at Greta's chart below. It illustrates a discontinuous growth pattern before 15 months. Looking at Greta's chart, a doctor might conclude at various times that she is gaining too quickly, or "falling off her curve." At different points in time, following standard advice, Greta's parents may have been told to get her to eat less, then a few visits later, to get her to eat more!

If there are no concerns with the child's physical exam and they are otherwise thriving, that's reassuring and it's okay to continue to monitor things. More concerning patterns that require investigation include steep ups or downs, as in Greta's growth after 15 months.

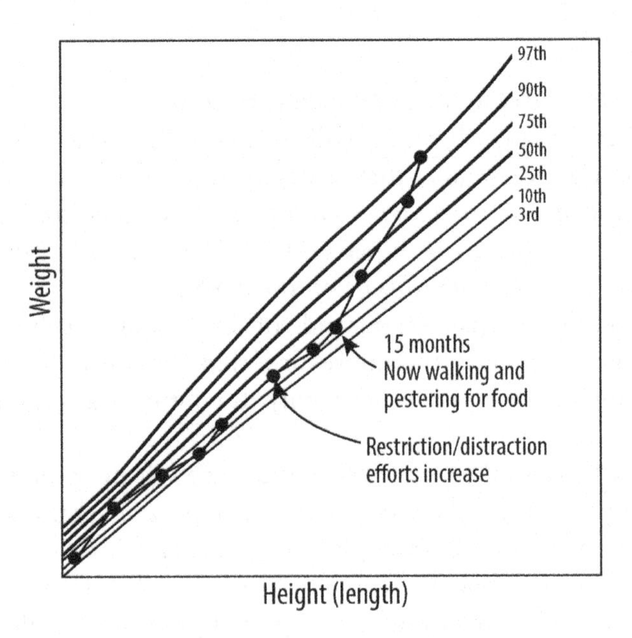

Figure 1.4: Greta's growth chart

Here are additional stylized growth charts to illustrate trends.

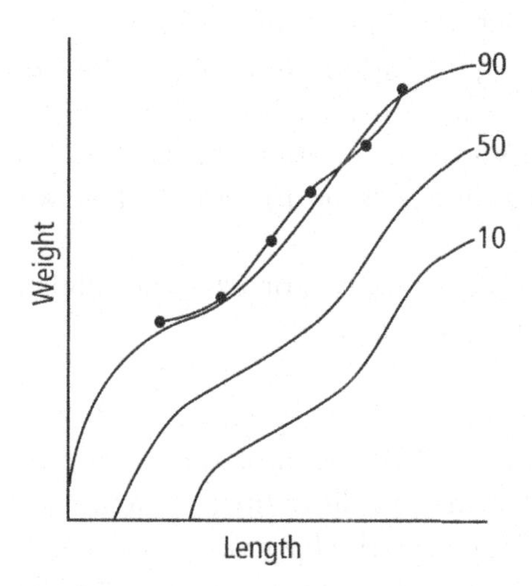

Figure 1.5: Chart A–High and Steady. This child is larger than average but is growing at a steady rate. If the child has healthy eating patterns and behaviors, this is probably healthy growth. Efforts to reduce weight are likely to backfire.

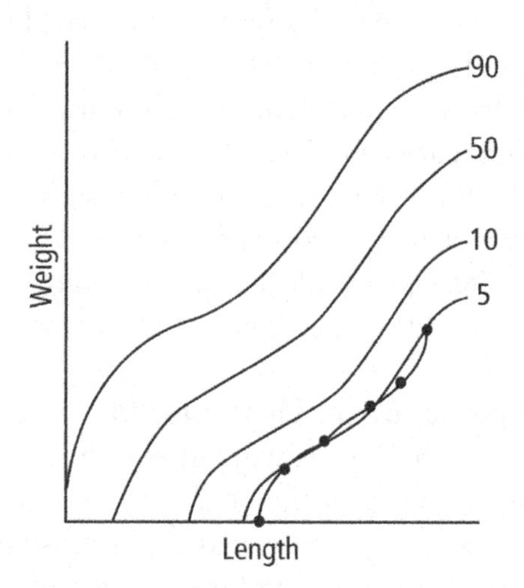

Figure 1.6: Chart B–Low and Steady. This child is small but growing at a steady rate. If a physical exam and evaluation of feeding and health behaviors don't indicate a concern, this is probably healthy growth, particularly if birth parents are smaller.

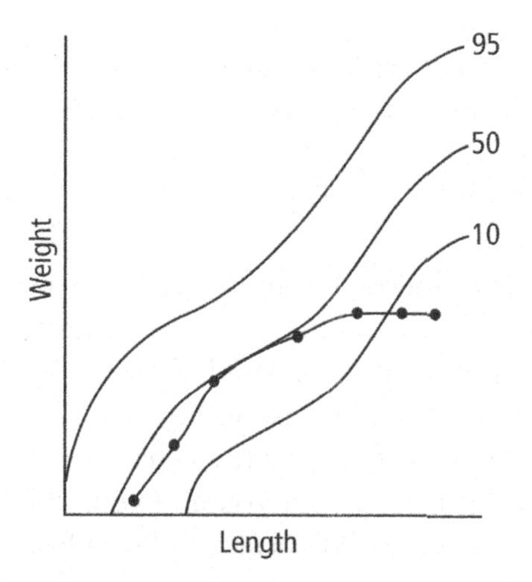

Figure 1.7: Chart C–Growth Deceleration. Note the clear deceleration. This child is rapidly crossing centile lines and needs further evaluation. Weight loss always needs to be discussed with a child's doctor.

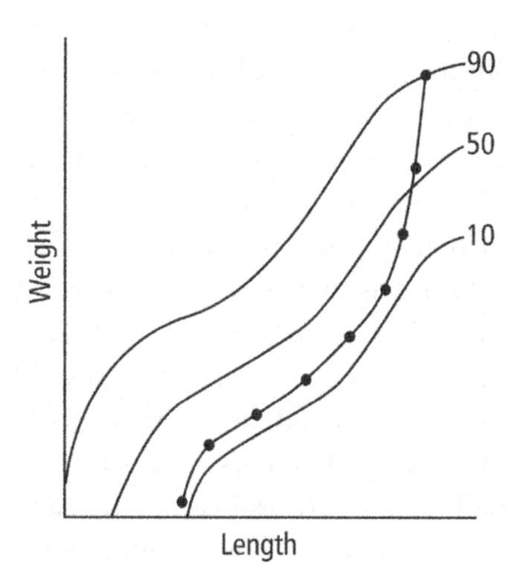

Figure 1.8: Chart D–Growth Acceleration. Note the dramatic shift across centile lines. Further evaluation is needed.

Growth Charts are Poor Predictors of Adult Weight

You may have been told that where a child is on the growth chart is where they will stay, especially with higher-weight kids. In fact, most preschoolers in the "overweight" or "obese" category will be "normal" weight as adults and 70% of "obese" adults were not higher-weight children (see page 170 for more). My own daughter's height curve has ranged from 100th for the first two years to 50th from age 2-4, then 85% for a few years, and then with puberty, she shot back up to 99th%. This was unproblematic growth for her.

The older children are, the more predictive the value is. For example, higher-weight older adolescents are likely to be higher-weight adults.

Following "Off the Chart" Growth

If your child is growing above the 97th or below the 3rd percentile (above and below the lines on the charts), your doctor might want to follow their growth using Z-scores, or percent change, because looking at the growth chart isn't accurate. Z-score represents how far away a child is from the mean (similar to average) on that Bell curve from a few pages back. For example, at the third percentile, the child is two standard deviations below the mean, so the Z-score would be -2. (An app called "Child Growth" calculates Z-scores and percentiles for you.)

Specialized Growth Charts

Regardless of the chart used, follow your child's own growth over time, with less comparison to the broader population.

If your child was born early, ask the doctor if a chart "corrected for gestational age" for the first few years is appropriate. A baby born 10 weeks early would be expected to grow behind their peers for some time.

There are charts specific to children with certain genetic diagnoses such as Down Syndrome but are not available for every diagnosis.

Questions may arise as to which growth chart to follow for gender-diverse youth. We don't have enough data yet on gender-diverse children and teens for specific growth chart recommendations. Clinicians should do a thorough history and physical; learn about how the child feels in their body; ask how they are eating; ask if they have access to safe play and activity, and support internally driven eating, healthy behaviors, and mental health and resilience. The care team, in consultation with you and your child, can decide how to follow growth and how to support your child's health and well-being.

Look Beyond Growth Charts

Parents of bigger kids are usually told to worry that their child is o*erweight and will be unhealthy, even if the child is healthy and growing consistently or having a period of accelerated, but unproblematic, growth (such as a growth spurt, catch-up growth, or with puberty). Conversely, parents of small children are told to worry and to get the child to eat more. Note: If your child is nutritionally compromised or may be losing weight, do not wait. Follow up with their doctor.

Maxine gave a clear example of the importance of focusing on the child, not just growth charts. *"Anya was 25th percentile for weight when she was placed with us at 16 months, but was clearly undernourished; she had hollow cheeks, almost translucent skin, no fat on her arms or legs, and dark circles under her eyes. My biological son was six months older and had always grown around the 5th percentile; but he had lovely full cheeks and some fat on his thighs. It was a striking lesson to me to look first at the child, not the number on the charts."* Sadly, the pediatrician showed more concern over the nourished child growing well at the 5th percentile.

As you're learning, health and wellness go far beyond a number on a scale or chart. Here are some signs that your child is doing well.

- Your child can play and has energy
- Your child is progressing in terms of development
- Your child has meaningful social connections
- Your child isn't winded with simple activities
- Your child is happy most days
- Your child sleeps well and enough
- Your child is eating enough food to grow and have good energy

On pages 203-206 you'll read about weight-neutral behaviors that support good health (reclaiming health section).

Puberty Is a Risky Time for Misguided Worry and Intervention

The accelerated weight gain of early puberty usually starts in the tween years. A common puberty growth pattern sees fat stores (especially in girls) and weight increase before height. Children can gain up to 50 percent of their adult weight during puberty. I've heard too many stories from adults saying that when they got a softer "tummy" around age 10, the pediatrician sounded the alarm—leading to decades of yo-yo dieting and negative body image. (See *early puberty* on pages 336-337 if you have concerns.)

Misperceptions About Nutrition

The final misperception category is nutrition. Many professionals only focus on *what* kids eat, and ignore *how* kids are fed and how they relate to food. In this section I'll cover the short- and long-term lens on nutrition as well as the energy and behavior connection. (Nutrition topics including salt and sugar are covered in Chapter 11.)

Variety, Nutrition, and the Food Attitude

Good nutrition is easier to achieve when we eat a variety of foods, but trying to *get* children to eat by prescriptive rules invites pressure or restriction.

Nutrition needs can be met with fairly limited diets (using supplements if indicated). There are different ways to eat that serve individuals. There is no one "right" way to eat.

Remember that the amounts children eat vary meal to meal, with most picking and choosing one or two options from what's available. Kids offered variety without pressure are more likely to consume a balanced diet over several days.

What's Important Now (WIN) is helping your child develop a positive attitude toward food. Kids who are calm and comfortable at mealtimes (short-term goal) and around food, are far more likely to move themselves toward trying and enjoying a greater variety of foods (long-term goal).

They don't need to eat squid by kindergarten, and you don't have to expose them to every possible food to "train" their tastes. I didn't try sushi until my twenties, but I approached it with a positive attitude and enjoyed it (starting with cooked shrimp rolls before venturing to raw fish).

While a number of factors (life experience, sensory profile, etc.) influence the foods someone is comfortable eating, the feeding environment is a big factor.

Blood Sugar, Behavior, and Nutrition

Eating fat, protein, and carbohydrates together helps to even out blood sugar and energy. Many "snack" foods are simple carbohydrates. For example, a snack of Goldfish crackers and juice may be followed about an hour later with a child's meltdown or whining for food. Carbohydrates offer quick energy and are necessary and favored (particularly by growing children); protein, fat, and fiber help children feel satisfied longer so they can make it until the next meal or snack.

Notice I did not say, *get* your child to eat fat, protein, and carbohydrates; rather, *serve* them. Your child will be okay if they mostly eat carbs, or from one food group, at some, or even the majority, of eating opportunities.

Next Stop on the Worry Cycle: Pressure and Restriction

With an introduction to misperceptions and worries behind us, we continue the Worry Cycle tour considering pressure and restriction.

If you have tried to get your child to eat more, less, or different foods, you're far from alone. The majority of American parents do so. Here's a list of tactics: "Typical negative food-related behaviors of parents with two- to five-year-old children: bargaining, bribing, and forcing; promising a special food, such as dessert, for eating a meal; withholding food as punishment; rewarding good behavior with food; persuading children to eat; playing a game to get children to eat; taking over and feeding children who refuse to eat; threatening punishment for not eating; and making children clean their plates."[30]

These efforts may work, in the short term.[31] For example, bribing with dessert or the "two-bite rule" might get a child to choke down two bites of broccoli (or lead to a 90-minute meltdown), but does it help your child willingly eat and enjoy these foods?

Any health benefits of a few bites of broccoli—in a body flooded with stress hormones, increased heart rate, blood pressure, and tears—is pretty much lost.

Even if you are careful with your words, **nonverbal cues can also pressure.** Anything you do or say to try to get your child to eat more, less, or different foods can backfire. Observing your child's reaction is key. *Even attention can pressure.* One mom lamented during a call that her son wouldn't try a hot dog. I asked her to describe the setting: Mom laughed and recalled that he was the only one eating, and as he was about to take a bite, he looked around at the expectant, excited eyes of his parents, grandparents, and siblings. He put the hot dog down and refused to eat.

Another anxious parent told me: *"But we don't pressure, we praise and encourage. That's what we were told to do."* There is an assumption that pressure only includes negative actions. Many parents don't "push," "force," or "threaten," but the child still resists. Smiling, cheering, and encouragement seem positive, but can feel like pressure. The following can also feel like pressure to some children:

- Giving Gabriella a sticker for eating her veggies.
- Clapping enthusiastically and commenting about how brave Jaxson is to try a food.
- Going on about the nutritional benefits and how it will make them strong can also pressure. (We'll explore pressure in more detail in Chapters 5 and 6.)

Is it pressure? Ask yourself...

- "Why am I saying or doing ________?" If the answer is to try to get your child to eat or engage with a food, it is likely pressure.
- "How will I feel if this doesn't 'work'?" If you're disappointed a child hasn't eaten or engaged in the food, you were likely serving pressure.
- "How did my child react?" If they resist or appear less engaged, they likely felt pressure.

And desperate parents bounce from one strategy to the next, *often in the same meal,* as each one fails to produce the desired result. It might start with encouragement, then a request, then a bribe, perhaps moving on to a threat, then pretending not to care, then a last-ditch negotiation, and finally, a sigh as the dishes are cleared. Mom Mimi commented on a reel I did on Instagram, *"I hated sitting with her because it was pressure all around no matter how 'fun' I thought I was making it."*

Unclear expectations mean children come to mealtimes wondering if they will have to eat one or two bites, or if they will earn dessert or not. This conflict and lack of consistency is stressful, disrupts connection, and decreases appetite and curiosity.

Kids Might Think About Praise and Rewards

Pediatric feeding specialist and researcher Hazel Wolstenholme, PhD said, "Children feel expectation on their eating in very nuanced ways—not just through 'pressuring' or 'controlling' feeding practices. They are very aware of their parents' mealtime actions, emotions, and goals."[32] They might think:

- "Hmm, Mom really cares about me eating broccoli..." (This information is useful to children if they are testing boundaries.)
- "This stuff must taste really bad if I need a reward to eat it."
- "They must not think I can do this if they're buying me a present."
- "Will they love me if I don't eat this tomorrow?"
- "Am I a 'bad' kid if I don't eat this again, since I was 'good' for eating it?"
- "I get so annoyed when they fuss over what I eat, I'd rather just eat alone in my room."
- "Will they be upset if I ask for more?"
- "I wanted to do it my way!" The persistent or independent child who wants it to be his idea may feel robbed of that feeling if he is encouraged or praised.

Even children who thrive on praise in some circumstances can resent attention on their eating. Jacky Lamenzo, who struggled with eating as a child, wrote this in a blog post called "All Eyes on Me": "I wanted everyone watching anytime I was doing a cartwheel or jumping into the pool. But not when I was trying a new food. Every time someone cheered or commented on me trying a new food, I felt pressure."[33]

Children Resist

Which brings us on the Cycle to children resisting. *Non*-responsive feeding (pressure and restriction) is associated with weight dysregulation[34] and decreased enjoyment of eating for children and parents, increased avoidant eating, and increased mealtime conflict.[35] Children push back; here are some potential reasons why:

- Maintaining a sense of bodily safety. If there was pain or discomfort with eating in the past, it makes sense that they will try to avoid it. (More in Chapter 6.)
- Autonomy, or protecting their body and ability to choose.
- It's their *job*. Saying "no" is developmentally appropriate to become an individual. Think of the "terrible twos" or the teen years.
- Temperament. One child will have no trouble with a "one bite" rule, another will resist.

- If they *can't* do what you want them to do, and they feel they will always disappoint you, they may stop trying.
- Rejection sensitivity dysphoria relates to the previous point. Newly described, it is associated with ADHD and autism, and is a distressing experience associated with feeling rejected or disappointing others. (Think intense shame spiral.) Trying to avoid this feeling can make kids give up or want to eat alone.
- Testing limits or boundaries.
- Not all children understand expectations, and they may get frustrated.
- Children may resist restriction and seek food if they are hungry, anxious, using food as a coping mechanism, or have a history of food insecurity.
- Conflict may be preferable and more stimulating than boredom for some individuals, including those with ADHD.
- Child has traits consistent with "pathological demand avoidance."

Pathological demand avoidance (PDA) is an evolving and controversial term, used to describe a proposed sub-type of autism. It is characterized by what seems like an extreme reaction to a "reasonable" ask (such as to stop kicking a chair). Sound familiar? When I first heard of it, I wondered if it could be called "demand anxiety," or as some in the PDA community refer to it as, "pervasive drive for autonomy," and author of *Brain-Body Parenting*, Mona Delahooke suggested *protective* drive for autonomy. Many autistic children are in compliance-based therapies which can be stressful and draining. School can overwhelm and traumatize from a sensory and nervous system standpoint, so their cup of tolerance or brain fuel (page 37) is already almost empty. Then a "small" ask of say, licking a food can lead to an intense fight-or-fight reaction. Prioritizing felt safety and reducing demands can help. Page 67 gives examples of language that minimizes demands.

Resistance Isn't Universal

Different children experience parenting differently. For example, praise isn't always off-putting. Take sisters Ali and Bea. Their mom Michaela homeschools Ali, her biological daughter, and her youngest, Bea, who is thriving in an open adoption. Michaela notes that with their schoolwork, Ali shuts down completely with praise or direction, while Bea takes direction and is eager to please.

Connecting their learning styles to their eating was eye opening: "*I realized we had been subtly trying to get Ali to eat more foods. We knew outright pressure didn't work, so we tried games, talking up nutrition, or praising when she tried something. Like with her schoolwork, any attempt to steer Ali toward something backfired. Bea, on the other hand, enjoys food and is more easily encouraged, but that can be a downside, too. She might finish her plate to please an adult rather than listen to her body.*"

Mom Connie also related that children didn't mind being encouraged to try a few bites of food and that it didn't lead to battles. If the "no thank you bite" or other things you do at mealtimes help your child enjoy variety, and meals are pleasant, do what works for your family. Often, though, a tactic tolerated by one child sparks epic battles for another. Then what? (Hint: Children who go along with pressure and encouragement generally do fine without.)

Break the Cycle with Responsive Feeding

The tour of the Worry Cycle showed how a child's challenges (or misperceived issues), plus worried and unsupported parents, can result in nonresponsive feeding. Not feeding in a responsive way "has the potential to undermine the child's trust in an otherwise responsive parent."[36] Pressure and restriction in most cases worsen feeding and growth issues. Like quicksand, the more you struggle, the more stuck you become.

Stress and mealtime battles make it harder for children to tune in to hunger and fullness cues coming from their own bodies, making them more likely to eat more or less than they otherwise would. In essence, parents unwittingly contribute to the outcomes they're trying to avoid. There is a lot that can slow down the process, but not much to speed it up—it's like trying to peel open a bud on a flower. Nisha offered an example of how attempts to speed things along can lead to setbacks: She shared how her food-avoidant son progressed so that at twelve he eats like many of his friends, but her own impatient father occasionally tries to bribe her son with a twenty-dollar bill to taste a new food. It upsets her son, whose eating worsens for a time, which she interprets as reclaiming his autonomy.

So if you can't bribe, praise, reward, or negotiate, what helps to raise children to do well with eating? How do you nurture your family when it comes to food? The answer is responsive feeding.

Chapter 2
Felt Safety and Connection Before Vegetables

"We are so much better connected, she is relaxed, we eat all meals together at the table instead of in front of the TV . . . It's a revelation. We spend so much more time giggling and chatting than before. It's improved everything."
— Mimi

Feeding children can't be separated from parenting. I've watched friends explain and offer choices to their young children all day, respecting the child's autonomy around say, a choice not to wear a coat, and allowing them to learn from the "natural consequence" of being cold. For some reason when it comes to food, it seems like these parenting values are replaced by a more authoritarian (*Do as I say!*) approach.

The worry and sense of responsibility over ensuring good nutrition are so strong (veggies and protein are the main focus), that bribes, negotiating, rewards, threats, and pleading define mealtimes. As you read in the last chapter, this doesn't work. And that's good news! You don't have to work so hard and you can enjoy your children more.

As Dr. Mona Delahooke wrote in *Beyond Behaviors*, "Instead of focusing on what we do to children we prioritize how we are with them."[1] This chapter lays out how a child's sense of felt safety, and connection is the foundation for better emotional and physical health.

There are many ways parents seek to understand and connect with their children; books and research use different words. A focus on calm and felt safety may be especially helpful if your child is highly sensitive, autistic, has brain-based differences, or is neurodivergent.

And before we dig in to how you can focus on felt safety and connection with responsive feeding, learning a little about the nervous system states and the brain-body is critical.

Brain and Body Are One

You may be familiar with the "states of arousal" as it refers to the nervous system and body. (This section takes from the work of Dan Siegel, Bruce Perry, Stephen

Porges, Tina Bryson, Karyn Purvys, Bessel van der Kolk, and others.) Brain and body are not separate. You *experience* emotions in the body. Your thoughts may fuel and reinforce emotions, such as with those middle-of-the-night worries.

You might awaken from a scary dream with your heart pounding; relaxation exercises might help you calm. A near miss on the drive home raises your breathing rate and blood pressure in a split second; it may take the rest of the ride to return to baseline. Maybe you wrestle with a traumatic event in your own past, even re-experiencing a memory as if it's happening in the here and now. Input from our senses alerts the primitive areas of the brain (not thinking rational thoughts) and triggers events that impact every part of the body—from digestion to muscle tension, to chemical messengers in the brain, and heart rate.

Check out the Brain-Body Connection diagram, where I've attempted to simplify these ideas while highlighting how they relate to physical health and digestion.

As you explore the diagram, consider that nervous system regulation does as much, if not more, for heart and physical health as vegetables. A focus on felt safety and connection does not ignore health; it's the foundation.

A Sense of Calm, or Felt Safety

Felt safety is a term often used to describe a "regulated" or calm state and is used by folks with a nervous-system focus. Felt safety is, well, felt. It's a feeling. A child may be perfectly safe but feel panicked. Kitty, an adoptee and adoptive mom, reflected on felt safety, *"That term really resonated with me. It matches that feeling that's hard to describe. That's how it feels—safe."*

Dr. Karyn Purvis, a child development expert and founder of the Trust-Based Relational Intervention (TBRI) program for children helped define felt safety: **". . . means that adults arrange the environment and adjust their behavior so children can feel in a profound and basic way that they are truly safe in their home and with us."**[2] I like that the definition focuses on what adults can do to support children to feel their best.

When parents are tuned in to the child's body and brain (nervous system), and adapt the environment to support the child's sense of calm, it helps children learn to feel good/better about food and their bodies, including how children think about their bodies (body image) and their experience of *living in* their bodies (embodiment).

"Calm" doesn't mean eating with children will look like a tea party with your children sitting with napkins on their laps, perfect table manners, and quiet voices. A regulated child can still be rambunctious, have a fidgety body, loud voice, and experience a range of emotions. Meals with young children often feel like barely controlled chaos. "Calm" refers to your child's nervous system, as explored in the following pages. It's important to have realistic expectations.

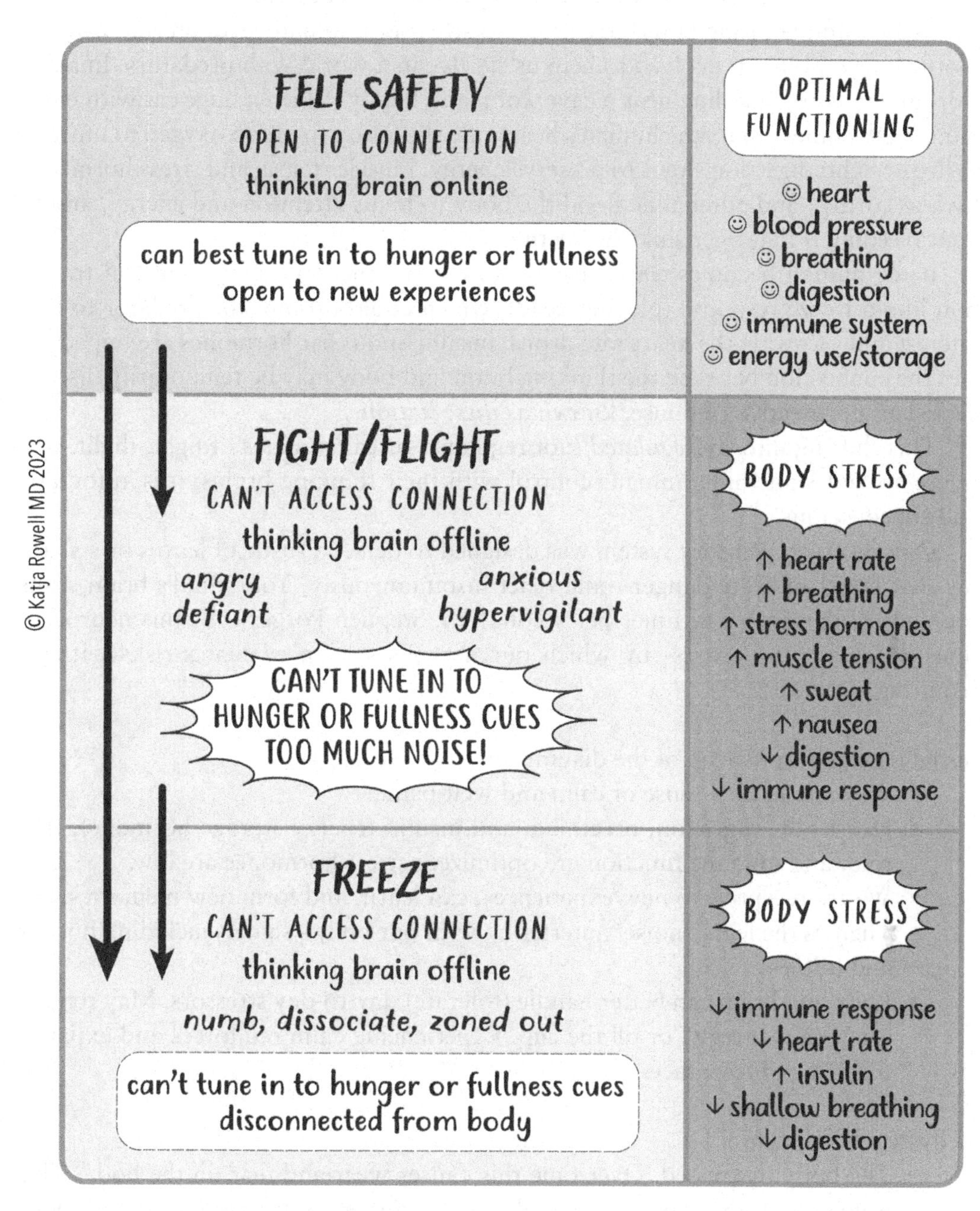

Figure 2.1: Brain-Body Connection diagram.

The next section explores nervous system states and their impact on eating and health.

Regulation (Felt Safety) and Dysregulation (Fight, Flight, Freeze, Fawn)

A classic example of the body's reactions to stress is a human encountering a saber-toothed tiger. Humans evolved to help us survive in a world with predators. Imagine a distant ancestor standing near a cave, calm and happy. When a huge cat with enormous teeth comes along, the human's heart rate shoots up to pump oxygen to muscles to flee or fight; digestion slows to preserve energy; muscles tense; and stress hormones such as cortisol and adrenaline flood the body to focus attention and energy, and to limit bleeding if that tiger sinks his teeth in.

If the human becomes trapped with no escape, the nervous system can transition into a freeze response (playing dead), which could prompt the predator to lose interest and go away; the heart rate drops; insulin and other hormones are impacted; and the connection between the thinking brain and body may be temporarily disconnected as a protective response, known as *dissociation.*

This shifting into *dysregulated* (not regulated or calm) states of fight, flight, and freeze are not something humans control with their thinking brains; it is automatic and subconscious.

Our ancestors' sensory system was designed to detect a rustle of leaves or a shadow that might indicate danger—and react instantaneously. Your child's brain scans for signs of danger many times per second! Dr. Stephen Porges calls this neuroception, which is "the process by which our nervous system evaluates risks without requiring awareness."[3]

In the regulated state (top of the diagram):

- We experience a sense of calm and well-being.
- Heart rate, digestion, breathing, and insulin (energy storage hormone), thyroid, and immune function are optimized; stress hormones are low.
- We are receptive to new experiences, can learn, and form new memories.
- There is the least "noise" interfering with our body's signals including hunger and fullness.
- Body and brain can better handle (tolerate) day-to-day stressors. May replenish "brain energy" or fill the cup. Experiencing calm reinforces and expands this zone of tolerance.

In dysregulated states:

- The body is stressed. Over time this causes wear-and-tear on the body. This is believed to be why adverse childhood experiences are associated with poor health outcomes into adulthood.
- Digestion slows or speeds up; there may be nausea, diarrhea and/or constipation.
- Appetite can be dramatically impacted.

- Curiosity, say to engage with an unfamiliar food, is limited.
- It's difficult or impossible to concentrate, learn, pay attention, or follow conversations.
- There is little capacity for connection and relationships.
- Interoception (feeling and figuring out what sensations occurring inside the body mean) is impaired. Chronic dysregulation may mean those signals aren't sent or sensed the same way, or aren't recognized as easily.

This threat-response system was designed for quick, life-and-death moments, perhaps up to 10 minutes of extreme stress. Once the tiger left, the body and brain recovered into calm.

In modern times we experience wear-and-tear on our brains and bodies when the threat (real or perceived) is prolonged; there is little recovery time. A person might flip back and forth from calm to fight, then back to calm, to flight, then freeze...

Under chronic and prolonged threats, it's not uncommon for individuals to bypass fight or flight and go straight to a freeze response. Some may rarely, if ever, fully return to or experience felt safety, and instead experience *hypervigilance*—always on alert and ready for that next threat. Bruce Perry of the Child Trauma Academy warned that, "Prolonged alarm reaction alters the nervous system."[4]

Prolonged toxic stress alters hormones, digestion, cardiovascular system, growth, and more. It's tough on bodies and undermines good health.

Signs of Regulation and Dysregulation

A big part of a responsive approach is being attuned to your child. While each child is different, the following are some common clues to let you know which state your child may be in:

Felt Safety

In a child experiencing calm and felt safety, you might observe a regular breathing rate, a relaxed and alert appearance, and the ability to engage in conversation and follow directions.

Fight or Flight

In fight or flight, you might observe: increased heart rate and breathing, flushed or pale skin, sweating, tense muscles, trembling, dilated pupils, and unfocused attention. Behavior you might notice:

Fight:

- Aggression
- Self-harm

- Anger and loud outbursts
- Automatic oppositional (seemingly doing the opposite of whatever is asked or expected) reactions
- Stimming (repetitive physical movements such as tapping hands or rocking) to self-regulate

Flight:

- Can be quiet or loud, big or small movements
- Anxious
- Hypervigilant or agitated
- Stimming (repetitive physical movements such as tapping hands or rocking) to self-regulate

Freeze:

In freeze, you might observe slow heart rate and breathing, or a child holding their breath. You might also notice:

- "Zoning out" or numb
- Yawning or acting sleepy
- Seeming frozen or almost paralyzed

Fawn:

In addition to fight, flight, and freeze, fawning is a more recently described reaction. One can think of it as a way of trying not to make waves, to avoid conflict, and to stay safe and in connection with caregivers. Children who cope by fawning seem well behaved. You might observe:

- Child seems unable to express how they really think or feel (an example is a tearful child, gagging on a food, but declaring, "It's yummy!").
- Always saying "yes," or trying to do as asked.
- People-pleasing, such as prioritizing others (they may give their own cake to a sibling, though they clearly want some).

Neurobehavioral Lens

Related to this framework of understanding the state of the brain (nervous system) and body, a neurobehavioral (brain and behaviors) perspective shifts how we view children and their sometimes challenging behaviors. This lens is helpful for all children, but especially if your child has sensory differences, is neurodivergent, or has a high-alert nervous system for any reason.

Eileen Devine, therapist, and founder of Brain First Parenting and The Resilience Room online community writes, "The neurobehavioral perspective is an organizing principle, not another 'diagnosis' to add to a list. Viewing your child as a tender-hearted child who is probably working harder than every kid around them is a powerful shift in perspective. That's where the curve starts; translating that lens of understanding to your everyday parenting . . ."[5] And that includes feeding.

It can feel overwhelming when your child has diagnoses such as anxiety, sensory processing disorder, or autism. Diagnoses are an attempt to describe observed behaviors within a medical model of understanding and are often necessary to access care. Psychologist Mona Delahooke wrote, "As we learn more about the value of focusing on these causes, labels become less significant and determining underlying causality becomes more significant."[1]

Devine shares that children do better with accommodation: "But it won't happen if they are distressed or overwhelmed, anxious, or expected to do things that don't match their skills."

Sensitized Nervous Systems, Starting with a Cup Half-Empty

Someone who has a brain that has spent a significant amount of time in fight, flight, or freeze, or has sensory or brain-based differences, may have a smaller *zone of tolerance* with a nervous system on high alert; this can be thought of as a *sensitized* nervous system.

The top of the Brain-Body Connection diagram can be thought of as the zone of tolerance. Minimal triggers can dysregulate the brain (with a cascade of effects on the body) into survival modes where that capacity for connection, thinking, and emotional and behavior regulation shuts down. Another way to think of it is using a cup analogy. Someone with a more typical threat response, has a cup that is usually pretty full; their zone of tolerance is wide. They can roll with a fair amount of stress and sensory input; access their thinking brains; more easily tune in to signals from their bodies; and be available for connection.

However, for many children, their cup of coping energy starts half full (the zone is smaller). Sensory onslaughts from situations such as school and demands to comply may use up their small amount of coping and regulating energy—and drain their cup close to empty. Asking them to hang up their coat when they walk in the door or eat carrot sticks before crackers may tip them into dysregulation (and you may be one of the few safe people they can do that with).

". . . many persistent and concerning behaviors are manifestations of physiological stress responses that occur when a child experiences a neuroception of threat. When I came to view problematic behaviors as *adaptive responses and not purposeful misbehavior* I shifted nearly all of my beliefs about how to help children and families."[1]
– Mona Delahooke, PhD

Felt Safety Undermined

Many factors can undermine felt safety, which impacts health.

Environmental and Social Factors

The Brain-Body Connection diagram from a few pages back highlights that toxic stress makes poor health outcomes into adulthood more likely. Regardless of whether your child is bigger or smaller than average, toxic stress harms.

Social Isolation Is Bad for Health

Research suggests that social isolation is as bad for you as smoking.[6] Humans are wired for, and feel safe and regulated in, connection with other humans. A war on loneliness and isolation is a health movement I could get behind. Love and connection are heart healthy.

Responsive Feeding and Food Insecurity

Food insecurity (FI) must be included in the exploration of environmental factors because it impacts how children relate to food and their bodies—now and in the future. We will take a deeper dive into the impact of FI in Chapter 7. Let's start with some context.

Food insecurity means not having reliable access to enough food due to any number of challenges, including a lack of a living wage and safety net, income inequality, to healthcare costs, and more.

The Food Insecurity Policy Research organization in Canada describes different levels of FI from marginal (less choice or quality, worry about running out) to severe with missed meals, and reduced food intake.

FI in childhood, particularly moderate to severe cases, creates intense focus and anxiety. Actor Viola Davis, a crusader against child hunger and spokesperson for No Kid Hungry, said in 2020, "The uncertainty of where your next meal will come from is a scary thing and it consumes every waking moment you have." She continued, "I still remember what it was like—the stigma attached to it and the shame . . . your sense of value and worth are taken away from you . . . You have no idea the potential we could tap into just by solving this one problem for kids."[7]

It is very hard to settle into felt safety if you are hungry, or worried about being hungry.

If you're experiencing or have experienced FI you may observe your child eating very quickly, focused on food, sneaking, food preoccupation, an intense focus on energy-dense foods, or negative feelings and even apathy (couldn't care less) toward food. Additional considerations:

- Food insecurity impacts more than one in five children in the United States (one in six in Canada), disproportionately harming children of color.

- Food insecurity is worse for families with infants and young children (and is associated with iron deficiency).
- It impacts every aspect of parenting; for example, depressive symptoms are more common in mothers in FI families, correlating with severity.[8]
- Food-insecure children experience more anxiety, attention issues, and behavioral outbursts.[8]
- It is associated with eating disorders; the more intense the FI, the more likely and severe the eating disorder.[9]
- It is linked with higher weights in children and into adulthood.[10] Children who participate in school meal programs have more stable weight.[11]

Feeding well, with reliable access to enough food, is one of the most important ways to help children settle in to felt safety—no matter what a child weighs.

If You are Experiencing Food Insecurity

If you're struggling to get enough of the foods you want to serve, I'm sorry you're dealing with this burden. There needs to be real, systemic change to address this all-too-common problem. In the meantime, here are some ideas that may help:

- Filling bellies is good feeding; big pots of pasta, beans or grains; or breakfast for dinner. Focus on enough calories and energy.
- Come back to thinking about variety when you're able to.
- Keep other things consistent if you can, stay with a routine.
- Acknowledge children's feelings. A *New York Times* article offered, "I know you're angry with me right now because you're hungry and your tummy hurts, I'm working and other helpers are working to try to get you more."[12]
- Reassure children that it's nothing they did and it's not their fault.
- Access food assistance if you can.
- See pages 76-77 for ideas on reducing food waste.

Connection, and good feelings at mealtimes and around the food that is served matters. Danielle, a pediatrician, grew up in a family experiencing marginal food insecurity but wasn't really aware of it. Things improved during high school, but in her early years, she remembers eating many meals of store-brand mac-n-cheese with hot dogs. "It's just what we ate. I remember enjoying that time together around the table." Though she wasn't exposed to a lot of variety in childhood, she enjoys a wide variety of foods now.

Support Felt Safety

It is ideal for people to eat when they feel calm because body systems, including digestion, work best. It's also easier to tune in to hunger and fullness, making it more likely that your child will eat well for growth and fuel. Eating may still happen at times when your child is dysregulated, though, and that's okay. Consider:

- Is my child in their window of tolerance?
- What clues are there so I can learn to tell?
- Am I regulated?

After an episode when your child was dysregulated, a meal was particularly stressful, or they didn't eat well, **get out your journal and reflect:**

- What was happening earlier in the day?
- Right before the meal?
- Had it been too long since the last meal so they were very hungry?
- Did they spill and get upset?

The goal is not to avoid dysregulation at all costs. That's impossible. The goal is to avoid unnecessary stress and conflict.

Connection Is a Biological Need

Being in relationships with others is a *biological need.* From early studies on attachment with primates, baby monkeys famously chose a minimally responsive wire-and-carpet "mother" over food—to the point of starvation.

According to the Self-Determination Theory in psychology, humans have three fundamental needs in order to thrive: being in relationship with others, a sense of autonomy, and a sense of competence. Responsive feeding aligns with these needs.[13]

Co-Regulation and Connection

There is more to regulation than the saber-toothed tiger analogy. A calm state makes meaningful connection with other humans possible. Addiction and trauma expert Dr. Gabor Maté has been widely quoted: "Safety isn't the absence of threat, it's the presence of connection."

We hear a lot about attachment and feeding for infants, with attention to skin-to-skin and breast feeding as critical to promoting attachment. But there are other ways to feed that are attuned and nurturing, including bottle feeding while offering eye contact and singing, or chatting with a grade-school-aged child over a shared snack. Warm, attuned relationships are critical to health and happiness at all ages.

Calm and connected is more important than tracking servings of vegetables.

Calm supports connection, a child tuning in to cues coming from their body, optimal functioning of body systems, and curiosity around new foods. How can we help children experience more calm? Children learn to self-soothe and regulate after hundreds and thousands of experiences of having their physical and emotional needs met. A regulated parent is more able to respond sensitively and to help a child back to a calm state, a process known as *co-regulation.*

Jo Cormack, PhD psychologist and feeding researcher recommends that parents practice scanning their own bodies for two reasons: first, to get a sense of what their own nervous system is doing and if they are also in felt safety; as well as to gain insight into what may be going on inside their child's body, as there is often subconscious mirroring. With practice, learning to read your child's cues should get easier.

Synchrony in the relationship between parents and infants was described by psychologist Chloe Leclère as, ". . .a matching of behavior, emotional states, and biological rhythms. . ."[14] Synchrony and connection facilitate co-regulation beyond infancy. Co-regulation, and then self-regulation, develop and reinforce the awareness of interoceptive signals and experiences.

When Children Learn To Relate To Food, Their Bodies, and You

The first few years are when children learn how to relate to food, their bodies, and you. As Mister Rogers wrote, "Knowing deep within us that someone is going to feed us when we are hungry is how trust and love begin . . ."[15]

If in general a child's needs have been met reliably, that supports tuning in to hunger and fullness cues over time. Feeding supports attachment, and attachment supports feeding; and in the early months you can't separate the two.

As I said earlier, how we feed kids in the early years reinforces and strengthens capabilities around internally guided eating, or it can undermine those cues.

And I don't want to raise your anxiety with all this talk about co-regulation. You can't do anything "perfectly," or all the time. Children are resilient. There's data on attachment and parenting that shows that you don't have to co-sleep, be available for co-regulation all the time, home school, or feed home-made organic rainbow meals exactly every 3 hours to raise a child who can thrive and do well with food.

And meaningful "connection" doesn't have to be fancy or take a lot of time; for example, it can be a one-on-one conversation in the car on the way to school, folding a basket of laundry with your child finding matching socks, enjoying a snack with phones silenced and your full attention, or watching funny cat videos together.

Self-Regulation and Interoception

The foundation of calm, connection, and co-regulation supports your child's relationship with food and with their body. It supports noticing and interpreting the sensations happening inside the body (interoception), which includes things such as emotions, hunger, fullness, nausea, and cramping. Interoception is important for self-regulation—of emotions, behavior, appetite, and intake. How?

The nerves inside our bodies are different from the nerves on our skin. *Visceral* (gut) nerve fibers are spread out and imprecise, which helps explain why lots of gas makes the whole abdomen hurt, while a paper cut hurts in exactly one spot.

The vagus nerve is an amazing nerve that sends messages back and forth from the brain, to the heart, to the gut, and finally... to the rectum! Branches of the vagus nerve raise and lower heart rate, make you sweaty and clammy, drop blood pressure, and more. (The vagus nerve does a *lot*. As part of the autonomic nervous system, it is explored in detail in Porges' evolving Polyvagal theory of neuroception for those of you using it in your helping professions, or if you're curious to learn more.)

Emotions are experienced in the same places in the body as hunger and fullness; for example, anxiety, food poisoning, and low blood pressure can all make you feel nauseous.

For children with sensory differences or sensitized nervous systems, relatively minor things can tip them into fight/flight or freeze; where it's difficult to tune in to their bodies. Over time children can have trouble differentiating cues coming from inside their bodies, and the response gets dulled. They might not know if they are hungry, full, content, cold, or have a full bladder.

Non-responsive feeding and therapies that take children out of felt safety sabotage appetite, and hamper tuning in.

It can take time to learn to get back in touch with those cues—not that they are *gone*. Many adults struggle with their own histories of dieting or having been pressured to eat, trauma, or food insecurity, which can interfere with the wisdom of the body. Brain-based differences, autism, and sensory differences can also make it more challenging for children to tune in to their bodies.

Seventeen year-old Ian has had a lot of support around co-regulation and regulation over the years. This is a lovely example of ways Ian has learned to help himself feel safe, how he is able to self-regulate as well as continue to seek co-regulation: *"I hate it when people say, 'take a deep breath'—that is so condescending. You can't tell neurodiverse people like me to do something without telling them why you want them to do it. It's better when you say, 'I am going to help you,' or 'are you willing to breathe with me?' To calm down, I like to just listen to music, be by myself, ask someone to rub my feet, head or hands. Then I can relax mentally and my brain comes back online."*

Being Able to Tune In Is Not All-or-Nothing

Erika Shira, a licensed mental health counselor, challenges the common myth that, "If someone isn't 100 percent confident or able to apply a skill all the time, then they lack that skill." Erika counters, "They may need guidance or accommodations, or it might be a skill they can access only when regulated, not that they *can't.*"

Knowing that the ability to sense hunger/fullness/satisfaction is not all-or-nothing is important. Too often parents are told, or they believe, the child "can't" sense hunger or fullness. While you read, keep in mind that this capacity is more than "on" or "off"; and you can figure out how to support tuning in.

A child who is nervous about school, excited to see a friend, overwhelmed by sensory input may have trouble accessing hunger or thirst, but be able to access and interpret those sensations at other times.

Appetite, Curiosity, and Sensory Threshold May Be Contextual

Another way of saying it's not "all-or-nothing" is that appetite, tuning in, curiosity, even gut discomfort and the sensory threshold may be contextual for your child; that is it may depend on the environment and cues around the child. It is also often heavily impacted, as we have been exploring, by what is going on inside the child's body. PhD, mom, and founder of *At Peace Parents*, Casey Erlich, realized that while her son had sensory differences, his loss of appetite and ability to eat, even nausea was mostly "related to his nervous system activation."

Rose, a 20-year-old autistic adoptee, had feeding challenges since infancy, including a feeding tube into her teen years and described her relationship to food as "very contextual." At home she often forgets to eat and is prompted by her mother. But there are circumstances when things feel better and more attuned. She and her mother identify these primarily as situations where she feels safe and accepted with supportive friends.

Rose shared, "*I had a friend who was a cook and he made the most amazing Asian rice bowls. I felt really happy, like he made this food for me. And it was really frickin' good! My favorite rice bowl had chicken and broccoli, amongst other seasonings and sauces. I gained weight when we were hanging out.*" Sometimes a full stomach felt unpleasant; other times, often with friends, ". . . *I could kind of lay down and it was okay. No big deal. It wasn't really unpleasant.*"

Her interest in connecting with her birth culture is another bridge to positive food experiences. "*I like watching cooking videos on YouTube or Googling recipes. I'm really drawn to Asian recipes right now. I think food is a way I'm exploring my birth culture in a way that feels authentic and that I can be independent with. The connections I make cooking and eating with others enriches my relationship with food.*"

For Rose, eating with friends and exploring Chinese cuisine supported her appetite, curiosity to try new foods, and even made feeling full less unpleasant.

We know that for many people, anxiety, or a dysregulated nervous system makes sensory experiences feel more intense, disconnected, or unpleasant. This can result in a vicious cycle of anxiety and sensory distress, and is why felt safety is so important.

> A mom wrote, *"Our OT says we have to work on her sensory issues and interoception, before we can deal with her food preoccupation and picky eating. I'm not sure."* Reassuring with food may be the key to a child feeling calm. You may see anxiety, sensory, and other challenges be less over-whelming, and other capabilities emerge by focusing on calm and responsive feeding from the start. You can certainly address other issues at the same time.

Responsive Feeding Supports Interoception

Responsive feeding will help children and teens learn to tell the difference between emotional and physical needs over months to years. How you feed them and react to their (and your) "mistakes" can help or hinder that process. Every interaction is a learning opportunity for you and your child, as in, *"I tried to make her drink milk with lunch and she raged and ate nothing."*

When you are locked in a power struggle over food, it is close to impossible for your child to differentiate emotion from physical sensations—and your relationship, their health, and nutrition suffers.

Anxiety impacts appetite (up or down) and can affect how nutrients are absorbed. People often experience anxiety as tension or tightness in the throat or stomach and gut which can get in the way of hunger signals.[16] Having a pleasant atmosphere around food and a supportive relationship with you, helps kids listen to signals from their bodies and discern, "Am I hungry, am I full, am I worried about tomorrow's quiz?"

Angry? Bored? Hungry? Full? The following can help your child learn to "hear" what their body is telling them.

- Limit exposure to food advertising, which can suggest to children that they are hungry if they are susceptible.
- Identify boredom. Many children, particularly with a history of restriction, will say they are hungry when they are bored. When this happens, you can say: "Snack time is soon; shall we play some Legos?" Avoid, "You can't be hungry, you're just bored." See how it goes. Offering the child something to eat if it supports felt safety is always an option.
- Offer language to begin talking about emotions; find resources online or from a school social worker or your child's therapist if they have one.
- Model emotional awareness and health. "I'm a little sad today; can we (insert activity here) together?"

Dr. Bruce Perry advises: 1) Helping the child understand that "all feelings are okay to feel—sad, glad, or mad (more emotions for older children)"; 2) "Teach the child healthy ways to act when sad, glad, or mad"; 3) "Begin to explore how other people may feel, and how they show their feelings: 'How do you think Bobby feels when you push him?'" 4) "When you sense that the child is clearly happy, sad, or mad, ask them how they are feeling. Help them begin to put words and labels to these feelings."[17]

Michelle Gorman, RD, tells a story about helping her then three-year-old listen to his body: *"He was crying, seemed really out of balance, and was asking for ice cream."* She asked, *"How are you feeling?"* When he answered, "I feel sad," she asked if he would like a hug. He didn't ask for the ice cream after they had time to hug and connect. Gorman recognized, *"It was sadnes he was responding to, not hunger. I believe it helped him to clarify and distinguish the difference between emotions and physical sensations."*

The following do not promote learning to separate emotions from physical sensations:

- Using food frequently as rewards for good behavior, grades, etc.
- Offering food first and regularly to soothe upset or pain.
- Pressuring or trying to get kids to eat more or less than they want.
- Praising children for eating or punishing when they don't eat.

For more on interoception, check out the index for where it appears throughout the book.

Will Sometimes "Using" Food Interfere with Interoception?

While I've just mentioned it's unhelpful to regularly reward or control behavior with food, there are some exceptions. For example, if you want to celebrate after a softball game with a team outing to Dairy Queen, or your child gets a sucker with an annual feared shot or uses candy to mask the taste of foul-tasting medicine, that's fine. (Studies suggest that sweet tastes lessen pain.[18]) However, if every time your child scrapes his knee he gets a cookie, he isn't learning other coping skills.

If you've had a rotten day and give your son cheese puffs to get through that Target run, do what you need to do! However, if crackers or candy are the only things that get you through every day, or every transition to daycare, you may need help coming up with other strategies.

Offering a child an extra snack (maybe a cheese stick or cereal bar) if you observe them getting dysregulated, is also okay. When you're attuned to their needs and reactions, this will help guide you.

Note that behavioral therapies that use food or drink rewards/reinforcers can interfere with appetite and interoception, and increase cavity risk.

Casey Ehrlich, PhD, has an autistic son with pathological demand avoidance, which she and others view as a nervous system disability. With her son's burnout, he had severe GI distress and a handful of accepted foods. She shared online how she used the "Transition Treat" to help with her son's chronically dysregulated nervous systems. I asked her to elaborate:

"When his threat response was so activated, he'd stop eating; he'd say, 'My body won't let me.' That's how I would know we needed to bring down that threat response. How can I accommodate this perception of threat?

When you hit rock bottom and you're afraid your child won't survive without a feeding tube, you're kind of beyond fear. There's a freedom to try things outside of the box.

Sometimes 'breaking the rules' helped to decrease that threat response – even if it's not a rule in our house. **So I experimented with letting him have a Tootsie Roll before breakfast and it helped him calm so he could access his hunger. There is the worry that the sweet will ruin his appetite, but after, he could eat. He didn't just keep wanting to eat sugar, it just brought his sense of threat down.**

We'd already done 'eat this first,' 'sit at the table to eat,' positive discipline, SOS [sequential oral sensory feeding therapy, see page 152] . . . I was in a constant state of anxiety about his eating. All the stuff we'd been told to do wasn't helping.

And, I was learning about how his brain works and thinking, let's follow the logic and figure out how to decrease the threat response... So we started using a treat to help decrease that threat response during difficult transitions. We did this starting 3 years ago. We don't need it as much now."

Casey offered the treat to help her son get out of fight, flight, and freeze. The transition treat is not a reward which can invite pushback and dysregulation for some kids. She explained, "It's not, 'If you get in the car you get the candy' because that's still me in control. I think of it as an accommodation to move through the transition, I offer it whether he gets in the car or not."

Casey shared, "We use food in a non-traditional way to support his nervous system that has not ended up in worse eating habits, in fact, over time, he's eating better and the variety he eats is increasing."

The Power of Accommodation

Throughout this book, I will recommend a practice such as supporting children to self-serve, and then suggest potential accommodations and flexibility. You are invited to observe how your child reacts—and reflect and adjust to help your child (and you) feel calm and connected.

Social worker Eileen Devine is a fan of accommodations. Between our interview and articles on her website, she describes the power of accommodation:

- Accommodations are right, just, and fair.
- Accommodations are an "intervention."

- Accommodations recognize that our child would do well if they could.
- Accommodations help preserve our child's "brain fuel."
- Accommodations are not "giving in." They are proactive and developed through observation and reflection.
- Accommodations help your child settle in their environment and experience less challenging behavioral symptoms.

Accommodation is responsive. Within the feeding relationship you have with your children, you observe, plan, feed, nurture, and adapt. The next chapter lays the groundwork for a responsive alternative to pressure and restriction.

Chapter 3 The Foundation for Responsive Feeding

Understanding the *why* behind what you *do* with responsive feeding prepares you for challenges. In this chapter, you'll learn about learn about shifting agendas, the mealtime environment, what words help or invite conflict, how long it might take, tips for managing expectations and behavior, and getting regulated before eating.

Why RF?

If we restore or establish a structured, reliable, and safe eating environment, we allow children the space to rely on cues to eat or not eat that come mostly from *inside* their bodies. Equally as important, when adults feed children reliably and with love, we teach children that they can trust and rely on us, and they learn to trust and rely on their bodies. Their bodies are worthy of being cared for.

Responsive feeding is supported by work in different disciplines, and grounded in the responsive parenting model.[1]

Researcher and psychologist Jo Cormack defined RF in her PhD thesis: "Responsive feeding is an approach to feeding children which facilitates autonomous eating in the context of warm, attuned relationships and appropriate structure. This is with a view to supporting the development of a positive relationship with food characterized by effective self-regulation of energy intake and optimized competence and eating enjoyment."[2]

Responsive feeding centers the attuned relationship between the parent and child and helps kids experience calm (where they eat, think, and feel their best).

Benefits of Responsive Feeding

You are more likely to:

- Look forward to eating with your child.
- Have confidence in your feeding choices.
- Enjoy more variety and (re)discover your joy around cooking and/or eating.
- Worry less about weight or size.

- Worry less about who is eating what or how much. As one mom put it, *"I get to be a mom again, not a food cop!"*

Your child is more likely to:

- Have stable and healthy weight (for them).
- Learn to eat based on internal (from their own body) cues of hunger and fullness.
- Eat a variety of foods and enjoy better nutrition, and feel more confident and competent in other aspects of life.
- Avoid disordered eating behaviors, and have a lower risk of eating disorders.

RF Is for All Your Children

Your toddler and your teen; your child with developmental differences; biological or adopted children; your anxious eater and your foodie; your bigger and smaller-than-average child—are fed with the same underlying philosophy and, without bouncing from one strategy to the next.

Consider Lila's dilemma. Lila had two girls. Her four-year-old, Martha, was growing steadily around the 10th percentile. At age seven, her sister Julia, who had grown at around the 75th percentile for years, had recently grown into the o*ese category at the 90th percentile. About a year earlier, alarmed by Julia's hearty appetite, Lila made some changes: Julia was not allowed to have fried foods, sweet foods or drinks unless they were sugar-free; and starches and meat were limited while she could have as much fruits and vegetables as she wanted. Most meals ended in tears—for everyone at the table.

Lila despaired, *"I'm shoving ice cream and milk shakes at Martha and keeping them out of Julia's hands. My husband gets angry if he finds out Julia had a treat and blames me for not controlling her. Julia is obsessed with dessert and candy. When we go to a friend's house, she hounds them for the stuff we can't let her have. It's embarrassing, and I'm worried she's heading for an eating disorder!"*

The message both girls learned is that they aren't okay as they are, they can't handle eating, and they can't trust their bodies. Feeding siblings differently sets them up for conflict, comparison, and resentment. Julia and Martha can both be trusted with eating despite their different bodies and appetites.

Kids Can Do It, Even with Challenges

Almost every child has capabilities, including around knowing how much to eat and the drive for variety. Some children have lost touch with this capacity for various reasons as you learned in Chapter 1. But those skills are there. The delayed child has skills. The child with a neuromuscular disorder or a genetic syndrome has skills. If we build on what children *can* do or learn to do, rather than focusing on what they can't, it helps us recognize that our role is to optimize the environment and provide *scaffolding* so children can do their best with eating.

For children with challenges to interoception, Chapter 8 covers optimizing the feeding environment, including gentle external support.

"I thought my child couldn't feel hunger; an OT told us as much, because he didn't seem to for years and had so many challenges. But as a teen, there are instances where he can and does enjoy eating and eats a good amount, usually with friends and not at a classic mealtime. It's fascinating. I wish I'd known more about it earlier so I could have explored how to support him then, but we are seeing progress. I have hope."
— Nico's dad

What Is Responsive Feeding?

Before diving into application of RF, it helps to examine the supporting values, as well as examples of what RF is not. The following is my interpretation and evolving understanding of RF, which may differ from how others describe it.

RF Guiding Values

Parenting (and feeding) decisions are easier to make when guided by your values, and you are clear as to what those are. This book won't cover every scenario you'll face, but reflecting on the values behind a responsive approach can help.

The core RF values that help children do their best with eating support the child's autonomy, relationships, internal motivation, and sense of competence with a whole child lens (from the White Paper on RFT that I coauthored).[3] Centering these values supports felt safety. And the values are intertwined; for example, not enforcing bite rules supports autonomy and decreases conflict, which allows for connection and the space for internal motivation to bloom. The following sections provide a bit more about each value.

Support the Child's Autonomy

Allow your child to have control when possible. **When parents support autonomy, kids do better *for* themselves and feel better *about* themselves.** This isn't a free-for-all with the kids in charge. A textbook on developmental psychology said this about supporting the "I do it" drive: "When people in positions of responsibility or authority—for example, parents and teachers—support the autonomy of those with whom they interact, the latter individuals tend to display enhanced autonomy, intrinsic motivation and self-regard. Overcontrol, conversely, is typically associated with diminished motivation and self-esteem."[4] Note that autonomy supports internal motivation, and self-regard that aligns with the value of competence.

Example: The independent or cautious child pushed to try a bite of pepperoni (thwarting autonomy) may refuse or take a tiny bite with intense emotion and fuss, but when he is at a party and sees a friend enjoying pesto, without pressure he may try and even enjoy it.

Center Relationship

This refers to warm and attuned relationships through connection.

Mom Mimi described how much she enjoyed mealtimes when she focused on connection and stopped all the "fun" tricks trying to get her kids to eat more fruit and veg. *"My kid put butter on her crackers tonight and I cannot tell you what a big step forward that is in her willingness to try new foods! Now we have a few bowls out and we chat about literally anything else but the food. She is inquisitive about my food and putting some new bits on her plate or plating them up for me. We are so much better connected, she is relaxed, we eat all meals together at the table instead of in front of the TV . . . It's a revelation. We spend so much more time giggling and chatting than before. It's improved everything."*

Examples: Cooking together, eating with a child, and decreasing conflict.

Support Competence

This has two parts: One is the child's sense of being capable (with or without accommodations); the other covers concrete skills in areas where a child may need more support.

Examples: A preschooler enjoys adding ingredients and stirring batter, or a child using an adaptive spoon beams with pride when she gets most of the yogurt to her mouth.

Whole Child Lens

Each child is unique and lots of things play a role in how they will feel about food, for example: school "growing food first" rules, nutrition lessons that label foods as "good" or "bad," social media, friends, and a need for accommodations.

Example: If money is tight, a tween might experience less anxiety composting leftovers versus throwing them out, another child may need noise-canceling earbuds to enjoy family meals.

Support Internal Motivation

Internal drives to eat include hunger, appetite, curiosity, pleasure, sensory input, and soothing or nervous system regulation. The desire comes from the child rather than imposed from the outside. Internal motivation is your ally in helping your child become the best eater they can be.

As Fred Rogers wrote, "There's a world of difference between insisting on someone doing something and establishing an atmosphere in which that person can grow into wanting to do it."[5]

This is such a critical value and enmeshed with other concepts that it needs a bit more fleshing out.

The Power of Internal Motivation, or I Do It!

The basic human needs of relationship, competence, and autonomy can also be viewed as internal needs driving behavior. Children want to grow up and do their best with eating. This drive from within is a powerful force. (Think of a child learning to walk who will pick themselves up over and over again...)

You can't replace internal motivation with praise, stickers, or therapy. For many children, external rewards and pressure undermine the true motivation to grow up and be capable. Jo Cormack PhD sums it up: "Internal motivation isn't the only way to get children to eat, but it's the best, most long-lasting, and authentic way."

When the child has a desire to succeed, rather than feel pushed or that he has to comply, it can work wonders. One dad after one week of not trying to *get* his four-year-old son (who has sensory issues) to eat wrote, *"Jaylen observes everything and understands now that he is not expected to eat anything he doesn't want. He remarks on foods, 'Hey, watermelon!' He's eaten some different waffles, which is great. I sense that he wishes there were more foods on the table he could eat."* I often hear this from parents. It is this motivation (curiosity in this case) from the child that, if supported with options and without pressure, will help children like Jaylen branch out.

RF Isn't...

Another way to help define something is to look at what it is *not*. To give you a general idea, here are a few examples of non-responsive tactics that don't align with the RFT values:

- Hard and fast rules that don't honor flexibility such as one-bite rules (undermine autonomy and individualized care).
- Pressure and restriction (undermine autonomy).
- Not advancing textures or hand feeding a child who may want to do it themselves (undermining competence and autonomy).
- Punishing a child by not letting them enjoy cake at a party (undermines relationship and connection).
- Protocol (one size fits all) feeding therapy (not individualized).

Responsive feeding also isn't just "eat when you are hungry and stop when you're full," or "let kids eat whatever, whenever"—two common misperceptions.

RF Isn't Just "Eat When You're Hungry and Stop When You're Full"

The advice to only "eat when hungry and stop when full" is not practical, realistic, or joyful for the vast majority of us. ("Emotional eating" is okay too! More on that soon.) It's common for eating to be guided by schedules, communal meals, daycare, and routines. It means we get to be flexible and accommodate. Our bodies can handle it.

You don't have to eat only when you are hungry and stop when you are full. Neither do your kids.

Here is an example of functional, attuned eating that happened while I was writing this chapter. I had a ZOOM meeting from 11–1:00, but I feel best when I eat at around 11:30 a.m. By 1:00 p.m., if I haven't eaten, I'm predictably ravenous, maybe headachy, and grouchy. So I had a sandwich before the meeting and brought cashews and water to my desk in case I got hungry. (Though I have never experienced food insecurity, I was restricted as a teen and dieted in my twenties. I tend to feel anxious about being hungry, so I try to always have something on hand.)

I ate when I *wasn't* hungry—and I consider myself a tuned-in eater. And I am able to plan ahead, connect what is likely to happen with past experiences, and plan the snack, etc. You may need to help a child or teen (or you!) think through this kind of scenario in concrete ways.

Eating beyond fullness (especially if your next meal may be delayed) is fine too. I was recently curious when I realized that I eat most dinners beyond fullness to slightly uncomfortable. While at first I felt badly about that, I realized that I wake up most mornings pleasantly hungry and tuned in. I figure my body knows it needs a bit more to make it the 12–14 hours between dinner and breakfast. Bodies are amazing!

RF Is Not "Let Kids Eat Whatever, Whenever"

Some think that RF means letting children eat whatever and whenever they want... which you already know isn't true. It's also not about making them eat. It's prioritizing calm and supporting the child's autonomy while you provide opportunity, structure, and reliability, and adapt based on your child's experiences and reactions.

Preparing for the Transition

You may be tempted to jump in with what you've learned so far. But I encourage you to read on before making major changes. I've had parents reach out after reading a blog post, or having listened to a podcast, with variations of the following:

"I tried this for four days, but our three-year-old ate more than my husband!"

"If I don't bribe with dessert, he'll only eat bread."

"We've been at it for over a month and we're still fighting all the time."

"We experimented with dessert with the meal, but he had to eat his vegetables before he could leave the table. It was still miserable."

"My wife is convinced this just won't help our child."

Responsive feeding is much more than a few tips or not pressuring. Consider this dad at a workshop. It was the second time I'd visited his early childhood support group, and in front of the other dads (most of whom were new to this info), he said, *"This doesn't work. I'm doing everything you said, and my daughter is still really picky, and we still fight at meals. It's been a year!"* It turns out that he and his wife were so worried about calcium that they forced their daughter to drink milk at every meal. They were still pressuring.

When parents pick and choose one or two pieces of advice and haven't had the time to understand the philosophy, self-regulation of energy intake, or how children learn to enjoy foods, they usually find that it doesn't work the way they'd hoped, or as fast as they'd hoped. When this happens, parents can feel more hopeless and that they and their child have "failed" again.

Learn as much as you can, get buy-in from your partner (if you have one), and believe in your heart this is what you want to do *before* you jump in.

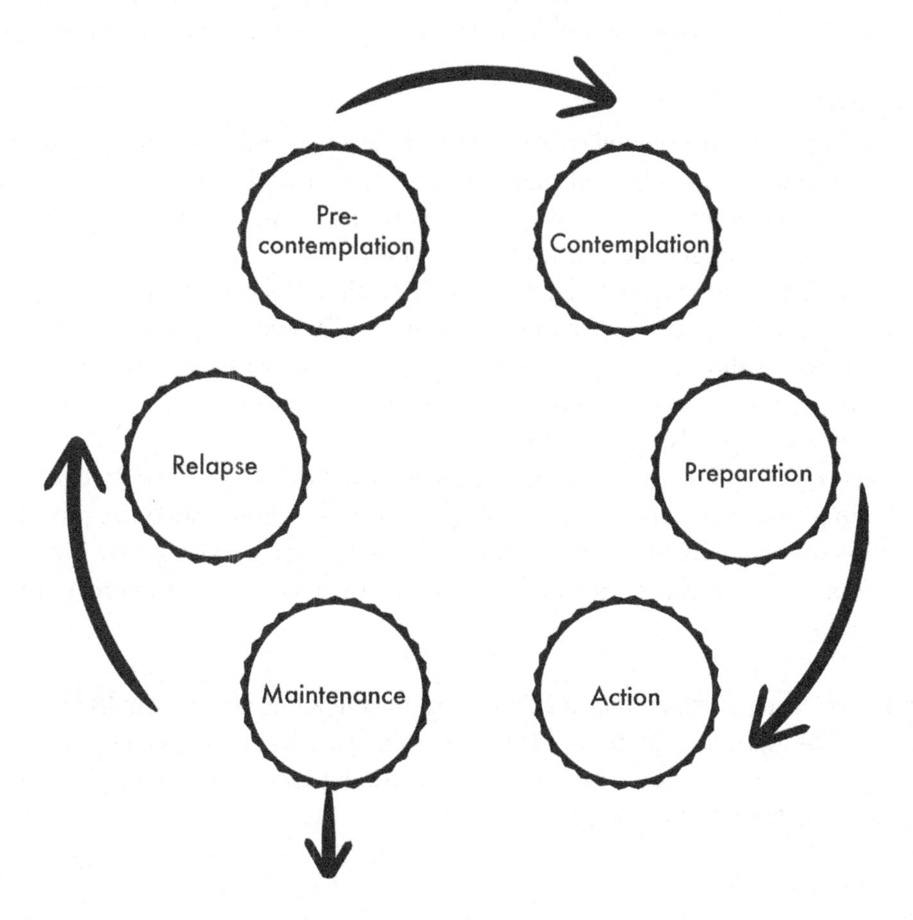

Figure 3.1: Visual representation of the well-known "cycle of change," coined by Prochaska and DiClemente in the 1970s.

Thoughts on Timing

When to start, how long it takes, and normalizing "relapse."

When to Start

Jo Cormack PhD, shares: "The change cycle is helpful. First, doing the prep work to be in the stage where you feel ready for change is important." This book should help with that.

Jo goes on to say, "If it's a particularly stressful time, it may be best to wait. And it's okay if you're still learning and thinking about not pressuring or not restricting, to start with other things such as structure, or getting proper seating, or trying to serve dessert with a meal and even self-serve meals."

If you're feeling overwhelmed, like *you* aren't anywhere near to feeling safe, dip into Chapter 12 and consider ways to support your own sense of calm as you begin to explore how you can offer support to your child. For some parents, data and research and jumping in with understanding and with action will help them feel confident, others will themselves need to consider doing their own work first. Do what helps you most.

How Long it Takes

It can take time to learn new ways of approaching food and mealtimes. You may already have structure, variety, and shared meals in place and want to work on serving family style or backing off on pressure. Or you may have nonstop grazing, intense conflict, behavioral challenges, or no family meals.

With growth or nutritional concerns, trusting this process feels even tougher and tends to take longer (and you may benefit from additional support). Once structure and responsive feeding is in place, which may take weeks or months, how long it takes for your child to begin tuning in to hunger and fullness cues, or branch out in terms of variety, depends on age and other factors.

For neurotypical children with problems such as "overeating" or "picky" eating, a toddler might take four to six weeks to see progress; a grade-schooler a bit longer; and a high schooler, maybe months or more. The process can take longer if your child has developmental or oral-motor differences, or other barriers to interoception.

We all want results... now! Some feeding clinics and therapists promise results on a timetable. Be aware that "progress" in the clinic setting (such as licking a food) may not translate into eating better at home. Pressure to get results can lead therapists and parents to push, which often slows the process.

Many parents notice rapid improvements. Jules had happier meals almost immediately after giving up on the "no-thank-you bite" rule. *"It wasn't working anyway to get them to eat vegetables and we all hated it. I dread meals less and she's happier and stays at the table longer. She's not coming back ten minutes after the meal is over, looking for snacks anymore too."* Sue says it took about seven months for her toddler with oral-motor and sensory differences to increase the variety of foods he enjoyed. Nora, whose daughter at age five ate less than 10 foods, had slow progress—with fits and starts—until about four years in. Nora says today, *"I actually think she is a better eater now than most of her peers."*

One mom told me her 15-year-old son started trying new foods because he was interested in dating and didn't want to "order off the kiddie menu." Another dad talked about his selective daughter who tried all kinds of new foods in her first year of college.

I have also seen a 10-year-old feeding clinic "failure" branch out and improve his attitude toward food in a few weeks, and "food-obsessed" toddlers happily leave food on their plates in less than a month (a sign of tuning in to fullness).

And children in the same family may react differently to change; one child loves self-serving and branches out quickly, while another observes and is slower to try new things overall.

Teens and adults with eating struggles tend to need longer to heal their relationships with food and their bodies—depending on the severity of challenges, and sometimes with the help of an eating disorder specialist. Some young people progress but still struggle with their relationship to food into adulthood (along with many American adults). That's okay. You may find it a relief to be reminded that, as mental health counselor Dawn Friedman says, "You don't need to raise a finished person at 18."

Relapse Is Part of the Process

You, the parent, may "relapse" and fall back to pressure or rewards after a few rough meals. But don't despair: "You learn by getting back in," as Cormack says.

Cormack and I both observe a pattern when there are more entrenched feeding challenges, in which things can get worse before they get better (you'll read examples later). "Then things may dramatically improve, which is wonderful, but sets up doubt when there is a plateau or a time when eating worsens again," Cormack observes. And it probably will during stressful times, such as starting a new school or the arrival of a sibling.

Cormack shares, "It's a time that's high risk because parents can lose faith and think, 'See? I *do* have to get them to eat vegetables!' and may fall back into pressure."

And stressed children may prefer the comfort of predictable foods for some time. Knowing in advance that this is typical of the journey can help you ride through challenges. A child who may rely on her preferred, comforting foods while adjusting to a baby brother, will be more likely to come back to a variety of foods if they are not pressured, and with a focus on felt safety.

Wagon Ruts: Change Takes Time

Think of how your child relates to food now as engrained, automatic pathways that have been reinforced over thousands of experiences, several months, and even years.

If you've ever seen wagon ruts, say on trails from the covered wagon migrations in the American West, there are actual grooves carved inches deep into stone. The wagon wheels (how your child reacts to food and eating situations) want to stay in these well-worn, familiar grooves. It takes time to forge new pathways (ways of interacting with food and eating).

In the beginning, challenges or sensory reminders will nudge those wagons back into the familiar grooves. **This is what can happen when a food-preoccupied child finally enjoys a cuddle and isn't thinking about food, then hears a food wrapper and hops up and runs frantically into the kitchen; or the child curiously exploring an unfamiliar food looks up to see the eager eyes of a parent only to make a face of disgust and throw the food.**

With more and more time in felt safety, and without pressure or restriction, which can nudge children back into familiar and anxious patterns, children (and adults) can discover new ways of relating to food and their bodies. (And those old paths are still there. So a child who was restricted or food insecure may always benefit from the reassurance of food on hand, or a selective child may gravitate to familiar and favored foods during times of upheaval.)

Preparing Yourself for Change

Before you begin new feeding strategies, write down where you are now. What are your days like? Do you start with a child screaming for a snack, or sneaking snacks from playmates while ignoring all else? How does it make you feel? How much energy is devoted to what does or doesn't go into your child's mouth?

As you go through this process, it will be easy to forget how things were when you started. **The journal has been invaluable for parents to notice clear progress when they may feel like things are going nowhere.**

Acknowledge Your Expectations and Feelings

"No one wants to feel angry with their child or dread every meal."

— Peggy, mother to Scott, age four

"I never realized how important it was that I not raise a 'picky eater' until I was struggling so hard to get him to try new foods. I had to question what the worst outcome could be. Would my mothering be a failure if my son never liked vegetables? I had to learn to lighten up my ideal of how I wanted him to eat, and just take things one bite at a time."

— Sue, mother to Marcus

"Almost all of our meals growing up were cooked by my mom and eaten together around our dining table. This instilled a routine of serving nutritious meals. While this was positive, it was also a stumbling block, as it fed my frustrations with a child who refused to eat in a well-rounded manner."
— Brigid, mother of Mena

"The most frustrating thing for me has always been when I go out of my way to make something for my daughter that she asked for or that she has eaten in the past—and then she refuses to eat it."
— Mishelle, mother of three-year-old Katie

A lot of the bad feelings happen when expectations don't match reality (I'm looking at you, rainbow Bento-box social media lunches!). Mealtimes aren't what you hoped for, and your child doesn't eat the way you want them to.

Moms often tell me they feel rejected and defeated when a child turns their nose up at a lovingly prepared meal. Acknowledge your feelings and know your child feels your love in many ways.

Sixteen-year-old Yiseth, a self-described picky eater says, *"It's not a personal rejection of love if a kid doesn't want to eat something their mom made for them. Maybe it's the pressure, maybe the food, but it's not coming back at the love. It's not about the love. I love my parents to death."*

It's okay to feel angry, disappointed, and even resentful. It's okay, but it can be a problem if your children sense your desperation, feel they are letting you down, or invite you into conflict. Addressing your feelings and expectations so you can be available for co-regulation, plus good company at mealtimes, will help your child's eating and everyone's anxiety (including yours). Find a way to work through your feelings. Fume (in private), talk to your partner, join an online support group, or consult with a professional. Acknowledging when you're overwhelmed, feeling anxious or depressed, isn't easy.

Sitting down to think about and understand where you are, and where your child is, as you undertake this process will be critical to learning to observe and be responsive to your child.

This book will also help adjust expectations to more achievable goals, which ones to focus on, and when. Felt safety first, vegetables later. (And as Sue mentioned above, your child can be okay without ever eating a vegetable, though that's a rare outcome.)

If you let your mood depend on whether your child eats something you made, or eats less or more than you wanted, you are setting yourself up for defeat.

A Shift in Thinking

Stepping back from pressure and restriction isn't easy. I wish feeding kids was as simple as insisting your child take a "no-thank-you" bite, or making smiley faces out of raisins. It involves consistency and effort, and often a major shift in the way you think about food, weight, your child and his capabilities, and your role in it all.

Our culture mostly looks at food in terms of what it can *do* for us or how we can control its consumption. There are a lot of rules: eat "superfoods," limit portions, do intermittent fasting, take expensive supplements . . . We are told to optimize our child's nutrition to influence IQ, behavior, and weight (with little evidence to back up these ideas).

When pressure and restriction don't produce the desired results, we are told to try harder, avoid another food group or macronutrient (carbs), or buy a different supplement. Doctors or feeding therapists may accuse parents of not doing as they are told, and parents (and their kids) feel like failures.

We may be able to get a few bites in here and there, but across the board, we can't sustainably control what or how much children eat or weigh (at least not without significant downsides). This can be difficult to accept, although you may already suspect it's true. Here are a few examples of how a shift in thinking, by leaving the agenda behind, might look:

From: How can I push (encourage, get) my son to eat more (less, different foods)?
To: How can I set up the best feeding environment and support so his natural capabilities with eating can emerge?

From: Why won't he eat vegetables?
To: What are my son's capabilities? What can he do? How can I support him?

From: How do I get more calories in her?
To: How can I offer appetizing foods at her skill level in a lower-stress environment so I can support her appetite and tuning in to her body?

From: The doctor said he's too heavy. How can I get him to eat less?
To: How can I feed him so he grows to have the body that is right for him? (With the understanding that it may not mean an average outcome.)

Do you see the difference? They will feel it and so will you.

And when this clicks and you get to the point of recognizing what is and isn't in your control, the relief will likely be immense (it was for me and for many of my clients). Remember the mom from the Introduction, after the workshop on starting solids? She said, *"You're saying I don't have to control how much he eats; that it's his job. This feels so good."*

If a feeding approach promises to get a child to eat more, less, or different foods, then it's not responsive. You can't do *intuitive* fasting, and *mindful* eating isn't a weight-control tool. During a popular training I attended, one feeding therapist said, "Someone has to teach kids portion control." I think that's wrong. This comes back to the idea of whether humans can self-regulate. It took me a long time to trust this concept. If we can accept that we don't all have to be in the "normal" weight range (for health or any other reason), then we can more easily accept that humans can self-regulate.

Seeing Things from Their Perspective

Putting yourself in your child's place can help. As one mom shared, "*When I learned to look at this all from my daughter's point of view, things got so much better.*"

Or, as 16-year-old Yiseth said with a twinkle in her eye, "*Think of it from the kid's point of view. It shouldn't be 'how can I get her to try this,' but 'how can I help my child do this at her own pace.*" Yiseth, the "picky eater," liked less pressure and more relaxed meals.

Prepare Your Child for Change

For children old enough to understand, it's probably wise to let them know things are changing. Focus on connection and enjoyment as the reason for changes, rather than perceived problems or blame. Try, "We haven't been enjoying meals. It's kind of stressful, and we can tell that you're frustrated, and so are we. We're going to do things differently and this is how . . ." Something like, "We will figure it out together," leaves the door open for adjustments.

Implementing Responsive Feeding

If Kailynne is engaged in a battle over how many bites of carrot earns an Oreo, her focus is on *the battle*. If she's upset, she can't imagine tasting a new food. There's too much going on in her body to tune in to hunger or curiosity. Start with felt safety.

"Since mealtimes have such deep meanings about relationships and love and giving and receiving, it's worth all the effort it takes to avoid turning mealtimes into bargaining sessions or battlegrounds."[6]

— Mister Rogers, Mister Roger's Neighborhood

Get Regulated Before Meals

Pause and set the stage for more connected meals. Saying grace or taking a centering breath is a way of signaling that things are different. With my adult clients, I also coupled the centering breath with them giving themselves explicit permission to eat what tastes good, and enough of it to feel satisfied.

Taking a moment after a hectic day helps on many levels. Alexis noticed that she herself ate quickly: *"I'm going 100 miles an hour to get the food on the table, and then I match my daughter's fast pace and I never slow down."* Reminding herself to catch her breath helped Alexis pay attention to her own eating, enjoy herself more at the table, and access calm.

As often as you can remember, pause before a meal to slow down and settle into your body and invite your kids to join you. This might mean a brief saying such as, "bon appétit, you may eat!" or a traditional blessing, a shared song, or perhaps a moment to thank the farmer, the cook, and everyone for showing up. When children lead this thank-you time, it can be an opportunity to learn something about their thoughts and what they value most.

This regulating moment, whatever it is for your family, can serve to:

- Include children in family rituals.
- Pass on family traditions, such as saying Grandpa's funny grace.
- Support starting the meal with felt safety before passing plates and serving little ones and others who may need assistance.
- Transition into conversation, such as, "What was the best part of your day?" or "How was gym?"
- Help you and your children tune in to hunger and fullness.
- Help connect you with yourself and your family; holding hands is nice, too.
- Make meals feel special. Maybe light a candle or two (real or LED), and let the children blow the candle out to signal the end of the meal.
- Share values, religious practices, and/or gratitude and appreciation for the food and preparers.
- Slow the pace for everyone.

For some food-preoccupied children or where there may be difficulties with impulse control, looking at the food while saying grace may increase anxiety. You can try to say the "thank you" while standing, then bring food to the table, or eat for a few minutes, then pause and connect.

The Mealtime Environment

If mealtimes have been really stressful, even when you stop pressuring or restricting, your child may still feel anxious for a time. Signal a change by altering the physical setting:

- Change the view. Move her place or change the painting on the wall.
- Change who sits next to her. For one family, Dad was battling over manners, so moving him to a seat not directly across from his nine-year-old helped.

- If your child is ready, get rid of the tray on the highchair and pull them up to the table.
- Get some new cups or throw out the plate your child has been staring at while gagging.
- Eat somewhere else (kitchen island, picnic table on the patio) for a time until you have some positive experiences.

The Case for Eating Together

Family meals are associated with good things. You have to eat, they have to eat, and it's generally better when you do it together. Ideally, meals would be with family members around a table (or on mats/cushions on the floor) facing one another. One attuned adult eating with a child is a family meal.

Children tend to do best with eating when they sit down with few distractions such as screens, toys, or books. Meals can be a fun time to connect. (See topics on flexible family meals, and when distractions can help with felt safety, in on pages 77-79.)

Eating together:

- Helps kids tune in to hunger and fullness and eat the right amount for them.
- Lowers choking risk.
- Helps children explore new foods; seeing someone they trust enjoy a food is an important step in the process.
- Builds relationship and connection.
- Is linked with overall success in life, more so than socioeconomic or educational milieu and after-school activities.[7]

Table Talk: When in Doubt, Don't Blurt It Out

I often get asked, "Is it okay if I say X?" I get it. I'm a talker. And parents are encouraged to narrate our days for language development or positive attention, and we seem to be talking, talking, talking.

Parents do this around food with kids *all the time,* usually with an agenda. All that talking can interfere with your child's curiosity and internal motivation, and it interferes with their ability to tune in to their body, while increasing anxiety and resistance. Here are some tips:

- Don't talk nutrition with young kids. A three-year-old doesn't need to know the word protein, and won't understand it anyway.
- Don't go on and on about how pretty a food is or how delicious. One comment about a red berry or a sweet taste is okay.
- Don't talk about portions or weight.
- Don't talk about "green-light" or "red-light" foods, "growing," or "fun" foods. All of those other names mean "good" and "bad" to a child. The child

who eats "bad" foods thinks he is "bad," inviting guilt and shame into the relationship with food.

- Don't ask questions that invite negativity (no) or refusal: "Do you like it?"
- Don't argue with their observations: "It's not too hot."

The wisdom is *within*, and children have a better chance of being able to *listen* to that wisdom if we support them with eating. One mom wrote on my blog that it was "irresponsible" not to teach nutrition to young children, for example, and that they will feel ill if they eat too much "junk food." I suggested that it is far more meaningful if the child learns that through experience, and they will, if we let them.

You can't teach kids this stuff with words or picture books. It's learned, meal after meal. Remember Mimi? I'm repeating her words here: "*. . . we chat about literally anything else but the food . . . We are so much better connected, she is relaxed, we eat all meals together at the table instead of in front of the TV . . . We spend so much more time giggling and chatting than before. It's improved everything.*"

When a child on occasion chooses to eat only candy for a snack, she will learn that she is soon hungry or has an upset tummy. If she chooses only to eat the Cheetos for lunch, she may not have energy for gymnastics class.

It amazed me on the day after Halloween when my then three-year-old turned down candy, saying, "I've had enough sweet today." She happily set the candy aside for the next day (this was within the context of filling meals and snacks with regular access to sweets for about 18 months). Another time in middle school after a sleepover where she enjoyed takeout and lots of pre-packaged salty and sweet foods, she came home saying she wanted stir fry for dinner since she hadn't had veggies in a long time.

Things you *can* say, and may need to repeat in a calm and gentle manner, include:

- "You don't have to eat anything you don't want to."
- "There will always be enough."
- "You can have as much as you want."
- "You don't have to eat it, but please be polite. Instead of 'gross,' please just say, 'no thank you.'" (One blog reader shared the delightful phrase, "*Don't yuck my yum.*")

The word "soon" can be particularly helpful (especially to avoid a "no"). And young children don't have a notion of time, so saying, "40 minutes," or "the day after tomorrow," makes little sense. Try:

- "We'll have mashed potatoes again soon. Tonight we're having __________."
- "Dinner will be soon."
- "Snack is soon, let's put some music on and clean up the paints."
- "I'm sorry we're not having ice cream again for dessert. We'll have it again soon. Aren't we lucky we get to eat so many wonderful different foods, like ice cream and potatoes and red peppers?" (Put all those foods on an even playing field.)

As always, observe your child. Some children prefer a concrete answer such as, "We'll have ice-cream again with lunch tomorrow." (Read on for more on talking to kids and expectations around mealtimes.)

Avoid discussing their eating at eating times. The less you say about how much your children weigh, or what or how much they eat, the less they will have to prove, disprove, disappoint, or resist. Try not to label or refer to children as "picky," "under-eater," "too small," or "too big." If children pick up on concern, they learn, "I don't eat right, and it makes Mom and Dad upset," or, "Something is wrong with my body." Be careful not to let them overhear you talking about your concerns with others. Wouldn't it be nicer to give the message, "You're great, exactly as you are"?

Mealtimes are for Connection First

Mealtime is not the time to discuss gloomy issues such as whether you have to put Fluffy to sleep, or your son's behavior report at school. If something comes up during the meal, it's fair to say, "This is kind of a tough topic. Let's talk about this later." (If a child needs specifics, offer options.

Try to cut down on screens, as they can interfere with connection. Perhaps allow screens with some meals or snacks, or eat for 15 minutes before turning on the TV. Find what works for your family. Often, by backing off pressure, children are less dependent on distractions to eat.

Four things are fed by you at a meal:
1. Love
2. Care
3. Connection
4. Food

– Charlie Slaughter, MPH, RD, in *Hungry for Love*[8]

Behavior at Mealtimes

One challenge around eating together can be behavior. The good news is that when you remove pressure and restriction, there are fewer opportunities for conflict and behavior often improves, even relatively quickly.

Sometimes, the expectations for children that come with mealtimes can drain already-limited reserves. For children who struggle with frustration or impulse control, who may have trouble following conversations or bristle at any request, it might take patience, creativity, and flexibility.

Managing Expectations Around Food and Mealtimes

Eileen Devine, social worker, and founder of Brain First Parenting, reminds that it's okay to have expectations of children. She recommends parents prepare children to be able to roll with small disappointments and frustrations. I've included some of her ideas to get started:

- Reteach rules and expectations more than you think you need to, and in the moment.
- Rules need to be clear, consistent, and simple to follow; consider visual reminders.
- Give one-step directions, not three to five steps. First say, "Please stop kicking the table," then, "Would you like to pick a fidget from the basket?"
- Right before a meal, you might remind with, "We will each get one corn muffin. There is plenty of other food to fill up on."
- Avoid vague or ambiguous words like "later" or "some." Here's a clear expectation: "We will save leftover food in this container for snack tomorrow after school. You can have it then." (This is different from my suggestion to use "soon." Some children do better with concrete language.)
- Help the child anticipate change and transitions (write it down or use visual cues).
- Increase supervision/connection to help with impulse control challenges.
- Use play/distraction to help the child get unstuck: when they get stuck in a loop, it's not rewarding the child, it's about settling and regulation.
- Accept that your child has "on" and "off" days when they know something one day and completely forget the next.

Devine described another helpful strategy: "You might have one parent 'on point' close by, focused on helping the child, maybe letting her whisper what she wants to say because she's afraid she will forget. Alternate that point person if you have a partner." If a child has had a tough day, the "on point" parent may even eat ahead of time so they are available, knowing the child may need the parent's full attention.

Katie, a family support specialist, reminds parents to prioritize the relationship. Here's an example from her own table: "*With a preschooler and a toddler, mealtime was a minor zoo. It was okay to draw on craft paper, maybe make a racetrack for your car while I helped the baby eat. The focus was on the connection and having a pleasant time.*"

While you are learning about RF and working toward lower-stress meals:

- Redirect, manage, and co-regulate.
- Do not punish or reward because of *what* or *how much* he is eating.
- Help them regulate by being proactive: try fidgets at the table, a weighted blanket, noise-canceling headphones, taking a walk during dinner, or even allowing an overwhelmed child to move with an adult or on their own to the breakfast nook if boisterous conversation is too much.
- Get help if you can. If you are not confident or consistent, or feel lost about how to understand and help your child with her behaviors, then you may benefit from additional support.

Limit Language That Can Invite Conflict

Avoid language that commands and directs, or invites resistance especially for that hair-trigger "no" or pushback (see PDA on page 29). Examples of language that invites resistance includes: "Come set the table now." "Take the potatoes and pass them on." "That's not spicy!" "But it's your favorite!"

Instead, try "declarative" language that encourages engagement and connection. Such as: "I'm going to wash and peel potatoes if anyone wants to join me." "I wonder if these are hot or cold?" "I didn't know cinnamon could be spicy too." (There is a growing number of online resources on language that is helpful with PDA.)

After the Behavior, Lessons to Learn

After a challenging behavior or experience, it's worth unpacking. What was the task or expectation? What skills were involved? Do the child's skills match the expectation? This can sometimes provide clues. Your journal can help uncover patterns and opportunities for healing.

Nisha figured out after tracking things for a while that the worst meltdowns were right before lunch. Adding a mid-morning snack made a huge difference since her son didn't have much of an appetite for breakfast.

Some parents try to avoid *all* conflict. One mother of a neurotypical child felt guilty for working long hours and only served what her selective six-year-old requested. *"I just don't want to fight, I want him to be happy,"* she agonized. But she described walking on eggshells and letting him eat whatever and whenever he wanted, and of course, he *still* got upset and was very selective.

More on Neutralizing Power Struggles

While trying to get a favored food and some negotiating is expected, mealtimes shouldn't feel like "45 minutes of hostage negotiations" with your child, as one parent put it. When you're battling over how many beans he needs to eat to earn dessert, your child's focus is on the struggle, he is likely dysregulated and disconnected, and is less able to tune in to cues of hunger and fullness.

"I had to learn how to lay off. It's really hard to resist. My biggest hurdle at the table is not getting sucked into power struggles. All day long, Mommy sets boundaries. To feel like it's not a parenting failure to let him tell me 'No,' and to know I don't have to have consequences for that—was a huge struggle.

— Riya, mother to Jackson

Can you imagine not fighting over food? Not trying to get your child to eat more, less, or different foods will eliminate most battles. Not allowing yourself to get sucked into power struggles gets easier. As Mishelle, mom of three-year-old Katie recommends, *"Be patient, and don't take it personally."*

Find What Helps and Do More of That

If a child had a particularly pleasant meal or snack and ate well, consider the circumstances. Your journal can help. Here are some prompts to help figure things out: Where was the child eating? With whom? What was different? Utensils? Condiments? Picnic on a blanket? What was happening earlier in the day? Right before the meal?

Reflect on what supported calm and connection, appetite, and curiosity—do more of that! For one child with avoidant eating, she had a great appetite at one brunch restaurant and at the park after swim class. Another child liked to eat meals from the takeout containers from her favorite restaurant. See what helps and do more of that if you can. Positive experiences reinforce listening to appetite cues, help children feel capable, and help you trust the process! Build new patterns to help children get out of those ruts you read about a few pages back. These feelings and capabilities generally then transfer to eating at home.

Letting Go of Control

Many religious traditions share this idea: *We suffer when we fight against that which we cannot control.* If you are a spiritual or religious person, this can feel like a test of faith or a spiritual journey. If that's you, leaning on your faith tradition can help. **Let go of what you can't control. Or rather, let go of the illusion of control.**

The following "Serenity Prayer for Feeding," borrowing from the famous prayer attributed to Reinhold Neibuhr, is about letting go:

Grant me the serenity to accept what I cannot change (a few examples):

- My child's genetic weight predisposition: It might be bigger or smaller than average.
- My child's temperament: An easygoing, curious child will more easily accept new foods than a cautious or strong-willed child.
- *My* temperament.
- My child's allergies.
- My own feeding, dieting, or eating disorder history.
- Factors that I can't change in the immediate future, such as finances or kitchen setup.
- My child's medical or developmental challenges.
- Other?

Grant me the courage to change the things I can, such as:

- Focusing on felt safety and connection.
- Feeding without pressure or restriction.
- Considering accommodations.
- Being reliable about flexible meals and structure.
- Striving to provide a low-stress atmosphere at eating times.

- Working toward offering a variety of foods.
- My attitude about my own and others' bodies.
- My attitude about my child's eating.
- Offering co-regulation to my child, when I can, and as needed.
- Appropriately managing expectations and behavior at the table, but not what or how much my child eats.
- My general parenting skills.
- Working to support my own resilience and emotional regulation.
- My communication with feeding partners, if I have them.
- My menu-planning or cooking skills.
- My own selective eating (one of my other books, *Conquer Picky Eating for Teens and Adults*, is a resource).
- Focusing on supportive behaviors, not numbers on the scale.

And the wisdom to know the difference. I am learning by:

- Trusting my child and supporting their autonomy.
- Looking for signs of progress (pages 130-131 and 197-199) and building faith.
- Finding support and resources as needed.

The next chapter dives into actionable specifics to begin (or continue and refine) your transition to a responsive approach.

Chapter 4
Implementing the Responsive Feeding Approach

A responsive approach is based on permission, nurturing, and providing. It's not about avoidance, *shoulds*, or *shouldn'ts*. It starts from where you are as a family and moves forward with changes that support felt safety and connection, that feel good, and are therefore more sustainable.

This chapter covers the basics of RF. It will start with flexible structure (a great place to start if you're not already there), what mealtimes can look like, a discussion about exercise (movement), and end with what to expect as this journey unfolds.

Structure and Eating Together

Reliable structure is one of the most important ways to help children do well with eating. It can also reduce *your* anxiety. When your child eats little for a meal or snack—which is likely—he soon has another opportunity to eat. You know it and they know it. Flexible timing of meals and snacks makes eating together more doable and enjoyable. Structure allows enough time between eating to support appetite with a bit of hunger, but not so long that a child is too hungry, or dysregulated. Structure helps ensure that kids will get enough.

"Daily life requires some structure and routine so that everyone in the family knows what to expect and can move through the day with some comfort and predictability."

— Fred Rogers, *The Mister Rogers' Parenting Book*[1]

With structured and reliable meals and snacks, children:

- Are more able to tune in to internal cues.
- Learn to trust that they will get fed, and let go of worry between meals and snacks.
- Can come to mealtimes with an appetite, which helps with internal motivation and curiosity around trying new foods.
- Experience more stable blood sugar levels, which improves energy and helps them stay in felt safety.
- Have lower risk of cavities, as frequent eating is a risk factor.

How This Might Look

See if you can work on the following suggestions:

- Serve food to younger children every two to three hours; roughly three meals and two to three snacks a day.
- Serve food to older children every three to four hours (sometimes sooner), at about the same time every day. This adds up to three meals with one to two snacks a day.
- If a child is food-preoccupied, offering food more frequently for a while may help their anxiety.
- Allow/offer mostly water between meals and snacks.
- Don't forget to pack a snack if you head to the park or other outing. It takes planning.

Flexibility During Short-Term Illness

When children don't feel well, it's harder for them to interpret what's happening in their bodies; especially for infants and kids who may have trouble communicating their needs. Children may be more whiney or clingy; are they crying because their ears hurt, or are they hungry? Medicines, particularly antibiotics, can taste bad and cause diarrhea.

In general, sick infants and children eat and drink less, and sometimes more frequently. Appetite changes can be an early sign of illness. My daughter would lose her reliable appetite a day or so before the runny nose or vomiting (yuck) started.

Let them nibble and sip throughout the day if they prefer. The infant who normally finishes a bottle in 10 minutes might suck for five, or for 40 minutes, and intake might drop. Kids don't have to eat much when they are ill for a few days. (If your child has underlying nutritional or medical concerns, monitor and keep your doctor informed.) Consider giving Popsicles, Jell-O, or watered-down juice as appropriate to boost fluid intake.

With severe or prolonged vomiting or diarrhea, contact your healthcare provider about rehydration. If your child is listless or acting "off," don't hesitate.

Have faith that their appetite will return as they feel better; contact a doctor if it doesn't. Ease back into your routine. Yogurt or foods/supplements with probiotics and live cultures may help with diarrhea or if your child is on antibiotics.

Make the Routine Work for You

Many parents serve a small afternoon snack in an effort to encourage eating at dinner, when the more challenging foods tend to show up. Some of the "witching hour" effect (as many parents call the challenging pre-dinner hour) is due to hunger and low blood sugar. Low blood sugar or anxiety associated with hunger can trigger challenging behavior—they're 'hangry!'

Often children have a large appetite right after school. Maybe plan a substantial snack and move dinner later, or plan for an early dinner and offer a snack before bed. Make the routine work for your family.

A Flexible Routine

There will be times when waiting two to three hours between eating is not what your child needs. You'll learn as you go. A helpful stopgap is a small snack (different than a regular snack, where the child is allowed to eat as much as he wants). You might use this "appetizer" if dinner will be later than usual or if the planned snack was at a time or place where your child was too distracted to attend to eating.

You can distinguish it from a regular snack. Try: "Here's an appetizer; dinner will be soon." Or "Here's a little something 'til dinner." I also used, "We'll save some hungry for dinner." Appetizers can be a small bowl of crackers or some baby carrots and dip. It should take the edge off the hunger. My daughter's favorite appetizer for years was a bowl of frozen peas.

Err on the side of providing. Observe what helps and what doesn't. I've heard some say that kids, especially those with brain-based differences, need to eat protein every 90 minutes. This can undermine appetite and routine and becomes another *should*. While offering protein at meals and snacks is a good idea, getting into battles over protein isn't. Avoid pressure, even if you think it's good for them. (More on protein in Chapter 11.)

"I can tell when Micah is about to tip into a full-on meltdown. A cheese stick usually makes a huge difference. I always have them on me. Maybe he didn't eat well at lunch, or his busy brain used up all his energy. It works for us.

— Ophelia, foster mom to Micah, age four

Some children do well with a cereal bar or some milk and crackers to help them regulate. If your child had a challenging day or their eating was off, offering something to eat may help them with low blood sugar, coping, and regulation.

Bedtime Snacks

A common question is, "They don't eat the healthy food at dinner, and then hold out and eat bowls of cereal before bed. Should I cut out the bedtime snack so they eat dinner?"

The answer is almost always, "Tell me more" and is rarely, just serve what they didn't eat for dinner again. Look at patterns, and the emotional energy around the question; a bowl of cereal or something else the child requests now and then isn't something I would fret about—regular meltdowns over dinner and frequent food requests in a chaotic bedtime point to opportunities to figure out a different approach.

Journal about what's happening earlier in the day, is the after-school snack too close to dinner, what kinds of food show up at dinner versus snack, is the cereal before bed in front of a screen where they feel relaxed and free from the one-bite rule at dinner? It's all connected. Get curious. It isn't the child being manipulative; it's an indication that there may be opportunities to work on what's happening throughout the day. Consider:

- Serve a filling after-school snack, then move dinner later in the evening, maybe even right before bath and bedtime so you know they will be fed.
- Move dinner earlier and routinely include a bedtime snack.
- Mix up favored and more challenging foods throughout the day. Some children eat best at snack because there are "snack" foods, which tend to be easier-to-like foods, while dinner is when the vegetables (and pressure) show up.
- Aim for bedtime snack at the table with a loving adult. (I've seen a few children try to delay bedtime and/or get more screen time by drawing out that last snack.)
- Incorporate the snack into the evening routine.
- For children on medications that lower appetite (such as stimulants for ADHD) who may be most hungry after medications wear off, plan a filling before-bed snack.

A bedtime snack can address your anxiety that they may get hungry, and theirs as well. It may also help you resist pressuring at dinner.

Feed Yourself Too

It's easy in the chaos of getting meals together for the adults to forget to eat. You are worthy of nurturing as well! This may feel extra hard if you didn't have that reliable nurturing growing up. If you can eat with your children, you are less likely to forget. Stress and chaos can decrease (or increase) appetite signals for adults too, especially if you struggle with eating or tuning in to *your* hunger (See Chapter 8). This may also help your mood and capacity to be there for your child.

Serve Family or Buffet Style if You Can

Eating together from shared foods, where children see, smell, pass a food, and see others enjoy it is part of the learning process. According to my clients, the number one piece of advice that neutralizes battles is serving food family style. Second is serving dessert with the meal (see pages 83-85). If you put a pre-plated meal in front of a selective eater, and he doesn't even want to *see* green beans, he may instantly fight or gag. A food-preoccupied child may panic if their portion is small. Starting a meal with intense emotions helps no one.

Skye VanZetten, a mom of two, one who had a feeding disorder, is the admin for a private Facebook group called Mealtime Hostage, which has over 19,000 members—mostly parents of children and teens with extreme picky eating. One post on her *Mealtime Hostage* blog recalls her experience with her son: "*Once he was given the option to choose what he wanted on his plate and permission to do with it what he wanted, family meals immediately took a turn for the better. Simply changing the way food was served made a huge difference in his anxiety."*

Here's how it looks: Put all the bowls, packages, and plates out on the middle of the table or eating area, let children (who are able) serve themselves. It may feel strange at first with a bowl of chicken nuggets next to a bowl of chili, plate of cornbread, and package of baby carrots, but foods served this way are on equal footing. Sometimes, help yourself from "their" food; put a couple of pretzels on your plate and enjoy them.

So if your child has been eating French toast fingers for breakfast, these are put on a plate in the middle of the table, and whatever you are eating goes there too, even if you *know* he won't take any scrambled eggs for a while. This lowers the emotional and physical barriers to a child trying something new and reminds parents to make it accessible.

This section is full of practical advice including utensils, children who do well with help serving, modifying meals to work for you, and questions about screens.

Serving or Pre-Plating

You may need to help young children or children with motor differences or other challenges serve themselves. Support your child having choice when possible. If they've indicated they would like to have a food, hold up the serving spoon with an amount that feels right (for some it will be bigger or smaller) and ask, "This much?" They can tell you more, or less. Then ask them to point to their plate where they would like you to put the portion. This helps avoid, "I didn't want it *there*! It's touching that!" Partitioned plates can help too.

Occasionally, some children prefer to have their food pre-plated. Self-serve can feel overwhelming; they may worry they will do it wrong or take too much, have trouble with motor initiation or experience decision fatigue. When serving the child preserves felt safety, it's the right approach. Reassure them they don't have to eat it all, they can have more, and they can self-serve when they feel ready.

Serving Tools and Utensils

Spoons and utensils can add frustration and get in the way of your child enjoying mealtimes and even how much they eat. Avoid pressure with utensils.

- Eating with hands is typical into grade school and is the cultural norm for many, as well as with certain foods such as pizza, naan, and injera. Anxious or sensory eaters may need or prefer that sense of touch to feel more comfortable.
- Offer choices: regular soup spoons and teaspoons, plastic or silicone, colorful forks, or different sizes and cups. Smaller hands (or those with fine motor delays) may need thicker handles. (If you're working with an OT or feeding therapist, they can help find the right ones.)

- For a child with a motor delay, you may need to help load the fork or spoon and hand it to her, offer a straw and a spoon with thin soups, or even feed an older child—with her in control, meaning the child leans forward and/or willingly opens her mouth to accept the spoon.
- Put paper napkins out so she can spit food out. The young toddler may just lean forward and spit food out, as is age appropriate. Teach children to discreetly spit food into a napkin when they are ready.

The Child Who Wants to Eat on Your Lap

If a child who is otherwise able to eat independently demands to sit on your lap and be fed, you can do so if it supports felt safety and you are able. Over time, maybe they can sit right next to you and eat from your plate, still touching if they need that, or they can eat from their own plate while sitting on your lap. Make small changes, and work toward the goal of having them in their own seat eating off their own plate.

No More Clean-Plate Club

Your child will end up with food on their plate that they decide they don't want to eat, for whatever reason. They are allowed to get more potatoes, even if there is something else on their plate they haven't eaten yet. No pressure means no more clean-plate goals, and they may need to explore food on their plates many times before they are ready to eat it.

Reframe and Minimize Waste

The idea of wasting food may be upsetting if you don't have extra or if you grew up with food insecurity or expectations around waste. Go into this knowing you might waste more food—for a while (though probably less in the long run).

Kids need permission to put food on their plates and not eat it. It's part of the process. A child who is allowed to *not* eat something is more willing to try something new. If your selective child orders something they are unlikely to eat, avoid the temptation to say, "You won't eat that; why don't you get something you can eat, like chicken fingers...?" Instead, think, "Well, I'm glad he's open to the idea; if he doesn't eat it this time, he can eat the cornbread and baked potato and I can take the leftovers for lunch tomorrow." And if resources are tight, it's okay to point them to a choice they are more likely to eat. You can explore variety in less costly ways.

Tips to reduce waste:

- Ask your child to serve themselves a small portion to start and take more if he wants: "Start with a spoonful and then you can have more."
- Try redefining "waste" like one of my blog readers did: *"I struggle with guilt about throwing food out, since I grew up with 'clean your plate' and had to*

retrain myself to know when I'm actually full. It helps me to define 'eating food I don't want/need' as wasting. It helps me realize that feeding scraps to the dog is better than eating food I don't want. If a kid tries a bite or two of a new veggie and the rest gets thrown out, is it really 'waste' if it provided an introduction to a food that she might later like?"

- Try new foods at grocery stores, such as buying small amounts from bulk bin sections, or samples. Beware of the big-box store trap of having your child enjoy the sample and then buying 64 of those fiber bars they probably won't touch again...
- Compost scraps and let your child "feed" the garden, or feed scraps to your backyard chickens (if you're lucky enough to have them).

Modified Family- or Buffet-Style Serving

Family meals can be chaotic, with siblings arguing over who got the extra muffin, or a child with motor differences anxious that there won't be enough for seconds by the time they finish their firsts. Perhaps the budget is tight, and everyone is eyeing that taco meat or the avocado. There are ways to modify family style to work for you. Here are a few ideas:

- Adults portion out high-interest foods. Each child gets equal taco meat, or one and a half corn muffins. If it's a food the child isn't keen on yet, you can serve it into a personal "serving" bowl or napkin near them so they have the opportunity to choose it.
- Make it a habit that before someone takes the last of something, that they ask if anyone else wants more. Model with, "I'd like to finish the spinach; did anyone else want more?" Maybe start with less-favored foods so it doesn't spike the "scarcity" effect.
- Pre-serve pricier, limited foods, with bowls of more affordable and filling items such as tortilla chips, beans, pasta, lettuce, etc. within reach.
- Allow children to sit or stand, have fidget toys or weighted blankets, or feet tucked under them to help them with sensory comfort.
- If you don't have a table or space for serving bowls, you can self-serve in the kitchen, and kids can get up for more or you can help younger children get seconds.

Family meals may look different (but kids decide how much they eat regardless) over the years. Aleesha says that with tweens and teens, most meals are served family style at the table, but for some reason, *"with spaghetti, everyone serves themselves at the stove, straight from the pot."* When she had toddlers, she sometimes fed them separately from the older kids when their schedules didn't line up.

Social worker and foster mom Renee felt that expectations and traditions helped: *"Expectations at the table provided predictability and a calm space for eating. First, no cell phones; second, music and screens were always off; and last, with sometimes up to seven people at the table, we made sure that everyone took a turn telling us about the 'best and worst' from their day without interruption and with the 'listening' attention of everyone else."*

Let Children Be Participants, Not the Focus

Parents tell me they spend the majority of time at meals talking about how much and what the child is eating: negotiating, encouraging, talking about nutrition, and bribing. That has to stop. In essence, try to "ignore" what and how much your child is or isn't eating. Over and over I have heard from clients that when the focus was off the child, perhaps when Dad shared about his day, or attention is on a sibling, *that* was when the "picky eater" slid a baby carrot onto their plate, or their food-preoccupied child stopped eating as quickly.

As mom Eliana said, *"The family meal is an adjustment, but now it is something we really enjoy."*

The child must be allowed to participate at meals, not be the focus. Attention on their eating invites conflict and anxiety, and decreases appetite and curiosity around food.

Also know that shared mealtimes can be a convenient, reliable, and enjoyable way to connect, but they are not the only way.

Creating Space at Mealtimes (Literally)

If your child is eating alone, a pressure-free invitation to join connected mealtimes may help. Casey Ehrlich PhD, a parent of a child with PDA and a feeding disorder whose son was down to a handful of accepted foods shared what helped: *"We had guests in our home who had experience working with traumatized kids and we shared cooking. My friend said, 'Let's just set a place for him even if he doesn't come to the table.' After a couple months he'd come and get his plate and leave, then come and sit with us with his iPad. He was enticed by the family meal. It's evolved over the last few years from there. Last week he ate fried fish that he had caught, and he now wants to incorporate new foods and ask to try something. He's added steak, bagels, grilled chicken, and fast food. Now he adds foods and doesn't drop others."*

They literally created a physical space for him, an open invitation to join in connection when he was ready.

Casey shared that the key ingredient was not trying to get him to eat or engage with the food. *"We all want our kids to be happy, our families to be connected, and for our children to be healthy. Paradoxically, what's facilitated connection and him being happy and eating healthier is me completely letting go of my agenda."*

Is It OK to Eat with Screens?

In general, eating with distractions is a barrier for many kids and adults to tuning in to their bodies, as well as to connection. Some kids may eat less, and others more, than they would otherwise. **Always start with curiosity, and ask WHY? Why does my child prefer to eat with a screen?** Observe your child and recognize if a screen is helping or harming. While no-screens rules work for many families, there are times when eating with screens is responsive.

Screens can help regulate: Screens may help some children get or stay in felt safety. If a screen with breakfast helps a child focus on eating while the rest of the household is in chaos getting out the door, then continue using it.

Screens can buffer: Screens can be a child's way of tuning out conflict, pressure, or attention on their eating. In this case, work on responsive feeding, and the screen usually is less needed as the child is reassured that they won't be pressured

Screens can support intake and weight in special circumstances: If low weight or intake is a serious concern (Chapters 5 and 6), such as with medications or conditions that dampen appetite such as anxiety or depression, then screens/distraction can help support intake while you work on RF.

Weaning Off Screens

You can work on structure and setting first, then offer the child some choices, maybe choosing one meal or snack to go without. Or no screen for the first 10 minutes, or screen right before or after eating.

Remember that all screen time is not equal. Social media apps seem worse, with mindless scrolling and potentially harmful content served up every 30 seconds or so. (Social media seems particularly bad for body image and eating.) Watching a movie together while eating takeout feels different than a TV that is always on, with commercials and news and unpredictable content. A teen putting the day in their phone planner during breakfast isn't the same as mindless scrolling.

Eating with Older Children

Eating together (family meal) presents a reliable time for older children to connect with parents and siblings. They may not want to join at first and bristle at no-texting-or-earbuds rules, but they will often grow to enjoy and depend on this time. Rose, a 20-year-old adoptee, reflected, *"In middle and high school, my mom enforced that we all ate dinner together. It was fun. It really helped my relationship with my siblings; otherwise we were all in our own rooms most of the time. Sure, sometimes it was annoying, and after a long day at school I might have just wanted to play video games, but it made us actually talk to each other. We each talked about our 'best/worst' of the day. When I shared my 'worsts' it made me feel less alone."*

Jennifer started with family meals when her girls were 13 and 16. She had struggled with selective eating with her oldest, Yiseth, for a dozen years, and had basically given up. A former "foodie," she was resigned to cooking the handful of dishes that Yiseth would accept. *"Not much changed until I did your webinar. From age 3½ to 16, the number of foods she would eat stayed at about 25, and she added only new flavors of ice cream to the list."*

On Fridays, Jennifer would call the girls before she left work and ask what they wanted for dinner: *"Chinese? Subway? Rotisserie chicken?"* Everything was met with complaints, and Jennifer admitted she thought, *"How ungrateful! I would have loved restaurant food as a kid."* Everyone was in a foul mood.

Reflecting on the conflict around those meals, she remembered to focus on connection and that it was her job to provide, and theirs to decide if and how much to eat. *"I stopped asking them and just brought home dinner. They almost never complained, and I even got the occasional 'thank you, Mom.' I think I was asking them to do something that was not their job. Just that change made such a difference."*

Jennifer now loves family meals, and within weeks of not pressuring or commenting, her self-described picky teen tried a few new foods. *"Dinner has become pleasant and relaxed, not stressful. Yiseth feels respected rather than hassled. She eats more than she used to, which has cut down on late-evening snacking. I enjoy cooking again. I really don't pay attention to what she puts on her plate and try to keep my husband from commenting. I wouldn't say that she has dramatically increased the variety of foods she eats, but it is in the range of normal now, and that is great. I think she will be able to go to college in 18 months and nourish herself independently with a dorm meal plan."*

Jennifer admits her friends think it's strange that her teenagers want to eat dinner with the family. *"This is such a treat. I love that my children want to be there with me."*

Jack shared this story: *"My son, a senior in high school, started dating a girl who kept wanting to make plans over our dinner time. Family dinner has always been a priority, so we told him he could go after, or she could join us. At first, she thought it was 'weird,' but pretty soon she was a regular and delightful guest at our table."*

Jennifer's tips for older kids:

- Serve foods family style. When Jennifer pre-plated foods she wanted Yiseth to eat, it caused battles and never worked.
- Enjoy each other and try not to worry about who is eating what or how much.
- Stick with it. *"At first the girls complained, but now we all like to eat together."*
- You decide what's for dinner, including what *you* want to eat too. (See "What and How to Serve" in Chapter 5).

When the attention and negotiating about who is eating what and how much is no longer an issue, the family table can be a place where kids want to be.

Conflict Identifies Opportunities
Flashpoints around food are like neon signs pointing out opportunities for healing. Where are you battling? What do you dread most? Where do you and your children experience the most negative emotions? Journal and reflect on your goals versus your child's. Are you trying to get your child to eat more or different foods? Are there unrealistic expectations?

High-Interest Foods, Including Sweets and "Treats"

Next we'll look at one of the most frequent sources of conflict and frustration: high-interest foods such as sweets or salty and crunchy foods. It's not a coincidence that these lightning rod foods are the "bad" foods that are restricted or shamed. While sweets are generally the most challenging, I'll use "high-interest food" (HIF) moving forward, since your child may seem out of control with Flaming Hot Cheetos.

How to Talk About Sweets/Treats

In the previous edition of this book, I used the word "treat," which I still use and don't find problematic. But there are those who criticize the term "treat" or even the word "dessert," as it can bring in moralizing around food, just like "red-light" foods might. I get it! I really dislike the terms "fun," "play," or "sometimes" foods.

For me, "treat" is something special; it's eating out, it's crab legs for a birthday, it's homemade lasagna, it's a fresh peach, it's Rice Krispies treats or a banana split. I also like "treat" because for some children, sweet foods are desired, while others prefer salty.

The meaning behind the words (your agenda) matters. Are you trying to get them to eat less or more? **One solution to adding unintentional meaning is to just describe the food. Foods are sweet, salty, fried, or fast; find the words that work for your family and culture.** Remember, how children feel at mealtimes matters more than the words spoken.

Every food has value, including nutritional (such as carbohydrates or fat for energy). Avoiding language that shames or judges can help children manage all foods in more positive ways.

Non-Responsive Strategies Backfire

Common tactics adults use to get kids to eat less of high-interest foods backfire and make children more interested.

Bribing or Rewarding with Dessert

Bribing doesn't help. A scene I witnessed at a buffet restaurant illustrated the contrast of "must eat" versus "dessert." At a nearby table, three adults sat with a preschool-aged child. The adults glared at the child, chiming in one after the other: "Colton, you have to eat two bites of chicken before you can have donuts. You know the rule..." This depressing scene, with Colton's grimacing, whining, and negotiating, and the grown-ups doing the same, came to an end when Colton choked down a bite of chicken.

Then, the adults transformed into smiling companions. One fetched a plate of donuts. Colton was praised, and everyone cheered when the donuts showed up. They had a grand time eating those delicious donuts.

The combination of sugar and fat is particularly yummy, but equally as reinforcing were the adults' attitudes. When the meal was present, it was miserable; when dessert showed up, it was rainbows and puppies. Bribing teaches powerful associations with different foods, and doesn't help children learn to eat and enjoy a variety.

Allowing sweet foods *with* the meal feels wrong for many parents. They tell me, "But I won't be doing my job if I don't make him eat some of his real food before dessert." Or, "How will I get him to eat veggies if I can't bribe with dessert?"

I ask parents to reflect on bribing with dessert:

- How is it working for you?
- Is it pleasant?
- Has it taught your child to learn to like a variety of foods?

Bribing with dessert generally has several unintended consequences. It:

- Teaches kids that dessert is the good food.
- Teaches that other foods are a hurdle they have to endure to get to the good stuff.[2]
- Sets up negotiation and conflict.
- Might reinforce eating beyond fullness.
- May entice them to eat a food on that occasion, but they like the food less.[3]

When we bribe kids, they are suspicious. They learn, "Huh, this stuff must be bad if they have to bribe me to eat it."

A One-a-Day Sweets Rule Encourages Sneaking and Lying

Some resources recommend allowing children to have one sweet option a day and they choose when. If that works for you, great! Most often I've seen this play out with children feeling they need to lie or sneak (and feel ashamed about it!) if they want more.

For example, children have lied about not having a cupcake or chocolate milk at school because they then knew they wouldn't get a sweet with dinner with everyone else.

Other countries don't seem to be as worried about sugar. Emiko Davies, a cookbook author raising her children in Italy shared on the podcast *Don't Salt My Game:* "Italian kids are just eating like cookies dipped in milk for breakfast and then going to school or having Gelato after dinner and then going to bed, and that was so different to what I had been brought up to think in Australia. But then when you look around there are no problems that seem to come out of sugar in Italian culture . . ."[4] She shared that it's common for the chef at a restaurant to prepare separate food for children, such as pasta with a simple tomato sauce, and that social connection is prized at mealtimes. Is the culture you are raising your child in protective or adding to your feeding challenges? What could we learn from other ways of relating to food?

Banning Foods Makes Them More Desirable

Banning foods almost always makes them more desirable, and predictably can lead to binging and shame, and predispose to disordered behaviors. Unless you live on a commune and never go into the wide world, children will have sweets in their lives, in school, at work, with friends—basically everywhere. Helping them enjoy these foods and not have a fraught relationship with them is important.

Note, this doesn't tend to apply to foods a family doesn't eat for religious or cultural reasons. With the whole family eating this way, and particularly if it is explained as tradition without shame or moralizing, such households often have a healthy attitude with these foods.

HIF Helpful Strategies

Certain foods, mostly sweets, are treated a bit differently. Particularly with very young children, this is the one area in which the adult usually guides how much. Why? Because sweets are so appealing that they can be difficult to learn to manage without a little more direction. If a child is allowed unlimited sweets with every meal and snack, it can result in less variety and balanced nutrition.

However, in order to deal with the potential "forbidden-food" phenomenon, in which the child becomes overly interested in HIFs, most children benefit from fairly frequent opportunities to learn to handle them. With the strategies of: 1) usually serving a portion of dessert with the meal; and 2) allowing regular snacks and opportunities when HIF foods are unlimited, they will lose their intense power, becoming a food to be enjoyed among others.

Step One: Serve Sweet Foods (aka dessert) with the Meal

Serving dessert with the meal creates an even playing field. You put the roasted cauliflower out at the same time as the cookies or pudding. Food is just food. It's all wonderful. At first, they will stare, shocked. You may want to prepare older children:

"Max, we haven't been enjoying meals much because we're arguing over dessert and not talking about much else. We're going to start serving dessert with the meal. You can eat it whenever you want."

If you have used dessert as a bribe for eating veggies, it will take them a while to understand. They will eat dessert first, for a few days or even weeks, but eventually you will likely see them lick a Popsicle, maybe eat a bite of chicken, then lick the Popsicle and poke at a carrot. They will probably eat dessert first for a while and not those two bites of veggies; so remind yourself that bribing with dessert wasn't helping. Things may seem worse before they get better.

There are times when dessert after the meal still works, such as holiday gatherings where the after-dinner dessert may be part of the ritual. Also, as they gain comfort and confidence with eating, you can transition sweets back to the end of meals if you prefer.

Dessert with the Meal Helps Selective Eating and Self-Regulation of Energy Intake

Serving dessert with the meal can reduce anxiety (no more negotiating or wondering how many bites to earn dessert) and frees up energy so the child can access curiosity about other foods. It also helps kids eat the right amount for them. Dessert is so yummy that if you serve it at the end of the meal, even if the child is stuffed, he may make himself eat it.

Hydee Becker RD, tells the story of a boy she observed at daycare. He was experiencing rapidly accelerating weight gain. The rule at daycare was that he had to eat his entire lunch before he could have his M&Ms, which were his "clean plate treat." Becker recalls him repeatedly saying, "I'm full," only to be reminded of the rules.

She watched for 40 minutes as he slowly finished his lunch *and all* the M&Ms. He was taught to ignore his body's signals, and he overate—twice. Over time this makes it harder for him to access those cues. This is another reason why I'm against school rules that make children eat certain amounts or certain foods before dessert.

For the first several months (to years), I recommend serving dessert with the meal. As your child gets older and more capable with eating a variety and regulating intake, you can move the dessert to the end of the meal or even later, and maybe allow seconds or as much as they want.

It's important to let your child know when there will be dessert. My daughter, four at the time, had eaten a lovely meal with friends who didn't serve dessert with meals. When the dessert came out after dinner, she said she was too full, and cried while others enjoyed it—but she listened to her body. I reassured her that she could have the dessert with lunch the next day. That was powerful to see.

Parents On Dessert with Meals

You may be thinking, "How will I get them to eat anything if I can't bribe with dessert?" or, "I can't accept that he gets rewarded if he hasn't eaten anything healthy first." But don't just take my word for it. Here are some parent testimonials from my blog post "Parents on Dessert with Dinner."

"Occasionally my 4-year-old will take bites of dessert, bites of dinner, bites of dessert. Sometimes I suspect starting with dessert actually stimulates my 4-year-old's appetite or at least lowers her resistance to the meal as a whole."

"My 18 month old usually seizes on dessert first and eats some of it, but then switches back and forth among different foods for the rest of the meal and often leaves some dessert. My feeling is she's probably going to eat some dessert whether she's hungry or not (at least if she's like me) so may as well let her weave it in with her hunger rather than stuff it in after finishing some prescribed portion of 'healthy food.'"

"I couldn't believe how well this worked. She would lick her homemade smoothie pop, then eat some beans, then lick the pop and go back and forth. Half the time, dessert melts now while she eats dinner!

"Back when we bought into dessert as a reward for eating dinner, both my kids were sweet tooth junkies. Now that dessert is just part of the meal, it's impressive to see how well they self regulate the sweets, and choose foods they appear to need over eating a lot of something because it's available for a limited time.

"It takes away bargaining. . . I love that part."

No Seconds on Dessert Most Times

"But I want more ice cream!" Dessert is generally one portion, and you can be matter-of-fact, avoiding bargaining or overexplaining. "We all get one scoop, and if you're still hungry, there are other options." Some days, dessert might be fruit salad or a bowl of grapes. Avoid anger or apologizing for limits, but you *can* acknowledge emotions. "I'm sorry you're upset, but we had ice cream yesterday. We're having fruit-pops today. We'll have ice cream again soon." It may reassure you to know that most of the families I've supported share that this is accepted without fuss.

There is room for flexibility. If your child is doing well overall and there are occasional extra servings of sweets, do what is necessary to preserve felt safety and get through the day!

Desserts That Melt

With an older child, you can put the Popsicle or ice cream in a bowl and let them choose when they want it. Sometimes it comes out at the beginning of the meal. Pre-scoop the ice cream and put the bowl in the freezer. Let your child know it's there, and she can help herself when she's ready. Children can wait until the end of the meal if they prefer. For younger children, if it melts during the meal, offer to put it in the freezer.

Your Sweets/HIF Approach Adapts to Your Child Over Time

How you approach sweets and HIF will depend on your child, how their interest ebbs and flows, their age, and how much support and structure they need.

For example, with my food and sweets-preoccupied toddler, we stuck to one sweet a day with dinner and included "treat" snacks a few times a week. This worked well for a few years. As she got older and was exposed to more sweets out and about, she ate something sweet a few times a day.

By middle school she started having dessert a few hours after dinner as a bedtime snack of sorts, as she was awake later into the evening. In high-school now, with a foundation of attuned eating firmly in place, she manages sweets as part of a variety of foods, enjoying them at times in large quantities, a portion after a meal, and at others times having no interest.

Trust what you know of your child.

When Parents Don't Eat Dessert

I didn't grow up eating dessert, but my husband did. I started serving sweets most days after our daughter was about two years old. Before that, she didn't really know what she was missing, and none of us missed dessert. Once we began going out more often and she was exposed to foods such as ice cream and cookies, I needed to be purposeful about helping her learn to manage HIFs.

For many years, my daughter was the only one eating dessert at dinner. When she first noticed and asked why, I explained that I would prefer to eat chicken, potatoes, or soup, and that I often had something sweet with coffee after lunch when she was at school. If your child is struggling handling sweets, you may want to serve dessert in neutral ways to help them. (More to come on sugar worries and how to talk about food.)

Step Two HIF Strategy: The "Treat" or Unlimited HIF Snack

When I hear from a parent whose child is sneaking candy or cookies, finding ways to bring them into the meal and snack rotation almost always resolves the issue. About one to two times per week, serve a snack where a HIF or formerly forbidden food is included, and he can eat as much as he wants.

Katherine Zavodni, RD, reminds that it can take time to get out of the cycle of sneaking between meals resulting in decreased hunger at meal and snack time, especially if stimulation-seeking may be a factor (as with ADHD).

Serving a few cookies with lunch, or a plate full of cookies with snack, helps get out of and avoid the sneaking and preoccupation cycle. If your child has been limited and is focused on the HIF, he will eat lots of it initially. He may eat so much that he feels sick, and rarely, even vomits. That is part of learning to manage the foods. Hovering and warning him not to eat too much can interfere with that experiencing (or make him want to assert his autonomy and eat more).

It might look like this: on a weekend afternoon, make a pan of Rice Krispies treats together. He can lick the spoon or sample marshmallows while making it. Then sit down and enjoy the treats with milk (or alternative) and maybe a favorite fruit so they have the option of getting some fiber. I recommend serving some fat and protein as well, which is why milk with fat is so easy (or make the treats with butter).

If the unlimited HIF snack feels scary for you, start with something that feels less threatening, such as homemade oatmeal-raisin cookies, and go from there. With time, you should see your child's frenzied interest in sweets decrease; they will likely eat a little less, perhaps slower, and possibly choose a banana or other options to go with it. I remember being amazed after we did this for a while that my daughter—after one or two Rice Krispies treats, milk, and half a kiwi—would stop.

What we might think of as "too much" sugar may be what's needed for a child to learn what their "enough" is, and it will likely be less than we fear when there is permission.

What if They Eat So Much They Get Sick?

If they say their tummy hurts, try not to lecture or use that to justify limiting them next time. Try, "I'm sorry your tummy hurts, want to sit on the couch with me? Will it feel better if I rub your tummy?" You might add, "I don't feel well sometimes after a really yummy meal when I eat a lot, but it will feel better soon. Your body knows how to handle it."

If they vomit, try to remain calm, and approach it the same way. Help them feel comfortable, reassure them that they will feel better soon. If they are vomiting frequently, or have other symptoms, talk to your child's doctor.

Some children may do okay with a gentle reminder, or even ask for limits around amounts. Focusing on your child and felt safety and connection will help you know how to respond.

Holidays

Handling the candy haul can feel particularly scary, and it's not just with Halloween anymore. It seemed that at every holiday, my daughter would come home from school with a bag of candy. Whether or not this is your experience, you'll have opportunities to deal with candy. I first learned the following strategy from Ellyn Satter's work.

On Halloween, we would eat an early dinner and then go out (sometimes with friends). My daughter got to bring her candy home, dump it out, and take out what she didn't like (I got the peanut butter cups!). She ate as much as she wanted. We usually sat at the kitchen table, or the floor, with a glass of milk. She sampled, spat out many she didn't like, and usually ended up eating three to 10 pieces (some years more, some less).

The next day, she again got to eat as much as she wanted, at snack time with a glass of milk—a HIF snack. After that she got to choose a few pieces to go in her lunchbox or with dinner. Usually within a handful of days she'd forget about the candy, and we'd add it to our candy container in the cupboard. It has been remarkably painless. If you are new to the process, your child might eat a lot more, but they also might surprise you.

Hydee Becker, RD, followed this strategy with her son. The year he turned five, he ate all the candy before bed, with nothing left for the next day. I loved how Becker approached it with curiosity: "I wonder what he'll do next year?" If they do eat a whole lot, avoid the temptation to intervene. Let the process play out; if overconsumption is routinely a problem, reassess if you are allowing enough "HIF snacks" or if you might be inadvertently increasing their anxiety, with for example lots of commenting about sugar being unhealthy.

"The whole 'how many spoonfuls of this do I have to eat to get my pudding?' thing is so tiresome. (Pudding refers to desserts in the UK and Australia). The first time I let Thomas eat his Easter stash, he ate and ate until I was sure he'd be sick, then he stopped two pieces before he'd eaten it all. Just like that. It was almost as if he had to test if I really meant that he could have as much as he wanted. My daughter didn't even want that much. And now, a couple of years on, their Easter chocolate lasts until summer. Not because I'm restricting it. It's available, but they don't often feel like eating it."

— Mira, mother to Thomas and Emma

Put HIFs Away

I learned a lot the year we ended up with two gingerbread houses, one we made at home and one from school. Sitting in the middle of the dining room, they were always in sight and on my daughter's mind. Though her food preoccupation days were past, she pestered me about the houses several times a day, occasionally taking a nibble when she thought I wasn't looking. (Occasional sneaking is developmentally appropriate. Habitual, secretive bingeing is not.)

It was becoming a source of conflict, so I knew I had to try something new. On December 26, she got to eat as much of the candy from the gingerbread house as she wanted. At snack time, she had about two teaspoons of scraped frosting and four or five pieces of candy with some milk. She had wanted some gummy bears, but said she was full. I didn't want her only choice to be to eat them now or throw them out (which could trigger the "scarcity effect" and make her more likely to eat even though she was full), so I told her she could have the handful of gummies with her snack that afternoon. We tossed the rest without incident. This story illustrates HIF handling, but also the concept of putting foods away and out of sight.

I'm seeing more advice to have HIF's out on display and always available to help neutralize them. Generally, kids who see candy or HIFs will ask for it, especially those who have been restricted or have known food insecurity. Parents of kids with ADHD also tell me that seeing the shiny wrappers as they walk by immediately draws their focus to and consumption of these foods rather than letting them forget about them between eating opportunities.

While some kids may lose interest and feel reassured with HIF on the kitchen counter, I generally don't recommend this approach or think it's necessary. Again, follow what helps your child feel less anxious. Keeping HIF in a cupboard and regularly serving them will help children learn to incorporate these foods in a more balanced way. (There's more on food preoccupation in Chapter 7.)

Responsive Movement

"I understand that my son shouldn't diet; how can I get him to be more active?"
— Oliver, father to Jeremy, age 11 years

"Movement is so important to his emotional and nervous system balance, but he pushes back when I want him to do it because I see him getting antsy."
— Benny, father to Orlando, age 5 years

Switching gears, let's ponder movement. Moving our bodies has benefits, from mood and nervous system regulation to fitness, and health. Similar to food, if we try to *get* kids to move, it can backfire. (I avoid the word *exercise* because it has negative associations for many and can feel like a chore.)

Thinking about the RF values from Chapter 3 can help; supporting a child's *autonomy* and *internal motivation* is central to a responsive approach to food, and movement. A better question Oliver, above, might ask is, "How can I support Jeremy so that he has the opportunity to move in enjoyable ways?"

Here's an example of external versus internal motivation with movement. One afternoon, I was pushing my daughter on the swings at a local park. A little girl with a glorious, toothless grin ran up, hopped on a swing, and started pumping her legs. A slender man strode over and shouted, "Sally! We didn't come here for lazy exercise! Get off the swings and run around." Sally's smile disappeared as she walked slowly away.

Perhaps he read on a handout from their pediatrician that children need "60 minutes of vigorous supervised exercise daily." Doctor's orders, right? But did Sally learn that movement is fun, or a chore? Did she learn to trust her body or to punish it? As a teen, will she comply or rebel?

We want to raise children who are as happy and healthy as they can be, who enjoy moving their bodies as they are able. We know that fitness is a better indicator of health than fatness, has many physical and mental health benefits, and can help with felt safety. So how do we help kids access movement without turning into a drill sergeant?

Trying to Get Kids to Move can Backfire

Trusting kids with activity, as with food, can feel tough. If you have a larger-than-average child who loves the swings, the impulse to make her get off and run is understandable. Your child's doctor, even family members, may lecture you. One parent commented on my blog, *"My two-year-old is big and loves to swing, but my mom only takes her to a park where there aren't any. Some days my daughter hops off the swings and runs around, other days she mostly swings. The important thing is she loves being at the park, and I don't want my mom to spoil that."*

This concerned grandma is trying to control how her granddaughter moves to get her to be thinner. This has a high chance of backfiring. And swinging may be regulating for this kiddo, or just fun! Other common tactics to get kids to move that may backfire include:

- Using a pedometer or fitness tracker. (One blog reader wrote that if her parents had tried that, she would have sat in the bathroom tapping away at the pedometer to add steps in an act of rebellion.) Fitness trackers have been shown to decrease enjoyment of activity; they can make eating disorders worse or trigger disordered eating.[5] Rose said this about her experience with a tracker when she was trying to add weight and build strength as a teen: *"I felt like a failure if I didn't reach the exercise goals."*
- Signing a child up for a class with weight management or loss as a goal. Movement should be about fun, enjoying a challenge, a social outlet, or building strength and fitness—but not with the desired (and rarely achieved in the long term) goal of weight loss.
- Requiring your child to run or do jumping jacks during commercials or on the hour. If it feels like a chore, it can lead to power struggles.
- Using equipment such as stationary bikes, which I have seen for children as young as three. Most adults find exercise machines boring, and they're less fun for kids. Again, if a child uses something like a "brain bike" for regulation (getting popular in schools) and it's overall positive, that's another story.

The Relationship with Movement

An individual's interest in activity is determined in part by genetics or an expression of temperament, and other factors. We all know the person who "doesn't feel good" unless they get in their run, or the person who recharges by relaxing with a good book. A study on newborns, with little bands around their limbs to record movement, showed wide variation of movement from "almost constant" to "very little."[6] (The leanest babies seemed to move the most, and interestingly took in the most calories, while their fatter counterparts seemed to move less, but also ate less.)

I think of my family: My father has likely managed ADHD with vigorous exercise since early adolescence, rarely skipping a run until his 70s, when he switched to biking. My husband could sit for hours reading or watching YouTube videos, and I'm somewhere in between. I rarely had time for exercise during my medical training, but now have more balance. I feel better if I move most days, preferably with a hike outside. Some weeks I move less, some more. (I am far more active than I was 20 years ago, and I'm heavier now.)

How much activity do you need to feel good? What about your kids? If you have a slight frame and a high metabolism, and your child is stocky, gains weight more easily, and doesn't love running like you do, are you fighting biology to try to get him to be a lean runner? It's hard to turn someone who loves and needs quiet reading time after school into someone who needs a couple of hours racing up and down a soccer field to regulate; and both can be healthy and happy.

Activity Varies from Day to Day and Year to Year

A child who prefers the stroller one month might run nonstop during the next visit to the park. The swing, the sole object of interest at the playground for weeks, may one day be forgotten.

Strict goals and limits, such as these examples from a pediatrician's handout rarely help: At least 60 minutes of supervised vigorous physical activity a day and don't allow more than 30 minutes of sedentary time in a row.

What if your child is doing homework, or watching a movie? Does he need to run laps around the basement every 30 minutes when a timer rings? What if they swim and play three hours one day, but prefer to read and rest on the couch the next?

I do think kids need way more opportunity and time to play and move, though with more testing and less recess, busy schedules, and perhaps for many a lack of safe places to play, we've gone in the wrong direction. With support and opportunity, kids may move more some days, less others.

It's been fascinating to watch my daughter, whose interest in activity has gone through cycles: very active as a crawler and toddler, less so around two and three years. Some days she sat and crafted and watched TV, other days she would run around the house in fairy wings, start games of bowling with cups and materials scavenged from the recycling bin, jump on the mini trampoline, and launch herself onto the couch.

During third grade, she and I were riding bikes on a camping trip when she said, "I need to get 60 minutes of exercise." I said, if she wanted to, we could ride more loops around the campground. I could see that she didn't want to, but she'd heard that she *should*. I reminded her that the day before she had played in a pool for three hours, and it evens out.

Be ready for children to come home with messages around food and movement that you may have to help them unpack. I didn't shame my daughter for not moving for 60 minutes or for feeling conflicted about it. We talked about how having a good time was most important, and how sometimes that kind of messaging, just like diet culture messaging around food, can make us less healthy and happy. She decided that laps were boring, so we went back to the camper.

Often, movement was tied to opportunity. My daughter was less active in later grade school, no longer happy on family hikes, occasionally biking, and ice-skating at the local park in Minnesota. Middle school sports teams were inclusive and fun (she learned to play tennis), and in high school, she was surprised to enjoy her weight training class and signed up a second time, even though it wasn't required. She grew to enjoy hikes during Covid lockdowns, especially if there was a photogenic Alpine lake involved (we have moved to the Pacific Northwest).

While sports have many benefits, be careful not to over-program your kids to the point that they regularly miss out on family dinners or don't get enough down time. Especially if your child or teen is struggling with eating, a sport that has them away from home from 7:30 am until 9 pm, and trying to manage lunch, snack, and dinner away from home can ask too much. Prioritizing isn't easy. Therapist Dawn Friedman reminds that knowing your core values as a family in advance will help: "Is a goal or value to enjoy movement? Then open swim time, or a body-positive dance studio, is more in line versus an intensive swim team that will undermine another core value of down time and family meals."

Supporting Activity

Children need to play and move their bodies, but at different levels. Movement, regardless of the child's size, supports better mood and nervous system regulation and improves other health markers. Just as with food, the goal is to avoid pressure and provide opportunity. Don't push it, and allow your child to find his natural rhythm and interests. (I'm impressed that our high school phys-ed program has options including a walking club, yoga, outdoor hiking, Zumba, team sports, weightlifting, and dance.)

Focus on having fun, being together, and feeling good. Be positive. Telling children they need to lose weight or not get fat is a great way to get them to be *less* active. Don't talk about weight or health, including your own. Try not to shame them if they are less active for a time, or compare them to more active siblings.

Be responsive to your child and consider their temperament and interests. Are team sports ideal for a social child, or geo-caching at a state park for the one who loves maps and treasure hunting? Help your child find something they like to do, and the time to do it. Limiting screen time helps kids move more than following them around like a personal trainer.[7] And remember to be flexible. Many families learned during the Covid-19 pandemic that sometimes more screen time helps get through challenging times (it sure helped ours).

Below are some ways to enjoy movement together or offer opportunities to your child, including some low-cost and free ideas.

Organized Activities

- Sign up for a class at the local rec center or gym, such as karate, dance, or swimming.
- Join a sports team or running club at school. Many waive participation fees if a child qualifies for school lunch.
- Train to participate in a fun run/walk or fundraiser for a good cause, such as a local animal shelter.
- Check out your local Audubon society for kid-focused bird-watching programming.

Nature is for everyone, but outdoor recreation hasn't always felt that way. You may find organized community programs, businesses, and non-profits in your area with the goal of helping children of color access, enjoy, and feel welcome in outdoor activities such as hiking and birding.

While there are few trails and playgrounds that are accessible to children and youth who use mobility aids, their numbers are increasing. There are also more online resources to find accessible trails and opportunities (such as the free AllTrails app).

Being Active as a Family

- Go for winter-lights walks. Bundle up after dark and bring a flashlight. Even if you have to bring little ones in the stroller or wagon for a while, get in the habit of moving together in a fun way, if you can.
- Let your kids see you having fun. Bring a basketball and shoot some hoops, or swing on the swing. (If you need to rest and sit on the bench with a book or podcast, that models wellness too.)
- Find child-sized rakes, snow shovels, and brooms so kids can join in and "help."
- Family walks or bike rides may help a child who is anxious.
- Ride bikes along a historical train track (search Rails-to-Trails online). Our family likes them because they are mostly flat, so not too challenging.
- Play in the pool at the local health club or recreation center.
- Go to family night at a local gymnastics center and bounce on the trampoline with your kids.

- Head to an indoor playground instead of, or before the movies. Minnesota, for example, has several of these in community centers and malls, given the long, cold winters.
- Plant a garden or sign up for a community plot, if available.
- Consider getting ice skates, snow pants, and boots for yourself. I found that my cold feet were often the limiting factor for outdoor play. Local schools and rec centers may have free ice rinks and skate rentals.
- Check out the free app Merlin Bird ID. Use it anywhere you can hear birds; Open a window on a walk to school, camping, or at a park. Just point your phone at the sky and hit record and it lets you know who you're hearing. See who can find the most in ten minutes, make bird bingo cards, or a scavenger hunt. Other free online resources help identify flowers and trees.

Make It Easier to Be Active

- Have a box in the trunk of the car with a few balls, bubbles, or a Frisbee. Stop at a park on the way home if you have time.
- Ask the person picking your child up from school or daycare to stop by the park and play on the way home.
- Encourage your school to increase play and recess time. Less testing, more play!
- Walk or bike to school if it's safe and you have time. Many schools are organizing programs to support walking to school.

Low-Cost Fun

- Move furniture so kids can jump on couch cushions, or try indoor bowling with empty bottles or toilet paper rolls.
- Play music and have a dance party.
- Learn Tik Tok or Fortnight dances (or whatever the current craze) with your tween.
- Make a list of scavenger items that they can either collect or mark off on a list during a walk, such as a fire hydrant, yellow house, manhole cover, mailbox, etc.
- Provide cushions and masking tape to make an indoor obstacle course.
- Check out your local recreation or community center's open gym hours for young children.
- Stock up on outdoor gear, an important consideration in northern climates. Hand-me-downs are great, but Goodwill, Once Upon a Child, and Craigslist are also good sources for cheaper gear. Snow pants and waterproof gloves prolong the fun.

Ideas from Parents

"We bought a smaller house in a walkable neighborhood. There is a park and corner store, and we can walk them to school."

"If it's not too many flights, we take the stairs. We race, and it's fun."

"I started workout DVDs at home, and they like to join in. My daughter loves yoga. Check out Namaste Kid."

"We found a cheap tumbling class, challenge our kids to race, or do silly things to get their energy out. We have a lot of fun."

"We belong to our local community center; the kids can play sports or work out there, too."

"Hula hoop and Twister. Then going to the park to throw sticks off the bridge and being in nature."

"Playground time. Bring snacks and water. It's lots of active, independent play."

"My boys love to play chase around the 'track' (our kitchen/living area). All it takes is a suggestion, and they are off."

Even Small Amounts of Movement Help

Even relatively little movement (1–3 hours a week) has benefits (unrelated to weight change), including on insulin, blood pressure, and mood.[8,9,10]

Movement broken up throughout the day improves health, and walking or gardening has health benefits. You don't have to go for "no pain, no gain." And rumor has it that the 10,000-steps-per-day number was a marketing gimmick picked by the inventor of the pedometer.

Just like with food, anxiety and shoulds around activity can get us stuck in counterproductive patterns.

Exercise Can be Dangerous

Boys are feeling more pressure to be "ripped" like their screen idols/social media influencers who work out for hours each day. The current pressure on girls is to be "toned," but still thin and "feminine." (No one is supposed to be fat.)

Consider 15 year-old Damond, who was determined to "get healthy" over the summer. He fantasized about starting school with a "glow up" and a six-pack. He started two to three hours of online workouts and stopped eating sugar. He got a lot of praise from his dad and football trainer who posted Damond's stats online, including his dropping body fat percentile. His mom started to worry, however, when he skipped hanging out with friends to work out. (Some call this unhealthy obsession with a muscular physique "bigorexia.")

Be curious about seemingly "healthy" changes. Compulsive exercise, exercising before school, not eating until they have exercised a certain amount, not doing anything without an activity tracker, anxiety with missed workouts, or skipping social events are concerning. (See Chapter 9 on eating disorders.) Conversely, if you notice your child/teen's activity falling off: A child who quit the swim team and now plays video games until three in the morning may struggle with depression or a situation with friends they don't know how to handle. Stay curious, keep communicating, and seek help when needed.

And now, back to food as we wrap up this chapter.

When Responsive Feeding Is New

Much of what you've been saying and doing around food you can let go of—maybe even need to let go of. **Building up the courage (or noticing the habit) to stop rewarding, bribing, praising etc. and then working on structure, felt safety, connection, what to serve etc. may feel both like you're doing a lot, and not enough at the same time!**

Make It Work for Your Family

I used to recommend that parents go "all in" with structure, family meals, no screens, etc. Many have had success this way. However, I've learned to trust tuned-in parents to make changes at a pace that works for them.

Children may need to be eased into new routines. Consider Samantha and then three-year-old Rosalia who had some sensory differences and feeding challenges. Samantha decided it was too overwhelming for her to make all the changes at once. Initially, Samantha removed the highchair and pulled Rosalia up to the table but kept everything else the same. Then Samantha focused on providing reliable and structured meals and snacks. Finally, they addressed the bottles. Previous attempts to go "cold turkey," as recommended by a dietitian, ended with Rosalia "catatonic" for two days (likely in a *freeze* response). This time the bottle was offered at mealtimes, at the table. Samantha followed Rosalia's cues and sat next to her with their arms touching. It wasn't long before Rosalia was happily drinking from cups.

Start with flexible structure, eat together if you can, and note where you might fall into pressure and restriction.

"We're Doing Everything You Said and It's Not Working!"

Working with clients with all kinds of challenges, this comes up regularly. And almost always there is still something (a look, a sigh, outright comments) adults are still trying to get kids to eat more, less, or different foods (it might not even be you).

This is an invitation to get curious. Ask yourself, "What am I still worried about? Am I still pressuring or not trusting the process? What is happening on weekends at her father's? What messaging is she getting from social media and friends?"

Remember that conflict helps identify opportunities. *Where are you the most upset, frustrated, and fighting over food?* Is there lingering worry about protein or that one bite of vegetable?

One study's authors wrote, "If there is a problem with compliance, identify the source of anxiety." (And they mean compliance with feeding, not the child's eating.)[11] Take out that journal and try to get honest about your worries and motivations. For example, I've heard, "If he doesn't finish his smoothie bottle, I panic and think he's going to die," or, "I just ask her to check in with her tummy before she has seconds to see if she is really sure her body needs more food." (The motivation is to persuade the child to skip seconds.) This indicates an ongoing worry about nutrition and size that fuels counterproductive feeding and is what the next three chapters tackle more in depth.

Other reasons for lack of progress might be a need for more flexibility and accommodation. Perhaps find an OT to support transitions and regulation. Consider why a child might not understand expectations, or struggle with motor initiation or other challenges.

It May Feel Like You Want to DO More

This is a process, with ups and downs, and sometimes progress is slow. It may even feel like you're not *doing* anything. **Not pressuring or restricting is not the same as doing nothing, or just letting them eat whatever, whenever they want.** You'll learn that you *do* by providing that scaffolding for your child's skills to emerge.

It may sound simple, but feeding well is work that you get to do for years. Struggling with feeding is even harder and the outcomes are worse. **The first few weeks and months when you transition toward a responsive approach are the most difficult. It's still a lot of thinking at six to 12 months, but at some point you'll likely marvel that you did it any other way.**

Chapter 5
Picky Eating and "Underweight": Pressure Undermines Progress

"I literally would throw myself on the floor with clown-like antics after every bite my daughter ate. It was exhausting, but I was terrified she wasn't eating enough."
— Olivia, mother to Janelle, age two years

"I hated sitting with her because it was pressure all around no matter how "fun" I thought I was making it."
— mom Mimi

"Years of trying to pack in calorie-dense foods had little effect. From what I could tell, she ate less. It resulted in battles. The day I finally gave all of that up was the day we started to move toward non-stressful mealtimes. Now at three-and-a-half, she eats a decent variety, and is still not quite on the charts, but is clearly healthy, and thriving."
— Beth, mother of Annabelle, age three and a half

Anxiety about weight and nutrition abounds, with apps tallying bites, or sticker charts tracking vegetables. One mother lamented, *"Parents today are really pressured: 'Make sure your child is getting enough of all the nutrients.' One book I read said that four- to eight-year-olds should eat eight to 10 servings of vegetables a day, a serving size being ½ cup—my child doesn't eat that much food in a day, let alone of vegetables!"*

Unrealistic expectations, and the social media that shoves it in our faces, doesn't help. Your child isn't drinking green smoothies!? Their bento box isn't filled with a rainbow of fruits and veggies?!

It seems to make sense that if you could *get children to eat more, or "healthier" food,* by any means necessary, she will eat more variety and grow better. "Good" parents make sure their child eats vegetables before dessert, right? Except it's not working.

And raising children who are significantly smaller than average; are picky, anxious, or avoidant eaters; or have developmental or sensory differences adds layers of worry. In the coming pages, you'll read about: typical picky eating; the growth and appetite worries that fuel pressure; what pressure and other unhelpful feeding practices look like and why they backfire; and what to do instead Then Chapter 6 will delve into more extreme picky eating (anxious and avoidant), when professional help may be warranted, how to find the right help, and more.

Typical Picky Eating

Picky (fussy, choosy, selective) eating is common. What children will or won't eat is a hot topic at daycare and preschool pickup, and online. In various studies (not just in the United States), about half of all children are described as picky. Knowing what to expect is important so that you can weather the typical picky eating phase, and not inadvertently make things worse.

With typical picky eating, the child:

- May eat well until around 15–18 months, when they become more choosy. This usually lasts through early grade school.
- Has favorites; usually carbs, sweet, or crunchy foods.
- Gets upset when a favorite food isn't served, but is able to settle and eat other foods.
- Eats a variety of textures.
- Stops eating some foods, adds others, and will come back to most of the formerly rejected foods over time (if they are served).
- Generally tolerates different foods being nearby.
- Will sometimes touch and taste new foods.
- Eats from all food groups, generally over the day or several days.

Even food "rejection" is nuanced. Most parents stop offering a food after a handful of tries. The process of learning to like new foods isn't predictable or rational. Remember the green bean study how the babies frowned while eating the beans, but ate more as the days went on? Though the infants ate the beans, the, "Mothers were apparently unaware of these changes in acceptance."[1] It's easy to put foods in the "they don't like it" category and fall into the habit of not serving them again. (I've done it too.)

Food Jags are Expected

Many children fixate on a few foods and ask for them at every meal. This can be challenging when suddenly they don't want their favorite mac-n-cheese anymore!

After an overnight with her grandparents, my daughter talked about how she loved "the cheese where you unwrap every piece," so we bought some. She ate lots for a few weeks with lunch or snack, sometimes up to four slices. Very soon, she would only eat one or two, and within six weeks the slices packed in her lunch came back uneaten.

Food jags aren't just for kids. Many adults say they eat a ham sandwich with lunch for weeks on end, and then suddenly aren't interested. I eat toast with peanut butter and jam 95 out of 100 breakfasts, most days with fruit or smoothie, and don't feel deprived; but I spend a lot of effort on and enjoy different recipes at dinner. There are many ways to enjoy variety.

The key is to not *only* serve one or two foods. **Incorporate the child's accepted foods into regular meals and snacks (more on this soon), allow children to eat as much as they want at those times, and continue to rotate in other foods.**

Temperament Plays a Role

Your child's temperament impacts how they approach life—including food. Temperament refers to the mostly innate characteristics of a child, such as how calm or reactive she is. While temperament is influenced by different factors, trying to change a naturally cautious or adventurous nature isn't likely to work. Another way of thinking about it would be personality traits. Is your child boisterous, or more of a quiet observer? Is she sensitive and cautious? Intense? Easygoing and able to let things roll off? Does your child accept help, say happily holding your hand to climb a sledding hill, or is she more likely to refuse your hand while crying in frustration—scrabbling and slipping so she can "do it myself!"

An easygoing child who is up for adventure may happily try a new food the first time they see it—and like it! A child with this temperament may go along with a "two-bite rule" with no fuss.

A 2017 study showed that some toddlers jumped in to play with new toys, and approached foods the same way, while more cautious and observant kids hung back with the toys *and* unfamiliar food.[2]

A cautious or anxious child, or one with sensory aversions, or say a history of medical trauma, may be suspicious of new people and experiences, including food. This child may react strongly to even the suggestion to try a new food. It may take dozens to hundreds of no-pressure opportunities to explore before a cautious child grows to like a new food. They may have to see others enjoy a food many times before they consider trying it. Other children fall between adventurous and cautious.

A child's temperament plays a role in their reactions to food *and* to pressure.

Observe and seek to understand your child's disposition, whether they are extroverted or introverted, and what kinds of sensory experiences they enjoy or tolerate. It can help explain why you have two kids who eat all kinds of food, but your middle child is highly selective. Keeping in mind that children approach foods differently *from infancy on* (including slower sucking patterns and different levels of interest[3]) might help you relax and resist pressure.

The Worry Behind the Pressure

You may remember from Chapter 1 that misunderstandings around growth and appetite can factor into feeding problems. These may be areas where you don't need to worry so much. Let's dig in...

About Growth

Remember, nature demands that children come in a range of sizes and roughly follows a bell curve distribution. Steady growth, even at the outer edges of the growth chart, can be healthy growth.[4] That, however, is not how many clinicians think about growth.

Healthy children can weigh well below average for their age. Many healthy infants and young children can even move downward on the growth curves, which means that the rate of gain has slowed. A 2014 study of almost ten thousand infants showed that 44% decreased one centile line or more and 25% decreased at least 2 centile lines on the growth chart (such as going from 50th to 10th percentile).[5] A decrease in two centile lines is often used to describe growth faltering, but can happen in healthy infants. This can be tricky for doctors to figure out.

Any weight *loss*, even in kids with bigger bodies, must be followed up with a healthcare provider. Weight loss can be a sign of a medical illness, and eating disorders and unhealthy weight loss behaviors are more common in individuals with higher weight.

A child growing below the third percentile on the growth charts can be followed with Z-scores. (See page 24.) Bethany shared how following Amari's Z-score reassured that they were on the right track. *"Her doctor had never heard of Z-scores. I reviewed Z-scores after calculating them online like you suggested, and her numbers definitely were improving with the weight gain, so it was helpful for me. Plotting weight-for-length was interesting too. She's pretty proportional, and close to the 'normal' range, especially for her current height."* Consider plotting growth on the WHO Z-score chart,[6] or use an app called Child Growth that calculates them for you.

Too many children are labeled incorrectly, their bodies turned into a problem to solve, and parents get kicked into worry. Remember that in 2011 the CDC warned of this possibility: ". . . overdiagnosis of underweight might damage the parent-child interaction, subjecting families to unnecessary interventions and possibly unintentionally creating an eating disorder."[7] If your child is healthy but small, a basic understanding of growth can help you protect your child from unnecessary interventions.

The "Failure to Thrive" (FTT) Label

Traditionally, "failure to thrive" (FTT) is used when a child's weight-for-age falls below the third percentile (though I've seen it used at or below the 10th percentile), or if there is a decrease of more than two centile lines such as from 50th to 10th (which isn't always problematic as you just read!). There is no real-world agreement on cutoffs, which vary by country, and frequently from provider to provider.

Note that from birth to two years, the WHO growth chart relies on different populations than the U.S. CDC chart. The WHO weights are comparatively lower before officially falling into the "underweight" or "faltering" cut off. (The WHO decided to remove data points above the 98th percentile in their sample population[7] and included only breastfed infants which may explain some of the differences.) If you're concerned and your child is on the low end of the growth chart, a thorough history and physical will help determine if there is an issue that needs addressing, regardless of which chart is used.

Most of the literature on FTT in children describes a broader picture of a child who is chronically undernourished, fatigues easily, and experiences impaired brain development. Yet, this label is frequently applied to healthy children based solely on small stature. An American Academy of Family Physicians (AAFP) guidance document[8] on FTT refers to low weight/growth and "malnutrition" interchangeably, which I believe is incorrect and confusing.

There is a movement to stop using the term FTT, as it is imprecise and confusing (countries such as the United Kingdom have largely stopped using it). Few labels are as painful for parents as "failure to thrive." Remember, children can be small *and* healthy. Not all children at the third percentile are healthy, but some are, and we must *do no harm.* I remember chatting with a teary-eyed father after a workshop while his preschooler ran back and forth, laughing with friends. Dad said, *"Failure to thrive? Sure, she's small and we're trying to figure out if something is wrong, but she's happy and thriving. It's like a punch to the gut."*

Kara tells the story of her son Griffin, who had always been small. He had a life-threatening food allergy and anxiety (no wonder!) with new foods. For two years, Griffin's pediatrician "diagnosed" FTT and lectured Kara to get her son to eat more. *"It was unbelievably stressful. I felt like a total failure. If Griffin pooped before a weigh-in, I was annoyed. That meant he would weigh less. How ridiculous is that? We switched to a pediatric allergist, who said that our son was not FTT and was growing steadily at about the fifth percentile.* ***I urge any parent dealing with an FTT diagnosis to get a second opinion. All that worry because the first doctor mislabeled our son.*** *Dealing with serious food allergies meant we already had plenty of anxiety. We so did not need this additional piece of constantly fighting to get more food into him."* (See navigating the medical system on page 341. Getting a second opinion may not be an option for all families.)

The label leads to worry, which leads parents to pressure, resulting in pushback from the child, contributing to the outcome they are trying to avoid—a child who eats and grows less well.

Signs Associated with Concerning Weight Patterns

A thorough history and physical should occur to rule out explanations for growth changes, or diagnose and guide intervention. Lab tests can be ordered if indicated.

These are some red flags and risk factors that should be looked into by a healthcare provider:

- Crossing centile lines (but should not be used on its own as a basis for diagnosis).
- Rapid shifts are more alarming. (See Chapter 1 for a refresher on growth.)
- Symptoms consistent with medical conditions (see the medical issues appendix). Coexisting conditions such as iron-deficiency anemia, elevated lead levels, or abnormal thyroid function.
- Low energy and listlessness. This raises far more concern than if the child is happy, energetic, and eats a decent variety of foods with little conflict. Consider overall health and wellness.
- Certain medications, such as ADHD stimulant meds, may suppress appetite.
- Poor mood. The child's mood, such as depression, anxiety, or chronic dysregulation, can impact appetite and digestion.

Steady growth, even if the child's weight is low on the chart, is reassuring if the child is otherwise well. Maintain or establish a healthy feeding relationship and address concerns if there is faltering growth.

"Lizbeth was born at the third percentile. The pediatrician was trying to get me to bottle feed formula, but she was steadily gaining, and had full cheeks and everything else was going well. I was also very small compared to peers growing up. She's always stayed around the 5th percentile and she's healthy and happy. I resisted all the attempts to try to get her to eat more. I have two other children, one is also smaller than average, the other is bigger, all have been healthy and are great eaters today."
— Eleanor, Mom of 16 year-old Lizbeth

Now that we've touched on growth, let's look at the related issue of how much kids eat.

Worries Around Appetite and Hunger

Many parents believe their children aren't eating enough. Frequently, children just eat less than peers or siblings, and it's not a problem. They eat enough to grow and thrive, even if they are smaller than average.

It may reassure you to know that studies suggest that children described as "picky" eat roughly the same amount, get similar macronutrients (protein, carbs, and fat) and grow just as well as children who are not.[9]

An especially challenging worry to address happens if parents believe, especially if they have been told by a feeding therapist or OT, that their child "can't" sense hunger. Let me reassure you that this is exceedingly rare; far too many parents are told their child can't.

There are many reasons why a child might not be hungry or eat much at some mealtimes. A child might not eat if they don't feel well, are dysregulated, have an appetite that is dampened by anxiety and stress, are experiencing a typical lull and will make up for it later, or are sensitive to pressure.

Researchers Black and Aboud remind us of the importance of autonomy: "*When caregivers misinterpret their child's refusal to accept food as a sign of poor appetite, rather than a signal for autonomy, the mealtime may become stressful, potentially leading to the child's feelings of frustration, inattention to internal cues, and lack of interest in communicating those cues to the caregiver.*" [10]

Hunger Cues May Be Easy to Miss

"*She's never shown me that she's hungry,*" said the mother of 10-month-old Olivia, while we watched her crawl and play. Olivia, a healthy infant transitioning to solids, soon became less interested in her toys and made her way to Mom. She stopped inspecting me, whimpered once, and played quietly with a ball in her lap.

She looked more serious than the smiling baby who had greeted me at the door. Minutes later, she whimpered again. Mom picked her up and Olivia nursed, though they had to go into another room to minimize distractions. Olivia did have hunger signals; they were just subtle.

In addition, a review of her feeding showed that Olivia was fed every 20 minutes or so over an hour in the morning, with a similar pattern in the afternoons—on Mom's, not Olivia's, schedule. Mom wondered, "*Maybe if I'm feeding her so often, she doesn't get a chance to really feel hungry?*" Once mom learned to follow Olivia's cues, and to offer family foods modified for what she could handle, Olivia's appetite picked up and her cues were more obvious.

Discovering Hunger

Mason's story is perhaps more suited to the next chapter as he grew below the curve and was diagnosed with a feeding disorder. Even in this more "extreme" scenario, Mason was capable.

Four-year-old Mason had sensory processing differences, ate fewer than 10 foods, and "failed" months of behavioral and sensory feeding therapies. His growth was steady, around the first percentile. An extensive medical workup turned up nothing; his chewing and swallowing were fine. Mom offered supplement drinks frequently, which he sipped for rewards.

Mason was described as, "cautious, not too anxious, and incredibly strong-willed." Mason had been small and "difficult to feed" since his earliest days. His parents were told by an OT when he was 18 months old that he "can't sense hunger." This seemed true, as he'd never indicated hunger or asked for food. That's scary! The fear is, if a child can't sense hunger, parents *have* to make the child eat, or the child could die. This is not an uncommon scenario.

Highlights From Mason's Intake Journal

6:30 – 7 a.m.: sippy cup milk—cuddles with Mom, Dad, and sister, who gets a bottle
8 – 9:15 a.m.: at table for breakfast (with cartoons)
10 – 11:30 a.m.: sips of supplement and crackers while wandering around
12 – 1:30 p.m.: lunch (with iPad)
3 – 4:00 p.m.: crackers while playing
5 – 6:45 p.m.: dinner, with Mom, Dad, sister; Mason eats slowly and is last to leave the table

From just this information, opportunities jumped out. Mason spent 7.5 hours a day at the table or eating on the go. He had a little something in his tummy all day, which sabotages appetite. Here's what I recommended after the first call:

- Put water in the sippy cup for the morning cuddle; could slowly water down the milk, but he tolerated going straight to water. (The milk spoiled his appetite for breakfast.)
- Limit meal and snack times to no more than 30 minutes; try to offer only water in between.
- No more rewards for eating or drinking.
- Can offer supplement drink during meal and snack times.

That was it! They kept the morning connection time with cuddles, and worked on structure, allowing Mason to have periods of time when he wasn't taking in fuel. Mom felt reassured that he still got the supplement. I got an email three days later from his mother: *"I have tears streaming down my face! He just asked for seconds and said, 'I'm hungry' for the first time!"*

This is not a complicated intervention. **Removing pressure and adding structure allowed his body to experience hunger.**

Support Appetite With Challenges

Some things can make interoception (tuning in to the body) more difficult, including medications, sensory differences, and dysregulation; it means adults need to take extra care to support autonomy, felt safety, and connection. Optimizing feeding gives children the best chance to tune in. I've seen many children and teens told they "couldn't" sense hunger, eventually be able to tune in (like Mason!). Here are a few considerations:

- Your child may not have the opportunity to develop an appetite if he is constantly encouraged to have small amounts of food, or supplement drinks.
- His cues may be subtle: a change in demeanor, a change in activity level or skin color, looking for closeness, etc.
- If feeding and mealtimes are characterized by conflict and distress, he may be less able to feel his hunger signals.

Non-Responsive Tactics and Picky Eating

This section digs into why you might get stuck in pressure, why it backfires, and how to spot it. The main worries you've read about behind pressure to eat is that a child is perceived as too small, not eating enough, or the right foods. Worry fuels the pressure, begging, and bribing—which backfires. As one feeding expert wrote, "Ensuing parent-child struggles around feeding may consequently increase parental distress and worry, leading to further attempts to make the child eat that cause further disruption to the feeding relationship."[11] (This is described in the Worry Cycle from Chapter 1.)

Reasons Parents Pressure

- You might feel scared:
  - "If I don't get my child to be adventurous, he'll be picky forever."
  - "He has to eat five servings of vegetables a day to be healthy."
  - "He needs protein every one to two hours so he has fewer meltdowns."
- You're told to pressure by those you turn to for help:
  - "Do whatever you have to, just get the food in!"
  - "Serve green beans and rice until he eats it."
  - "I've never heard of a child who would starve himself; just keep trying."
  - "Let's see how far we can push them."
- Everyone around you pressures.
- It's how you were raised.
- Pressure "works" in the short term—to get those two bites in.
- Occasionally getting that bite of vegetable in can make you feel like you did your job, and it may relieve some of your anxiety in that moment.

Pressure Makes Things Worse

Pressuring involves a lot of effort and leads to conflict and disconnection. Research shows it doesn't work.[12] Consider:

- Children pressured to eat more tend to eat less, and may not grow to their potential.
- Pressure leads to stress, which can kill appetite.
- Stress interferes with cues from their bodies about hunger and fullness.
- Stress leads children to seek and rely on familiar and comforting foods.
- Children pressured to eat more fruits and vegetables tend to eat fewer of them, and eat more high-fat foods.
- Pressure leads to slow eating, more negative emotion at mealtimes, and early satiety (getting full fast).

Lots of Downsides, Little Benefit

Being forced to eat is scary and unpleasant. In one study (aptly titled, "You Will Eat All of That!"[13]) college students described being forced to eat as children and ". . . identified the most aversive aspects of this scenario as lack of control and feelings of helplessness." They also wrote, "**. . . most respondents (72 percent) reported that they would not willingly eat the target food today. In some, the forced consumption episode appears to be a unique situation in which distasteful food combines with interpersonal conflict to result in long lasting food rejection.**" Unlike peanut butter and chocolate, food and conflict do not go well together. Conflict undermines connection and autonomy, and makes children feel less capable. And it didn't get them to like the food!

"Trying to make her eat, creating any kind of battle—I would lose. The harder I tried, the worse it got. I cheered, stood on my head, played games . . . all of it made her eating worse."

— Renee

What "Pressure" Looks Like

Encouraging kids with eating is the norm in many cultures, so it can be unclear if what you're doing is helping or not. (Hint, observe your child!) The following are some common ways parents pressure. Check off how many you've tried:

- ☐ Bribes or rewards: "You can have dessert if you eat two bites of chicken," or "If you eat half a bagel every day, you'll get a sticker and earn a prize at the end of the week."
- ☐ Demanding compliance: "You have to eat two bites of everything on your plate," or "You have to take a 'no-thank-you' bite."
- ☐ Negotiating: "Okay, two bites of this, then one bite of that. No? OK, three small bites of this one then..."
- ☐ Catering: "I made rice like you asked for! You don't want rice? Want buttered noodles?"
- ☐ Guilt: "Think of all the children who don't have this wonderful food," or "It shows Mommy we love her when we eat the food she makes."
- ☐ Overselling: "This mac-n-cheese is soooo delicious! I promise you'll like it. Look! I just had a bite, mm-mmm!"

Some attempts to get kids to eat have more negative energy.

- Begging, as in, "Please, just take one bite. Please."
- Physically placing or forcing food into a child's mouth or holding a child's head or hands while feeding.
- Punishing kids by withholding food, making menus of only rejected foods, or threatening to take away screens, toys, or your affection to motivate a child to eat.

"'Just make them eat'—that one gets me every time!"

— Sherry, mother of a five-year-old selective eater

"We praise and beg and reward when she eats, but it's not helping."
— Franny, mother to Dora, age four years

Pressure Can Be Subtle

Even subtle pressure, including "positive," kinder, and gentler tactics, can backfire.[14] An example may be buying three different kinds of pesto on the way home from the restaurant where your child tried it, then serving it multiple times over the following days while reminding them that they like it. Here are a few more less-obvious ways parents pressure, ways to avoid them, and what to try instead:

Distraction

Examples include relying on screens or toys to get kids to eat. Parents describe an almost "dissociative" state in which children only eat if they are "zoned out." This can also be an outcome of feeding therapy that uses screens to get bites in. Another example is feeding infants only while they sleep, relying on the suck reflex to get calories in. (Sleep-feeding typically falls apart around 4–5 months of age, when the suck reflex diminishes. If an infant only feeds while asleep and you aren't able to transition to feeding while awake, contact the child's doctor.)

Over time, "zoned-out" eating can be a barrier to tuning in. Many children with sensitive nervous systems have trouble connecting with their bodies, including signals of hunger and fullness. Some children will eat less, some more, with tuned-out eating.

Ideas to handle screens/distractions: See page 79 for tips on weaning off screens and try to be consistent about eating without screens for a while. Once children seem to "get" the process and capabilities emerge, you can have occasional snacks or meals with screens. See how it goes. Maybe it's a snack during a movie, or dinner on trays while watching the game. She may eat more or less than she otherwise might have, but since bodies self-regulate intake over more than one meal or snack, it should even out.

Remember, screens can help with regulation and also be useful in some cases to support intake. Please see the index for mentions of screens for a fuller picture of how screens can support eating—or not.

Rewards and Praise

Sticker charts, toys, high-fives, and "You're so good, you ate your pancakes!" are common, even in feeding therapies. Rewards can help with things like transitions or helping a child set the table. Rewards and praise with eating can pressure and make a child feel less confident.

Sophie's experience with her son's feeding therapy illustrates the limitations of rewards. Her son was eating a few more foods in sessions (after 18 months of "desensitization") but still relied on 10 foods at home. She described how he was rewarded with toys at therapy, which she knew wasn't working when he asked one day, *"I wonder what they'll give me today if I lick broccoli?"*

Empathy builder: Think of a time when you vomited, or had a bad experience with food, maybe choking. How long did it take before you wanted to eat that food again? Thinking about it now, do you notice any sensations in your body? A tightness in your throat? Are you frowning? What reward would have enticed you to eat that food shortly after the event? Money? Praise? How would it have felt if you had to eat that food before you could have other foods?

The praise, stickers, and toys are external (outside their body) motivators, and provide an opportunity to resist. If the motivation is internal (tapping into the child's drive to do their best with eating), there is nothing to fight against, and the child will very likely branch out—when she is ready.

Health or Nutrition Lectures

Trying to rationalize with children doesn't work. Avoid, "Protein makes your muscles grow. You want to be big and strong, don't you?" and definitely stay clear of vague and scary health warnings such as, "You have to eat vegetables so you don't get diabetes."

One study showed that when children were told a cracker was "healthy," they chose it less often than the cracker not labeled that way.[15] It seems that kids have likely absorbed the message that "healthy" food tastes bad. Other studies have found similar results.

Ashley Rhodes–Courter, in *Three Little Words,* articulated her resistance of nutrition messaging from her adoptive mother Gay, "I knew Gay was trying to please me, but for some reason, I resisted every attempt she made. She made chicken nuggets in the oven so they'd have the KFC flavor, but not as much fat. They were quite good, although I was annoyed by the way she preached to me about eating healthy foods."[16]

Overselling or Praising Food

Generally, commenting on what someone is or isn't eating, with an agenda, won't help. Skip the lectures and sales job: Children eat because they are hungry, it tastes good, or for other reasons we've explored. Rarely do they eat because it's "good for them" or because you are trying to convince them they will like it. The less you say, the less they have to push back on.

Hiding "Healthy" Food

With the internet full of "sneaky" recipes like mac-n-cheese made with squash, you may be tempted to hide nutrient-dense foods in accepted foods.

Samantha, a self-described reformed picky eater was left as a child to fend for herself and her brothers to get meals, was rewarded with food, and was served a limited variety. During a visit to her grandmother, she ate a stew, only to be told afterward that it was bear meat. She became so suspicious of anything served at her grandmother's that she only ate crackers, cereal, or individually wrapped items.

Sherry, another mom, told me about baking blueberries into brownies. She baked at night, taking the blueberry container to the garage trash to hide the evidence—like cleaning up a crime scene. She was jumpy hiding the "healthy" food, because she knew that if her kids found out, they might not eat her brownies again, or anything else. It felt wrong, but she didn't know how else to support their eating.

Sherry says, *"The information I read was completely unhelpful. 'Hide veggies in her meatballs,' but she won't eat meatballs, and it's impossible to hide veggies in plain noodles with butter."*

A Facebook reader warned, *"I tried to sneak riced cauliflower into his scrambled eggs and now he won't touch eggs. I'm heartbroken. It was probably the most nutritious food he would regularly eat."* **Trust takes time to build, but can be destroyed in a moment.**

Instead of hiding: If you don't want your kids to know you're putting blueberries in the brownies, reconsider. Chances are, they might not care either way, so if you do choose to add foods to support nutrition, do so in the open so you are simply preparing food. If you do mix in nutrient-dense foods, or use shakes and frozen pops to support nutrition, also offer the foods in different ways. (See ideas on supporting nutrition later in this chapter.)

What's Important Now (WIN) is to protect the trust that you have and are building with your child; don't risk it for a short-term nutritional goal. Don't even try the old trick of sneaking in a spoonful of veggies between those sweet pears for the infant learning to eat solids. It will make them wary and prone to refuse foods.

Not Providing Opportunities

While not exactly pressure, the following represent mostly missed opportunities to support emerging competence:

- Allow the child to dictate the menu, hoping she will eat something.
- Routinely offer other foods or regularly allow the child to get something else after food is on the table.
- Only serve foods that the child readily accepts.
- Allow the child to drink milk or other filling beverages throughout the day.
- Feed only accepted foods separate from the family so he isn't around other foods.
- Lose structure and allow the child to nibble throughout the day. The child doesn't have the opportunity to develop an appetite between meals and snacks. (Many parents are told to push the child to eat frequently. I remember one call when the mom was out of breath. She explained, *"Oh, I'm just chasing Mathew around with his sausage from breakfast."*)

Games

I'm seeing social media posts from nutrition experts that say things like, "Don't pressure your child to eat! Instead, get them to eat vegetables using these strategies..." Even if it's playful, it can still feel like pressure:

- Let's see who can eat it the fastest!
- Let's use our dinosaur teeth!
- Who can crunch the loudest?
- Let's see if we can make stamp art with the blueberries!

These were the "fun" tactics Mimi was trying that didn't work and that felt awful.

Too Much Attention (i.e. the Lunchbox Interrogation)

Remember the boy who stopped mid-bite with the hot dog because he had an expectant audience (from Chapter 1)? Frequently commenting on your child's eating while they're in earshot, or reporting what they ate the minute your partner walks through the door, sends your child the message that their eating is a big deal—and they're not good at it.

Another reinforcing event is the lunch interrogation. When you pick your child up from school or daycare, avoid the temptation to rummage through his lunchbox and greet him with, "Did you eat all your sandwich?" If it's the first thing you ask about, you send a message that his eating matters most, and that he can't handle it on his own.

Instead, pretend you aren't concerned (look in his lunchbox later); ask about art or if he played tag during recess—anything but food. Many daycares report intake at pickup. Colby, a client whose son Frank was a selective three-year-old, had to ask childcare staff not to give the report in front of Frank. She also asked them not to encourage or scold Frank about his eating. (More on "meddlers" in Chapter 10.) Colby met with the daycare staff to explain their new approach and the staff agreed to text her instead, which took about the same time as the verbal report. The information helped her plan after-school snacks and meals as well as make sure things were on track, as his weight gain was a concern.

Supplement Drinks Can Undermine Appetite and Curiosity

While not necessarily "pressure," supplement drinks such as Boost or PediaSure (even home-made smoothies) can sabotage appetite and variety. It's one of the first "solutions" many clinicians reach for when a child is smaller or eats a limited variety. If we think about the RF values it can limit internal motivation, and even their sense of competence.

"We were handed a coupon for PediaSure by my physician when I tried to discuss my child's picky eating. We served it with meals, and my son didn't want or need to eat

any other foods, it seemed. Now, a few years later, I have banned PediaSure and am now struggling with an older and pickier eater."

— Alice, mother of Mitchel, age six

You may have seen PediaSure ads, which fuel worry. (I read somewhere that, "The ideal consumer is a scared mom.") In one commercial, a girl turns her nose up at some fruits and vegetables while the slogan plays: "Be 110 percent sure!" How could you *not* want to "feed your child's potential?" Supplement drinks are a potential problem because:

- If sipped throughout the day they can undermine structure and appetite.
- They are sweet and may be easy to like for a selective child, who may fill up on them and limit their exploration.
- They are rarely necessary; most children described as picky get enough variety and grow fine. Supplements may be an answer to a problem that doesn't exist.

That is not to say that supplements are the 'easy' way out. Parents with feeding struggles are often desperate. If your child truly is limited with her intake, a supplement can support nutrition. But most often I see families stuck using shakes and supplements in a way that sabotages eating.

Almost all the children I've worked with who relied on shakes for most of their intake had feeding differences, and experienced intense pressure to get them to eat more. Usually the parent was told to follow the child around with a PediaSure to get as much in as possible. This undermines structure, and if their tummies always have something in them, it robs children of the opportunity to develop an appetite.

Another couple I worked with would make their child sit in the highchair for up to an hour at each sitting, hoping to get in a few more bites, then follow each meal with eight ounces of PediaSure. This child vomited several times a week. Within days of stopping the post-meal PediaSure and offering four ounces at a time with meals, her vomiting had almost completely stopped.

Using Supplements in a Responsive Way

Some children benefit from supplements to support nutrition while addressing feeding:

- If you rely on drink supplements and are scared to stop, first incorporate them into the meal and snack routine.
- Serve regular meals and snacks that offer a variety of textures and flavors.
- If your child truly is not getting adequate nutrition, that can affect appetite. Be sure to work with an RD, follow growth, and have support. (See the next chapter).
- Consider nutrition-boosting versions of accepted foods, such as fortified juice, bread or pastas, or other supplements. Work with an RD to identify nutrition needs.

- Consider making your own smoothies or shakes with ingredients such as dairy milk, soy or almond milk, yogurt, vegetables, fruits, protein powders, or nut butters. Ask your pediatric RD for recommendations. One mom wrote, "*We wound up making her homemade smoothies with almond milk, instant breakfast mix, baby rice cereal, peanut butter, bananas, and mangos. She loved it.*"

There is more than one "right" way to meet nutritional needs, and this may change for your child over time. Supplement drinks can help provide good enough nutrition. One mom shared, "*Eddie's autistic and never enjoyed eating. If he could take a pill instead, he would. He eats okay variety, but breakfast is tough for him and he does well with a Boost every morning.*" Eddie's nutrition is adequate and this works well for them.

Pushing High-Fat or High-Calorie Food Can Backfire

Similar to supplements, only offering high-fat or high-calorie foods and drinks can undermine appetite and curiosity. I usually see this with more avoidant eating and in lower-weight kids (more in next chapter). In an effort to get calories in to increase weight, parents may be advised to only allow the child to drink high fat smoothies (never water), with fats added to all foods. This can be an important tool if a child has high metabolic demands or tires quickly with eating (with heart or lung defects for example), has lost weight, or is in treatment for anorexia nervosa. However, this should rarely be necessary, and parents should have support if it is.

Kids often don't like eating this way. Think about how you might feel after many fast-food meals in a row. You might have less of an appetite facing your tenth meal of pizza or a burger and fries. Or on a hot day you might want water, but are only allowed to drink whole milk with cream added.

For many of these children, the first foods they want to eat are ones they weren't allowed to have. Ironically, plain fruits and vegetables are the formerly forbidden, high-interest food! This happened to Jacob, who was being followed for below-the-charts but stable growth. His Mom was thrilled to report to the GI (gastrointestinal) doctor that Jacob discovered he actually liked plain cucumbers. The doctor scolded, "Not enough calories. Douse them in ranch dressing and then give them to him."

Jacob showed a glimmer of internal motivation; for the first time, he *self-initiated* eating and experienced pleasure with food! By dismissing and spoiling those first steps to a healthy relationship with food, his GI doctor probably did more harm than good. Offering high fat options along with meals and snacks is responsive: cream, avocado, oils, nut butters, fried foods, whole dairy can offer calories and fat.

Maren, mother of Katia, shares how this recommendation played out for them: "*With my very small but ultimately healthy daughter, who was picky from the start. . . we were supposed to put syrup or cream on everything sweet, and oil and butter on everything else. For a couple of years, I added oil to almost everything. But she loved (and still loves) plain fruit, and I refused to mess with that, even though her doctor disapproved."*

Like Katia and Jacob, many children often branch out first with foods they haven't been pressured to eat. Four-year-old Shawn's first new food in over a year was a homemade treat for a neighbor's dog. The next new food he tried was nuts from a bird food mix. Perhaps he felt safe trying foods that no one expected him to eat.

Pocketing or Cheeking Food Can Be a Response to Pressure

Pocketing, or "cheeking," refers to keeping food in the mouth, usually tucked in the cheeks for prolonged periods. I'm including it here, as it can result from pressure. Pocketing is usually ascribed only to sensory-motor causes. If pressure is removed and the pocketing resolves, that helps you know that pressure was the culprit.

There may be a combination of factors, including sensory-motor challenges; a child may not know how to chew and move food around in his mouth, or he can't sense where the food is in his mouth. Frequently, kids pocket or gag (assuming they have the skills to safely chew and swallow) when they are fed when they don't want to eat.

Jacob was labeled "failure to thrive" with years of "failed" feeding therapies. Doctors found no explanation for his low appetite and slow growth. Jacob screamed at the sight of his highchair, which was in front of the TV, where he spent hours each day as his mother tried to get in a few more bites. A speech therapist found no concerns. When the parents filled in the intake analysis, insights emerged. Mom wrote: *"I put the cracker in his mouth and walked away. I came back 20 minutes later and he still hadn't swallowed the cracker. He knew if he didn't swallow it that I wouldn't put anything else into his mouth."*

When kids get into gagging and vomiting, it can become almost reflexive. Amari (more on pages 132-133) was likely pocketing because if she tried to swallow she would vomit. Once Amari's mom, Bethany understood it as something frightening that Amari couldn't control, she was able to stop pressuring. When Amari trusted that no one would put food in her mouth, her gagging and pocketing quickly improved.

If a child pockets, ignore it when possible, and stay calm. If there is a safety concern, offer the option, "You can spit it out (while handing over a napkin) or swallow it (offer a glass of water), but it's not safe to play with food in your mouth." You can develop a shorthand such as, "Let's do a quick cheek check." (See page 147 for red flags for sensory motor concerns and if an evaluation may be warranted.)

If kids pocket and rechew the food, or swallow and bring food up to chew again, this may be rumination and is discussed in the medical issues appendix.

Wrapping Up Pressure

No matter the tactic, from force-feeding to following the child around with high-calorie shakes, most attempts to try to get your child to eat will backfire.

"Our daughter was a tiny baby and didn't breastfeed or move to solids well. She was, and probably always will be, skeptical of new foods. So we made the classic 'mistakes.' We were so concerned about how much she was eating that we only served foods she ate a lot of, which of course are now the only foods she eats. We were so freaked out about variety that we tried again and again to get her to try foods, laying on the pressure, lots of fighting. Exhausting and stressful for everybody."

— Nora, mother of Suzie, age five

As we wrap up the discussion about pressure, it may help to note that almost all humans have a drive for variety in foods and will eventually tire of eating the same thing, if we let them.[17]

From Pressure to a Responsive Approach

Jo Cormack, clinician and PhD researcher focused on pressure and feeding, is direct with parents: "You're working really hard and it's coming from a place of love and concern. Yes, you might get that extra bite of carrot in with bribes and tears, but research is very clear that it is making things worse. It's not your fault that you didn't know that."

Once parents have that understanding, Cormack shares, "We can harness the energy of that love and concern into not pressuring and responsive feeding." She finds it is compassionate to be direct. I agree. Parents usually seek help knowing that what they're doing isn't working (as I did). We will transition now into what you can do instead of pressure.

Protect Your Child's Autonomy and Internal Motivation

Pressure undermines your child's autonomy (and leads to conflict and undermines internal motivation). But autonomy can be a tricky idea.

We might confuse allowing children to get any food whenever or wherever they want as supporting their autonomy. However this kind of "autonomy" isn't developmentally appropriate, especially for young children, and can increase their anxiety. With a responsive approach, the parent provides the scaffolding for the child to do their best with eating. The child's autonomy is expressed within a supportive feeding environment.

A useful construct around supporting autonomy is the Division of Responsibility, or DOR. The essence of DOR is that the parent is in charge of what, when, and where food is served, and the child is in charge of how much at those times.

A responsive approach allows for flexibility in your jobs of the what, when, and where, while virtually always ensuring that the child decides how much.

See if you can tell where the jobs have been confused around autonomy:

Scenario 1: Marion makes dinner with a salad, canned fruit, bread, and stew. While she cooks, she asks her son Ryder what he would like. He asks for plain pasta, which Marion prepares. When she is serving up their plates, he cries that he wants rice instead. Marion snaps at him that he asked for pasta.

Answer: Mom did part of her job—the when and where—and got everyone to the table and served a variety of foods. (Bravo!) But her son decided the what—pasta. Per usual, he changed his mind (developmentally appropriate), and they argued through the meal. Also, Mom pre-plated the food. Mom could allow Ryder more control (autonomy) and neutralize battles by letting Ryder serve himself.

Scenario 2: George gets takeout Chinese food with plain rice and a few entrées. He also opens a jar of applesauce. Nine-year-old Joshua gets up from the table and helps himself to crackers from the cupboard, saying, "I hate takeout! You never listen to me!"

Answer: George allowed his son to decide the what. Joshua normally likes rice and applesauce, and one entrée was a mild chicken dish that he has enjoyed in the past. Joshua had options on the table he could have eaten. George could have said, *"I'm sorry you're upset. You don't have to eat anything you don't want to; we will have crackers for snack tomorrow. Come sit with us."* Or, if Joshua had an exhausting day at school and was nearing meltdown, they could take some time before coming to the table to connect and calm, or George could have allowed him to put the crackers in a bowl on the table.

Scenario 3: Morning snack was finished and put away 15 minutes ago, but four-year-old Susie gets herself a granola bar. Mom Deborah, and Susie argue over the bar.

Answer: Susie decided the what and when by getting it on her own. Deborah could have given Susie the choice to save the granola bar for afternoon snack, or to eat it with lunch. Susie could even carry the granola bar if it helps. (See page 192 on letting kids carry of have access to food, or the 'stash.') If this happens frequently, looking at the morning routine may offer clues. Stress or pressure can kill appetite, resulting in kids seeking food shortly after meals end when they are more regulated and can tune in to hunger.

Scenario 4: Six-year-old Tom wants dessert, but he has to eat two bites of chicken and a bite of corn first. He's whining and trying to negotiate down to one bite of chicken. Answer: Tom's parents are trying to control what and how much Tom eats. Once the food was on the table, Tom's parents could let him decide what, *in what order*, and how much he ate.

On Assumptions and Accommodations

Jo Cormack PhD, psychologist and child feeding specialist wrote a blog for feeding professionals. The following is adapted with permission:

I worked with the family of ten-year-old Amy who is autistic and has sensory differences. Amy attends a local school and is into video games and netball. Mum explained that **Amy was only able to eat alone in the living room, playing video games or watching TV.** This raised two questions.

1. Amy is neurodivergent. Is it an appropriate goal to have her join family meals when she is clear that this doesn't work for her?
2. Why is Amy finding family meals hard? Maybe it's the sensory or social aspects of meals… maybe she's always eaten in the other room, and the change wouldn't feel good. Or perhaps she's experienced pressure in the past and needs to eat where she knows her autonomy will be respected.

Question two informs question one. Neurodivergent or not—we need to understand WHY a child is finding something hard in order to decide whether and how to address it. We need to be cautious about making assumptions and unquestioned accommodations. Assuming children "can't" do something means we don't dig deeper. This risks failing to see the individual and missing out on healing opportunities.

On the other hand, what am I trying to gain by exploring whether Amy can join the family table? Am I imposing cultural norms, the notion that "sitting at a table" is the correct way to eat a meal? Do I want Amy to "act neurotypical"? What is genuinely in Amy's best interest?

What if Amy's need for a separate space to eat is more important than potential benefits of eating with her family (connection, opportunities to experience different foods, the benefit of modeling, etc.). If felt safety is compromised, she won't benefit from all of that anyway, and aversive experiences increase negative associations with being at the table.

If I decide sitting at the table is a goal BEFORE I've got a nuanced understanding of what's going on for Amy, then I'm imposing my agenda. However, if I get an understanding first, then reflect on which goals may be appropriate, I'm able to understand Amy in context and view her as an individual.

The solution: Mum thought Amy needed the distraction of the screen to eat. This seemed plausible. I chatted with Amy, who laughed at me for not understanding. "Well it's obvious!" She said. I asked her to tell me more. She looked at me quizzically, and said, "Why would I want to be at the table with cold toes?"

And this was the crux of it. The living room had a soft carpet. Amy couldn't stand socks or slippers because of her sensory preferences, and the floor where the family ate had cold tiles. She didn't like how it made her toes feel. No one had asked her about this before, so she'd never shared it. Amy and Mum went rug shopping and from then on, Amy happily joined the family for evening meals.

The takeaway isn't that floors need rugs. Neither is it that autistic children should necessarily be encouraged to sit at the family table. The point is, we should neither decide what is right for a particular child or what is going on for a child, without really diving deep into it first.

When parents stop trying to get children to eat more, less, or different foods, the battles mostly stop—and the mood improves, often quickly. It doesn't mean that the intake or variety improves right away; in fact, they may worsen initially, as you will learn below. But ending battles is the first step to felt safety and tuning in to curiosity, hunger, and fullness.

Confusion Around Autonomy and Taking the Lead

Increasingly, parents express confusion because flexible structure, any limits on any food, or efforts to address variety are portrayed by some as diet culture or not honoring the child's differences or autonomy (see above). For example, a dietitian online might tell you that putting sweets in a cupboard and limiting a young child's access to mostly meal and snack times reinforces diet culture; when for most kids, out-of-sight sweets support tuned-in eating (more in on pages 88-89).

There can be an overcorrection from too much pressure or restriction to not enough support. Both can undermine a child's comfort and capabilities with eating. But parents can model and take the lead with a calm, matter-of-fact eating environment that acknowledges and accommodates differences.

Self-described "clean eater" Ilse shared that seven-year-old Axle hadn't joined family meals for over a year. Mom felt this was due to Axle's anxiety around noise, though he wasn't distressed eating with friends. Axle increasingly refused previously enjoyed foods to a worrisome degree. Ilse was unsure how to handle sweets, his frequent filling up on energy bars and pouches from the pantry, or how to eat *with* Axle and if that was an appropriate goal given his sensory differences.

Ilsa worried about nutrition, and their feeding relationship was anxiety-ridden. Here is an excerpt from a follow-up email a few days after an initial call: "*I felt paralyzed—like would saying no to food whenever he wanted it make him lose touch with his hunger signals? Is it respecting his sensory needs to have his iPad whenever he eats? Should I never allow screens? Ack! I'm getting a sense that it won't hurt him to have appropriate-for-him expectations. He happily sat with us for breakfast yesterday (and it was loud). You'd be impressed . . . I didn't make any comments about the food. I have a lot to learn, but I feel more confident knowing it seems to help when I'm the adult taking the lead!*"

Responsive Flexibility

How you approach scenarios will depend on many factors, from the timing, your own capacity, what is happening with other children, and what patterns you observe (journaling helps here).

What Else Can You Do to Help Your Selective Eater?

Here are more tips geared to the issue of picky eating:

- Offer the foods you want to eat as a family, including high- and low-fat foods and sauces.

- Serve foods from different containers, bowls, etc. Try to avoid serving directly from the original container until they are doing better with eating. Some children will refuse a food if the label changes. (Go slow if they are stuck on packaging as removing it may increase anxiety.)
- Change up cups, plates, or mats. Some children with "rigid" preferences (often observed with autism, or anxiety) can fixate on the visual presentation and might only eat from the purple placemat. Try to avoid this issue from the beginning by rotating mats etc. If they do get "stuck" on one plate, try to buy a few extras, just in case.
- Avoid scraping your infant/child's face with a spoon or washcloth to clean dribbling foods, wiping her hands, or otherwise unnecessarily touching her while she eats. Important: You can wipe her hands with permission if she seems distracted or unhappy about messy hands, but try to avoid it if she doesn't seem bothered by it. Wiping a child's face without permission can be unpleasant, and increase rejection and avoidance.
- Have a damp washcloth available if she doesn't like messy fingers; she can be taught to wipe them herself.

Paper Napkin: They Have to Be Able to Spit Food Out

Children are more likely to try a new food if they don't have to swallow it, particularly if they gag or vomit frequently. Let them know they may spit out any food they don't want to swallow into a paper napkin. They have to have an *out*. If a child doesn't have the skills, a feeding therapist can teach them to spit food out.

Mentioning the paper napkin once or twice to let them know it's there is fine. However, this is a prime example of how **support turns into pressure:** Mentioning it several times during a meal, as in, "Hon, don't forget about your tasting napkin!" or, "Look, Mommy doesn't want to eat this bite, so I'm spitting it in my napkin!" or, "I don't see you using your tasting napkin! Remember you can try something and spit it out! Try the burger!" This invites resistance. Did you sense that as you read the multiple reminders?

Ideas on What and How to Serve

Here are a few ideas to get started.

- Texture can be more of a stumbling block than flavor. If you're moving slowly with texture, remember to introduce flavors (drinks, ice-cream, Jell-O, gum, sauces, etc.).
- Serve one or two items your child usually eats at every meal and snack.
- Include dips, sauces, toppings, and sprinkles. Ellory explained her approach with her selective three-year-old: *"One day I put out several small bowls of rice (she was unfamiliar with rice and would not eat it), and let her put different toppings on each bowl. She loved the rice with soy sauce, and that's how we added a new food."*

- Serve dessert with the meal.
- Occasionally serve sweets or other favorites with a snack and let them eat as much as they want. (These last two points usually elicit the most "yeah, rights" from parents. For more, see page 86.)
- Find ways to serve and enjoy fruits and vegetables yourself if you can. This is an important predictor of a child learning to like fruits and veggies.[18]
- Experiment with different settings such as restaurants, samples at the grocery store, or outings where food is available—but not the main activity. One mom shared on my blog, *"She watched another young child request seconds, thirds, and fourths of pasta and pesto. She would not try it that day, but soon after, her curiosity got the better of her and she ate some. Pasta with pesto became a staple for years, and is still a favorite."*
- If low appetite or weight is a worry, let them eat preferred and familiar foods, even if it's only ice cream and a handful of carbs. Renee shared the advice of their beloved pediatric GI doctor: "A calorie is a calorie." This helped take the pressure off. Otherwise, *"Trying to push vegetables (as their other doctors were doing) when a child is literally starving is terrifying and made it all so much worse."*

Many Ways, Many Times

My mantra with serving foods is ***"many ways, many times."*** Let's take blueberries. Go ahead and bake them into a brownie (in broad daylight), but also:

- Bake them into half of a batch of muffins or buy a blueberry muffin.
- Make some of your pancakes with blueberries.
- Try offering frozen blueberries if your child has the oral-motor skills to eat them safely. Children sometimes prefer frozen fruits or veggies straight from the freezer.
- Serve freeze-dried blueberries for crunchy textures.
- Serve blueberries in yogurt or buy blueberry-flavored yogurt of a brand your child already likes.
- Try blueberry jam.
- Make yogurt or ice cream, or oatmeal "sundaes," and have different bowls of toppings, including blueberries.

Canned, frozen, and freeze-dried are not second best. Some kids prefer the predictable size, texture, and flavor. Add them to the rotation if you don't already. Your child will benefit from the nutrients, and it introduces new flavors and textures.

Condiments Are Your Friend

Parents may avoid sauces and dips, worrying that the child "won't learn to eat foods plain" or that ketchup has "too much sugar." One study showed that kids who had a little sugar with grapefruit juice on the first try later liked the unsweetened juice more than children who had initially tried an *un*sweetened version. Another study showed that children ate more vegetables when served with ranch dressing.

So the myth that sugar and condiments limit variety is just that—a myth. Ketchup, even sugar for that matter, help *increase* variety.[19,20] Think of sauces and dips like training wheels.

You probably won't have a teenager pouring ketchup on rice. And... is it *wrong* if an adult likes ketchup on rice? I wonder if there would be less suffering and shame with more acceptance. People can do their best with eating in all kinds of ways; like my uncle who never eats seafood or veggies, but enjoys meals and is still playing tennis at 80. Or the autistic person who feels best drinking smoothies and a handful of foods to meet their nutrition needs.

The bottom line is that condiments *help* many children learn to like new foods:

- The familiar flavor of condiments can bridge to a new food. If a child likes chicken with ketchup, she may enjoy another meat with ketchup.
- For tougher-to-chew foods (such as meats or dried fruit), dips and sauces add moisture and make them easier to manage.
- Have a variety of options, such as ketchup, ranch dressing, homemade dressings, or hot sauce.
- Put one or more accepted condiments, dips, and spread out at every eating time.

In our book, Helping Your Child with Extreme Picky Eating, Jenny McGlothlin SLP and I wrote about "bridges" to new foods. **The bridge or connection may be a condiment (like ketchup), a sprinkle, preferred temperature, favored smoothie, color, special plate or restaurant... something familiar that helps make that positive connection to a new food.**

Let Kids DO

Dips, sprinkles, and spreads are another bridge. Children who prepare foods tend to eat more of them.[21] When children *do*, it gives them a sense of control (autonomy) and a feeling of competence. If your child prepares food *with* a caring person, it also offers connection. Consider:

- Cinnamon sugar in a shaker may make apple slices, buttered toast, or yogurt more appealing.
- Candy sprinkles can bridge from ice-cream to frozen yogurt, and from yogurt to applesauce.
- Dip spreaders for whipped cream cheese, Nutella, or nut butter.
- Yogurt, whipped cream, or melted chocolate may make strawberries or banana chunks more appealing.

- Prep simple no-cook recipes, bake, or have kids help wash or cut veggies for stir-fry (with age-appropriate knives, see page 253).

Plan to Serve at Least One Thing Your Child Can Eat

If eating together is new, start with the foods you eat now, place the serving bowls in the middle of the eating area, and eat together. Do this until you get the hang of schedules and not pressuring. If choosy eaters come to the table and see *something* they can eat and know they won't be pressured to eat other foods, they feel reassured and can begin to relax, look around, watch, smell, pass and poke, and eventually try new foods. Serve at least one familiar food, which might be bread, rice, bananas, pasta, naan, or tortillas.

It might feel odd to have the rotisserie chicken Mom brought home, next to microwaved frozen peas and mashed potatoes, next to a bowl of pretzels, but this is part of the process of helping your child learn to like new foods.

How we talk about food informs how we feel about food. I prefer "familiar," "preferred," or "accepted" versus "safe" when describing food around a child. Saying "safe" implies other foods are "unsafe" and can reinforce or introduce anxiety. If a child or teen refers to a food themselves as "safe," that is the term I use with them. (I also introduce neutral descriptors.) Similarly, I don't use "clean" to describe food, as the alternative is "dirty."(A food a child is allergic to can clearly be called "unsafe.")

Yes, That Includes Serving "Processed" or "Junk" Food

When I recommend serving a child's preferred foods, or ones they may be fixated on if they are limited, parents frequently object with, **"It's not healthy, and I don't want my other children to only eat the processed stuff either."** This common worry hasn't panned out over the years. Yes, at first other children (and adults) may be interested and choose these foods; but trust that they will tire of it and continue to eat the foods they were eating beforehand. This assumes these foods aren't "forbidden" or shamed.

Kitty shared, *"I come from a cooking home. Believe me, serving Kraft mac-n-cheese was hard at first."* Serving packaged or fast foods might stretch your comfort zone, but it is important. I've seen far too many families ban these foods in an effort to improve the child's nutrition, only to see the child become fixated and struggle.

Over time, keep serving familiar foods and add something new like canned pineapple, or make your favorite chicken chili knowing they probably won't try it (but they won't *ever* try it if it's not available). Serve new foods with something your selective eater generally likes, such as tortilla chips or rolls and/or microwaved corn.

If you have a child who only eats, say, seven things initially, *every meal and snack must include one or two of these foods.* Planning what to put on the table is tricky for families who are used to serving only accepted foods at separate times. Here are some ideas.

- Fill in the Food Preference List starting on page 350.
- Or, on a sheet of paper, in one column, list your child's favored or almost-always-accepted foods. Make another column of foods your child usually eats. Include a third column of foods he has eaten in the past.
- Observe if your child prefers salty, sweet, crunchy, or smooth tastes and textures.
- List any accepted condiments, sprinkles, toppings, or dips.
- Also make a list of what you like and want to try or eat again.

Put the lists of favored and sometimes-accepted foods, as well as the foods you are interested in serving, on the inside of a cupboard/notes on your phone or where you can see them. Refer to these lists when planning and shopping as a reminder to rotate foods for variety and opportunities to explore.

When you're planning what to serve, *you* may think, "Hmm, he ate mostly cheese at snack, so I'll make his favorite sweet potato fries for dinner with chicken," or, "Sam hasn't liked my chili before, so I'll include cornbread and a fruit he usually goes for." This is great, but don't let your kids in on your thought process.

For example, you don't need to say, "We're having corn muffins because I know you probably won't eat the chili, but at least I know you'll have something you like." That gives something to push back against, and they don't need to think about it anyway.

The Whole Family Benefits

Interestingly, siblings often benefit and branch out as meals are commonly and unintentionally limited to the preferences of the most selective child. Many parents tire of "kid" foods and are happy to rediscover their own joy and pleasure around food. When planning meals and snacks, include foods *you* want to eat, and foods you want your other children to learn to like. As one dad explained, "*We put out lentils, chicken, bread, and corn. While our daughter ate mostly bread and a little corn, we were surprised that our younger son loved the lentils. I don't think he'd ever had them, and he's two. This process made us aware of not limiting his opportunities.*"

Sample Preferences List

Here's a sample list for Kayleigh, an eight-year-old selective eater. Note: For younger kids, I use the descriptors *favored, accepted,* and *refused;* older children who may help make the list can use the descriptors shown in parentheses:

- Favored (eat now and enjoy): crackers (Ritz, Club), pretzels, plain pasta, rice, French toast fingers, McDonalds plain hamburger, chicken nuggets, vanilla tube yogurt, maple instant oatmeal made with water.
- Accepted (eat now but don't enjoy): canned mandarin oranges, seedless red grapes cut in half, vanilla yogurt from a cup, Wheat Thins, plain peas, 2% milk (for planning purposes, I consider milk to be a food, as it has protein and fat).
- Refused (can't imagine trying): fresh fruit or vegetables, anything with mixed textures.
- Prefers: sweet, salty, and smooth.
- Condiments: ketchup and ranch dressing.

Sample Menu for Kayleigh's Family

- Breakfast: French toast fingers, yogurt from a cup, and cut-up bananas (allow the child to cut with a safe knife, if willing and able). If you're eating, say, scrambled eggs, put them on a serving plate and serve yourself, maybe make a little extra (knowing Kayleigh is unlikely to take any for a while).
- Morning snack: Pretzels, canned mandarin oranges, and 2% milk.
- Lunch: Whole-wheat Club Crackers, whipped cream cheese with a spreader so she can apply it, turkey deli meat, and grapes. (If children are old enough, they can eat grapes whole or cut them themselves with an appropriate knife.) You may want to eat pita bread and turkey with avocado, so slice some avocado and put it on a plate on the table so she can see it and can help herself if she wants.
- Snack: Cut-up apple with half of the slices peeled, cinnamon-sugar shaker on the table, vanilla yogurt from a tube, pretzels.
- Dinner: Chicken nuggets, plain rice, rotisserie chicken, microwaved peas, pan or air fried pre-sliced frozen onions and peppers with bottled teriyaki sauce, ketchup on the table, vanilla frozen yogurt (or ice cream) for dessert.

Each meal and snack has one or two items from Kayleigh's favored list, while everyone gets used to structure and no pressure. Once they have been doing this for a while, they can try one meal or snack per day without a "favorite" and see how it goes, but serve something from the accepted list, knowing that in a few hours Kayleigh will have the chance to eat a favored food again.

Be Responsive with Menu Planning and Cooking

- Hold the spice or chopped herbs; let everyone add their own.
- Serve a favored side if you're making an unfamiliar or unpopular main dish.
- Serve different preparations of favorite foods; for example, serve half the pancakes with blueberries or chocolate chips.

- Serve deconstructed meals: maybe plain pasta, a side of sauce, and some cheese rather than mixing it all together. Many meals can be served this way. My co-author for our books on "extreme" picky eating, Jenny McGlothlin, SLP, calls these "pile-ons." While Jenny ate a traditional baked potato with sour cream, cheese, and bacon, one of her children ate potato with butter, cheese, sour cream, turkey bacon, sunflower seeds, and pineapple. Another child ate cucumbers, potato (without peel), cheese, avocado, and tomatoes. He ate the pineapple last for dessert.

Support Nutrition While Working on RF

With a focus on vegetables we can miss opportunities to support nutrition. Here are a few ideas:

- Serve fortified versions of accepted foods, such as whole-wheat Goldfish crackers, protein or fiber-fortified white bread, orange juice with calcium, or drinks fortified with omega-3 such as DHA.
- Serve canned, frozen, and freeze-dried fruits and veggies.
- If your child enjoys smoothies, offer options to introduce variety. They can put a blueberry in the blender to see if it changes the color.
- Try homemade frozen pops and include nutrient-dense ingredients. You and your child can experiment. Many children like frozen pops because of the temperature and consistency, and they can hold them and control the eating.
- Remember—don't sneak!

Don't forget about fruit. It's easy to focus on vegetables, but fruit also provides fiber, vitamins, and antioxidants. Many picky eaters enjoy a fruit or two. Fruit is not inferior to veggies. Serve them and don't worry about fruit sugar.

Veggie Tips

And, you don't have to ignore vegetables… Veggies can be yummy. Here's some ideas:

- Serve some veggies you're cooking raw in a little bowl with the meal.
- Include dips, ranch or yogurt dressings, ketchup, or other condiments.
- Find different ways to serve veggies; your child might reject a baby carrot but eat carrots cut into coins, shredded, or cooked with a honey glaze.
- Add fat, flavor, and even sugar. Studies show that adding a little sugar can help with the bitter taste of some vegetables.[19] Simmer chopped carrots in a little chicken broth, ½-1 teaspoons of sugar or honey, and some butter.
- Add crunch: freeze-dried veggies, crunchy toppings, or roasting with panko bread crumbs and parmesan adds flavor and crunch (may be especially appealing to sensory seekers).
- Serve frozen veggies in a small bowl. At my daughter's elementary school salad bar, they served frozen peas because the kids ate more of them!

- Take advantage of convenience foods: precut veggies or frozen stir-fry mixes.
- Keep serving veggies, without comment.

Remember that pressuring (even playful tactics), bribing, and begging kids to eat veggies will probably make them like veggies less.

Ian, age 17, who describes himself as an "Autistic, ADHD, 2e [twice exceptional], extreme introvert" shares his wisdom around preferences and meeting nutritional needs. It is also a reminder that we don't all have to eat the same way to do well with nutrition. "Its not the flavor or anything, just the texture. Honestly, I am not too much of a food person. I don't need exquisite meals to be satisfied. I'd just eat a rice cake with peanut butter and a peach and be satisfied. I could literally have like 14 meals to eat on a two-week rotation and be happy. I like predictable textures and flavors. I just don't need flavor variation. I respect needing variety for nutrients, but can't you get that with like 14 different meals plus snacks? One food I am particular about and am willing to spend time preparing is a really good layer cake. I also prefer separated foods, just let me mix them myself if I want to. Using a recipe is easier for some things, but it's much more fun to experiment and be creative in the kitchen. Like, I'd take a can of black beans and mix in some steamed carrots. That actually sounds really good."

Planning Meals and Packing Lunches Away from Home

If your child doesn't eat well at school, it can feel really scary. "*Our son is a slow eater and doesn't eat much lunch. I dread opening his lunchbox when I pick him up and seeing his sandwich still sitting there. He complains about everything I pack, even if it's something he likes.*" If he's staying on track with growth, there may not be much to worry about, though it's awful to think of our little ones going all day at school without eating much.

Sometime away from the situation, ask him about what eating at school is like; maybe he's upset because he only has five minutes to eat, or they have to eat in their snowsuits to rush to recess, a lunch supervisor may be hovering and reminding him to eat, or he's nervous because math is after lunch. Maybe a phase of being less hungry at lunch, or distracted, has now turned into something more. There could be an opportunity to help that you weren't aware of. Checking in with his teacher may provide more insights.

Here are some ideas to help if eating away from home is a challenge:

- Offer breakfast with accepted and filling foods.
- Pack a few accepted or preferred choices that are easy to open and eat.
- If he's drinking milk with lunch (flavored may help), he'll get several grams of carbs and protein and a little fat.

- Send high-energy drinks such as smoothies or liquid supplements, along with accepted foods.
- Pack a favored cereal or energy bar.
- Think outside the box. If sandwiches don't get eaten, try sending an insulated container with microwaved corn, edamame (shelled or not), or leftovers. Try a handful of crackers and cheese, with rolled up turkey or sliced pepperoni.
- Add a sweet item that offers fuel, such as a mini-Snickers, fruit snacks, cookies, or Go-Gurt.
- Involving children can help, but even if you involve them with shopping, cooking, growing, or packing, that is no promise they will eat. Avoid saying, "You chose those crackers, now eat them!"
- You might want to cut down how much you pack until the issue improves, or accept more food waste for now (see page 76 for more on waste). Sometimes foods are eaten, sometimes not.
- Some kids like more options, some feel overwhelmed where packing fewer choices may help.
- Invest in insulated containers, bags, and ice packs to keep foods at desired temperatures. Help maintain temperatures in a Thermos by leaving it in the freezer overnight (take the top off first), or by preheating it with hot water before filling it with hot food.
- Consider tucking in the "lunchbox card" (see Appendix) to help your child fend off interference (more in Chapter 10).

Plan on a filling snack right after school. Let him eat as much as he is hungry for—it might be a lot! Making him eat leftovers from lunch (if other options are available) feels like punishment and becomes a battle point. Remember not to ask him what he ate or rifle through his lunchbox first thing; give him the message that he can manage his eating, even if he's still learning.

Breakfast Tips

If children don't eat well at school, that puts more pressure to get something into them in the mornings! Some children aren't hungry in the morning or are distracted by the hectic pace and nerves around school, which can interfere with appetite. Here are some ideas to consider:

- Start breakfast a little earlier, maybe move up bedtime.
- Plan easy-to-eat foods, such as nut-butter toast, breakfast burrito, yogurt tube, protein bar, smoothie, or the supplement drink he'd been getting in the afternoon.
- School breakfast programs can be a great option if your school has them.
- If kids are up especially early for childcare or bus schedules, they may not be hungry; pack a well-liked option that they can manage.

- Err on the side of extra snacks or food if you're not sure.
- I advise against young kids eating in the car, due to risk of choking, though many kids do. If they are eating in the car, make sure the foods are easily chewed and swallowed, or switch to smoothies.

If you're transitioning away from pressure and encouragement with a child with a low-appetite and/or limited variety who is eating in the mornings, maybe keep breakfast the same while you address eating away from home. Let them continue to eat favored foods (perhaps keep the screen) for breakfast so you can release that worry while you get settled in with structure and not pressuring.

Stages of Progress

Because early progress won't be your child suddenly eating vegetables, it's tempting to fall back into old patterns. **It's critical to know what early progress looks like so you don't miss it, and it can help you have faith in the process.** I've observed that progress follows a general pattern, but remember that children have better and worse days (or weeks).

Earliest Progress Is Yours

Initial successes will be yours, and are worth celebrating (out of your child's sight). Pat yourself on the back when you:

- Get people together to eat.
- Get options together, including a familiar food for your child.
- Start serving family or buffet style.
- Allow your child, without comment, to not put a food on their plate.
- Allow your child to serve themselves seconds and thirds of a preferred food while not choosing a vegetable, even if it makes you anxious.
- Don't have to play food cop and can yourself begin to enjoy mealtimes.
- Didn't allow yourself to get sucked into a battle or react angrily when your child insists they don't like bananas, when they ate two the day before.
- Focus on felt safety and get yourself regulated before meals.

Stage One: This Is Scary

With selective eaters, a predictable response to removing pressure is that **your child's eating may get worse before it gets better.** Without dessert bribes, you might not get that reluctant bite of carrot. The good news is that while the variety he eats may be the same, parents almost always say that conflict decreases. More enjoyable meals is one of the main goals parents have. This is a big step; not to be underestimated. Note it in your journal.

Things Parents Typically Observe Early On

- Your child is calmer at the table, experiencing fewer meltdowns.
- More connection at mealtimes, more smiles and conversation.

- "He starts with dessert and only eats that, plus maybe one or two bites of bread or a favored food."
- "She eats even less than she used to." (See next chapter for more.)
- They eat only one or maybe two things from what you serve.
- Behavior usually improves.
- You used to be able get him to eat a bite or two of veggies with the dessert bribe, but now he won't eat any.

This stage can last a long time—or not—and as with other transitions, it will pass more quickly if you believe in the underlying philosophy and stick with it as much as possible.

How to Get Through Stage One

- Pray. (If you pray, or read "Serenity with Feeding," Chapter 3).
- Bite your tongue (or squeeze your lips closed)—when every part of you wants to encourage him to eat one bite.
- Scan *your* body for tension or signs of dysregulation. Put both feet on the floor, take some deep breaths, and recognize that this is tough.
- Hold hands with your partner (if you have one) under the table.
- Set up a call or text a friend or family member right before or after a meal. Tell them in advance what kind of support you're hoping for.
- Keep a note on the fridge to use it as a mental mantra, such as "Trust Jacob" or "Connection over carrots." (If your child can read, maybe tuck this away.)
- Tap into feelings of relief or confidence in the process and/or remind yourself that everything else you've tried hasn't helped.
- Look for signs of progress and write anything down in your journal that's going well.
- Ignore, or pretend to ignore, how much or how little your child is eating.
- Focus on connection and felt safety.

See Chapters 6 and 7 for more on what the transition and progress look like with low appetite and selective eating, and with food preoccupation.

Stage Two: Emerging Skills

This sometimes surprises families, as children can blossom in a matter of days. The first thing you might observe with structure and leaving pressure behind is that the child has less anxiety or strong emotion around eating. DO NOT underestimate the importance of this. As you all get the hang of things, you may witness the following with your child:

- They notice and express an interest in foods, even if they don't put any on their plate or try them yet.
- He might pass a food to you and watch you intently as you eat it.

- She might lick a food.
- They might ask for food or wonder when a meal is.
- A child with anxiety or sensory issues may be more tolerant of foods on the table or nearby.
- He visibly relaxes and fusses less at meals.
- Patterns emerge in intake—more food some meals, less at others, an indication that they are learning to tune in to hunger and fullness.
- She might eat a "large" meal on occasion, or at least a "normal" portion.

Two Steps Forward, One Step Back

The journey may feel like two steps forward and one step back (see page 57 on "relapse"). Be prepared for gradual and subtle progress. Your child is probably not going to suddenly and reliably eat the quantities you hope for, of a variety of foods.

"We are working at removing pressure, tweaking mealtimes, etc. and are seeing signs of progress, like her commenting on food smelling good, her moving to eating grilled cheese sandwiches that have a little bit of mozzarella mixed with the other cheese."

— Sally, mother to four-year-old Anisa

"I feel so hopeful when Ruby has a bigger meal, and then dashed when she goes back to nibbles for the rest of the day. It isn't easy to keep the progress in mind, and there has been amazing progress in only one week: saying she's hungry, being happy at the table, one time eating an entire egg, but then there are still those meals that go by and she eats so little."

— Carrie, describing the process as a roller coaster

Mom Bethany found it helpful to look back at her journal to note how far they'd come: *"Compared to where we were a month ago, this is a huge improvement. It's hard not to want it to go, well, faster. It helps to remember how miserable we were and how none of what we'd tried before helped, and where it got us. No sense going back to that."*

Bethany and Amari's Journey

Bethany and Amari's journey illustrates how even an "extreme" presentation can improve with RF. (The following chapter covers feeding therapy and severe picky eating). Amari, age two, was adopted at age 14 months from Ethiopia. After being in the U.S. for about 10 months, her eating changed dramatically. While feeding was never easy, with no identifiable cause, it became an all-consuming nightmare. While underlying medical causes were being ruled out, Mom and Amari needed help. The following are excerpts from Bethany's notes, taken the first few months after reading a draft of the first edition of *Love Me Feed Me,* then with a few emails and phone calls for support.

February 10: A few months ago, Amari started to get pickier and ate less and less, eventually eating about five bites at meals and down to two cups of milk a day. She would pocket and take an hour to finish those bites. In one year home, she grew four inches and gained only nine ounces . . . We saw a nutritionist who told us how to sneak calories into her. A speech pathologist determined that the issue was "psych" and barely glanced at her. In the last week, Amari has gotten SO much worse. She hardly drinks 1-1/2 cups of milk per day, drinks nothing else, and takes about three bites at meals. I can force feed her more, but she gags constantly and has developed a tongue thrust. I've gone back to infant spoons only about half full if I want the food to stay in her mouth. I do think this is mostly a psych issue, though I wouldn't mind her having a better exam. She gets distressed, with this glazed-over look in her eyes (we have parented deeply emotionally disturbed children through treatment foster care before and I have seen this look too many times to not recognize it) after a few bites and completely disassociates. We have tried EVERYTHING. We have ignored the issue, we have put her in a quiet room with no distractions, gotten angry and screamed. We even tried to punish her (I know, bad move, but we just thought . . . maybe?!?). Now she's puking all her food at least once a day. I'm screaming inside. I don't want to do this anymore. I'm tired. This is sucking the joy out of parenting. I need to know what to do. We have an appointment to see a psychologist—a month away.

February 12: We are just allowing her to eat as much as she wants (one or two nibbles) and offering food regularly throughout the day. It goes against everything the nutritionist said, but this is not a "normal" situation . . . While I cannot be 100 percent certain this is a psych issue, I am about 95 percent sure that it is—or that it has become one. In other words, if she has a physical issue, psychological trauma is still presenting itself through this issue . . . I am weary.

February 14: I've read about half the book. We are totally willing to try this, but I am leery about whether or not this will work with our daughter . . .

February 18: Vomiting has stopped, in one weekend! Seems to be pocketing less as well. I'm not sure if it's because feeding overall is more relaxed or because she hasn't put something in there that she doesn't like. If only she'd start eating more. I am appreciating less stress around eating, but I still feel so defeated at the end of the meal when she's only had a few bites. It is very tempting to feed her again to get just a few more calories in, but I know where that leads, so hopefully I can avoid it . . . Eventually she'll have to start eating more. Three bites, three times a day isn't going to get her to grow.

February 23: I wonder how much she needs to gain weight? For lunch, she ate 1/2 slice of bologna, one ounce of cheese, one teaspoon of hummus, and two crackers. Breakfast was 1/3 of a banana a 1/2 cup of oatmeal. I don't think that's enough, but maybe it is?! It's certainly better than three bites. I have helped her to take a few extra bites at both meals, but she did so happily. So glad I reviewed her Z-scores, she's definitely improved with weight gain, so it was helpful for me. She's close to the "normal" range, especially for her current height.

February 26: Good days and bad, good meals and bad. I still really struggle with what to do when she cheeks food. I know the simple answer is to let her spit it out, but it angers me. I know she can swallow it—she just swallowed other bites. I don't know how to mentally get past that to let her spit it out. I've tried, I swear I have. My husband has the same struggle. For now, we're just having her sit in her highchair until she swallows it. She eventually does, but it can take a LONG time.

March 12: Amari is doing much better. She only ate three bites of food for breakfast, but she was asking for food two hours later. I had her wait until lunch and she ate half a cheese stick and about 2/3 of a hot dog plus a few crackers and other things. We're seeing about one full meal per day and she's happily eating more like six bites most meals—versus three before . . . If she has gained weight (I think she has), we don't want to see GI. I'm afraid that will traumatize her and set us back. I'm not seeing her dislike any certain type of food like before. She even asked for chicken the other day and took and swallowed two bites without any prompting.

March 12: Sometimes Amari refuses to try something that I know she will like. I have asked her to lick these things and then she always wants a bite after that. So far it doesn't seem to upset her, but I don't want that to turn into a battle, ever. I feel like I am better able to gauge and respond to her reactions. (This is roughly six weeks after the initial consult, and Amari has gained 10 ounces, more than in the previous year.)

April 3: And . . . just like that, she eats normally for 3/5 meals. Amari still likes to cheek things and it still drives me crazy, but it no longer seems to cause any kind of backslide for the next meal when she does that. I would honestly say that MOST days she eats two decent meals. They're small, but so is she. She will never be big. Her Z-score is going up and she's almost on the regular charts. I call that a HUGE win.

Bethany's words illustrate the anxiety and how unpredictable the process can be. There is also dramatic progress with relatively minor adjustments; the example being no more vomiting within days after they stopped putting food in her mouth.

The final section of this chapter explores common obstacles that trip parents up along the way.

Handling Common Obstacles

Your child may love the new approach, or push back. They may be figuring out the new rules and deciding if you really mean it this time. They may be thriving and curious about new foods, or they may eat less variety. You may feel confident or more anxious without bribes or rewards. Hang in there. Each challenge, or meal where you think, "What do I do *now*?" is an opportunity for reflection, checking in with the responsive feeding values and your family's priorities. Ask yourself when scenarios come up: *What is the worry?* Here are some common questions and scenarios:

- *"Every time I put food on the table, he immediately says, 'Yuck, that looks gross.' It's so discouraging. I remind him he loved it last week, but it doesn't matter."* That is typical. Rationalizing, convincing, or explaining usually prolong battles. Try: "You don't have to eat it, but please say, 'no thank you.'" Then move on.
- *"Everyone says introduce a food at least 10 times before he'll like it. Our feeding therapist has us keep track, and with a big smile, remind Jeremee that he has to try it TEN TIMES! He refuses, and then I serve the same food 10 meals in a row. We're sick of it."* I would be too. The idea is you'd have a checklist and cross off each try—which he would agree to after your rational explanation—and he'd like it? If only it were that simple! It hasn't worked so far and almost certainly won't. It may take dozens of neutral opportunities (as described, these are not neutral) before liking a new food. And there are some foods they'll never like. My mantra "many ways, many times," can remind you to serve foods you enjoy and hope he might too. Even the "adventurous" child might take years to learn to like spinach or tuna. Serving it 10 times in a row puts the focus on the food and the child, not on enjoyable meals. Serve foods you want to eat, as frequently as you want. Think about his accepted foods when menu planning. Then wait. As my friend Pam Estes, RD, said, "They don't, they don't, they don't, then suddenly they do!" I'd routinely get calls from clients six months to a year after one or two sessions, with cheerful news of breakthroughs. Hang in there.
- *"We noticed a few times when a serving bowl was almost empty, and I'd say, 'I'm going to finish the peas if no one minds,' he would suddenly want peas, or would put them on his plate. Can we trick him into trying stuff by doing this more often?"* What you're seeing is scarcity mindset. That is, when something is limited (as in "ONLY ONE LEFT!" advertising), it makes us want it more. I've seen it at my table as well. It's a common reaction that is tempting

to exploit. You're examining your motives and worries (maybe "I want him to eat more because I still think he's too small"), and it feels wrong because it's a "trick." If you do try it, chances are he'll figure it out, and it will slow the process. Also, if your child has experienced food insecurity or restriction in the past, this may increase his anxiety.

- *"Can we pressure just at breakfast?"* Some feeding therapists recommend pressuring some meals but not others. Jo Cormack, PhD, explains why this may not help: "I think it confuses children. When expectations aren't clear, it is likely to add to the anxiety and emotional and nervous system dysregulation." Reflect; "Why do I want to pressure at some meals, what is the worry?"
- *"We're frustrated with how slow this is going. He hasn't tried more than a few new foods for weeks. We eat after the kids are in bed so we have couple time. We don't eat together much."* If he is eating by himself regularly from mostly favored foods, he's missing out on key opportunities. It's like trying to teach a child to swim in only an inch of water. After watching you eat something, he might pass the bowl and let it sit next to his plate, or look at it when no one's watching; poke it with a serving spoon and smell it. Maybe after a while, he'll put some on his plate for a closer look. He might dip a favored cracker or lick some off his finger. A few weeks or months later, he might pop it into his mouth, chew it, and spit it out. This is the process of "trying" it, where he's having positive, no-pressure opportunities to explore. (Another child may learn to like it more quickly.) It might be weeks, months or even years, before he chews and swallows a challenging food. Focus on keeping the table low stress, offering a variety of foods, and not giving up. Review this book. Might you be pressuring without realizing it? Have you slipped back to rewarding "brave" bites, praising, or bribing with desserts? It's tempting! If you have slipped, learn from it and move on.
- *"He wants to play with his food, and he's four."* Playing with food shows comfort. If it's exploration and fun, and he might never have tried to smear applesauce or bite a noodle into a fish shape, let it slide. Playing with food is part of learning how to eat. You can also offer food play outside of mealtimes, such as with potato stamps or pudding paint. There are tons of ideas online, but only if he wants to and with no pressure to try the food. Play and familiarity with food can help cautious eaters.
- *"Our family sabotages our efforts, especially around structure. Grandma dropped by with a cupcake the size of his head right before lunch. Give it to him? Tell Gran to keep it?"* Managing unexpected foods will get easier. You can let him eat a treat from Grandma now if it's not happening often. If it frequently sabotages appetite and your routine, you can teach your son to say, "Thank you," then give him a choice, "Do you want to save it for snack, or dinner tonight?" You're not saying "no," and you're giving him some control. He may argue at first to see if he can get you to cave in. Grandma might

too. Try to stay firm and calm. You can also decide to serve the cupcake as a "high-interest food snack," say with milk and a banana (see "Sweets and HIFs" in Chapter 4) or half for dessert with dinner, and half the next day. You can tell your family you appreciate their kindness, but suggest they bring stickers instead, or maybe they can bake with your son. Look for and support ways they can have special time together.

- *"What if he doesn't want to eat anything for snack or dinner?"* That's okay. He might be testing to see if you meant it when you said you wouldn't make him eat, or maybe he's not hungry (and he'll likely make up for it when his appetite is better; see Figure 1.2 in on page 12). Remind him there will be another opportunity to eat in a little while, but not as a threat to try to get him to eat, as in, "Are you sure you don't want to eat now? There will be no more food until dinner!" Consider a "bedtime snack" (see page 73). If you need to, you can decide to serve the next meal a little earlier. You can say, "You don't have to eat, but we'd like you to sit with us. You can leave in a few minutes." When parents do this and don't pressure the child to eat, they usually report that within a few minutes, the child is eating something and is partaking (even happily) in the meal. If your child is becoming dysregulated, allow them to leave the table and accommodate to prioritize felt safety. (See Chapter 6 if your child regularly skips meals.)
- *"My son eats better at daycare. At home we're always fighting over what he eats."* Start with curiosity. Why might this be? Maybe he's pushing back if there are more expectations or pressure at home; or, the friends at daycare and increased autonomy help him tap into curiosity. Fake it at first if you have to, but try to stop caring whether he eats his broccoli tonight. Over time, with strategies in this book, the fighting and his variety at home should improve.
- *"He tried mashed potatoes the other night and was looking for praise. We've praised his eating for years. It feels weird not to."* Follow connection, not what or how much he's eating. Maybe he's excited and perhaps proud, or looking for a familiar reaction? While praise has not helped his eating so far, maybe he was sensing that things were changing, was more open to explore foods, and was looking for feedback? Share his excitement without spoiling his sense of accomplishment. You can say, "I'm so happy you're excited!" Focus on how he feels, not on the food. Praising his eating can feel like pressure and can lead to outright pushing, as in, "What a big boy for trying that carrot. Maybe you can try the tomato now?" If he does try something new, talk to another family member or pretend you don't see it. It sends the message that he is capable of trying new foods. Parents tell me they see their child nibble that carrot when no one is looking.

Other day-to-day challenges will come up. My hope is that as you consider the values and incorporate RF practices, you will feel more confident; it gets easier with time.

Chapter 6
"Extreme" Picky Eating

"The amount of stress this was causing cannot be underestimated. Feeding your child is primal; it's a fundamental responsibility of parents to provide food, and when your child won't eat, it's devastating."
— Carrie, mother of three-year-old Cassie

This chapter explores more severe feeding or growth challenges, and considers physical development, medical conditions, feeding history, temperament, trauma, and attitudes toward food.

Because I can't know potential issues your child is dealing with, I am repeating the disclaimer from the Introduction: This text is not intended to replace careful observation, evaluation, diagnosis, or ongoing medical or nutritional care for a child.

Children want to do well. If there are concerns, delays, differences, or challenges with sensory-motor skills and eating and digesting, they will impact every other issue you may face around food. My intention is to prepare you for possible challenges so you can understand why your child struggles, support them more confidently, and find help if needed.

You will learn about: 1) how feeding problems might be evaluated and diagnosed; 2) support and intervention options; and 3) how RF at home helps.

If your child receives professional services, this chapter aims to empower you to recognize when an approach is not helping so you can advocate for the support you need. Even if your child has challenges that impact feeding, the feeding relationship at home is where most healing happens. It's not a choice between formal therapy or doing nothing.

Responsive feeding and responsive feeding therapy are not just for neurotypical kids. With their emphasis on supporting autonomy, and prioritizing felt safety and connection, they may be even more necessary for children with challenges.

For some of you, this will be new information; for others, it will delve into a therapeutic world you have been immersed in for some time.

Beyond Typical Picky Eating

While about half of children are described as picky, just over 10 percent are considered to have more problematic or persistent picky eating.[1,2]

There are varying criteria for diagnosis. In the last several years, we've seen "feeding disorders" with six proposed subtypes: "problem feeder," "neophobia," "food aversion," "behavioral feeding problem," "avoidant restrictive food intake disorder" (ARFID), and most recently "pediatric feeding disorder." (Page 234 has a brief discussion of ARFID.) Interestingly, the same child could qualify for any or all of these labels depending on who is doing the evaluation and at what age they were seen. A diagnosis may be necessary for formal support, and I believe that a responsive approach is appropriate with all of these labels.

Remember that diagnostic labels describe what is observed. Increasingly, labels are questioned as they likely include behaviors that are protective stress responses or are associated with sensory differences or neurodivergence.

Generally, if the amount or variety your child eats is so little that it impacts his physical, social, or emotional growth, then I consider it more "extreme" picky, anxious, or avoidant eating. If you spend a lot of energy worrying about your child's eating, you need support.

I've seen children eating fewer than 10 foods who improved steadily with comfort, skill, and variety, without professional intervention; and I've also worked with a child who ate 40-plus nutrient-dense foods, but was so anxious eating away from home that it had a major impact on the child and family's well-being.

Though it's difficult to draw a clear line where on one side is typical eating, and on the other is a feeding disorder, I view it as existing on a continuum. Here are some general characteristics of more "extreme picky," or anxious and avoidant eating:

- Eating problems start earlier, not infrequently from the earliest days and months of life, or when transitioning to finger foods, table foods, or purees.
- Eat a limited variety, frequently brand specific or prepared precisely one way.
- May refuse to eat unless off a certain plate or with specific utensils.
- Described as "rigid" and inflexible when approaching new or nonpreferred foods.
- Gets upset out of proportion, melts down, rages, panics (dysregulation can be fight, flight, or dissociation) when interacting with a nonpreferred food.
- Reduces the number of "accepted" foods and doesn't add more.
- Refuses whole categories of foods, most commonly vegetables, fruit, or meat.
- Eats mostly highly processed foods that don't require a lot of chewing.

- Experiences sensory differences, often associated with autism or ADHD.
- Described as low appetite or "never" hungry.

Rigid Eating

Children described as "rigid" in their approach to food, could be experiencing anxiety, sensory or cognitive differences, or OCD. Professionals have unique lenses: The OT may think "rigid" eating is due to sensory issues and do desensitization therapy, a behavioral therapist may think a cognitive behavioral approach will help, a psychologist may recognize anxiety or dysregulation. Mental health counselor Dawn Friedman shared this: "The question, 'Is what I'm seeing because of the trauma or ADHD' really doesn't matter. We will try to help children function the best they can."

Eating Is Complicated

Eating is complex and impacted by:

- Every sensory system, including sight, touch, smell, balance (vestibular), taste, sound, proprioception (where the body is in space), and interoception (what's going on inside the body).
- Gross and fine motor skills, including holding a spoon, core muscle strength for holding the body upright, muscle tone around the jaw and tongue, and coordination of swallowing.
- The digestive system, including swallowing and digesting, and the gastrointestinal (stomach and intestines) experience: Infection, allergy, constipation, and emotions may be associated with discomfort and/or pain (see the appendix on medical conditions).
- Relationships with adults (now or in the past) who feed or share mealtimes.
- Behavioral, developmental, and cognitive differences and challenges.

Why Children May Struggle with Eating

Anything that makes it difficult, painful, uncomfortable, or scary to get food into the mouth, chew, swallow, and digest can increase the odds of food avoidance and anxiety. This could include a child born early (premature), or with:

- A chromosomal abnormality or genetic syndrome.
- Sensory differences or neurodivergence.
- A neuromuscular condition.
- In-utero exposure to toxic stress, or epigenetic trauma (passed down through generations) can potentially impact eating. This is a relatively new area of understanding.
- An anatomic abnormality such as cleft palate or malformations of the airway or esophagus (swallowing tube).
- Heart defects, lung problems, or other conditions that increase calorie needs.

Nutrient Deficiencies Can Affect Feeding in the Following Ways:

- Iron deficiency can cause weakness, anemia, and sleep difficulties, and potentially dampen appetite.
- Severe vitamin D deficiencies (rare, but higher risk in northern climates especially combined with darker skin, and with exclusively breastfed infants) can lead to rickets, which can be painful, impacts mobility, and perhaps behavior and mood (research is ongoing).
- Inadequate calories and fat lead to fatigue, listlessness, difficulty concentrating, mood dysregulation, and can impact growth and weight gain.
- Rare and extreme vitamin deficiencies, such as Vitamin C, can lead to mouth sores and more.

Medical Issues

It is critical to rule out and address medical conditions that can affect hunger, appetite, digestion, and well-being.

Whether you're dealing with multiple medical complications or an occasional ear infection, if your child doesn't feel well or his body is stressed from illness, it impacts eating. (The medical issues appendix has a partial list of relevant conditions.)

Eating is a Sensory Experience

Sensory differences relate to the senses and nervous system, including touch, taste, smell, sound, sight etc. (Interoception, the sensations around what is happening in the body, will be discussed separately.)

Input from the senses is interpreted and experienced in the body and brain in a range of ways, and individuals respond differently as well. A useful frame of conceptualizing this is the concept of Dunn's sensory quadrant, which proposes a continuum of a sensory threshold. For example, a child with a low register (think of a stereo dial set to 1), may not notice taste or texture and not be bothered or motivated by that experience. Another child with low registering of input may seek more, perhaps adding hot sauce to all foods or preferring crunchy foods (sensory "seeker").

One child with high registering (the dial turned up to 11) may not be bothered, while another will try to limit the overwhelming (to them) sensations. An example may be a child who experiences crunchy foods as painful as in, "*Eating chips feels like chewing glass.*"

Emotion and regulation states can lower or raise the sensory threshold and change how negative or positive an experience may be. (Chapter 3 has more.)

Sensory processing differences are present with diagnoses including autism, ADHD, anxiety, and developmental differences,[3] as well as with trauma and sensitized nervous systems.

Sensory challenges may present as the child avoiding certain textures, not wanting to get messy hands, or seeking input such as carbonation or crunch. Smells may be overwhelming, or the sound of others chewing (misophonia) can feel dysregulating. Understanding your child's experiences and preferences will help you navigate mealtimes. Pediatric psychologist Dr. Mona Dalahooke wrote, "Our ability to understand sensory preferences helps us develop supportive approaches across the lifespan."[4]

While sensory differences play a part in eating, I believe it is often oversimplified. Sensory diagnoses result in almost automatic (sometimes unnecessary) referrals to sensory-focused therapies. Consider a child who appears fearful of a bottle or food who is labeled with a "sensory aversion" and then treated with desensitization. I have seen many cases in which the aversion (anxious and avoidant reaction) was *caused* (or exacerbated) by coercive feeding or therapy. As a research paper stated, "Children may present with sensory aversion, which we believe is usually a complication of a long-standing feeding disorder."[5] Whether it's "usually" or sometimes, it must be considered.

What appear to be sensory aversions can be protective responses to negative experiences, or existing sensory challenges can be worsened with non-responsive feeding (see Frieda's story on page 146).

Extreme reactions to foods are often the result of anxiety, pressure, forcing, or previous painful or frightening experiences—not the bowl of applesauce on the table.

Children are generally better able to tolerate sensory input when: 1) they are in felt safety; and 2) they initiate the experience, rather than being directed by adults. **Sensory processing differences do not mean a child is incapable of learning to expand tastes and tolerate or even enjoy different sensory inputs.**

Signs of Sensory-Motor Differences with Eating Include:

- Sensitivity to temperature, texture, or smells.
- Increased awareness of flavor.
- Difficulty manipulating utensils.
- Spills a lot.
- Chews with mouth open.
- Bites tongue and fingers when eating.
- Dribbles or drools regularly and at a later age than typical.
- Is unable to sustain attention to eat adequate amounts.
- Frequently wipes hands and mouth or doesn't seem to notice food on face or hands.
- Prefers carbonation or high sensory-input foods, for example with crunch or intense spice.

- Accepts only smooth or uniform textures.
- Is a very slow and cautious eater, takes tiny bites, and/or chews for a long time before swallowing.

Pediatric dietitian Hydee Becker, who was part of a children's hospital feeding team, comments on lists like these: "In different stages, these can be issues all children have." And for children who have traits from this list, intervention isn't always needed.

When Smells Are a Challenge

Lara, mother of Brian, adopted at age two, noted his severe sensory distress. She explained, *"His brain is misreading cues."* When helping her cook over the years, he'd tie a handkerchief loosely over his mouth and nose to make odors more tolerable. Lara noted: *"Brian's almost 13, and in the last year we have seen incredible improvements with the variety he will eat."*

If a child has difficulty tolerating smells, here are a few ideas you could try. Your child might come up with others:

- Place a small fan near the child at eating times to blow smells away.
- Consider a handkerchief or nose plug (commonly used with swimming).
- Place the smellier foods farther from the child, or pre-plate those foods in the kitchen (accommodation from classic family style).
- Try aromatherapy with vanilla or peppermint oil on a cotton ball or the back of their hand.

Don't shame or downplay their reaction. Try to stay calm. Lowering the emotional energy may make smells more tolerable.

Empathy builder: Is there a smell you find off-putting? Imagine it under your nose while you eat. At breakfast, our daughter finds the smell of waffles unpleasant. My partner and I marvel at how the stir-fries she re-heats for breakfast make us lose our appetite, when the same aroma made our mouths water the night before! Our senses, and how the eating context interacts with them, are complex and fascinating.

Felt Safety Can Increase Sensory Tolerance

Six-year-old Ulysses had sensory processing differences and an ARFID diagnosis. Eighteen months of sensory-focused feeding therapy hadn't helped. At the school cafeteria, he would sit under the table and cry that it was too loud and smelly, so he was allowed to eat lunch in a classroom with a staff helper. He missed his friends.

When we dug further into the cafeteria experience, it turned out that an adult would sit next to Ulysses and try to get him to taste foods, as recommended by the OT. Ulysses' parents had realized that attempts to get him to interact with food spiked his anxiety. With that in mind, he was open to an experiment where he went back to the cafeteria, with accepted foods from home and with *no adult intervention.*

Within a few days Ulysses was happy to be back with his friends in the cafeteria—and the smells and sounds didn't bother him! Perhaps the anxiety from the adult pressuring him lowered his threshold of tolerance, or maybe he used sensory language ("It smells!") to escape the pressure. At any rate, a few weeks later he tried a new food—sweet potato chips shared by his friend.

Parents tell of children refusing to sit next to someone eating a "squishy" food. **For many children—when the pressure is off and they can trust that no one will try to make them touch or taste those squishy foods—their tolerance of those foods rapidly improves.** Carla, nanny to four-year-old Paul, explained with excitement that within days of reassuring him he wouldn't have to interact with any food he didn't want to, for the first time, he happily sat next to her while she ate oatmeal.

I'm not saying these children don't have sensory differences; I'm suggesting that decreasing anxiety, and supporting autonomy and connection can decrease sensory sensitivity and distress.

The Sensory Spectrum

Over the years, our nephew, a competent eater, has preferred foods at room temperature; reacted strongly to smells (balking at any fish smell, though he occasionally eats it); refused mixed foods (typical of the toddler phase); felt carbonated drinks were "too spicy"; and bit his fingers and, not infrequently, his tongue while eating. He hates auto-flushing toilets; will not use air dryers in public restrooms; cries with loud, startling noises; does not like tags in his clothes; and only wears socks pulled up past his knees. All of these preferences have been included on lists of indications of sensory disorders.

My friend Dana is also sensitive to loud noises and doesn't like crowds. But both my nephew and Dana are happy and thriving with their unique ways of experiencing the world.

In general, if your child is doing well, and these traits do not interfere with their overall happiness and development, you could choose to think of it as part of the spectrum of human experience and address sensory comfort with accommodation.

Is Being a "Supertaster" a Sensory Explanation?

Picky eating is frequently blamed on being a "supertaster." However, I think its practical importance is overstated, and I wouldn't change the overall approach. We can think of this as part of the sensory picture. Interestingly, about as many people (one in four) are considered "non" tasters,[6] with fewer taste buds, which may mean they get less pleasure from eating, or they may seek more flavor.

Melanie Loomer, a psychologist in Alberta working with eating disorders and feeding challenges at a children's hospital shares how she works with the idea: "I do find that supertaster is a helpful concept to share with parents because it resonates and helps address the guilt they're feeling. But if not explained carefully, parents or children may use the idea to avoid trying new foods. True example from a young client, 'I'm a super taster, my body is telling me I won't like this food.' Gulp, not what I intended!" (This is a great reminder to professionals reading this that our intentions when sharing information may not be clear. It's good to check in to make sure you're on the same page.)

Melanie continued, "I apply the term carefully and add that it does not mean you cannot try or like new foods it just means that you can sometimes taste what other people can't. I have a whole shtick I do about super-tasting being your superpower which kids love, especially if they're into the Marvel movies (like I am). I tell them that supertasters kept the community safe when we were cave people. It helps turn a negative into a positive and reframes the conversation. But the conversation has to be done skillfully and thoughtfully."

Wrapping Up the Why

In summary, if we think about it from the child's point of view, they might avoid eating because:

- "It hurts!" Gut or medical issues, allergies, cavities, mouth ulcers (now or past).
- "I can't!" Sensorimotor, neuromuscular (nerves and muscles).
- "I don't like how that feels, tastes . . ." Sensory, or just preference.
- "I'm scared!" Choking, vomiting, anxiety, being forced to eat.
- "I don't want to!" Temperament, autonomy, PDA, etc.
- "Ewwwww!" Disgust.
- Usually one or more of the above.

Jenny McGlothlin, speech-language pathologist and feeding program director at the University of Texas-Dallas Callier Center says, "Whatever the child's behaviors are, there is a reason behind it. Be careful about labeling the child as having a 'behavioral' feeding problem (or letting someone else label them) and then beginning a behavioral feeding program where they try to get children to eat, without a thorough understanding of why the child approaches food the way they do."

Hopefully you may now have some ideas that could help explain why your child has a hard time with eating.

Formal Therapy May Not Be Necessary or Helpful

When non-responsive practices are replaced with responsive feeding, and children/teens are given time to trust that their autonomy will be respected, enjoy more pleasant mealtimes, and have the space for appetite and curiosity to emerge, things often improve. Rushing to evaluate and intervene if your child is otherwise stable with nutrition and growth, and they are not getting worse, may not be necessary and can even harm.

"While I chose not to pursue therapy, I had an understanding of Jack's needs and I knew what NOT to do. It helped me relax and worked well for our family as Jack learned to eat."

— Lucy, mother of Jack, age two

We are in a strange time (in much of the United States at least) when many children with mild or misperceived feeding problems receive therapy (which can make matters worse), whereas many children who could benefit from help aren't able to access it. Children are at risk of being over-pathologized and over-therapized. The next sections hope to clarify if you need more help, and how to support your child if you're waiting for a referral.

Feeding Therapy

If it's determined that you would benefit from a feeding evaluation and potential treatment, the following pages aim to help you find the right help. Feeding professionals working with children care deeply and do what they believe is in the best interest of the child. There has been a big increase in the last few decades in providers offering feeding therapy. Differences in treatment philosophies confuse parents trying to make sense of contradictory advice from different providers they turn to for help, such as, "Make them eat non-preferred foods," and "Never force a child to eat." (Sometimes they say, "never force a child to eat," and then provide activities that contradict that advice!)

For full disclosure, my bias toward responsive therapy is in part because most of the children I see have "failed" sensory-focused and behavioral feeding therapies, often for months and years. (I would argue that the therapy fails the child). I don't hear from families who were helped by these therapies. To address my potential bias, I reached out to, learned from, and partnered with STs, OTs, RDs, and therapists as we develop responsive feeding therapy.

Parents tell me they wish they had known that the therapy they were referred to could set them back, or even that there were other options. As Lara warns, *"Bad therapy is worse than no therapy."*

There's a lot to consider when working with feeding, and some professionals have neither a broad understanding of feeding nor adequate training/experience. Recent graduates with OT and SLP masters degrees may have only had a few hours of training focused on feeding. Then they might start providing feeding therapy after attending a single feeding workshop, with huge pieces of the puzzle missing.

Early Feeding Support

Primary care providers need better training. They miss opportunities to help early on, or refer inappropriately. And they regularly dismiss parents' concerns, as in: *"My three- year-old only eats purees or really soft and processed foods and gags all the time,"* and the doctor just says, *"He'll grow out of it, his weight is fine..."*

Consider this call (one of several like it) I received from the parent of a 10-month-old as an example: *"My child isn't taking the spoon anymore! My pediatrician said he might have an oral aversion and referred us to the feeding clinic, but our appointment isn't for six weeks. I can't get him to eat!"* After determining that the child wasn't at immediate risk, I explained that this is expected during the transition to self-feeding solids (usually between eight and 10 months). Children tend to want to do it themselves!

I suggested that until their appointment, they could look into baby-led weaning (page 247); mash foods that he can get in his mouth with his hands; or hand him the spoon, load another one, and *let him have control.* As childhood development expert Maria Montessori famously said, "Help me do it myself." And above all, not to force or pressure.

I heard from the mom a few days later, saying with immense relief that her son was eating well and they'd canceled the evaluation. She was upset that the pediatrician didn't offer this information. (So was I.)

How else might this have played out? While waiting for their therapy appointment, the parents might worry that something was seriously wrong, while trying to make the child eat. At the evaluation some weeks later, the child might be diagnosed with an "oral aversion." **Was the oral aversion there in the first place, or did it develop because of forceful feeding?**

Here is a clear example in which feeding resulted in an apparent oral aversion: A father I worked with had been given the harmful advice, "Do whatever you have to, just get food into her." Dad forced a bottle of pumped breast milk repeatedly into baby Frieda's mouth, at times holding her head in place, while she screamed, thrashed, coughed, and gagged. Frieda was evaluated at a children's hospital feeding clinic and diagnosed with a "nipple aversion."

Frieda had been seen twice for "underweight" and feeding concerns before she was five months old, although she was growing steadily at around the 10th percentile. When the ST diagnosed an "oral aversion," Dad was advised to put an oral stimulation brush into her mouth several times a day to desensitize her mouth, which she fought.

Frieda's dad said no one had asked *how* he fed her.

By the time I saw them, Frieda's intake was down and she would only take the bottle while sleeping. Dad was told she had a "sensory processing disorder" and to not make eye contact while feeding to avoid "overstimulation."

As a feeding team noted in a paper (emphasis mine), ". . . nearly all IFDs (infantile feeding disorders) develop through a common pathway involving food refusal **and an attempt to circumvent refusal or poor feeding by the use of pathological feeding methods.**"[5] These methods included nighttime feeding, forced feeding, distractions, and prolonged meals.

With a home visit, I observed a feeding and watched as Frieda woke up, cooed and smiled at her father, pushing the bottle out of her mouth to get his attention while he stared straight ahead. Frieda was more interested in having him look at her than eating. *She was seeking connection, not overwhelmed by eye contact.*

The happy ending is that once Dad's fears were addressed ("she's too small"—nope, just smaller than average), he was able to trust that his daughter would be okay. With a bit of education and coaching, they figured it out together. He learned to watch for and respond to her cues by offering and not forcing the bottle, talking and interacting when she initiated, and offering the bottle again a while later. Within three days, Dad fed Frieda while she was awake, and her intake was up. No desensitization needed. (Frieda's avoiding the negative experience and protecting herself from choking was misinterpreted as a nipple/sensory aversion.)

Red Flags: Talk to the Child's Doctor

Here are some concerning signs that may prompt an evaluation with a qualified ST and/or OT:

- Abnormal chewing pattern; for example, chewing only with front teeth well past 12 months of age, or if the tongue thrusts out of the mouth with chewing.
- Uncoordinated suck/swallow.
- Anatomic abnormalities such as cleft palate or tongue tie.
- Slow weight gain and/or any weight loss with no other explanation.
- Apparent pain or discomfort with eating.
- Formula or liquids are lost frequently or continuously from the mouth.
- Breathing problems or frequent lung infections may indicate that food or liquids are getting into the breathing tubes or that there is a swallowing problem.
- Child appears anxious or distressed with eating with no other explanation (such as medical, history of scary eating experiences, or coercive feeding).
- Frequent choking, gagging, vomiting, or food frequently tucked into cheeks long after eating is over with no other explanation.

Parents should get CPR trained and know what to do if their child chokes. This is particularly true if your child has oral-motor or swallowing problems.

Who Might Evaluate a Concern?

Note that many can support responsive feeding, if trained to do so.

- Speech–language pathologist or speech therapist (SLP, ST): Observes the child eating and swallowing a variety of textures to assess oral-motor function, including looking for tongue-tie; recommends ways to improve safety and advance skills by matching foods with abilities. (SLP-As, or assistants, and school-based SLPs may not be qualified.)
- Occupational therapist (OT): Assesses sensory, gross, and fine motor skills as well as core strength, positioning, and feeding skills. May recommend oral-motor supportive techniques, adaptive seating, utensils, and other equipment.

May be most helpful in tasks that support eating without food-specific interventions (can pressure). This could include activities and accommodations that support sensory regulation and felt safety, daily-living activities, and executive functioning.

- Pediatric registered dietitian (RD): Assesses growth, intake and nutritional status, energy needs, and macro- and micro-nutrient intake and deficiencies if indicated. Some assist with tube-feeding management. (Note, a "nutritionist" in countries such as the United Kingdom is similar to "registered dietitian" in the United States. A "nutritionist" in the United States does not require formal training.)
- Pediatric gastroenterologist (GI doctor): Diagnoses and treats medical and functional conditions of the gastrointestinal tract, including the esophagus, stomach, and intestines.
- Pediatric ear nose and throat (ENT or otolaryngologist): Evaluates concerns with anatomy and infections of the ears, nose, and throat; for example, enlarged adenoids and tonsils can impact feeding.
- Pediatric dentist: Addresses concerns if poor dental health/cavities or malalignment play a role. Qualified dentists can also assess for tongue tie.
- Psychologist or therapist: Supports the relationship, helps children stay in felt safety, and addresses brain-based behavioral concerns, resilience, and more. Evaluates feeding within the context of family dynamics if trained in feeding.

Occupational Therapy Can Support Interoception

Suzanne Stratford, an OT and owner of Whole Kids OT Northwest, shares these observations: "In terms of what an OT can 'do' to address interoception, I believe our most essential role lies not in mindfulness exercises, systematic desensitization or sensory food play. Rather, our unique role and perspective of exploring in depth with parents and other helpers, what a '24 hour-day' looks like for a child, to identify not only the challenges, but importantly, those moments of connection, finding those things that are going well within a child's daily lived experience, and then helping to find ways of building upon these strengths offers powerful opportunities for healing. This includes bringing elements of what is going well into the mealtime experience (in the case where mealtime relationships have become stressful).

"The most successful outcomes that I have witnessed with feeding challenges, occurred when the parent was ready to incorporate the responsive parenting/responsive feeding approach into daily routines with their child. Whether it is being held and read to at the beginning of the day, going for a walk, playing at the park, singing together or snuggling before bedtime, moments of connection create a deep inner sense of security and trust that lay a strong foundation for the development of interoceptive awareness in the growing child. *In these cases, it has consistently been my experience and observation, that a child's interoceptive sense, including that of appetite and hunger, emerges naturally.*"

Team or Solo Provider

Some clinics have a team of providers including a dietitian, a GI doctor, and an ST, OT, or physical therapist (PT), often at children's hospitals. The team may or may not include a behaviorist or psychologist, and sometimes includes a social worker. Many of these programs use behavioral approaches (ABA, described soon). An advantage of this arrangement is that the child has the evaluation and treatment in one place, and can improve team communication and coordination of care.

I've seen excellent care provided by solo practitioners with a thorough understanding of relevant factors, and effective communication between specialists.

Cindy recalls that when her 18-month-old daughter Marissa's growth slowed, it was reassuring to have a team assessment saying there was no concern in terms of anatomy or development. When she was given the "all-clear," however, she still felt let down: "*We were still circling that black hole. I desperately needed more than a handout to help us figure this out.*"

Don't Get Talked into Feeding Therapy

If things are going well (well enough or improving) with feeding, don't let yourself be talked into unnecessary and potentially harmful therapy.

At age three, Sara enjoyed a good enough variety of foods and ate amounts that supported stable growth. When Sara was evaluated at a private therapy practice for sensory distress and anxiety, Pam was asked repeatedly about feeding: *"I felt a lot of pressure to sign up for their picky-eating program, like they were looking for a reason that she would qualify."* Sara showed improvement with therapy around anxiety and transitions, but she didn't need feeding help.

For a time in the United States, there was an insurance incentive to diagnose feeding challenges as it helped get coverage for other therapies, and my colleagues and I have heard stories of unscrupulous businesses looking for income. There may be incentives, other than your child's best interests, to diagnose a feeding problem.

Finding a Therapist

Helpful feeding therapy can: 1) identify your child's skills; 2) help you provide foods that are safe and offer appropriate challenge; 3) help your child progress with their eating; and 4) help you feel confident and supported at home.

A personal recommendation from a trusted healthcare provider, therapist, or fellow parent can help. The Mealtime Hostage private Facebook group and Positive Parenting for Picky Eaters are online resources that have tens of thousands of followers and may be a source for local referrals.

Harmful Interventions: What to Look Out For

Knowing what *not* to do is step one. Some therapies can do more harm than good.

(This is a hard section to read, with descriptions of coercive therapies.) Here are some signs of nonresponsive therapy:

- Any time food is forced or placed in the child's mouth against their will.
- Making a child take more bites after vomiting or gagging, sometimes multiple times during a session.
- Putting food in front of the child's mouth or on his lips until he gives in (known as nonremoval of the spoon).
- Eating or therapy tasks upset the child (dysregulating or shutting down).
- Holding, restraining, shaming, or punishing the child.
- Bribing the child.
- Keeping the child apart from parents unless she eats.
- Not allowing parents to interact with (including eye contact) the child unless she eats.
- Insisting your pre-adolescent child (or any child if that is not what you or the child want) is separated from you during therapy.
- Recommending that you avoid force-feeding or pressure, but use techniques that do just that.

If a technique or "homework" recommended by a therapist increases gagging, vomiting, power struggles, or anxiety, or moves your child out of felt safety, it's likely not helping.

"Our OT insists that our son has to eat two bites of non-preferred food before he can have a preferred food. Every meal and snack, we end up yelling. The worst part of my day is coming home for dinner."
— Dan, dad to a four-year-old

"At age three, she started desensitization, which we did for 18 months and then almost a year with a psychologist. When we did the techniques we were told to do, she vomited or gagged almost every meal. They told us it might take years for her to improve, but they never helped us with the vomiting and power struggles. We gave up. Now she gags when we ask her to try a new food. She's into dance and I'm terrified this will all lead to an eating disorder. The way she is around food is so messed up."
— Cori, mother of seven-year-old Louise

"The OT didn't seem to know what to do. Basically, she was giving him a lot of candy. After a few months with no progress, she gave up working on his eating."
— Amber, mom of a preschooler

Keira began feeding therapy at age two for "sensory aversion." The therapist held the spoon near Keira's mouth until she gave in and took a bite, offering no eye contact or interaction unless she ate. If she took a bite, he would reward her with attention, praise, toys, and stickers. Keira's parents were advised to do the same at home.

Keira's mom found it profoundly disturbing to watch her cry and gag down a bite of food, desperate for interaction. It took a few sessions for Keira's mom to get up the courage to take Keira out of treatment—but she did.

Interventions that separate you from your child (or ask you to withhold your attention and nurturing to get your child to eat) undermine felt safety and your relationship with your child. If it feels wrong, or you are disturbed or doubtful of an interaction, trust your gut.

Sometimes children comply and take bites in therapy. Here's how Elisa's mom described an intensive behavioral program: *"Elisa cried and fought back for several hours over two days. By day three she gave up and tried to do what they wanted, while gagging and whimpering. It broke my heart to watch from behind that two-way mirror. Things only got worse at home."*

By discussing harmful therapies, my wish is not to make you feel bad if you followed recommendations, but to empower you to choose the best course of action for your family. (See "Let Go of Guilt" on page 317). The good news is that children are resilient, and I have seen remarkable improvements when parents have had responsive support.

Questions You Can Ask a Feeding Therapist

Qualifications/training:

- How long have you worked with feeding?
- Were you exposed to a variety of feeding therapy approaches in your training?

Treatment Philosophy:

- How do you help families integrate your advice at home?
- Do you separate parents from children or ask parents to withhold attention or affection to motivate children to eat?
- What do you consider "successful" treatment?
- What criteria determines when treatment is no longer needed?
- What resources do you recommend?
- What can you offer if therapy meals or suggested techniques result in conflict, gagging, or vomiting?
- Do you ignore, show disapproval, or use negative reinforcers if children don't comply?
- Do you use physical "prompts" such as mandibular pressure, holding lips closed, or non-removal of the spoon? (These are nonresponsive.)

- Do you use rewards such as stickers or toys to motivate children to eat?
- Can parents observe a treatment session or watch a video?
- What do you do when children show distress?
- Are you trauma-aware and observing children for signs of distress?

A Brief Review of Options

I have researched and attended training for various therapeutic approaches as well as collaborated with different specialists. But I've gained the most insight from the families I've worked with. Parents have described their experiences as mostly a mix of behavioral and desensitization techniques.

As I've said, my clients tend to find me after "failing" other therapies. I don't hear from many parents for whom approaches other than RFT go well. Every provider has bias in that sense; I want to be transparent about mine. Here are four (somewhat artificial) categories of therapeutic approaches:

Desensitization

This is sensory focused. Most parents say they have used the sequential oral sensitization approach (SOS). The OT or SLP works with the child alone, with other children, or with the parent present.

The basic idea is to take a child who might cry at the sight of applesauce or a puree and desensitize his response by decreasing pressure and anxiety, allowing the child to have a positive experience—to first see the food, smell it, play with it, kiss and lick it, and eventually eat it—a hierarchy broken down into many steps. This tends to be a high-energy activity, with play and praise and without the usual negative reinforcements. In the words of a therapist using the SOS approach, the therapist "works kids up the hierarchy."

Parents may be asked to do "therapy" snacks or meals, in which they prepare foods that are similar in shape or color and try to move a child to accept increasing variety. They are told to talk about the flavor, praise the food, and reward the child with big smiles and gestures. "Spit" bowls, or blowing food into the trash at the end of a meal, is encouraged to try to get the child to put food into or near the mouth without the pressure of swallowing it.

"Exposure" is Complicated

Some psychologists and behaviorists use a form of desensitization or exposure therapy known as "response" or "escape extinction," meaning the child is not allowed to avoid or escape the unpleasant act of, say, eating. Crying, gagging, vomiting, and screaming are viewed as "behaviors" to extinguish. Ask for clarification if words such as "exposures" or "desensitization" are used.

I used to use the word "exposure" to describe no-pressure opportunities to encounter and engage with the food, usually at a meal or snack, cooking etc. I've stopped using "exposure" to avoid confusion as well as the negative associations associated with classic food "exposure" techniques as described above.

Behavioral Modification (ABA, Applied Behavioral Analytics)

Programs are largely run by psychologists who oversee treatment, while technicians (BCBAs and techs) run sessions. In a classic behavior-modification approach, the therapist works with the child using both negative and positive reinforcement to motivate the child to comply with the desired behavior—usually drinking or eating. Many have no training in oral-motor or sensory feeding challenges, the feeding relationship, or trauma. Children are usually separated from the parent; then the parent is trained in the techniques. The child is generally in a chair where she can't get down, and many are upset during sessions. Escape and response extinction are commonly used.

One parent described the first day of her son's behavior modification program as, *"the worst day of my life."* Rose (who shared earlier how her eating is contextual), now age 20, recalls her months in an ABA program less than fondly: *"I remember them putting food on spoons, then squeezing my cheeks and forcing my mouth open and force feeding me. But not much food would go in since they were squeezing my cheeks. It was really uncomfortable. If I let them do it, they'd check my mouth to see if I swallowed and then I'd earn a check mark toward a reward. It didn't help."* Of note, data on autistic adults indicates higher rates of PTSD with ABA therapies, though not necessarily looking at feeding.[7]

This approach may "work" initially to increase volume and even texture accepted, but over time, my colleagues and I observe that the rewards lose their power and the negative consequences are increasingly painful to enforce.

Some parents and therapists have observed that many programs do not support parents on how to transition away from reinforcements (external motivators). Children may have significant difficulty becoming self-motivated to eat. Those of us practicing RFT do not use these compliance-based techniques. As Segal wrote, "These methods can be traumatic (extinction therapy) . . . and all do not attempt to treat the underlying causes that led to the development of IFDs (infantile feeding disorder meaning onset before age 2)."[5]

Food Chaining and Fading

Chaining and fading are routinely incorporated into other therapies. An example of a food chain is to start with an accepted food such as chicken nuggets and linking to a different brand, then perhaps to fried chicken, and on to breaded fish. *Fading* involves making small changes such as adding a small amount of wheat flour to pancakes, or strawberry flavor into milk. Proceed with caution: one client tried fading vanilla yogurt into her son's pudding without him knowing (she thought the yogurt was "healthier"). Once he noticed, he stopped eating the pudding, one of his most nutrient-dense foods. Both concepts can help in terms of what to offer.

"The chain looks like: mozzarella cheese pizza -> provolone cheese pizza -> pasta sauce on a bun-> cheddar cheese with sauce on a bun... something logical like that. Earlier this year, TJ decided to try mint chocolate chip ice-cream. The next day he ate chives from my garden. Perhaps the ice-cream planted the seed that green things are safe to eat? Who knows!! TJ often makes connections and chains with food that make sense to him that would never occur to me . . . I realized he does a much better job guiding his own eating than I could ever encourage him to do."

— Skye Van-Zetten Mealtime Hostage Blog

Responsive Feeding Therapy

The clinician (may be an ST, OT, RD, therapist or a combination) evaluates the child and educates and supports parents with specific oral-motor skills and food preparation ideas in the clinic as necessary, setting parents up to help the child at home. McGlothlin explains: "I have many clients whom I touch base with by phone or email but see only occasionally in the clinic setting to gauge progress and help problem-solve." (Some clinicians, like myself, do not work with children directly and rely on a thorough assessment to determine whether referrals are necessary, and the child may have already seen other providers.)

Jenny describes modeling strategies for parents that show a child how to use her molars, or "chewing teeth." Groups of families may go through a feeding program together. McGlothlin explains, "I run 10-week sessions with three or four families. They support each other and see that they aren't alone; they share what helped, such as booster chairs, utensils, etc." Program setups may look different, but this is the general flow. We adapted this approach in our book *Helping Your Child with Extreme Picky Eating,* in which we outlined five STEPs that dovetail with the values of responsive feeding therapy, including autonomy, relationship, competence, intrinsic motivation and whole child lens. The STEPs will sound familiar and are: 1) decrease anxiety for child and parent and lessen power struggles; 2) establish a routine; 3) move toward eating together and family meals; and 4 and 5) focus on what to serve and how to bridge to new foods.

When Sandra fostered Angel (a 17 year-old who ate mostly bagels and cookies), he arrived with stunted growth. Part of why Sandra opted not to pursue intervention was due to a terrible experience with another child in feeding therapy: "*There is so much talk about chaining or fading to try to get kids to eat variety. I knew from my other kids that when I pushed, things got worse. I just kept the house full of variety. I didn't push, lecture about nutrition, or try to influence. One day he just picked up an orange and ate it.*"

She described Angel at age 20 as "adventurous," that he likes experimenting, and does best with social eating situations. While he still has difficulty articulating preferences, he's made huge strides.

A Brief Discussion About Feeding Tubes

Few children depend on a feeding tube for nutrition. Unfortunately, some healthcare providers use the fear of a tube to motivate parents to get the child to eat. One dad was told at every visit for two years, "If she doesn't gain weight by the next visit, she'll get a feeding tube!" (During this time, she grew steadily, just well below average.)

Practitioners' threats can fuel desperate measures from parents, worsening feeding challenges (ironically making a tube more likely). However, in certain situations, feeding tubes support nutrition, and reduce pressure and anxiety for kids and parents.

This section includes discussions of medical trauma. Please take care.

Beverly's son was born with a rare chromosomal disorder, and fluid entered his lungs while he was eating. His early months included multiple surgeries, time on a ventilator, weight loss, and at six months, the placement of a feeding tube directly into his stomach. Beverly expressed surprised relief: *"I finally knew Danny was gaining weight and getting what he needed. It was scary to deal with the tubes, but ultimately helpful."* The agony over trying to get him to eat when he struggled to breathe was over. His surgical healing requirements meant he needed good nutrition, and the only way to get that reliably was a tube; he slept better, was more consolable, and even got chubby cheeks.

At 18 months, he could sit, began to crawl, enjoyed purees from the spoon, and joined family meals. His strength and coordination improved, and he began feeding himself adapted table foods (with guidance from their ST).

Danny's parents and pulmonologist decided to keep the tube through flu season. By his second birthday, he ate enough variety and amount to support his needs, was curious and happy at the table, and the tube was removed.

Feeding tubes (also known as gastrostomy, G-tube, or PEG) deliver nutrition directly to the stomach or small intestine (J-tube). Placing the tube is a relatively quick and common procedure that should involve minimal pain. Feeding and tube care takes time. Some parents find tube feeding easier than meals, and vice versa. Attention is needed caring for the tube and ensuring that supplies are consistently available.

A nasogastric tube (NG) is a thin tube that goes through the nose into the stomach or small intestine, and many feeding experts believe is best used short term (based on experience with clients and research). NG tubes are taped to the face, can be easily pulled out, and irritate the nose, throat, and skin, and potentially worsen reflux. It's also quite traumatic for parents to replace them every two weeks. If a tube is needed for more than a few weeks, a G- or J-tube should be considered, but policies vary. Some hospitals won't let kids go home with an NG tube, at all. Some GI practices leave them in for up to a year.

McGlothlin tells of a little boy with a long history of "failing" feeding therapies. "Even coming to therapy is pressure for kids who are traumatized," she says. "This boy resisted everything, and therapy was not helping. He ended up needing nutrition through a tube, using homemade-blended formula, which helped Mom feel empowered. We stopped all therapy, and once his nutritional needs were met, it helped Mom trust him and support his learning to eat. Within three weeks with no pressure, he started showing interest and asking for foods, and even ate a slice of pizza. Every kid is unique."

Feeding Tube, or Not?

If your child is seriously faltering with oral intake, growth, and nutrition needs, perhaps due to a cardiac condition, severe oral-motor or sensory issues, anxiety, or a combination of reasons, transitioning away from pressure will feel more scary. Sometimes, children take in less for a while. A child who does not have nutritional reserves may not be able to transition without the support provided by a feeding tube.

Heidi Liefer Moreland, SLP, and Jennifer Berry, OT, run Thrive, a tube-weaning program. They suggest having a discussion with the medical and feeding team to get everyone on the same page:

- Reach out to the member of the medical team that you have the best communication with and explain what you are trying to do and why.
- Ask for parameters, "We know weight can fluctuate with this process. What is an amount that he/she can go down? What is a time frame that we can work with, is it a month? 2 months?"
- Try to avoid a "check-in" weight unless there are other concerning signs. Even if they mean well, it adds lots of pressure.

Some parents, in consultation with their medical and nutrition teams, decide to place a feeding tube to support nutrition while working on skills and physical therapies, rehabilitating feeding, and dealing with medical issues.

Other times, healthcare providers and parents resist the tube and continue with desperate and dysfunctional patterns, such as in Allison's situation. Allison, mother of five-year-old Ava, shared that while intensive behavioral therapy "saved" her daughter from a feeding tube at age 18 months, Ava's current eating is characterized by severe anxiety, frequent vomiting, and continued worsening weight and nutrition concerns. Years of pressure and therapy have not resulted in anything close to normal eating. Allison now wonders if placing the feeding tube when Ava was a toddler may have allowed them the peace of mind to rehabilitate her relationship with food. They avoided a tube, but at what cost?

"I've let myself imagine the thing I was most scared about—that is, a feeding tube. I am finally at rock bottom. I actually think a feeding tube would be better than this."

— Amanda, mom of a three-year-old not gaining weight

Supporting Your Child with a Feeding Tube

If your child does need a feeding tube, it can free you to focus on felt safety, and your child can explore food (per their capabilities) without pressure. Support your child's skills and relationship with food and their body so they are best able to eat when it's time to transition to oral eating (if that is an option). Feed responsively, and:

- Incorporate tube feeds into mealtimes.
- If transitioning to oral eating, perhaps start with food by mouth as he is able, until he loses interest, or the feeding is no longer pleasant, then meet his nutritional needs with the tube. Your feeding team can guide you.
- Make best use of schedules, amounts, and what you put in the tube. I've seen families left guessing while managing tube feeds. Ask for an experienced pediatric dietitian (RD) to help, particularly weaning off tube feeds and trying to balance nutritional needs with allowing her to develop an appetite.
- Conversely, some families are frustrated by specific amounts and schedules that lack flexibility—for example, continuing full feeds even if a child experiences frequent vomiting due to potential overfeeding or with a viral illness. Keep detailed notes of your observations for a day or two so you can share them with the team if you are looking for adjustments. Take brief video clips of what you want to share with the team.
- Try not to be too hasty about wanting the tube out—anxiety and pressure can slow progress.
- Under the guidance of an RD, consider homemade blended formulas for the benefits from whole foods such as fiber, and to introduce your family's foods and tastes he might pick up from the modified taste receptors in the esophagus and stomach (cool!). Or use ready-made formulas made from blended foods; supplement drinks offer good nutrition as well. The Homemade Blended Formula Handbook (Dunn Klein and Evans Morris) is available online.
- The Thrive with Spectrum podcast and Instagram Lives are excellent resources for tube feeding and weaning.

Rose (from a few pages back) had a feeding tube into her teens and recalls her experience when the tube was removed: *"I'd go back and tell my mom and the doctor not to be afraid to think about what happens after the tube comes out and not to focus all on that goal. It was all on me. That fear of what happens if I don't eat enough. And it felt like there was this end point of getting the tube out, but there is a next chapter. No one really prepared me for how to eat after the tube came out, like I'd made it, but still there is not much progression or growth. I'm a little lost, trying to figure out how to gain weight after the tube."*

Sue and Beverly's Successful Therapy Journeys

Sue adopted two children from Russia. Mary was adopted first at 13 months and had significant growth delay and selective eating. She had difficulty chewing, with poor strength in her cheeks, tongue, and jaw muscles (low tone). Because Mary feared and refused liquids, it was guessed that she had been coerced to drink and possibly aspirated fluids (into the breathing tubes and maybe lungs).

Initially, through early intervention (a program in the United States for children birth to age three who need support in various areas), the OT who came to her home twice a week tried to address Mary's eating. Sue remembers laughing about a report that stated, ". . . by 18 months, Mary should be proficient with utensils." Sue says, *"I'd be thrilled most nights if my husband would be proficient with utensils."*

The OT tried to get Mary to eat meat. *"I knew in my gut that it was uncomfortable. The OT was prompting her with harder foods. I backed off. I figured she's going to eat meat eventually; maybe we're pushing too much. I'm going to keep offering it, but I won't push it, even with a game. She's smarter than that."* (Note: Chewing meat is a "late" skill as grinding molars come in around 18–24 months, with all 20 baby teeth in by around age three.)

A swallow study was recommended where Mary would swallow different textures, filmed by a special X-ray machine. Mary had undergone several surgeries, and Sue knew that her terror in medical settings would make the test almost impossible. *"Our OT didn't seem to know what to do beyond the basics. She suggested sticking a toothbrush in Sue's mouth before meals, which was really unpleasant."* The fact that "desensitizing" with the brush in Mary's mouth resulted in battles was a clue that it wasn't the right approach. Sue doubted herself and the therapists who tried to help.

Sue found a better fit when her pediatrician recommended Paula, an SLP. One issue was that Mary couldn't sense where food was in her mouth and what to do with it once it got there, a problem that McGlothlin calls a "blip in the sensory-motor connection." Sue recalled: *"I had a gut feeling that Paula would be a great match. She really listened and agreed that a swallow study wasn't immediately necessary, so we tried other interventions first and had a plan if they didn't work."*

And that "blip" worked itself out. *"Mary's real growth and mastery happened at home. When we did our 'homework,' she never realized there was therapy going on. When the OT pushed Mary during sessions, with 'here, try a piece of pepperoni,' her response was 'no.' Mary would get irritated, agree at first, and then push back."*

Sometime after Sue began working with Paula, she brought Mary's half-brother Marcus home at age 15 months. Marcus also had a rough time with eating, and Sue was relieved to have Paula from the start. Sue agrees that it's critical to listen to your gut, but admits, *"Relying on my gut didn't always help. When Paula said, 'Forget trying to get veggies in and serve dessert with the meal,' that went against how I was raised. But I realized that though my gut didn't feel good with this, what we were doing wasn't working, so I had to try it. I trusted Paula."*

Sue's experience with Marcus shows that a diagnosis may not matter. Marcus had only one visit with Paula, who watched him pick up, mouth, and swallow various foods. Marcus was believed to have some mild chewing delay, as sometimes he'd hold food in his cheeks (pocketing). Paula helped primarily by ruling out serious issues, reassuring about nutrition, suggesting appropriate foods, and helping Sue to respect her children's autonomy.

Sue continues, "*We never got to the bottom of how much of his stuff was sensory. It felt more like his behavior had to do with stubbornness and/or fear and mistrust. We didn't do anything sensory-related for him other than introducing a variety of textures and reintroducing periodically, whether he liked a food or not.*"

Sue got the support she needed to feed with confidence, and the family thrived. They met with the feeding therapist once a month. Paula explained how to prepare foods that were safe and how to advance as they gained skills; gave specific advice on appropriate cups and utensils; and offered recipes and ideas to support nutrition.

Jennifer Berry, an OT and responsive feeding specialist, said this on Instagram: "Our job is to uncover the barriers to that internal competence, and to not do *for* or *to* a child . . . but to allow them to come into their own so they can do for themselves."

Beverly, mother to Danny, who had complex medical needs and developmental delays, found her trusted OT through early intervention. "*Our OT was great. She offered suggestions and was open to finding something we could integrate as a family. If Danny wasn't game, we didn't fight it. I didn't have the nerves for fighting it with all his other needs.*"

Beverly notes how helpful it was for the ST to point out his lip closure, which she might have missed. Though progress felt slow, seeing it helped Beverly continue her efforts at home. This was the second therapist for Beverly as well, since the first wasn't a good fit. "*I learned to get over worrying about hurting someone's feelings. Our current therapy center is a godsend. Everyone is interested, and it feels right.*"

With oral-motor or swallowing challenges, children need close supervision while eating and drinking. You may need to give a few small, manageable pieces at a time or supervise with thickened liquids. Your ST should guide you. Beverly shares, "*'Family meals meant I was sitting monitoring him closely for his safety. Now, a year later, he's doing much better and I can eat too, but I still keep a close eye on him.*" **You may not be eating with your child, but you're setting the stage in a supportive and safe way.**

"*We only saw our therapist a handful of times. Most of the work was at home applying what we learned. The little nubby stick that she could dip into food was a big help. She liked feeding herself with that, and the nubs helped with desensitization.*

The support was so helpful, knowing it wasn't something I had done wrong. She improved pretty quickly."

— Kelsey, mother of Madison, who wasn't eating solids at age one

Feeding Therapy Isn't Just "Fixing" the Child

I have great concern when the goal is "fixing" the child. Many parents felt like Tatyana's: *"I brought Tatyana to feeding therapy twice a week for months, but got no real support or instruction about what to do the rest of the time."*

If it sounds too good to be true, it probably is. If a therapist claims he will produce "results in weeks," or that he "never" suggests a feeding tube, or has a technique that "always takes care of the problem," beware. Those who say "never" and "always" may not be open to following the child's lead. This expectation invites pressure.

In many therapeutic approaches, all the talk about food, the games, negotiating, and cheerleading centers what the child is or isn't eating during every encounter with food and, frequently, of family life in general. This, and aiming for compliance, robs children of the opportunity to learn by watching; feel capable and trusted; and grow skills and confidence. And therapy homework frequently leads to conflict. Lindsay, mother of Axel, lamented, *"It felt so forced, and it ruined meals. He was supposed to have spit bowls, or to blow food into the trash—he fought every bit of it."*

Therapeutic strategies that compromise connection and felt safety can make things worse.

Responsive Feeding Therapy Is Tailored to Each Child and Family

I don't refer families to "protocol" or one-size-fits-all therapies. One child may need relative quiet or a weighted blanket on their lap, another prefers background noise and hot sauce on almost everything. SLP Jenny McGlothlin agrees: "The most important thing is that your therapist makes decisions based on what's happening with each child in the context of the family, versus what some protocol tells them to do. Your therapist or doctor needs to listen to you and work with you, always following your child's lead."

Even siblings differ. For example, while Mary responded to encouragement to chew with her "big-girl teeth," this backfired for her half-brother, Marcus. Sue recalls, *"Any suggestion that he eat something, or if I even put veggies on his plate, meant an instant tantrum and the meal was over. We tried to do 'lion teeth' with him, but he said 'no' for months. Finally, as he learned to trust us, miraculously one day he watched and tried chewing with his molars, on his own."* With the help of a psychologist working on transitions and building trust, things were improving.

When You've "Failed" Therapy

When parents and children don't reach goals established by therapists or insurance companies, parents may be accused of not putting in the work or "doing it wrong," and the parent and child feel they have failed—again. Trying to *get* a child to comply, even with "small" tasks such as playing with a noodle, fails to take into account the power struggles, temperament, and neurodevelopment.

In my experience, when children "fail," parents mostly want to stop fighting. One mom shared, *"Mealtimes are so much more pleasant now that Natalee eats alone in her room."* The way they resolved the conflict over what she was eating was by letting Natalee eat her accepted foods alone, with no plan on how to bring her back to the table.

Happily, you know there's an alternative to fighting over bites or giving up. Responsive feeding taps into the child's natural motivation to mature and grow with eating, *even with challenges.*

Not Doing Therapy Is Not the Same as Doing Nothing

With this basic knowledge of feeding therapies, let's circle back to helping your child at home. Not pursuing therapy may be the right choice for your child and family, and is *not* doing nothing. (And not all families have access, whether due to economics, medical insurance, time, or where they live.) With supportive feeding, the child will have the opportunity to see, smell, touch, taste, lick, spit out, chew, strengthen muscles, and enjoy increased variety.

Lara was tuned in to her son's needs: *"We didn't do recommended therapy meals. It was one more thing that interrupted our time together as a family."* By focusing on felt safety, avoiding unnecessary conflict, and maintaining their connection, she found a responsive approach intuitively.

"There would be no quick fixes with Brian," she said, and worked on providing meals, structure, and connecting through cooking. Many families who choose not to pursue feeding therapy, even for children with sensory differences, can help their child progress with eating and learn to feel good about food. Later, at 13 years of age, Brian enjoyed a wider range of foods, including homemade salsa, which Lara never dreamed he would eat.

Kim explained her nonintervention approach: *"It took a while to adjust to new textures and tastes. Susan would take a hamburger apart and had trouble with lunchroom smells and textures. I even had school lunch with her a few times, sent lunch with her, and tried not to make a big deal out of it. With time, it got better."*

Another mom, Lucy, explains how **having a plan and knowing the next steps made all the difference.** At 15 months, her youngest son, Jack, had delays typical of boys with XYY syndrome (an extra Y chromosome). Lucy sought information before pursuing a feeding clinic referral suggested by her son's physical therapist.

Jack had some developmental differences, and low muscle tone and core strength. He vomited a small amount about twice a week. Jack had no problems with breathing, infections, or other red flags, and his growth was steady—all making serious oral-motor or swallowing problems unlikely. That the pediatrician found nothing of concern was reassuring.

Jack was happy at the table in a supportive highchair. He was undisturbed by his vomiting, though it bothered his father. Jack intensely wanted to feed himself (Lucy says he's "stubborn") and ate an adequate variety. Lucy worked hard to provide pleasant meals and a routine for her children.

Lucy and I talked it over, and she felt a watch-and-wait approach was reasonable. I encouraged her to try to be calm when Jack vomited, and to follow his lead. I cautioned that power struggles over food would probably slow things down.

If things backtracked, she'd reach out to her pediatrician. If things didn't progress, she would re-evaluate in a few months. Lucy shares, *"It felt good knowing I was choosing not to intervene, knowing what my options were, and knowing I had a plan. Equally important was knowing what NOT to do; not to freak out, pressure, force, play games, or reward him to try to get him to eat."* Six months later, Lucy happily reported that his vomiting was nearly resolved, and his eating was progressing, *"on his own timetable."*

After a workshop, a parent-education specialist shared how her wait-and-see approach worked out. Her daughter, born prematurely some 50 years earlier, had a feeding tube for a month. As she transitioned to solids, Mom wondered how her daughter would learn to eat, as she was far behind her brothers at that age. The pediatrician (finding no other concerns) calmed Mom's fears: "Don't worry. Pull her up to the table with you and her brothers, and she'll figure it out because she'll want to do what they do." This doctor and mother trusted she would learn, and (while monitoring growth and progress) that's what happened.

Rachel, mother of a child with a chronic severe illness, low weight, and digestive problems, explains how she supported her child at home after stopping therapy: *"My son is two-and-a-half and won't eat anything soft other than pureed prunes, which he loves, thankfully, because that's how he takes his meds. Anything else 'wet-looking' he won't even try... YET. It took almost nine months to try a hamburger bun. Now he loves it, and loves telling the story about the first time he tried it. I still offer all kinds of foods and look forward in another who-knows-how-many months to him beaming when he finally decides to try yogurt or cottage cheese or applesauce. Until then, I'll keep enjoying them myself, keep serving them at meals and snacks, and pretend I'm not paying attention.*

The Power of Internal Motivation: Sara's Story

The most powerful motivation comes from within. Parents provide the opportunity and scaffolding that allows children to succeed.

At age five, Sara was seeing an OT for sensory challenges. During therapy, Sara refused for months to take off her shoes and walk through a pan of dry rice. Pam recalls one afternoon at the park watching Sara and a friend playing in the sand. When the friend pulled off her shoes and ran to the slide, Pam watched with wonder as Sara pulled off her shoes and socks, gingerly at first, but then ran through the wet sand and played happily—barefoot.

This was a task they'd worked on in sessions without progress, and here she was doing it on her own! Similar happened with showering: After months of Pam trying to get Sara comfortable in a shower, Sara followed a friend into the communal shower after a swim at the local YMCA. Perhaps therapy made these breakthroughs possible, but just as likely, the key was providing Sara with enjoyable opportunities to be challenged. Breakthroughs came when Sara was playing (felt safety), she was *connected* with other children, and it was her idea (internal motivation). This seems to be a magic combination with eating too, as many teens and young adults especially, explore food in supportive social situations.

Felt safety + social connection + "I do it" = powerful motivation

Children can be taught skills or "desensitized" in the therapeutic setting, such as getting Sara to walk across that pan of rice. But *why* would Sara want to walk across a pan of rice? In theory, Sara would walk across the rice and desensitize her feet so she could run and play; but when there is no authentic *why* for the child, meaningful progress can stall. Children want to do well, and we need to support that drive any way we can.

Play Versus Playful

Play is where children learn best; the child feels safe, and brain connections are made more quickly. Maybe there is intense focus and the child is happily lost in make-believe or organizing their car collection. In the example above, in *authentic* play, Sara felt safe, calm, connected, and engaged. Her autonomy was respected.

Mr. Fred Rogers, in a well-known quote, said this of play: "Play is often talked about as if it were a relief from serious learning. But for children, play is serious learning. Play is really the work of childhood."

Let's come back to Sara's story. While therapy was *playful*, with cheering, clapping, bubbles, and cartoon characters on the wall, there was still an adult agenda to *get* Sara to walk across the rice. She resisted, tolerated, and tried to comply with most tasks, but she wasn't smiling and authentically engaged for many of the sessions.

Play therapy can be transformational, if there's authentic connection and autonomy support. *Playful* therapy that the child resists is not the same and won't have the same long-lasting positive impact. Having children do games or coloring pages with ketchup or pudding with adult-directed food "play" is not the same as a child deciding to smear apple sauce on a highchair tray, or giving a forkful of spaghetti a haircut with their teeth. Adult-directed food play (with an agenda) can pressure, and keeps the focus on the child's eating.

Progress at Their Own Pace

Pam feels that it was critical to both accept her daughter's strengths and determine where she needed support. For example, the OT's help with transitions was key to establishing a routine that made family meals easier.

Pam says, *"As a society, we think everyone should do everything in the same time frame. Maybe my daughter wasn't swimming at age three, but at five, she was on that soccer field. When I can relax and realize that this is where we are right now, this is the support she needs right now, and it might be different in six months, that is when things seem to go better. It's baby steps."*

Whatever path you choose, it takes almost three years for a typically developing child to learn to eat. It may take even more time to rehabilitate a difficult feeding relationship as your child draws on internal motivation and trusts, heals, and progresses with eating. The pace of progress varies widely. Some children I've worked with, even "feeding-clinic failures," tried and liked new foods within weeks. Frequently, I see major improvements six to 12 months after removing pressure and feeding in a more responsive way.

Here are five examples of how long things can take to improve:

- Mary's eating, described above, was greatly improved in about seven months.
- Marcus had frequent meltdowns and resisted the slightest ask. After about a year, he had far fewer outbursts and more accepted foods.
- Brian, with his distressing sensory issues and brain-based differences, needed several years of support and was much improved as a young teen.
- Ashlee's sensory comfort took about four years of steady and slow improvement; she now enjoys more variety than many of her peers.
- Oscar, who at 10 had "failed" feeding therapies and relied on a handful of foods, tried two new foods within a few weeks of supportive and pressure-free family meals.

This process can take what may feel like impossible patience. If you try to push or hasten things, you are more likely to slow it down.

Will They Always Be Picky?

While a selective eater may improve in terms of variety and nutrition, they may always be less tuned in, or get less pleasure from food, than their peers. It's okay. If you are a foodie and imagined shared delight over a sushi dinner or afternoons spent exploring recipes, it may be another expectation to grieve and let go. It's okay for your child to not be a foodie. They can still be happy and healthy. Your child can grow up to have a good enough relationship with food.

If you have a teen or older child, consider checking out *Conquer Picky Eating for Teens and Adults,* which I co-authored with feeding specialist Jennifer McGlothlin.

You can work with them on the exercises, or they can try them on their own or with peer or professional support.

Supported with Responsive Feeding

Regardless of the feeding differences or challenges, responsive feeding reduces anxiety and power struggles and sets the stage for the child to do their best with eating.

Chapter 7
Food Preoccupation and Concerns About Higher Weight

"She isn't interested in anything but food: 'Will I get fed again? Will Mommy be upset that I'm angry that I can't eat more? Will Mommy be impatient with me? Will she try to distract me with another stupid toy? Why does my brother have a banana?'"

Six weeks later: *"This feels so good. You're telling me I can treat her like everyone else, which is all I ever wanted to do!"*
— Rebecca, mother of Adina

This chapter is about supporting children who are food preoccupied, with a focus on higher-weight children (though children of all sizes can be food preoccupied). With families I've supported around this issue, generally, the child is larger than average and healthy, and enjoying decent nutrition. Then a parent or healthcare provider labels the child as o*erweight or o*ese and sets off a Worry Cycle: the child is (or will become) too big.

The worried parent is advised to (or on their own decides to) try to get the child to eat less or different foods to influence weight (restriction); the result can be food preoccupation and weight acceleration. It's important to have an understanding of these dynamics, especially how restriction can create and reinforce the anxiety and preoccupation, before learning about how to help heal the anxiety.

There are parallel fears for parents of larger, food-preoccupied children and smaller, picky children (previous two chapters): For the child who resists pressure, parents say, "If I don't make him, he wouldn't!" Parents of large and/or food-preoccupied children believe, "If I didn't limit him, he'd never stop!" You've read that smaller children can be trusted—bigger children can be trusted too. A major goal of this chapter is to reassure you where possible, and help you release anxiety where you can.

We'll look again at the Worry Cycle, this time around exploring misperceptions around weight and health; and why restriction and our current weight-focused health model backfires. We'll touch on food "addiction," puberty, and the impact of medical and cultural weight stigma on health and wellness. You'll see examples of growth charts and intake analyses.

The chapter then pivots to how to support a food-preoccupied and higher-weight child and how a responsive, weight-neutral approach can be applied with medical concerns, and finish with what you might expect in the transition. **Everything you've read so far about family meals, routine, menu planning, or serving sweet options with dinner still applies.**

If you are higher-weight or were a fat child, this chapter will cover topics that may be painful. I'm sending you love, and hope you have the support you need.

What Is Food Preoccupation?

I consider it food "preoccupation" (particularly applied to young children) when a child's interest in, seeking behaviors, and focus on food gets in the way of the work of childhood (play; emotional, social, and cognitive engagement; and growth...).

"Her food obsession scares me to death. I struggled with an eating disorder, and I feel like the only thing she thinks about is when and how much she will eat."
— Kathy, mother of Destiny, age 3

Here are examples: a child at a party is glued to the buffet table whining for food; a child gets frantic and cries when a parent is preparing food; or they might not go more than five minutes without thinking about or seeking food. You might observe:

- Eating quickly or stuffing food.
- Sneaking or hiding food. Note: Occasional pestering for sweets or for food while you cook is developmentally appropriate.
- Not eating at mealtimes, but eating secretly or alone.
- Eating large quantities.
- Becoming upset (or dysregulated) if someone eats off their plate or shared bowls.
- Getting upset (or dysregulated) if food is limited or taken away.
- Eating faster if asked to slow down.
- Eating only familiar foods.
- Clinging during meal prep, frantic around food.
- Focusing on eating rather than play at playgrounds/parties.
- Exhibiting high emotion around meals.

When a child is food preoccupied, so are the parents (this can be especially anxiety-provoking for parents with a history of, or who actively struggle with, an eating disorder or their own body image and weight). As Daisy's parents said, "*We can't hang out with friends because if she sees them eating, she freaks out.*" Parents frequently go to great lengths to distract children or keep food from them (encouraged by those they turn to for help). This might include:

- Not talking about food or reading books that mention food.
- Planning outings or vacations based on where food can be most controlled.

- Feeding other children, infants, and even pets separately from the food-preoccupied child.
- Not eating or drinking anything in front of the child.
- Keeping the child away from the meal or highchair with games, screens, bribes, and other distractions.

Worries That Fuel the Cycle of Restriction

For the restriction worry cycle, children still bring sensory differences and anxieties, and the seeking of nervous system regulation and safety into the dynamic. But the most important factor for parents on the worry cycle for this issue is the child's size and how much they eat, and the perceptions around weight. Let's explore.

For decades, our approach around kids and weight has been to: 1) believe that higher weight is inherently bad; 2) label kids and scare parents and kids about potential (often exaggerated) future health consequences; and 3) try to get kids to eat less and move more. This approach results in needless suffering, more weight divergence (moving up or down on the growth charts), and worse health.

Labels Imply Health Risks

Chapter 1 introduced how labels are problematic. Labels refer to arbitrary cutoffs on growth charts and are not a diagnosis. The child at or above the 85th percentile is currently labeled as "overweight," while the child at or above the 90th percentile is "obese." Consider:

- Does it make sense that when an o*ese American child travels to London, he becomes o*erweight? He didn't lose weight on the flight; the two countries just use different cutoffs. This is a clue to the practical utility of the labels.
- Until 2010, 90th percentile was "at risk of becoming overweight." In 2010, the bar was lowered to 85% for "overweight" and 95% for "obesity," with no change in weight or health status. For adults, the cutoff for "overweight" was lowered in 1998. Almost 30 million adults went to bed "normal" weight and woke up in o*erweight bodies, with no change in weight or health.
- In a child, a few pounds can span the label of "normal" to o*bese, and 1/8 inch can change the category as well.

While the clinical importance of a few pounds is likely insignificant, the label is not. Labels other than "healthy" make the child's body a problem to solve, essentially demanding intervention.

BMI Is a Bad Screening Test

The BMI (supposed to reflect fatness) is used to label children, despite both the Centers for Disease Control and Prevention (CDC) and National Institutes of Health (NIH) asserting that "BMI is not a diagnostic tool." Our healthcare system uses BMI as a proxy for fatness, which is supposed to indicate higher health risk. To more accurately assess health, a healthcare provider would need to assess "skin-fold thickness measurements, evaluate diet, physical activity, family history, and other appropriate health screenings."[1]

BMI Doesn't Accurately Reflect Fatness

Particularly in children, BMI mislabels o*erweight and o*esity when compared to measured body fat. A study in children under age six indicated that almost 60% of the children labeled o*erweight, and almost 2/3 of the children labeled o*ese did *not* have higher levels of fatness.[2] Other studies show similar findings.

BMI Does Not Predict Adult Weight

More than half of higher-weight preschoolers will not grow up to be fat adults.[3] The majority of adults with BMI above 30 were not higher-weight children.[4]

BMI in Children Does Not Accurately Predict Poor Health Outcomes

BMI as an indicator of health is estimated to mislabel one in three adults in terms of perceived risk,[5] similar is likely true for children. (Remember the study in Chapter 1 where 12/25 ten-year-old boys were mislabeled.[6])

A 2016 meta-analysis also said that BMI is "woefully inadequate" to determine the efficacy of health interventions as it misses measuring potential real benefits.[7]

I can think of no other widely used screening tool that offers so little information, gets it wrong so much of the time, and with so many negative consequences. When I first entered medicine, we didn't use BMI. I believe it should not be used in clinical care.

BMI Harms Black, Hispanic, and Indigenous Kids More

There are trends in body build (trunk diameter, bone density, body fat for same BMI) between ethnic groups, e.g. Caucasian, Inuit, Mexican, Japanese, and Indigenous Australian.[8,9] Diné (individuals of Navajo descent) tend to have a more dense build, and data on Hispanic-American children suggests similar.[10,11] In 8- to 20-year-olds, BMI particularly overestimated fatness for Black and Hispanic youth,[12] meaning more will be mislabeled and subjected to unnecessary and harmful intervention.

Misperceptions Around Weight and Health that Fuel Restriction

This section may defy long-held beliefs that our culture and most medical practitioners hold as true (as I once did). In addition to the misperceptions around BMI that you just read about, the following misperceptions, or "myths" offer opportunities to release worry and promote healing.

Myth #1: Fat Children Will Be Fat Adults

As you read above, child BMI is not reliably predictive of adult BMI.[13] According to a 2005 report from the U.S. Preventive Services Task Force, "a substantial proportion of children under 12 or 13, even with BMIs higher than 95th percentile, will not develop adult obesity.[14] There is increasing predictability as BMI increases, and the older the child. Not that anything is wrong with big kids growing up to be big adults, but many won't.

Consider Nora, who was above the charts for years. With her puberty growth spurt, she ended up in the "normal" range, around the 75th percentile, with no intervention. If we try to get higher-weight children to be smaller, we are likely interfering with natural growth patterns, undermining internally driven eating, and raising the risk of eating disorders and mental and physical health problems in the future.

Myth #2: Knowledge Leads to Lower Weight

School report cards don't help. With over a decade of BMI report cards to try to decrease child weight, it hasn't, and it likely caused harm.[15] Trying to get kids to eat less results in more conflict, shame, disordered eating, poor body image and self-regard, and usually, weight gain.

Labeling children has not lowered weight or improved health. Regardless of actual weight, children *labeled* as o*erweight or o*ese feel worse about themselves,[16] exercise less, and are more prone to have disordered eating, diet, and gain weight.[17] Parents who perceive their child as too heavy, or worry the child will become so, *regardless of weight* (some were in the "normal" range to start), end up with heavier kids.[18] Parents who are told their child is o*erweight tend to try to get the child to eat less.[19]

Myth #3: High Weight and Bad Health Go Hand-In-Hand

It's commonly accepted that every "extra" pound shortens your lifespan—that weight is linearly related with death and disease. It is not. There are healthy people at a range of weights. This fear was my main stumbling block to trusting my o*ese toddler, and I hear it from the parents I work with.

Yes, some conditions *correlate* with higher weight (mostly BMI higher than 35 or 40), but when studies control for factors such as fitness, activity, nutrient intake, weight cycling (yo-yo dieting), and socioeconomic status, the increased risk associated with higher weight disappears or is significantly reduced.[20,21,22,23,24]

Correlation Is Not Causation

If you look at a graph of ice cream sales and shark attacks, it could look like ice-cream causes shark attacks, when in reality hot weather is a factor in both; ice cream sales "correlate," or are associated with shark attacks. Population health research is good at uncovering associations.

Risk associated with higher BMI is reduced or eliminated when people of all sizes adopt healthy behaviors such as being active 12 times a month, eating at least 5 fruit and veg a day, not smoking, and consuming low levels of alcohol.[25] You can be fat and fit. If you feel a strong reaction to this statement, you're not alone; I literally scoffed the first time I heard this.

Large meta-analyses actually showed the lowest mortality in the o*erweight range.[26] In addition, a growing body of research confirms that blood pressure, blood sugar, and cholesterol improve with healthy behaviors, even *without* weight loss. And what you think about your health matters as well (more on placebo and nocebo soon).

This book can't review stacks of research; nor can I convince you in the next few pages of something that took me years to grasp (I'm still learning). My main point is that if you hear yourself saying, "But she *can't* be healthy and o*erweight," I urge you to learn more. Otherwise, it can be difficult to trust your children with their eating. Here are additional studies that helped me challenge my anti-fat beliefs:

- In children, fitness was more predictive than fatness for fasting insulin response.[27] (Abnormal fasting insulin is an early sign of impaired insulin function, indicating a higher risk for diabetes.)
- The thinnest older adults have the highest mortality. There is a correlation between illness, mortality, and weight beyond a BMI of 40 as well as at the lowest range of BMI.[26]
- Fat people survive heart attacks in higher numbers than their thin counterparts.[28] This "obesity paradox" has been observed in other health scenarios as well. (This "paradox" of fat people doing better in certain scenarios is so shocking to the biased medical community that it is labeled as a paradox—literally, "a seemingly absurd or self-contradictory statement.")
- Women who report to have followed low-fat dietary recommendations for seven years were no thinner than women who did not.[29]
- A child who maintains stable, even high, BMI into adulthood is less likely to experience health problems such as diabetes and hypertension than the "under" or "normal" weight child who gains as an adult.[30]
- A study banning sodas in schools made no difference in intake or BMI, and also found that the fat and thin children drank the same amount of soda.[31]
- A several-year study in California found that children who gained more weight over time ate no more calories and/or "junk" foods, and were not breast or bottle-fed differently. Parent worry about weight and a difficult feeding relationship in the preschool years predicted more weight gain.[32]

You don't have to believe all of this to stop restricting your child. For me (and many of the parents I've worked with), seeing my child's anxiety decrease and capabilities emerge motivated and inspired me to learn more and keep going.

Resources such as the podcast *Maintenance Phase* and Ragen Chastain's newsletter *Weight and Healthcare* dig into the data behind harmful myths around weight and health.

Myth #4: Fat Kids Eat More than Thin Kids

As a group, higher-weight children eat the same types and amounts of food as their lighter counterparts.[33,34,35] Study authors express surprise at their findings; whether results revealed that thin and fat children drink the same amount of soda, or that children who drink whole milk have a lower BMI than those drinking fat-free.

Myth #5: Long-term Weight Loss Is Simple–Calories In vs. Out

The belief that cutting a few calories here and there adds up, like a math equation, to a certain number of pounds lost is everywhere. Shoot, I even remember telling a patient if she went from two little cream packets to one in her coffee she would lose five pounds in a year. The only thing she lost was the enjoyment of her afternoon coffee.

Intentional weight loss fails 90–95 percent of the time; most people lose weight only to gain back more over time. We know this with the same certainty that smoking causes lung cancer. Studies on adults who have cut calories to lose weight experience hormonal, metabolic, and even muscle fiber changes.[36,37] Bodies become more efficient and metabolism slows, so it takes fewer calories to maintain weight, and *more* restriction to lose. A 2015 review showed that most weight is regained, metabolism slows, leptin decreases (can be thought of as a fullness hormone), and ghrelin increases (a hunger-signaling hormone).[38]

These changes drive seeking of energy dense foods, and the body stores energy (fat) more efficiently. The body perceives starvation and does everything it can to get back to pre-starvation weight. These changes last for years.

In her article titled, "How Fatphobia Is Leading to Poor Care in the Pandemic," Virginia Sole-Smith wrote, "The misconception that body weight is a matter of personal choice and willpower has long been debunked by science."[39]

> "It's not that weight gain is, in and of itself, the problem. The problem is that dieting changes a person's physical and mental response to food and movement and can lead to health issues from the many issues associated with weight cycling to perpetuating eating disorders . . . there's nothing wrong with people being fat or getting fatter, but there is something wrong with giving a supposed medical intervention that has the opposite of the intended effect the majority of the time."
>
> – Ragen Chastain in *Weight and Healthcare* newsletter[40]

Myth #6: Shame Motivates Healthy Behaviors

Bullying and shaming are often justified to motivate weight loss. Take the popular Biggest Loser show: contestants were screamed at, belittled, and hospitalized in the name of "health" and entertainment. Many contestants have regained the weight and suffer from eating disorders or chronic conditions.[41]

> Very thin children may be teased—and thin folks can struggle with body image. No one should be shamed about their bodies. And, as Aubrey Gordon wrote in Self Magazine, "Skinny shaming is bad. But it's not systemic exclusion or oppression."

In our shame-full war on o*esity, Americans have not slimmed down over the years. Shaming people thin doesn't work; it traumatizes. Continuing to present weight loss as a matter of personal choice (when we know better) promotes bullying, harassment, and job[42] and healthcare discrimination.

Weight bias harms and it's gotten worse, according to the Harvard Implicit Bias test.[43] If you spend any time on fat-positive social media you'll see the death threats and vitriol fat people endure when they dare to wear a bathing suit, go for a walk, or just eat in public.

A recent article[44] summarized research showing that *weight-based oppression* negatively impacts: perceived health, health-related quality of life, depression, anxiety, self-worth, self-esteem and confidence, self-compassion, body image dissatisfaction, physical activity, motivation, perceived social isolation, disordered eating, and binge eating disorder. The following increased: using drugs or alcohol to cope, avoiding preventive and treatment healthcare services, dementia, worsening blood pressure, arteriosclerosis, diabetes, metabolic syndrome, allostatic load (metabolic dysregulation, glucose metabolism, inflammation), cortisol and inflammatory markers and oxidative stress... Phew!

Growing research suggests that a significant proportion of negative health outcomes associated with higher weight can be attributed to the experience of living in a bigger body in a culture that devalues and dehumanizes fat people. This has an even greater impact on women, especially women of color, disabled, LGBTQIA, and women with lower socioeconomic status.

And weight is the most common reason children are harassed.[45,46] Even worse, research suggests that more than one-third of bigger children are belittled by family members.

Myth #7: Any Weight Loss Is Good, and the Sooner the Better

Weight cycling or yo-yo dieting (weight is lost and regained on repeat) is credibly linked with many of the things we are taught to blame on higher weight including inflammation, high blood pressure, high cholesterol, and insulin resistance.[47] Dieting is one of the most common predictors of developing an eating disorder.

If weight cycling is the most common outcome of intentional weight loss, which research suggests is bad for health, why would we want to start it *earlier*? The 2023 Academy of Pediatrics Guidelines for the management of o*esity claimed that there are effective treatments and recommend intentional weight management (lifestyle, medication and even bariatric surgery for teens) starting at age two. In the same document the text on a diagram indicating the child's weight going up and down like a wave stated, ". . . treatment intensity and support vary to address relapsing and remitting nature of obesity disease."[48]

Many nutrition and eating disorder practitioners point out that this describes weight cycling. (O*esity was categorized as a disease when the American Medical Association voted to label is as such in 2013, *against* the recommendation of their own expert panel on the issue.)

Poor Support and Bad Advice

You've just read about the pediatric guidelines that I believe are harmful, which brings us to the section on the Cycle looking at poor support and bad advice for worried parents.

Like the rest of us, clinicians tend to focus on *what* and *how much* children eat and ignore *how* they are fed. They *assume* a child with high or accelerating weight drinks too much soda or eats too much sugar.

Many cling to misperceptions, as I did. Biased research reinforces fat bias. Dangerously, fat bias is documented among a significant proportion of healthcare providers. Doctors and nurses have described fat patients as "lazy," "sloppy," and "non-compliant," and that they feel "disgusted" by fat clients. These doctors make assumptions about health and lifestyle based on appearance, resulting in missed diagnoses, poor care, and even death. (Adina's story, woven throughout this chapter and on page 342, is an example of medical weight bias.)

A look at the evidence around weight loss and weight loss medications often exposes: conflicts of interest for the researchers (funded by drug makers or weight loss businesses); high drop-out rates for study participants; concerning side-effects (look up fen-phen); lack of long-term follow-up; and modest weight loss with questionable significance, and regain. Several weight loss medications have come and gone over the decades, none thus far proving safe and effective in the long term.

Their approach, predictably, will be to cut intake or try to get the BMI below the 85th percentile (even if higher may be right for that child). A pediatric dietitian shared that the goal at the weight-loss center she worked at was for *all* the children to reach the 50th percentile—that goes against basic biology!

Becca offered a personal example of the harm of weight-centered care, *"I looked like everyone else (or pretty darn close) in the photos of my softball team from when I was a kid. But after that doctor visit where I was given a calorie list and told I was too heavy, I was convinced I was a hippo. I stopped every sport and activity I enjoyed. It's so sad! I don't want that to happen to my daughter."*

My colleagues in healthcare want what is best for children, but I believe they are misinformed, with serious consequences. And it's tough to admit that you may have caused harm when you wanted to help. Despite level-A (highest quality) evidence that intentional weight loss fails for the vast majority, doctors recommend it all the time. In my training, I never learned of the research showing that restricting children tends to backfire. I had to seek resources and extra training.

Focus on Weight Instead of Health Harms

In 2016, the Academy of Pediatrics recommended that pediatricians not discuss weight[49] (and should discourage dieting) with children and teens, but many still do. (There was no explanation as to why the 2023 guidelines ignored the risks of dieting outlined in the 2016 expert advice.)

Gabi's 14 year-old son has a blocky "Mayan" body and has been diagnosed as "pre-diabetic" (see page 330). Every time he sees the endocrinologist and dietitian, they harp on his BMI. Afterward, *"He sleeps more and plays more video games. I don't see him binging, he seems to eat the same amounts, and he eats pretty healthy, more so than my other kids who are smaller. I think the stress impacts his hormones, the cortisol, etc. and he seems to gain weight after these visits. It never helps and seems to make things worse. They are always telling me to limit portions and try to get him to eat less. I don't. I know it would backfire. He's one of the more tuned-in and regulated eaters in the family."* (Sunnyside Up Nutrition has a template letter for your child's doctor that I co-authored with an eating disorder specialist, asking the doctor not discuss your child's weight/BMI in front of the child.)

Jill's son Ethan was a swimmer with a muscular build. His BMI at his 8 year visit was 90th percentile. Jill was livid when the pediatrician talked to him and said he weighed too much and recommended he cut out sugary drinks and get more exercise! *"I'm fat, and I feel like the doctor assumed we eat poorly and don't exercise. Ethan was asking about it on the ride home and it broke my heart. He sleeps great, is constantly moving, I enjoy cooking, and he eats a great variety. But all the doctor focused on was that number."* The pediatrician mislabeled his actual health risk, and inappropriately recommended (ineffective) intervention.

Similarly, Ashlynne, age 9 had always grown steadily around the 70th percentile. Recently, a doctor said she was "almost overweight" and recommended "cutting a couple hundred calories a day." Ashlynne is a worrier and into numbers. Mom saw that very quickly she became obsessive about reading food labels, talked about calories in foods and drinks and started to withdraw socially, especially when food was around. Ashlynne's mom called her friend who worked with eating disorders and found help.

Remember that with discontinuous growth, perhaps if they had simply waited six months, Ashlynne would have had a growth spurt in height and the trajectory would have leveled off. Here again, misinterpretation of growth invited unnecessary and harmful intervention. She may have also gained weight in early puberty, which is normal.

As a teen, Kitty saw a weight-loss doctor: *"I wasn't going back to that doctor; he was mean and degrading. I felt like I was worth nothing. I felt like I was being punished."*

One mother reached out with questions after the RD at a pediatric hospital "weight management" program recommended diet soda as a "preferred" beverage for her two-year-old. After following "red-light-food" limits for six months, her daughter was more food "obsessed," and her weight was accelerating.

Weight-focused care harms.

If you're a healthcare provider, how does it feel to practice in the current weight-centered approach. Does it consistently lower weight long term? Do you dread talking to families about weight? Are you confident that it isn't harming? These were the questions that helped me have a more open mind. I was not satisfied with my outcomes, and it felt awful for me and patients alike. Supporting parents from a weight-neutral, responsive approach is more compassionate and health-promoting.

The youngest age at which I've seen restriction recommended was for four-and-a-half-month- old Mia, an exclusively breastfed baby. The pediatrician told Mom that Mia was o*ese, to cut nighttime feeds and make Mia wait 30 minutes when she seemed hungry. Mom cried in one room; Dad held Mia, screaming, in another. Within weeks, mom's milk supply was down, and these parents now had a child who drank frantically and screamed when bottles were empty. When Mom reached out to me—just after Mia's third birthday—she shared that she enjoyed cooking and family meals and Mia enjoyed plenty of activity, but they continued to limit portions. We had one visit and a few follow-up calls and emails, mostly to reassure Mom that Mia could be trusted. Within a few months of letting Mia decide how much to eat at meals and snacks, Mia was happier and far less food-preoccupied. The recommendation to ignore baby Mia's cues, and feed in nonresponsive ways to try to get Mia to drop into the "normal" BMI range, set up their woes.

Mental Health Providers Are Biased, Too

Mental health professionals also hold anti-fat attitudes. I've had too many parents and children working with therapists (usually not food related) who were given harmful advice. In *Heavy*, a memoir by Kiese Laymon, he shares how the main advice a family therapist offered young Kiese and his mother was for them to count to 10 when they felt upset, and *to cut sugar and carbs.* Kiese went on to battle what was described as binge eating and anorexia for years, compounded by early food insecurity and trauma.

You may have to advocate (again?!) for your child: "I'm sorry. We aren't here to talk about sugar. Can we talk about how to help him with his anxiety?"

Next on the Worry Cycle Tour we'll examine what restriction looks like and see examples of how children respond.

What Restriction Looks Like

Anything you do or say to try to get your child to eat less to weight less can be felt as restriction. Sometimes it can be hard to tell if you're restricting. Calorie counting and limits are obvious restriction, as is smacking a child's hand as they reach for a cookie.

Kinder and gentler language such as "wellness" and "lifestyle changes," even phrases such as "just don't let them gain any more," don't help. (See page 221 on moderation.) A diet (success determined by weight) by any other name is still a diet.

Most clinicians no longer use the word "diet" while recommending restriction. Businesses and social media influencers have caught on: Weight Watchers rebranded to WW, "wellness that works," and NOOM app spends lots of money trying to convince people it's not a diet, while using behavioral strategies and calorie limits that every dieter recognizes.

The bottom line is: If you're trying to get your child to eat less (or less of some foods) to weigh less, it will almost certainly increase their: 1) interest in food; 2) weight; and 3) risk for other harmful consequences (such as eating disorders). Looking back on the restriction she used with Adina on the advice of the pediatrician to "prevent o*esity," Rebecca wondered, *"If I had given her a few more ounces here and there and let her decide when she was done, maybe she wouldn't have developed such a serious food obsession."*

While the following list could go on for pages, here are a few (regularly doctor and dietitian-recommended) tactics adults have tried to get children to eat less:

- Use a highchair tray longer than necessary to keep food out of reach.
- Pre-portion foods.
- Make the child wait 20 minutes before they can have more.
- Push low-calorie, "green-light" foods, limit "red light" foods, and apps that use this basic approach. Ban favorite high-calorie or high-fat foods (red-light foods). As in, "We don't restrict, he can eat from the fruit bowl or the 'yes' veggie drawer in the fridge any time he wants."
- Fill the child up on water or vegetables before a meal.
- "Run out" of favored foods. Leah, a mother of two said, *"I was told to lie to the kids by our dietitian. It felt absurd. My kids were smarter than that.*

They figured out that I only 'ran out' of the stuff they really liked and wasn't supposed to let them have, like rice, pasta, meat..."

- Teach about "health" and "nutrition."
- Comment on how much a child eats or weighs at eating times.
- Ask children if they "really need" seconds or to "listen to their body" when adults think they should stop.
- Use smaller plates or portion-control education.
- Weigh a child frequently or before meals and linking it to how much they can eat.

Smaller Plates, and Portion Education Don't Help

"Portion control" sounds reasonable. Posters show "correct" portion sizes in school cafeterias, and books recommend using small plates. (FYI, an influential researcher had to retract several papers on topics including eating from smaller plates, having bowls of fruit out, or calling carrots "X-ray" carrots to promote weight loss in kids. An article on the controversy was titled: "'Small Plates Help You Eat Less' and Other Nutrition Lies Were Based on Bogus Research."[50]) Here are two studies that contradict the myth about portions and small plates.

- Portion control: In one study (participants thought it was about rating sauce), adults were told before a meal how much pasta was a "half" or a "whole" portion. Portion-size information didn't change how much participants ate.[51] They were not dieting; hunger predicted how much they ate as well as how much they liked the sauce. (This may explain why structure helps selective eaters. Allowing kids to be a little hungry for meals helps make food more appealing. You may have heard, "Hunger is the best sauce.")
- Plate size: Barbara Rolls, Ph.D., replicated in three scenarios that participants ate the same amount no matter the size of the plate.[52] Hunger and how the food tasted determined how much they ate.

This is good news. Both studies challenge relying on external cues. If you want to eat off smaller plates, that's fine. But using a small plate to try to trick a child into eating less probably won't work. It's better to raise a child to eat based on internal cues.

Restriction Through Teasing, Bullying, and Shame

Parents sometimes tease or playfully talk about a child's big appetite or tummy to try to influence them to eat less. Sometimes it's not so playful. A parent may think "tough love" is needed to protect their child (see Biggest Loser earlier in this chapter).

I remember one pediatrician insisting that he, "brings down the hammer" around higher weight. He admitted it didn't seem to help with weight loss or much else, but he had to *do something*. (He could try challenging his biases and learn about weight-neutral care.) I suggested that his oath to "do no harm" was one to consider. "Tough love" isn't love; no research shows that it helps, and it's likely to harm.

Your Child Will Let You Know if They Feel Restricted

Noemi had three sons. Her middle son was sweets-preoccupied while her other two sons weren't bothered with the one sweet-a-day rule. As we worked to help her middle son, she realized that the rule made him anxious, encouraged him to sneak, and didn't help. Her other two sons ended up being fine without that rule (none of them ate sweets in out-of-control ways with more regular access and less talk about it…). The way her middle son reacted to the rule indicated that he felt restricted. (We don't really know why some kids feel restricted with the same rules and others don't, much like with picky eating!)

Adina and her mom Rebecca offer another example. Rebecca had been advised to cut back on how much she fed Adina, to get her lower on the growth curve. How Adina responded indicated that she felt restricted. Rebecca wrote: *"She begs for food all day, but the pediatrician reprimands me because she thinks I'm not trying hard enough, and scares me about her health. This all feels so wrong."*

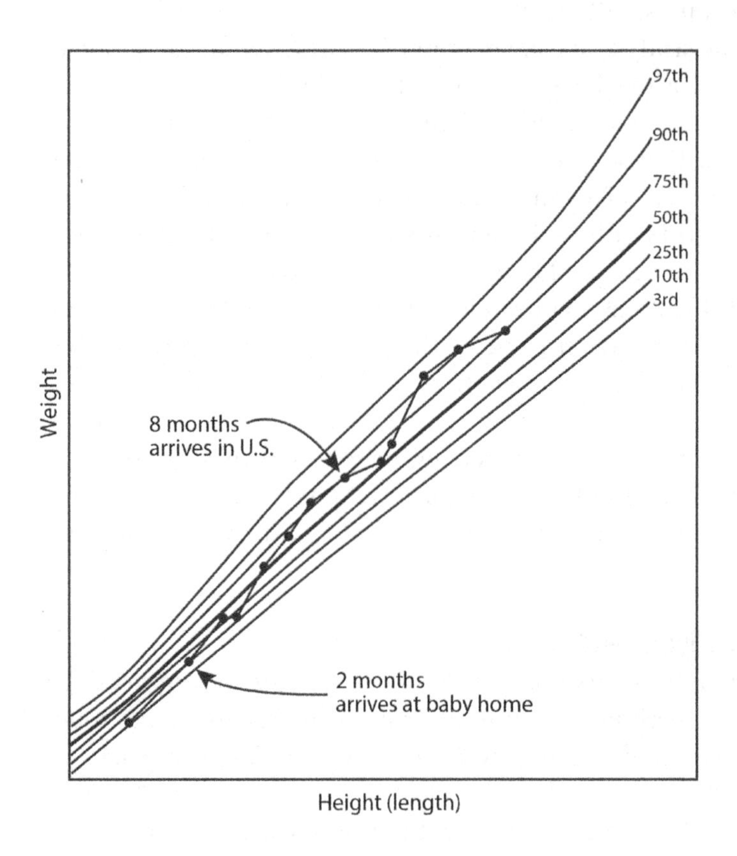

Figure 7.1: Adina's growth.

Rebecca was not encouraged to observe how Adina reacted (see page 168 for a list of things you might observe in a food preoccupied child) or to prioritize felt safety and connection. Parents are often advised to ignore a child's very clear cues of distress, as in, "She'll get used to normal portions."

Adina finished every bottle and cried for more—a story I've heard repeatedly. Adina's pediatrician didn't know: Restricting a child (especially with a history of food insecurity like Adina experienced) will heighten her anxiety, impact felt safety and attachment, and almost guarantee she will overeat when given the chance.

Food Preoccupation May Look Like "Addiction"

With no other explanation or support, Adina's mom began to wonder if Adina was addicted to food. Here's another myth: food preoccupation is not addiction (but can look like it). Yes, sugar lights up the same pleasure centers in the brain as recreational drugs, but so does a hug, hiking, donating money, or playing a game. (Pages 280-284 have more on sugar.) I've seen a child from a home that banned sugar eat it straight from our sugar bowl as fast as she could (while baking cookies with my daughter).

A 2016 analysis found "little evidence to support sugar addiction in humans."[53] Rat studies show addictive behaviors with sugar when the rats had "intermittent access." (Kind of like the girl eating sugar; banned at home, when it was available she ate it in an out-of-control way.) With unlimited access, the addictive behaviors in the rats stopped.

Most research on and behavioral treatments to "manage" food cravings or "addiction" don't consider past restriction or dieting; and we have plenty of research to suggest that restriction leads to increased interest and binging.

What convinced me most that food is not addictive is that with permission and without shame, the food loses that power. As Mikalina Kirkpatrick wrote with eating disorder specialists Hilary Kinavey and Dana Sturtevant on the *BeNourished* blog, "Most eating disorder professionals know that the most effective way to treat any eating disorder, including binge eating disorder (BED), is by *reducing* restriction and dieting behaviors, allowing for more flexible eating, and reincorporating once 'off limits' foods back into normal eating. This, coupled with destigmatizing larger bodies and offering support to HEAL relationship with food and body, is a less pathologizing and more supportive and liberatory approach."[54]

Children and teens themselves may fear being out of control. Dawn observed how children interact with play foods in her play-therapy space: "They create fantasies of all the foods they want to eat, they gravitate to the plastic burgers, pizza, and ice cream, and talk about how bad they feel because they want to eat it, sharing, 'My mom would not like this...'" Children experience shame around these foods, which we know fuels the binge cycle in adults.

Dawn's child clients wrestle with shame and anxiety, and experience how transformative permission can be: "I have chocolates in my therapy room. Early on they are very focused on it, even sneaking some or watching me to see what I do if they take 'too much.' For many of them, over time, the chocolate is just there. It takes kids a while to realize that I mean it when I say they can have as much as they want, and there is no judgment or shame."

Greta's Story

Research shows that when parents worry their child is, or even will become, fat, they restrict more often (as I did). In addition, parents in bigger bodies tend to restrict. It makes sense. The parents have been told that *they* eat too much, and parents desperately want to do better for their children, so they try to get the child to eat less. But restriction tends to lead to higher weight, as you already learned.

Greta's parents, Mike and Alexis, worried that Greta would grow up to be fat like her birth mother. This fear motivated how they fed. While genes predispose a certain body build, there are hundreds of genes (if not more) influencing energy storage and appetite. From day one, after Greta eagerly finished the recommended number of ounces, she wasn't allowed more. By the time Greta started solids, her interest, enjoyment, and the quantities she ate were impressive; even her grandparents commented, which upped the anxiety for Greta's parents. Alexis and Mike decreased portions and distracted her to get her to eat less. The more they worked to get Greta to eat less, however, the more food-preoccupied she became.

Greta's Food Preoccupation

When I first heard from Alexis and Mike, they'd been intensively limiting Greta's intake since she was about nine months old. At age 2½, Greta was "food obsessed." The fear that Greta would always struggle with food and weight terrified Alexis—her stress was "ten out of ten." Greta would cry, cling, and fuss as adults prepared food. She skipped playing if she sensed the possibility of food and whined for more most of the day.

Greta's Growth

Growth charts can reflect feeding. Before Alexis and Mike started seriously restricting, Greta grew around the 25th percentile with some variation typical of discontinuous growth that you learned about on pages 21-22 (the wavy pattern). As their struggles increased, rapid weight acceleration started when she was about 15 months old.

When toddlers become more mobile, tantrums and "pester power" can wear down even the most determined parent. One client caved in to a cookie demand after six hours of the child's whining. As many of you know, this anxiety-driven food seeking can be relentless.

Note: Early in the transition, weight acceleration may continue, and then tends to even out. Some will see a decline in BMI, while others will stay high and steady for some time. Greta's growth surprised Alexis and Mike. They weren't worried about her weight, but as Greta was in the 90th percentile, she would be labeled o*ese at the next doctor visit. Their observations that something was seriously wrong with her eating showed up in Greta's growth acceleration.

Greta's Intake Analysis

With many of the food preoccupation situations I work with, families serve "good" foods, parents cook, and families eat together—thought it's rarely pleasant.

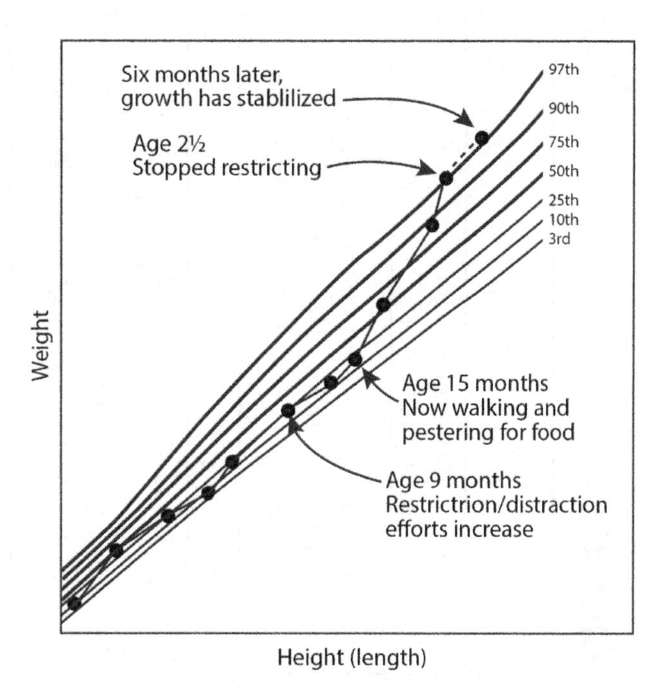

Figure 7.2: Greta's growth.

Greta's analysis by a pediatric RD showed a slightly higher intake for calories and fat than "recommended." **It may surprise you to learn that more than half the analyses I see for kids with food preoccupation or high weight have intakes within the recommended ranges for calories and fat, or even below it, as is the case with Adina.** (Remember from a few pages back that as a group, higher weight children eat the same types and amounts of food as their lighter counterparts.)

Take a moment while we are at Greta's and Adina's charts to note protein intake. It's common to see kids get far more than the minimum. You may find this reassuring. (See protein in Chapter 11 for more.) Greta and Adina's intake journals are on the following pages.

Greta's Macro analysis		
BMI 90th%	Actual Intake	Recommended Range
fat (% total calories)	30%	30-40%
protein (grams)	71.4	> 15
calories	1,511	1,100-1,500
veggies (cups)	2.4	1
fruit (cups)	2.3	1

Adina's Macro analysis		
BMI 75th%	Actual Intake	Recommended Range
fat (% total calories)	38%	30-40%
protein (grams)	42.9	>16
calories	1,188	1,300-1,500
veggies (cups)	0.8	1
fruit (cups)	2.1	1

FEEDING AND INTAKE JOURNAL

Name: Greta

Meal/Snack	Time of day	Food(s) and/or beverage(s) offered	Amount(s) consumed	Notes
(pre-breakfast)	6:30	8 oz 1% milk in a bottle	8 oz	Wanted more (she drinks in bed w/us while reading books)
brkfst	7:40	2 slices toast with peanut butter	2 slices 1 Tbsp PB, whole apple	Made 1 sl toast. Cried for more toast before finishing first slice (begged for more apple, toast); 1 apple eats fast, doesn't take time to chew well
snack	10:30	dried pear snack	1 bag	Begged for more
lunch	12:00	chicken broccoli sweet potato avocado	2 1/2 oz 1/2 cup 1/2	Eats quickly at all meals, asked for more and had another 1/2–1 oz chicken and 3 pcs broccoli. She is upset when we tell her lunch is over. Use distraction, favorite toys to get her to leave the meal
snack	3:30	home-made choc. pudding/yogurt popsicle	1	
dinner	6:15	1 serving Trader Joe's Shepherd's Pie 1/2 cup grape tomatoes steamed kale plum avocado	1 1/2 cups 1/2 cup 1/4 cup 1 1/4	Wanted more of everything, Watched Disney movie during dinner which helps slow her down. Always eats every single thing. Never leaves any food on her plate. We don't put food on the table bc if she sees it she cries. We have to hide all evidence of food in the kitchen or she whines for it
snack	7:15	1% milk	1 cup	

Name: Adina

FEEDING AND INTAKE JOURNAL

Meal/Snack	Time of day	Food(s) and/or beverage(s) offered	Amount(s) consumed	Notes
brkfst	9:00-9:45	almond milk with vitamins rice thins almond butter hard boiled egg apple blueberries	2 oz 3 1 Tbsp 1 1/2 medium 1/4 cup	Cries and whines for bottle on waking, Frantic until gets it. Bottles are on lap. Meals in kitchen in highchair, Screams while I get breakfast ready. Use toys and TV to get her out of highchair. Let her finish her apple wandering around to get her down. Whines for food and clings to me most of morning.
snack	12:00	sunflower seeds	1/4 cup	She loves them, is always asking for them
lunch	1:00	tortilla chips hummus applesauce strawberries	about 15 3 Tsp (?) 1/2 cup 7	Tantrums as I get her to leave the table. Feed other children first so she isn't screeching and begging for their food. Most of afternoon sits on my lap sucking her thumb. Occasionally asks for "snack." Doesn't play with other kids.
snack	4:30-5	rice chex	1 cup	Snack while walking around
dinner	6:30-7	gluten-free pasta tomato sauce (jar)? meatballs (beef, homemade) carrot sticks	1 cup 2 avg. sized 8-10 small	With the whole family. Dread it. Always begging for more, reaching for others' food. My older kids don't like family meals. All I do is manage Adina. I don't even eat. Never slows down even after all this food! I distract again to get her out of chair. Cries for bottle at bedtime, I give her bottle with water.

Intake Information Offers Opportunities

While an intake analysis by an RD can be helpful (in my experience, mostly to reassure parents), the majority of the opportunities around structure, variety, and other changes are clear before the analysis! In fact, I rarely refer for a full breakdown of nutrients.

Greta and Adina's Journals (previous pages) Show Common Opportunities:

- **Inadequate snacks.** See circled snacks such as dried pears and Rice Chex that don't have enough energy, fat, and little protein. Parents have been told that snacks "spoil" appetite. Adina was *hungry* and likely to eat more at the next opportunity.
- **Foods offered are too low in fat.** In an attempt to control weight, parents are advised to avoid fat, such as by serving low-fat dairy, or just fruit or veggies. But 30 to 40 percent of calories for the toddler should come from fat. While it's great to *include* fruits and veggies, they are generally not enough fuel on their own.
- **Too much time between eating—up to six hours.** By this time, the child may be very hungry, probably grouchy, and prone to "over" eat. (Given their hunger and lack of certainty about when they will be fed, eating large amounts is an appropriate response.) Frequently, parents try to skip snacks if a child is busy, in a misguided attempt to limit calories.

My first piece of advice to parents of bigger, food-preoccupied children often surprises them: Serve more food, more regularly.

From the intake analysis and growth information, as well as fleshing out the picture with Greta's parents, opportunities emerged to support them as they moved away from trying to *get* Greta to eat less.

And you don't need an official analysis to get started. Many insurers don't cover dietetics services. Parents pay out-of-pocket for an RD evaluation, which can range from $150 to more than $300. I'm hoping this book will be enough for most of you. You don't need an RD to look at intervals between meals and snacks or think about variety. And sadly, many RDs recommend restriction if they work in the weight-centric model. (Questions to ask an RD on page 299 should help you find appropriate support if needed.)

Lack of Variety and Nutrition

Lack of variety offers opportunities. For example, the intake of one six-year-old showed high saturated fat intake. This was clear before the analysis, because most snacks were cheese. The parents served cheese because she liked it and it was easy, and they viewed it as healthy. It is a perfectly good option, but offering only cheese several times a day meant that variety was lost. Snacks that include high, medium, and low-fat options, as well as different food groups, help balance things out, without limiting cheese or switching to fat-free.

When I do recommend an analysis, it's usually to help parents address sticky nutrition worries. For example, parents commonly push protein, but almost every analysis (even with a diagnosed feeding disorder) has shown that the child gets enough. It allows parents to see that their child is actually within the recommended range for nutrients, calories, and fat, or if there is too much or too little of one thing overall, it can be addressed by dealing with structure and adding variety, not by trying to cut foods or limit portions.

Even with Challenges, Children Can Thrive

Fannah, adopted from Ethiopia around her fourth birthday, experienced malnutrition, then catch-up growth: when Fannah arrived at the orphanage at three months, she had scarcely regained her birth weight. Her weight increased but was well below average; when she came to live with Elsa in the United States, she was 3rd percentile and wanted to eat *all the time.*

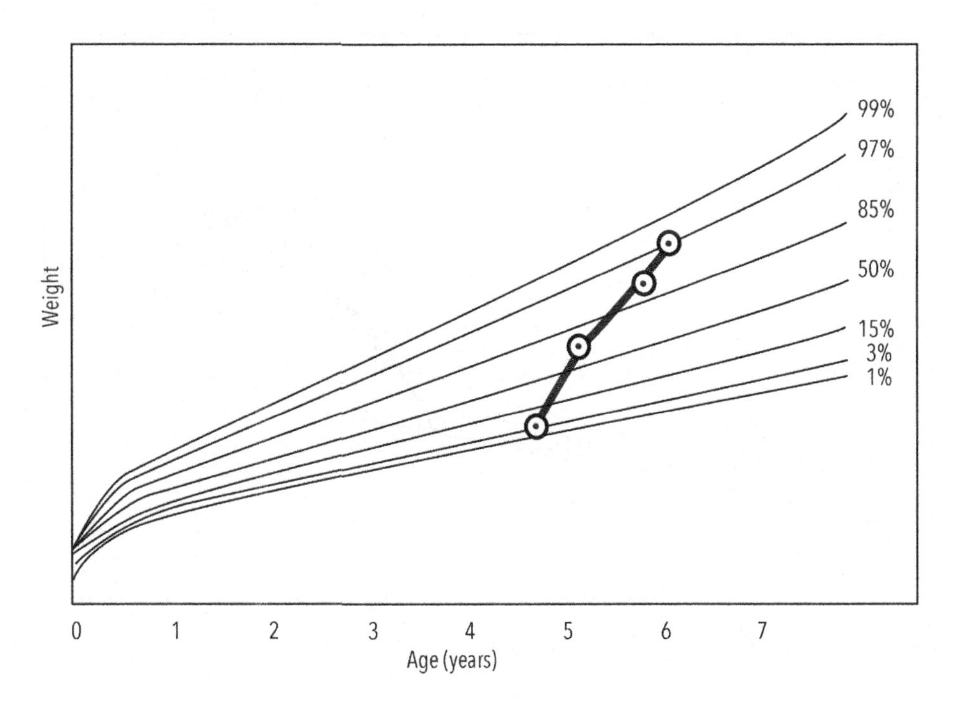

Figure 7.3: Fannah's weight.

Fannah was adjusting well, joining in meals and ate everything as fast as she could. Malnourished children can grow at 20 times the typical rate. At first, family and physicians were delighted with Fannah's growth, but within months, she was labeled o*ese at the 90th percentile. Her pediatrician asked how many sodas she drank (answer: none) and warned she would get diabetes. Although Fannah was already eating more slowly and was less frantic around food, the doctor recommended changing to skim milk, limiting sugar, and cutting portions.

Luckily, Elsa looked for more information. I shared some resources and we talked about trusting Fannah. Reviewing growth showed that her weight acceleration was slowing while her height continued at an accelerated pace, apparent only when the more sensitive Z-scores were calculated (see page 24). Fannah was still experiencing catch-up growth, and cutting her intake might have affected her adult height and resulted in worsening food preoccupation.

Fannah's mom said, *"Right now we're focusing more on her heart needs than on her weight."* This was over 15 years ago now, and we can think of "heart needs" as felt safety and connection. They continued to use a responsive approach and rejected the restrictive advice. In a few months, her weight acceleration stopped and her growth moved towards average, as children at the extremes often do. Fannah is capable of self-regulation of energy intake.

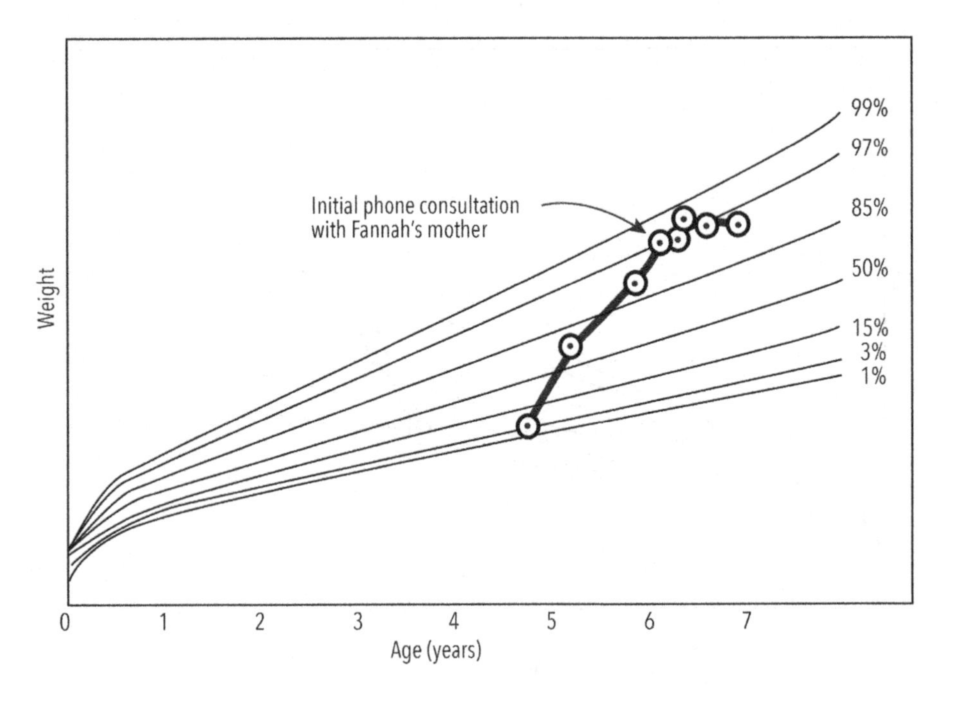

Figure 7.4: Fannah's follow-up weights.

Some Children Are Coaxed to Eat More, Then Less

Occasionally, children who are coaxed to eat more will do so. Problems arise when the child is deemed "too big" and is then restricted, which is why I'm mentioning it here.

This scenario is commonly seen with children who were born early; were smaller than average at birth; had medical challenges that impacted early growth; or had early feeding challenges or developmental differences. There is frequently a focus from the medical team to get the child to grow: concentrate formula, add fats to foods, and get calories in. As we explored in earlier chapters, while this backfires for many children who then eat less, others, for whatever reason will comply. (This could be due to wanting to please; liking food more; experiencing less discomfort with fullness; disconnected from their bodies; or other reasons.)

Hydee Becker, RD, saw this with young children with rapidly accelerating weight. "These were often preemies who had been tube fed, and then the parents were sent home with instructions to concentrate and add fats and oils to everything. The parents worked really hard to get these kids to gain weight. It seems like someone forgot to tell them they didn't have to keep doing that. These children had never been trusted to eat based on what their bodies were telling them, and some learned to eat more than they needed."

A NICU nurse in charge of follow-up care described increased rates of both higher and lower weights in former preemies. It seems these children were either put off eating or accepted eating more than they needed. In almost all cases, the early anxiety and focus on weight, as well as the fact that these kids were fed based on external cues, meant they were not fed in a way that supported self-regulation of intake.

Then, as their weight creeps up, rather than supporting them with RF, the intervention applied is restriction... It must confuse children who were encouraged for as long as they can remember, pushed and praised for being a "good" eater, to suddenly be told, "Eat *less.*" Externally motivated eating further separates children from internal cues and undermines healing.

Puberty (and Pre-Puberty) Is High Risk for Inappropriate Intervention

Weight gain in preparation for, and during puberty is necessary. Many parents begin to worry and restrict around this time. Children gain up to 50 percent of their adult weight, and tend to gain weight before height. Therapist and adoptive mom Dawn Friedman shares her observations: "It's common for families to present with power struggles around food in the tween/middle school years. Often, the child is visibly putting on weight, and it spikes the parents' anxiety. It's also when kids are looking more to peers for more independence, and these other shifting dynamics add to the stress."

And, puberty is earlier on average for Black girls. Even if pediatricians are aware of this, they may not consider it when looking at growth charts, which can show prepubertal weight gain as early as seven or eight. This earlier weight gain can trigger inappropriate labels and intervention. (See page 336 for more on premature puberty.)

Ironically, well-meaning parents who wish to spare their children from feeling bad about their weight may be the first to make it an issue. Dawn shared her experience as a pre-teen on her then blog (edited for length). *"They told me I was putting* *on a little too much weight, that maybe I needed to watch it a little because I was getting, well, I was getting chubby. This is what stays with me: The cold, cold shame freezing my stomach and making my vision turn wide then small. And my shock because no one—*NO ONE*—ever told me I was fat. The irony is that my parents wanted to protect me from the cruelty of other children, but the only people who had ever told me I was fat were my parents who were telling me now."*[55]

With hormones, changing bodies, and peer influence—basically the throes of adolescence—children need unconditional love and support.

Responsive Feeding with the Larger or Food-Preoccupied Child

For the higher-weight child, the key is to still nurture in terms of food. Everything you've read so far applies no matter the child's size. *You* provide, plan, and serve food so your child can let go of the anxiety that makes tuning in to internal cues more challenging.

You get to think about and plan food, so they don't have to.

"This makes sense. I did similar in my recovery from bulimia: Fill your cupboards, including all the food that wasn't 'good.' I remember feeling relieved that I wouldn't run out. Our kids need that same reassurance. In the times we've had plenty of food on the table but it looked more bare because of limited serving dishes, or because it's all combined in a casserole, I'm aware that to my daughter, it may feel scarce and scary. Sometimes I put stuff out, like grapes, to fill the space."

— Emma, mother to Nussa, age three

Many of the following tips will sound familiar. When a child can satisfy hunger at eating times, she can stop thinking about food as much. This helps with anxiety, trust, and felt safety.

Felt Safety and Kind Regard for the Body

- Create an environment where everyone is valued and consistently given messages that they are safe and cared for.
- Accept your child as they are right now, including their size and how they eat.
- Focus on felt safety and connection—not weight.
- Work toward bedtime routines and adequate and regular sleep.
- Aim for a flexible routine, with regular meals and snacks—generally every two to three hours for younger kids, every three to four hours for older kids.

What to Serve

- Always provide at least one food they are likely to eat. They need to feel that their hunger will be satisfied.

- Invite children and teens to help cook and meal-plan. You might say, "We're having chicken and lentils for dinner. Would you like cornbread or tater tots with that?" Resist the urge to argue or pressure, even if they refuse food they chose.
- Serve dessert with the meal. (See pages 83-85 for more.)
- Two to three times a week, serve a "high interest food" snack that includes formerly "forbidden foods."
- Include low, medium, and high-fat choices, and different food groups.
- Don't "accidentally" run out of the high-calorie, or "red-light" foods.

How to Talk About Food

- Don't shame them for foods they like. Try not to use words such as "junk" or "crap." Try neutral words such as "fast" or "prepared" foods.
- Don't talk about foods as "good" or "bad," "healthy" or "unhealthy." This invites shame.
- Offer reassurance: "There will always be enough food." (See page 39 if you struggle with food insecurity.)

Eating Environment

- Let them know they may spit out food they don't want to swallow into a paper napkin.
- Don't battle over manners. Lead by example.
- Serve foods family-style so a child can serve themselves and feel more in control. (See page 74.)
- At meals and snacks, they get to eat as much or as little as they want from what you provide. Even if they eat a lot initially, this sense of control will reassure them.
- They don't have to eat certain foods to earn others, as in they can have seconds on chicken even if they haven't had any veggies yet.
- Limit eating times to generally no more than 30 minutes.

It's okay to limit time at the table. In the first few weeks, parents are often shocked by how much children eat. One parent who had heard of the idea to let children eat until they are done expressed dismay: *"He will sit there for two hours, eating really slowly until he looks so uncomfortable he will finally leave the table."* Limiting eating times to 30 minutes or so supports routine and appetite. It will feel different for them to hear, "In five minutes we will play Legos," versus "You've had your sandwich, that's enough food." If your family or culture lingers at the table for hours, you may need to play this by ear. Perhaps limit mealtimes for a while until they are more firmly in the later stages of healing.

Reassuring Anxiety About Getting Enough

Being reliable about regularly providing food is powerful comfort. In addition to the tips above, some children will benefit from additional reassurance.

Letting Kids Carry or Hold Food

Letting kids carry or hold food is a common strategy in the foster and adoption world (sometimes called a stash). I recommended against using it when I first started working with families, but soon learned from parents that it can support felt safety and connection during the transition period.

There is no one-size-all advice, though the common advice to literally put locks on cupboard doors is one I recommend against; locks erode trust, don't address underlying challenges.

One mom shared, "*We chose not to have food available day and night. I didn't think it would reassure them. I fed them regularly and sat and ate with them. They pretty quickly learned to trust they would get fed.*"

Parents may offer a stash, or not, and see how things go. If a child melts down when his granola bar is taken away, allow him to carry it.

In addition to three meals and two snacks a day, letting Daisy take food from the table or hold on her walk home from pre-school helped with her anxiety. After a while she didn't need to carry food. "*Daisy brought the rice cake to the living room and held it while she started drawing. She left it on the table after about five minutes, I just picked it up and threw it away.*"

There Will Still be Some Limits and That's Okay

You may fret that any limits will trigger anxiety and your child will feel restricted. I had this worry. I remember when we stopped restricting M as a toddler, one of her favorite snacks was peel-and-eat shrimp—but I didn't want to spend $9 on shrimp for snacks too often! I learned that I could limit shrimp and she was fine: "Shrimp is expensive, so this is how much we have. I also brought crackers."

It's been my experience that the WHY behind the limits matters most (the parent agenda). Parenting, and living in the world we live in, means kids will have (and in some cases do better with) some limits. Supporting structure, such as by limiting time at the table, or asking a child to wait a bit if you're getting a meal ready doesn't tend to trigger the same anxiety (you can also offer an appetizer snack, see page 73). Limits around cost as in, "We can't get onion rings because they're $7, but I'll share my fries," or because you just ate out and you want to eat at home aren't the same as, "No onion rings; they're a red light food."

Mom Carrie asked a related question in my DMs, "*Should they have anytime access to all their snacks (kept down low)? He's eating so many chips and fruit roll-ups!*" More and more I see advice to allow children to have access to a "yes" box of snack foods, usually foods parents feel less anxious about like applesauce pouches or granola bars. (If you're doing that and it's working for your family, keep it up! It may also help with older children and teens who are home alone after school.)

From my own home to the families I've supported with children who've experienced food insecurity, neglect and abuse around food, to typical toddlers, to autistic kids and their autistic parents, for the majority, not allowing unlimited access to food has worked out well. Here are a few of the reasons why I think this is so:

- Appetite and internal drives including curiosity are usually best supported when kids have a little bit of hunger before meals and snacks.
- There is some evidence that not having frequent eating times and the spikes in insulin are better for health over time.
- Many wrapped foods are appealing, and when kids are bored, food can become entertainment. There is nothing wrong with that on occasion, but I've seen kids spend the whole day dipping back into the snack drawer when bored.
- Parents may feel like they don't need to provide regular meals and snacks if kids have access. This can mean missed opportunities to eat together and be around new foods. It can also undermine balance.
- For kids with anxiety around food and eating, this can keep food always in mind, and may not decrease their anxiety (or yours when they choose to only eat chips for 3 days in a row).
- This kind of snacking is often on-the-go and distracted which may mean less ability to focus on internal cues and lead to overall eating less or more than the child otherwise would. For many, it does not support internal regulation.

It's okay to say no sometimes and have limits. Consider the motivation behind the limit. Saying, "We'll have lunch in ten minutes, can you wash hands and set the table?" supports appetite, structure, learning to wait, and shared mealtimes. Almost all of the families I've worked with have found that increasing structure around eating times (with flexibility), making sure the kids had enough food, including high-interest foods at those times has worked really well to address their concerns around food preoccupation or picky eating.

And it lets kids forget about the pantry and food in between eating times for the most part. Many parents (myself included) felt it greatly reduced anxiety (theirs and the child's) and the child's focus on food when the adults thought about and prepared it, rather than having kids in charge or fending for themselves. We can think of it in terms of screen time or sun exposure. We might be thoughtful about placing a parameter around both in ways that support our children.

Zinneah's son had recently weaned off his feeding tube. He was still very anxious around new foods. With the snack pantry, he often ate small amounts of crisps and skipped meals. As she moved towards more regular meals without pressure, he joined in. Once he was comfortable there, she transitioned away from the snack pantry open policy. *"If you'd like something to eat, let me know and I'll fetch it for you and we can sit and eat it."* She also noted that when she sometimes offered a meal or snack that didn't include his favorite tortillas, he was now trying some of the other foods she had put out. *"I was always monitoring the snacks and worried about what he was and wasn't eating. It was less of an ordeal to get rid of it than I thought it would be, I think partly because he was happy to sit and eat."*

And sometimes the designated drawer is what your child needs. One foster mom had a little boy she couldn't keep out of the fridge, so he had his own drawer stocked with familiar foods. She reassured him that the drawer would always be full, *but* he could not take food at random times. He checked the drawer repeatedly, with Mom's reassurance that it was his, and he could choose from it for meals and snack times. Gradually he forgot about it.

Toni used a similar approach: *"We said we would keep the snack drawer full, and we did. I'd sometimes call my husband so he could pick up food on the way home from working the late shift if we were at risk of running out."*

Here is where the flexibility comes in. See what helps you and your child stay in felt safety. If things are improving, you're on the right track.

Advanced RF: Parties and Get-Togethers

Get-togethers are especially tricky. As one mom wrote, *"We've been at this for a few days, and he's eating a lot. We're supposed to go to a party with a buffet, and I don't know how to handle it."* You may be tempted to limit how much your child eats to avoid judgment, but doing that can confuse them. Early on (read about Stage One on the following page), they will probably eat a lot at parties and not play.

This is also about your comfort and anxiety. You have choices. You can skip the party if it's too much to deal with publicly right now. That's a fine option! (Obviously, if your child is excited about it, reconsider, or don't let him know why you aren't going.) Or go—and see what happens. You may or may not want to tell family and friends what you are up to with their feeding/eating in general.

Your child may regularly check in, not believing at first that they can eat as much as they want (as long as they're not depriving others). One mom decided to skip a cousin's party because she didn't want to deal with comments and explaining about her toddler's eating to her diet-loving family. Another mom went to a party and admitted she felt embarrassed by the amounts her daughter ate, while yet another was surprised that her daughter mostly played with her friends.

How Transitioning to Responsive Feeding Usually Unfolds

Just as I advised parents of small or selective children, start a journal. This process is characterized by progress and what appear to be setbacks. Progress sometimes feels slow. Write down where you are now, what your days are like, how much time and energy you put into keeping food from your child, and how it impacts you, your child, and your family. Use the journal to help you reflect, be curious, and learn how to respond to your child. It can help you through difficult times when you see how far you've come.

Once you institute structure and stop restricting, the transition typically unfolds in two stages.

Stage One: "This Is So Scary"

Predictably, at first your child will seem to prove he can't be trusted with eating—that he indeed can't stop. This is when, without preparation and support, you might give up. Many I hear from have "tried" to let the child decide how much but found the transition too scary. In these situations, I've mostly observed a lack of understanding of the layers of responsive feeding, or a deeply ingrained fear of having a child in a bigger body. Only changing one aspect, such as letting them eat until they stop, leaves out a lot of support.

For example, Jules, mother of Teresa, age four, commented on a blog post, *"We did it for four days, and I couldn't stand it. She ate more than my husband, so we went back to pre-plating her meals."* Another mom wrote, *"Our three-year-old eats so much. Sometimes I have to leave the room, it makes me so anxious. My husband is better at handling all this."*

Alexis, Mom of Greta (from earlier in the chapter) described the anxiety early on, *"We've been shocked with the amounts, like eight bowls of cereal with yogurt for breakfast yesterday."* A few weeks later, Greta showed signs of recognizing what it felt like to be full: leaving food on her plate and moving on from meals without extraordinary measures. *"Today at lunch, she didn't eat much, asked for more of something, then as soon as we gave it to her, she said she was done,"* her mom observed. *"Another day, she left the table voluntarily to go play, something she'd never done in her two and a half years."* Journaling these successes helped Alexis see Greta's emerging skills.

Getting Through Stage One

The approach for getting through the first stage (eating may look "worse" for a time) is almost identical to the list on pages 129-131, because it's an act of trust.

- Pray if you do or read the Serenity with Feeding section (page 68).
- Squeeze your fists, bite your tongue—hold onto the chair when every fiber in your being wants to comment or take her plate.
- If you have one, hold hands with your partner under the table. If you don't have a partner, consider having a supportive peer you can text before or after a meal, or an online parent group.
- Keep a note on the fridge with phrases such as,"Trust Greta," or use it as a mental mantra. (If your child is able to read, you may want to tuck this away.)
- Knowing that your child needs to "overeat" to learn to tune in will help you get through it.
- Tap into feelings of relief; or read your journal to remind you of how long you've been struggling, that all you tried before this didn't help, and that it can't get worse (some parents call this "rock bottom").

- Try to focus on early progress, such as a happier child and less anxiety and conflict, rather than how much they are eating.

Early on, your child will likely eat more than you're comfortable with. Try not to react. Don't count crackers, and don't comment. This is tough. You'll want to say, "That's your fourth piece of bread. Honey, isn't your tummy full?" (See index for mentions of interoception.) This is likely to make her want to eat more, and it distracts from internal cues.

When you pick her up from a play date and her friend's mom says with a frozen smile, "She ate six pieces of pizza," try to deflect and say, "It sounds like it was a great party. Thank you." Avoid explaining or apologizing, especially in front of your child. Stay calm and send your child the message that you trust her, and she will figure it out.

"In a way, it's easier than I thought. I've spent two years trying to not let her eat. I'm scared, but part of me is also relieved. That burden of having to constantly try to get her to eat less is lifted. It's such a relief, I can't even describe it."

— Rebecca, mother of Adina, now age two-and-a-half and in Stage One

"Normal" in the Transition

Knowing what you might expect will help you get through it. Your child is aware that things are different and is trying to figure out the new rules, such as by asking if she can have more chicken, even with chicken already on her plate. She is learning to trust that she is in control of *how much* and that she doesn't have to be preoccupied about when she will eat next, because you are taking care of that. This all helps her learn to tune in to her body, instead of being ruled by anxiety and feelings of scarcity.

"I'm beyond thrilled . . . seeing her play with her food, biting a piece of toast and saying, 'it looks like a fish—watch him swim!' There are so many more subtle (but significant) signs that she is finally feeling more secure around food—something I thought I'd never see. We were at a play date the other day, and she saw the food, had two crackers, and GOT DOWN TO PLAY! We'll keep working on this, and even though it may take a while, we're on the right track."

— Rebecca, mother of Adina, four months into stopping restriction

Stage Two: Emerging Skills

Seeing glimmers of self-regulation emerging and less food preoccupation and anxiety, builds faith in the process. Stage two is characterized by increasing signs of emerging skills, but she may still "overeat" and seem food-focused much of the time.

"We've noticed a bit less urgency before meal and snack time."
— Alexis, mother of Greta, two weeks into the transition to RF

"We went for a burger and she had about half the bun and one bite of meat, and said she was done. We were so surprised. I've learned that what she loved one day does not mean she will like it in the same amount or at all the next—which is a change, because she used to eat anything and everything in large quantities."
— Alexis again, now in Stage Two

"A month ago, she ate two whole bagels with cream cheese. Today she had a quarter of a bagel, said she was done, and went to play. This is a totally different child. She still eats a lot most meals, but seeing her have meals where she leaves food without a fuss is a big deal."
— Brittany, mother of two-year-old Sarah, one month after leaving restriction behind

Signs of emerging skills to look for and journal:

- She's less frantic or preoccupied with food.
- His rate of eating is slowing down.
- They are playing with food.
- He's opening up to the idea of sharing, as in, "This is for my brothers," or "I had mine, now that is Daddy's." (Even if he goes on to eat the food, acknowledgment is step one.)
- She may savor foods more, rather than stuffing.
- They'll leave food on their plates now and then.
- He will leave a meal voluntarily.
- She's more choosey (picky) and discovers preferences.
- He consumes large meals and smaller ones, as in, *"He ate a huge amount at dinner, and it was really scary, but I noticed he ate less at breakfast the next day."*
- She's engaging more (connection) at eating times, as the anxiety and focus on food decreases.
- They're starting to have patterns, such as eating more after nap and less mid-morning.
- He's a little more "naughty" at the table. This can be reassuring, as he's less preoccupied with how much he can eat and is looking for autonomy and exploring limits, like any other child.
- Playing for longer periods of time between food seeking.
- Not immediately seeking food when upset or frustrated.
- Not upset or immediately seeking food when they see mention of it (in a book, billboard, or TV show) or see others eating.

Remember that these are *emerging* capabilities. She will still pester you about sweets and perhaps eat quickly or "overeat" at times. Most children will beg for sweets and "overeat" on occasion.

You Can't Rush It: Learning to Tune In Is Experienced

When children continue to eat large meals, even with signs of progress, this can tempt parents to try look for something else they can do.

Rating Hunger or Tummy "Check in" Can Backfire

I often get asked along the lines of: "Is it okay to ask her when she slows down, 'Is your tummy full?' or 'Is your tummy still hungry?'" First, *why are you asking*? If it's out of anxiety and a desire to get her to stop, she'll feel it, and it's likely to backfire. But you can try it and see how she reacts. You can model, "I'm still hungry, so I'm having more beans," or "No, thank you, I don't want more; my tummy is full." One or two mentions are okay, but more might feel like restriction.

You can ask if she's had enough, and if she would like to move on to the next activity, such as coloring, reading a book, or watching a show. Generally, the less talk about appetite and how much they eat, the better. You could ask, "Did everyone get enough?" Max's mom wrote, *"I know now not to discuss eating at all, or tummies, or nutrition. The less we talk, the more relaxed I feel and the better he does."* (You'll read more about Max soon.) But it's so hard to resist. Asking children to "check in with their tummies" or talking about healthy portions, nutrition, or asking children, "What's your body telling you?" will tend to backfire.

The thing is, right now they have no idea how to check in or even what they're feeling; the talk gets in the way. They understand it's usually said to try to control their eating. **And when they say, "I listened to my body and it needs ice cream," you're kind of stuck.**

Popular social media accounts advise parents to use visual scales or try to rate hunger. One parent asked: "Can I train my three-year-old to recognize when he's full? My friend talks about 'starving, kind of hungry, hungry, not hungry, full, stuffed,' and has her kids use a chart to point to what they're feeling." I don't recommend these scales either, and especially not for a food-preoccupied child. It's possible that all he feels is "starving" or "stuffed," and he can't even tell what that means. From my experience, children learn to tune in to and interpret cues with:

- Time.
- Permission to eat and "overeat."
- Regular, filling meals and snacks.
- Coming to the table in felt safety.

After structured meals and snacks, with toddlers, I usually see capabilities begin to emerge in about 4–6 weeks (often sooner)—without charts or any talk about it. Children with sensory or brain-based differences can generally tune in, though it may take longer and they sometimes need additional support. (Read Suzanne Stratford's words on page 148 on tuning in.)

Experience is more meaningful than trying to explain vague concepts (especially to young children who aren't developmentally able to grasp what you're expecting). They might think there is a right or wrong answer, which invites anxiety and fear of disappointing. With an older child, these kinds of charts and direct techniques may or may not help. I still don't generally recommend them. If needed, these issues can be explored with a non-diet eating disorder specialist.

Free from Worry, Room to Play

It's a thrill when parents observe in their child a decreased focus on food, and an increase in spontaneous play—even in Stage One. The child who in June wouldn't leave her mother's side at the beach, is splashing in the water by August. They play at the park instead of wandering from one parent to the next, looking for snacks.

"It's as if his mind is freed of food and now he realizes he can move... who would have known? We actually cancelled a physical and occupational therapy evaluation after seeing just the few days of improvement."

— Adan's mother

"She was playing with the applesauce she picked up with the spoon. She was licking it, offering it to her doll, and talking between bites—as opposed to her usual nonstop putting food in her mouth."

— Toni, a mother seeing emerging skills

"We were sitting at the table talking when she announced she was DONE and wanted to get down to play. I let her down with no comment, of course, but I was jumping up and down inside!!"

— Rebecca, mother of Adina, age two-and-a-half

Max's Journey with Food Preoccupation and Mom's Fear of Fat

The following are excerpts from Mom's journal, emails, and calls on how the process of healing went for three-and-a-half-year-old Max. For context, Max's doctor labeled Max as o*erweight and recommended portion control when Max was 18 months old; an RD recommended red-light and green-light rules. Mom had been a larger kid who slimmed down with puberty. She worried Max would grow up to be fat. Their story illustrates so much around the anxiety with health and weight, judgment, the impact on the parent-child relationship, professionals unfamiliar with this issue, early progress and the relief and happiness and connection this can unlock. Of note, Max is raised by well-resourced biological parents. They read the first edition of this book some weeks before our first call. I've underlined some signs of progress throughout.

How Things Were Going: His teacher came to me with tears in her eyes and said, "I love Max, but something is seriously wrong with him." If food came up in a story she read, Max would spend the rest of class asking for food. She referred us to a child psychiatrist who said Max has OCD (obsessive compulsive disorder), but we found a different one who is going to do play therapy and see what comes up. Max never says he loves me; doesn't hug or cuddle like his brother did. He's always pestering for food. He kicks and hits when he gets really mad if we don't give him food. My friend is a psych nurse. She says it's probably a medical issue. Max has seen an endocrinologist and everything was normal.

Early November, first call notes: We started about eight weeks ago letting him eat as much as he wants at mealtimes. I can't watch. He eats SOOO much. I've snapped a few times. I cry after meals. I see that he's happier and more relaxed, but he'll never stop eating. He eats until his tummy hurts. I don't know if I can decide to let him be happy but o*ese or miserable and healthy. His doctor lectures us about diabetes and heart disease and mentioned food addiction . . . We can hardly get him away from the table. <u>Sometimes he sits and plays with his cereal after he's eaten two bowls. Before, he would eat any food in front of him and never left any. Is this the beginning of him listening to his body?</u> He puts food on his plate and looks at me, almost like a challenge, just to get a rise out of me. He screams within five minutes of snack being over. He screams for fruit and crackers. I know I'm not supposed to, but I give it to him. <u>The first few weeks he would eat it and ask for more, but now half the time, he just carries it around.</u>

Late November, second call: Max said "I love you" for the first time, and he even climbed onto my lap. He stayed for about five minutes and let me tickle his back. Then his head snapped up and he said, "I'm hungry." It was like he forgot for a few minutes and then remembered again. My heart broke. I was so excited, but he can't stop thinking about food.

Mid December, third call: We hired a new babysitter, and we've told her a little of our struggles, but she hasn't noticed anything! I was able to play Matchbox cars with Max for more than an hour while she cooked and helped my older son with his homework. This was the first time in Max's life that we played like this. Ever. The first time someone was in the kitchen and he wasn't right there . . . The phone rang, and it was amazing. He looked up, kind of blinked and said, "I'm hungry!" My mother notices that Max is doing so much better. She's totally supportive of our new approach. It's still really hard to get Max to leave the table at home, but apparently there he hops down and plays. Why is Max doing this to me? He still pesters me for food and it makes me crazy. If I eat anything in front of him, he has to have it. With my in-laws, he ate a huge meal and complained about his tummy hurting. I was so embarrassed. I don't know how I can trust Max. I think he's gaining weight. It terrifies me. I know he's happier but I worry about his health. I don't think I can be okay with having a fat child. I feel stuck.

Email: He's eating huge meals, I can never trust him. He's as happy as I've ever seen him but I can't stop crying. Strangers will comment about how thin his brother is, and how "big and strong" Max is. I know people pay attention to how much he eats, and he does have that little tummy. There is just so much talk about my kids and their bodies. If I try to suggest dinner is over, he puts up a fit. I'm so embarrassed. I know my in-laws judge us.

January, fourth call: Things are so much better at home. He never carries fruit around anymore. I have to really think about it or I forget how much progress we've made. I wonder if my anxiety sets him off so he eats more, or if him eating more sets off my anxiety. I can't tell which comes first. He still sometimes eats really big meals. Will he ever be "normal?" We went to the grocery store and he saw the candy and immediately asked for it. I said, "Sure, choose a candy," and he picked M & Ms. Normally I would have told him he could have maybe five, and he would have pestered me the whole way home for more. He asked how many he could have and I said he could eat as many as he wanted. I honestly felt so relaxed, I didn't care if he ate the whole bag. Then he ate four or five and said he'd save the rest. I let him know he could eat them all and we could always buy more another time, but he just kept them in his hand and put them in the pantry when we got home. It blew my mind. I'm happy now that he is actually pestering me for more "normal" foods like candy or ice cream and not begging for pasta or chicken. He asked for seconds on noodles, and I gave it to him, and I was cutting his meat, and then he just said, "I'm done." Pasta was the one food I thought he would never turn down, he always begged for more of it. I almost cried tears of joy.

Late January, sixth call: I used to think he wasn't affectionate. But he is. Max now climbs onto my lap, says, "I love you" all the time. Our psychiatrist says he's doing great. No need to see us anymore. I know now not to discuss eating at all, or tummies, or nutrition. The less we talk, the more relaxed I feel and the better he does. My husband and I were always fighting over Max's eating. It's so much better now I can't believe it. My husband has noticed how much calmer I am too and more relaxed, but it's still not easy. No one understands this. I know this is the right approach now. My biggest challenge will be my in-laws. They're both slim and focused on healthy eating and exercise. They talk about how much Max eats and his tummy all the time. His teacher pulled me aside and said he's like every other kid now. He can share snacks, he plays, she thinks he is learning better too. Getting him down from the table after dinner isn't a problem anymore. Sometimes we share an apple after dinner and he just says, "I'm full." And gets down. It feels like a miracle.

If Anxiety Spikes

Rarely, I've heard from families where, rather than seeing decreased anxiety after letting the child decide how much to eat or serve themselves, it appeared to be dysregulating. These were cases with more challenging brain-based differences, as well as children with multiple diagnoses such as OCD, autism, anxiety, ADHD, complex trauma, and FASD. A few children have even asked for parents to serve them and control portions, becoming upset when allowed to serve themselves.

Follow your child's lead and consult with their care team. If your child asks anxiously for you to serve them, continue to do so, while working on structure and removing pressure and working toward less conflict. Hopefully, with time, they may be able to trust the process and access those internal cues.

Sometimes, children need gentle external support until they're old enough, possibly into adulthood, to potentially work with eating disorder professionals to gently get back in tune with their internal cues and figure out ways to eat that work for them.

Parents Reflect Back on the Journey

"I no longer think about Sarah's eating. Her little brother eats more than her, and he's in the 50th percentile for weight. Food isn't the focus of her day. We were at a birthday party on Sunday, and I had to pull her away from the sandbox to get her to eat some pizza. A lot of times she refuses to eat dinner, and as frustrated as my husband gets, I'm secretly glad to see some 'normal' preschooler behavior. Don't get me wrong, she still loves food and often eats more than the other kids, but it's no longer an issue in our house."

— Brittany, mother of three-year-old Sarah, one year in with responsive feeding

"We're three years out with this process. I can tell you it was hard for a while. My husband and I had to simply believe it would work. Knowing that everything else we tried failed so miserably helped. We saw small meals sometimes, and pretty big meals at others. He was way off the charts, and it's taken years, but slowly he's coming down on the percentiles—but still in the 'overweight' category. I try not to think about his weight, since I know I can't control it. I'm just grateful he is strong, healthy, and happy. Grateful we turned this around."

— Pia, mother of Antoine, adopted at age 16 months, now age five years

"It was really tough to trust it in the beginning, but now almost always this feels really right and natural. I have to admit, occasionally I watch her eat a huge plate of pasta and think I should stop her, but I know better; she's proven she can be trusted. It's just hard to undo all that training where we think we have to limit portions or control what our kids eat."

— Mary, mother to Cindy, age eight years

Reclaim "Health"

I'm not asking you to ignore health for the sake of felt safety and connection. It's not, as Max's mom thought, a choice between "happy and o*ese" or "miserable and healthy." ***Focusing on felt safety is an intervention. Felt safety is heart healthy.*** Dietitian, author, and eating disorder specialist Leslie Schilling writes, "Relationships, food security, and access to non-stigmatizing healthcare are more predictive of health than what you eat or how you move. Health is complicated. Let's stop pretending it's as simple as diet and exercise."

Remember that many of the poor health outcomes blamed on higher weight are strongly linked with factors such as social isolation and the wear and tear of toxic stress.

And, our beliefs about health, our bodies, and our capabilities matter a lot. See Chapter 8 for more on how our thinking impacts our bodies, from hunger hormones to exercise capacity. Challenge the doom and gloom messaging around weight and health. Send the message that your children are capable and can access well-being and health. Let kids enjoy the documented health benefits of placebo and self-healing. It's good for them!

> Be careful how you talk about "health." Kids know that most of the time when people say "healthy," they mean "thin." Focus on how our bodies *feel* and what they can *do*.

That is a hopeful message! Diets don't work, but there is a lot you *can* focus on to support your child's well-being.

Tuned-In Eating, and Weight-Neutral Healthcare Support Well-being

Research shows that a weight-neutral approach and support of tuned-in eating is more effective in improving various aspects of physiological and psychological well-being than weight-centered models of eating and care.

Addressing what we do (behaviors), rather than weight, is associated with meaningful improvements in areas such as blood pressure, cholesterol, disordered eating behaviors, mood, and improved self-esteem. (You may see related eating and health frameworks described as Health at Every Size®, Intuitive Eating, Eating Competence, non-diet, or weight-neutral.) Regardless of weight, you can improve your child's odds of enjoying better health and well-being, and feeling better in their bodies

Two attuned eating constructs are supported by a growing body of research. "Intuitive Eating" is linked with: better cholesterol profiles; higher self-esteem, well-being, optimism, body appreciation, and acceptance; proactive coping skills and psychological hardiness; unconditional self-regard; pleasure from eating and variety of foods eaten; and lower internalized thinness idealization, eating disorders, and emotional eating.[56] "Eating Competence" (ecSatter) is associated with: less weight dysregulation, lower BMI, less dieting and disordered eating, better social and emotional skills, more activity, better fitness, and favorable cholesterol profiles.[57]

Beware of "Mindful" Eating

Mindful eating has been hijacked by diet culture—touted as a way to get people to slow down and pay attention... so they eat less. The implied result is weight loss. I don't recommend typical mindful-eating exercises (such as taking 10 minutes to eat a raisin with intention) with most children, especially if they are food preoccupied or experienced restriction or food insecurity. Responsive feeding will help children learn to tune in. Perhaps outside of mealtimes when children feel more secure, there are ways to explore food with taste tests, or looking closely at a grape-fruit cross-section. Approaching food with curiosity, without an agenda, is crucial.

Supporting Children in Bigger Bodies

Hillary is 14. She's always been big, with a joyful personality, and she enjoys food. Hillary is an athlete. Hillary's mom, April has worried about her weight since Hillary was a baby, but more worried about how to help Hillary have a happy life. And that meant unpacking her fears that her daughter would struggle with weight. Hillary is built like her grandmother, strong and solid; April takes more after her lean father. April watched her own mother diet and despair, lose and gain, starve and binge... her whole life. She dreams of a different future for her child.

Hillary's mom found support early on and has been feeding Hillary responsively for years. And Hillary is still in a bigger body. Mom sought resources to help Hillary deal with bullying and teasing. Hillary eats a good variety of foods, has friends, is on a travel volleyball team, and she's getting into weight lifting and track and field.

Nothing is wrong with Hillary. She's healthy and strong and supported and loved. (And there is nothing wrong with fat people who aren't healthy or athletic, everyone is worthy of love and respect.) And it's not easy to be teased. April does a lot of listening and talking, and sometimes Hillary sees a weight-neutral therapist that she can talk to when it's too hard to do that with mom.

And it's hard for April. She's gotten a lot of judgement from family (especially her mother) and friends, and even Hillary's doctor. And that sucks. Leslie Schilling, RD, author of *Feed Your Self,* works with parents of bigger kids. She says that along with supporting healthy behaviors and mental health, she also sometimes just "sits with parents in the suck."

The answer to bullying problems isn't weight loss. It's changing our culture. There are many of us in the field working to do so.

Caution with Genetic Testing

As genetic testing becomes more common, "genetic causes" for higher weight will be diagnosed more often and likely used to justify interventions such as medication and bariatric surgery. Try to access weight-neutral resources and providers. The Association for Size Diversity and Health has a growing list of providers and resources. Ragen Chastain's Weight and Healthcare Substack offers data on the interventions. (See page 221 on how genetics information can harm.)

How to Help

In addition (with some repetition) to what you've read so far in this chapter, here are more tips for helping children to connect with their bodies, and tune in to hunger and fullness cues:

- Offer unconditional support and felt safety in the body they have now, which means stopping attempts to change it.
- Find help to support mental health and address bullying.
- Support social connections, perhaps join a choir or club at school.
- Support a sense of purpose. Can he volunteer at an animal shelter, or is there a faith tradition he can lean on?
- Work toward a routine and helping kids get better sleep.
- Model wellness at all sizes, avoid shaming or weight talk.
- Nurture, reassure with enough food, and provide regular, filling meals and snacks with all kinds of foods (not just "healthy" ones).
- Don't shame her when she eats a lot or sneaks on occasion.
- Eat together when you can.
- Offer opportunities for embodied activities with movement or breathing:
    - Singing, making music, or music therapy.
    - Dancing, yoga or Tai Chi, tumbling, or Tae Kwon Do.
    - Swinging, bouncing, or spinning—an OT can provide suggestions for a child's sensory preferences if necessary.
    - Meditation or breathing exercises (find nervous-system centered and trauma-aware apps and online resources).
    - Walking a dog or playing a sport (individual or team depending on preference).
    - Learn some Tik Tok (or current popular social media) dances together.
- Therapy focused on play or somatic (body) experiences.
- Support variety in their diet by serving variety.
- Offer support if he wants to explore recipes to try.
- If she is on social media, look for non-diet, fat-positive influencers that she can relate to, particularly music or fashion pages, hikers, painters, or fat athletes, depending on her interests.

- Hold off on social media for as long as you can. Monitor and discuss use of social media, parameters, and safeguards.
- Make art or attend art therapy.

Emotions and Coping

You'll hear criticism of "emotional eating." But emotions and eating go hand in hand. We eat to celebrate and to gather, and sometimes when we are sad. Certain foods can be linked with bad memories (or good memories mixed up with grief) and trigger dysregulation; conversely, sometimes eating can help regulate. With other coping strategies and ways to be in felt safety, emotional eating can be part of a healthy relationship with food.

Amelia and Emily Nagoski (one has a doctorate in music, the other in psychology) wrote a book called *Burnout*.[58] They shared that suffering comes when we get stuck in emotions or toxic stress. The book includes practical ideas to "complete the stress response cycle," to signal that you are safe and to get unstuck. I've pulled out their top recommendations: 1) find some kind of movement; 2) breathe; 3) seek connection and social interaction; 4) laugh; 5) access affection, such as a hug; 6) cry to reset the nervous system; and 7) engage in creative expression.

While the authors are twins, they find safety in different ways. Find what works best for your child, and you.

Oral Stimulation, Coping, Self-Regulation, and Weight Worries

I'm concerned when occupational therapists (OTs) claim to treat o*esity. OTs and feeding therapists should NOT advise weight loss as a goal. If a child is soothed with oral stimulation, looking into Chewelry or other ways to meet that need can help. Eating food for soothing, stimulation, and regulation is okay. An OT may be able to help parents find ways to support nervous system regulation and offer movement that is safe and fun—without focusing on weight. (See Chapter 4 for movement.)

Helping Your Child Have a Good Relationship with Their Body

Positive body image is associated with psychological health and well-being; better self-esteem, compassion, optimism, and life satisfaction; physiological conditions; and intuitive eating and physical activity.[44]

A key protective factor is parents' support. Learn to be a safe person for your child to talk to about weight, bullying, and address it at school if it is happening. It means you may have to examine and challenge some of your beliefs about weight and health.

Virginia Sole-Smith wrote in her *Burnt Toast* Newsletter: "Your child needs radical acceptance of his body. He needs to know he'll have access to his favorite foods, even if you're serving less-preferred options alongside them. He needs time to pursue the activities he loves without worrying that they aren't physical enough. He also needs space and support to explore ways he might enjoy moving his body—but he won't feel safe doing that if he's worrying about what his body represents to you, or to other people around him."[59]

And *body-positivity isn't enough*. It's hard to will yourself into loving your body if it's not thin, white, and able-bodied in a culture that prizes that as the ideal. Self-love won't make others treat fat people better or grant them access to compassionate and competent healthcare. It's important for healthcare providers to challenge their biases, as well as the rest of us who may be teachers, bosses, co-workers, neighbors, friends, and family.

Finding Clothes That Fit

Sometimes a barrier to kids participating in activities they love is finding comfortable clothes that fit. It's hard to find plus-sized clothing for kids, but it's getting better. One example is the company Ember and Ace that specializes in active wear. They also have a plus-sized kids (PSK) shopping guide with tips and recommended brands.

Challenging Our Weight Bias

Even if you believe your child can be bigger and healthy, raising a bigger-than-average or fat child in a fat-biased culture, more than any other issue I've worked with, gets to the core of worthiness and what it means to be *enough*. When kids get bigger or aren't slimming down, "It's another way parents think they have failed, or the child has failed," therapist Dawn Friedman explains.

"We start with an understanding that parents love their children totally. And they need a place where they can say out loud their secret fears, 'I'm afraid my child will be ugly,' 'will my child be loved,' and even, 'can I say I was a good parent if I have a chubby child?'" It's incredibly challenging work in a culture that judges parents for what and how much kids eat and weigh. I can hold their anxiety with them about their child having second or third helpings."

Dawn loves her work with children, but finds that, "If parents are stuck in wanting children to eat and weigh less, it's hard to make progress." Sometimes, she shares, parents are able to dig into their own histories. Many mothers recall that their first negative experiences with body image, and the first of many diets, was at around age 10 to 11. Sometimes when parents are able to make these connections for themselves, they can imagine a different path for their children.

And parents may need to grieve when they realize that their child is likely to stay fat: "It takes a while for parents to realize that they can't control their kids' bodies," Dawn says. But she adds there *is* something parents can do, and that is to "contribute to how the child feels about their body." And children who feel good about their bodies tend to treat them better, to move more and have healthier habits, less dieting and disordered eating, and to be happier.

Dawn recommends that parents and teens (depending on social media access), follow body-positive and fat-positive pages (not just thin influencers who slouch to prove that they too have stomach rolls). "At first, seeing fat people in beautiful clothes, laughing on the beach, or in bikinis may feel challenging, but you get used to the images, and learn to see the worth and beauty in everyone."

It's a matter of "retraining" our brains and biases. Addressing our automatic negative feelings around bigger bodies can help with the anxiety when a child has a second serving, or trust the process of allowing a child to have dessert with dinner. (Consider taking the Harvard Implicit Bias test.)

It's why Dawn's office is filled with images of Wonder Woman represented in all sizes. "It's a great way to begin those conversations. There is so much internalized fear and loathing of fat bodies, even the children will say, 'I don't like that Wonder Woman; she's fat.' Then we can begin to explore that. Not shame, but explore those feelings and how they make sense in our culture, and we can begin to challenge that."

Parents often benefit from working on negative feelings toward their own bodies. Sometimes finding the empathy and compassion for their children is a door into their own healing.

A resource if you're understandably struggling with this section is the book *How to Raise an Intuitive Eater: Raising the Next Generation with Food and Body Confidence* by eating disorder specialists and dietitians Sumner Brooks and Amee Severson. They offer compassionate support around challenging weight bias. They also share words you can use with your children. For example, "We live in a world that sometimes wants us to feel unlovable. What do you need right now to feel comfortable in your body? What can I/we do to help you? Above everything else, I want you to know I'm here for you and I love you in your body today."[60]

Higher Weight and Medical Issues

I'm adding a few specific medical issues to the section of caring for kids in bigger bodies. Higher weight children and teens are told to do things for weight that would be diagnosed as eating disordered behavior in a thin body. Needed care may be delayed until "weight loss" is tried, or helpful care (such as medications) are denied if a side effect may be weight gain.

A useful question to ask may be, "What would you recommend if my child was slim?" (Also see "Tips for Navigating the Medical System" on page 341.) Ragen Chastain and others offer online support on advocating for medical care for higher-weight folks.

Medications and Weight Gain

When medication causes weight gain, it is complex and painful to navigate in our culture. There is no easy answer. I remember a discussion with a school-based support professional who said they had a teen boy who was blossoming on a medication and therapy: He was happier, no longer violent, catching up on schoolwork, and making friends. Unfortunately, the medical team took him off this medication because he gained 40 pounds into the o*ese range. The support professional was heartbroken, as the student again became easily dysregulated and his violent behaviors returned. He was convinced that this young man was heading toward a life in and out of prison. As the teacher saw it, the medical team would rather accept the possibility of juvenile detention, than allow him to live in a fat body.

This is not an isolated example. Fat adults have shared online how they encounter practitioners who think the side effect of weight gain is worse than the suicidality the medication was helping with.

If your child/teen is on medications that increase appetite and/or lead to weight gain, felt safety is still the priority. Apply what you're learning in this chapter. It is reasonable to explore if there are medications that could be effective that may have less of an impact on weight, or when it is safe to taper off medications. Having conversations around mental health and well-being, and not removing medications due to weight without a thorough look at the whole child is a minimum. Weight-neutral resources can help, and are often still hard to find.

Medical Challenges

I've heard a mom say, "Well, now that my daughter has prediabetes we need to get her to lose weight." While the fear is real, and the temptation to look for a solution in weight loss is a pull that's hard to resist, we do not have safe ways to achieve weight loss long-term. (Weight neutral care supports health without weight loss as a goal. Sometimes weight stays on a similar trajectory, sometimes it settles in at a different centile.)

Higher-weight teens diagnosed with steatohepatitis (fatty liver) have been put on 1200 calorie a day diets, which is less than inmates in Guantanamo Bay Prison are allowed to be fed. Very low-calorie diets harm. Decades of research show that they fail, and this teen will likely end up more depressed, angry, heavier, at far higher risk of an eating disorder, and less connected with her family. This is bad healthcare (and unlikely to meaningfully lower liver disease risk over time).

Brooks and Severson sum up a weight-neutral, and I believe more medically sound, approach in their book, *How to Raise an Intuitive Eater:* "If there is a nutritional concern, inadequate nutrient intake, medical diagnosis, or disordered eating, those can all be addressed from a weight-neutral approach. This means we don't ignore health and medical concerns simply because weight loss isn't the answer; we find ways of actually addressing the health concern, separate from assuming weight loss is the best thing, because we know that intentionally pursuing weight loss is harmful for children of all ages. It poses a risk in and of itself for worse health outcomes down the line."[61]

As the popular endocrinologist Gregory Dodell, MD, shared on his Instagram @everything_endocrine: "Treat people, not numbers." Remember that centering felt safety and connection supports health, as we reviewed in Chapter 2.

It's Okay to Like Food or Need Reassurance

You may have sensed intuitively that trying to get your child to eat less to weigh less isn't helping, and now you have a roadmap for a better way forward. As with the chapter on low appetite and picky eating, I end here with a reminder that children who get pleasure from food and enjoy eating, are likely to grow into adults who do the same. They may plan weekend trips based on restaurants they want to try, or enjoy menu planning. There's nothing to fear about getting pleasure from food; shame and guilt are far more damaging.

Children who have been food preoccupied may always have some residual focus or anxiety around being fed and need a granola bar or a snack within reach all their lives. This is especially profound if there has been an experience of food insecurity. Dieting can produce similar lingering anxieties.

For example, I was mildly restricted and teased by my family about my weight, starting with my puberty weight gain, and occasionally dieted through my twenties. To this day, I need to know when and where I will be eating or I experience anxiety. It took my husband a while to understand that that's just how I am; I'm not going to be on a trip away from home and just wing it with meals! And, I always have snacks on hand just in case. I'm also a super taster (which I found out thanks to my high schooler's biology class genetics section!) and I just really enjoy the pleasure associated with food. And that's all totally fine.

Common Questions and Challenges

As we wrap up this chapter, here are additional common obstacles you might face.

- *"She eats so fast. Can we tell her to slow down so her tummy can catch up?"* When a child is told to slow down, it can trigger anxiety and they eat faster. If that is what you observe, be patient. Try to eat at a comfortable pace yourself. With time, rapid eating or stuffing usually improves on its own. Support your child so they can eat in felt safety if possible. Sometimes, if overstuffing doesn't get better with reliable feeding, it could be sensory-seeking behavior; maybe serve a fizzy drink or crunchy foods to offer additional input. If you worry about choking, talk with them away from mealtimes and brainstorm some ideas: maybe cutting food into smaller pieces, or having a smaller "serving plate" that they can take smaller amounts of food from.
- *"But I don't want him to wrestle with his weight like I did. Will he lose weight if we do this?"* Maybe. Maybe not. Responsive feeding is likely to lead to more stable weight. Some children will still be fat, while some will grow into thinner bodies. RF and a non-diet approach helps children avoid dieting and potentially years of weight cycling, which tends to lead to weight gain over time and a whole lot of suffering, health complications, and wasted energy. Consider: If your child continues to be restricted, food-preoccupied, and bingeing when he gets the chance, what do you see for their future rela-

tionship with food and their body? Review the section on supporting children in bigger bodies and look for support.

- *"Do we sit with her the entire time? She keeps eating and eating after we finish, so one of us (sometimes both) gets up to start clearing dishes."* Play it by ear. At eating times, try to be available for connection. Eat with her or sit with some tea and chat; then life goes on, and if you need to load the dishwasher, you can. You are still available for connection. A food-preoccupied child might sit and nibble for hours. *When* you cut off meals is up to you. A general guideline is that 20 minutes or so is adequate for snacks; 30–40 minutes for meals. If you need to get moving sooner, your child will know the difference in terms of your motives. It feels different to her to hear, "Dinner is almost over," versus, "You've had enough!" Children may need lots of repetition and teaching. Prepare her in advance for transitions: "In five minutes we'll go do some coloring." She may eat more rapidly with the warning, but that's okay. Over time she will trust that you aren't trying to get her to eat less.
- *"She will say she is done, then when we carry her plate to the sink or if there are scraps we want to put in the trash, she panics."* Throwing out food can trigger anxiety. This should improve with time. Try these ideas: put the scraps in a container even if you end up throwing them out later; allow her to cover her plate and put it in the fridge, or save leftover food for the next meal or snack. One family had success when their child would "feed the plants" and put the scraps into a composter.
- *"She always asks for more, even after eating a huge amount."* She may be testing to see if you mean it when you say, "You can eat until you're done." I have heard from so many clients that the urge to cut the child off is strong, but that often after giving the child more, she takes a bite or two and declares she is full. The important thing is that *she* decides how much she eats.

Planning a favored activity for right after mealtimes can help end meals with less distress as children learn to trust they will get enough. "In five minutes we'll go feed the chickens (or watch Disney)."

- *"My toddler has a huge belly. People comment on how fat he looks."* If there seems to be pain or discomfort or your child is constipated or has gut symptoms, contact your child's doctor. However, many healthy children can look "pregnant." Smaller than average children can have a round belly too. Children have relatively underdeveloped abdominal muscles. If your child has low muscle tone in general, this can look more pronounced. Find stretchy pants and tops that allow movement. Most children will outgrow this by grade school. My friend Elizabeth laughs at her gymnastics photos from when she was eight, with muscular arms and legs and her round little belly. And if your child has belly fat, see earlier in this chapter for supporting kids in bigger bodies. I also recommend lots of belly kisses, blowing raspberries, and laughter—which is great for strengthening abdominal muscles.

- *"I'm scared to let her have her snack with as much as she wants of her favorites like cheese or cookies."* When you try that "high-interest food snack," she will probably eat large amounts at first. Consider serving it with a favorite fruit or vegetable if that helps you feel better. She will be okay with high-fat foods, and she does need access to formerly "forbidden foods" at meals and snacks. Maybe start with something you find less scary, such as homemade oatmeal raisin cookies versus Oreos. You need to feel comfortable with this process as well, but if you have trouble serving your child high-interest foods, you may want to examine your own eating and attitudes (Chapter 12).
- *"Even if he ate until he was 'done,' he'll say, 'I'm hungry' if he's bored or anxious."* This is an almost automatic response. (See wagon wheel rut callout on page 58.) Remember, it may have been a big part of his life to worry about food, or a reliable way to self-soothe. Like those wagon ruts in Chapter 3, until he's had time to develop new ways of relating to food and trusting he will be fed, the automatic response may be the anxious and seeking one. Avoid, "You can't be hungry, you just ate!" Reassure him that snack time is "soon," and redirect to another activity. You can always offer some food if this doesn't help. When kids who experienced food insecurity or restriction are bored, stressed, dysregulated, or even anxious about being hungry in the future, they commonly default to "I'm hungry."
- *"If we give her a pudding pop or a couple Oreos with her meal, and she wants more, do we give it to her?"* Dessert with the meal is usually one portion. "That's your share, and we'll have (that dessert) again soon. If you're still hungry, you can have more corn, potatoes, or chicken." This typically ends up being pretty quickly accepted, or met with an age-appropriate upset. However, if your sensitive child is going to have a 90-minute meltdown over it, use your judgment. Journal around what happened and see if you may need to increase access to sweets, add more calming activities before eating, or remind about expectations pre-meal.
- *"He acts out more now at the table."* Some of my clients have been dismayed at new behavior issues, such as throwing utensils. This could be a positive. Free from the anxiety and stress around food, he can now interact with others at the table. Part of that means testing *other* boundaries. Use your "time-in" or whatever your preferred teaching and connection strategy is. If she protests over food, you can say, "I'm sorry you're sad we aren't having rice. We'll have rice again soon." As Dr. Dan Siegel says, "Connect then redirect." If she needs help calming down and co-regulating, you can do that, and then let her finish the meal. Ask your therapist for support and suggestions if you need help.

- *"He still seems anxious that he won't get enough."* Use simple reassurance such as, "There's always more if you're hungry." Don't get too caught up in words; actions over time matter most. And he may grow up to be an adult who likes to know when and where he will eat, find that an empty pantry triggers anxiety, and always needs a snack tucked in his bag, or car. That's okay!
- *"What do we do when he eats several servings, says he's 'done,' gets down, and then when we start cleaning up he says 'more dinner?'"* Short answer: When eating is over, it's over. You might try to remind him before he gets down, with something like, "That was yummy. We'll eat again soon." When he comes back for food, you can say, "Lunch is over, we'll eat again soon. Let's play." You can look at the dry-erase board with the times and menu. It is different from, "You've had enough!" You are doing your job, which is having a flexible routine. He is figuring out the new way of doing things. If he's getting dysregulated, consider the "stash" as you read earlier, or offer him food. Often this is an anxious "wagon rut" response (page 58) that will improve with time and as he forms new ways of thinking about food.
- *"He won't eat a lot of the vegetables he used to eat. Can I make him eat those? I know he likes them."* Becoming more picky is common, but frustrating. It's a positive sign. Children who frantically ate everything now feel secure enough to have preferences, and can consider what they like and don't like; becoming more like their peers. Review Chapters 5 and 6 on picky eating. Making them eat veggies is prone to backfire. Keep serving them without pressure and they will likely come back to most of them!
- *"What if she wants more shrimp, but I want my share? If I say 'no,' will that trigger her anxiety?"* You are important too, so if you want some, you can have it. She is going to learn to share and will know the difference between being told, "You can't have more because you've had enough," versus, "Poppa likes shrimp, too. I'm sorry you're sad there isn't more for everyone. There's more rice if you're still hungry." (Sometimes, when a child sees that you are going to finish something, the resulting "scarcity" effect may lead to them trying a new food.) You can model asking if you can finish something, such as, "Does anyone mind if I finish the shrimp?" I thought it was a hoot when my then four-year-old used the phrase she learned from her cousins, "Am I depriving anybody if I finish the shrimp?" Find your own words. Acknowledge feelings of disappointment. And sometimes you'll feel like giving her your share.
- *"Maggie wakes up groggy, and we don't have time for breakfast. I worry she'll feel restricted if we hurry her."* Rushing at breakfast won't spoil your other efforts. She will get that she is fed reliably; it's not you trying to get her to eat less. (See pages 128-129 for breakfast tips.)

- *"He vomited last week after overeating pizza. Come to think of it, we did miss snack that day."* He will "overeat" and, rarely, vomit. It's not common, but it happens (more in the beginning). Try to be calm if it does. It can be part of the learning. If he is vomiting frequently, be sure there isn't a medical reason. Look again at structure and make sure he's not feeling restricted (are you giving a look, sighing when he has seconds, or is he overhearing you talking about his eating, etc.?). I have not seen eating to the point of vomiting continue to be a problem once children are fed reliably and in a responsive way.

Part 2:

Filling in the Gaps:

Common Pitfalls and Navigating Healing

Part I introduced the positive impacts of felt safety and responsive feeding, including with low appetite and selective eating, low-weight worries, food preoccupation, worries about accelerating weight, and supporting kids in bigger bodies.

Part II addresses a variety of issues that parents commonly grapple with. These include: the effect of feelings, the concept of food addiction, nutrition education, feeding stages and day-to-day challenges, shoring up resilience, the impact of a parent's eating history, common nutrition worries, feeding responsively with a special diet, and much more.

Chapter 8
The Eating and Feeding Experience: Mindset, Food Addiction, Shame, and More

Now that you've got the basics of responsive feeding down, including with challenges, there are still plenty of ways that families get stuck. From the idea of food addiction to nutrition education, emotions and eating, your own eating history, and interoception, this chapter offers additional strategies to help you feed with more confidence.

Tuned-In Eating and the Food Attitude

Tuned-in eating is not measured in calories, micronutrients, or sugar avoidance. Rather, it describes how we relate to food and our bodies, and our attitudes and habits related to how we provide ourselves with food. Two constructs briefly mentioned earlier are Eating Competence (EC) and Intuitive Eating (IE).

Research in adults shows that those who score as "eating competent" had better blood sugar measures and cholesterol levels, and tended to have a lower BMI—in spite of higher energy intake.[1] EC adults tend to diet less and have more stable BMI (measured in the research), eat a more balanced intake, experience less disordered eating, and enjoy better nutrition.[2] Research on IE shows similar benefits.[3]

And responsive feeding is a way to raise children to be adults who relate to food and their bodies in more compassionate and healthy ways.

Feeding *You*

One thing we haven't talked much about is the importance of modeling a positive relationship with food and body. Put another way, your children watch what you *do*, as much or more than what you say. You matter; not only because your modeling teaches children how to value themselves, *but because you just do*. You deserve to feel better about food and your body as well.

Plan on feeding yourself a variety of tasty and filling foods at regular intervals as best you can. The good news is that because you are already doing the same thing for your child, or working toward it, you can hopefully join in.

You, too, have inborn capabilities with food. Those capabilities might be buried from years of dieting, a history of an eating disorder or food insecurity, or struggling to have enough food now, but those capabilities are there.

Michelle Allison, a Canadian nutritionist and author, on her blog at *The Fat Nutritionist*, described that learning to feed her body with trust has, ". . . meant a lot of letting go of external rules and expectations around nutrition, and finding my own guidelines. I've discovered that I have a real, internal desire to do things that are good for my body, and that I don't need a drill sergeant to 'get' me to do anything. I will actually eat vegetables on my own, but I will also call it good enough. My focus is on preserving my long-term relationship with vegetables instead of force-feeding myself in the moment."

When you consider and work toward tuning in to *your* hunger and appetite, acknowledge pleasure, and turn your back on shame and deprivation, you are more likely to enjoy improved nutrition and health, and feel better in your body.

One of the most exciting aspects of working with families is that the child's eating can motivate parents to grow curious about their own relationships with food.

After Halloween, a comment posted on my Facebook page said it all: *"Honestly, watching him manage his stash so well has totally changed how I view candy too, for the better. No more bingeing because it's there. If I want a piece, I choose my favorite and actually enjoy it."*

If You're Neurodivergent or Have a Sensitive Nervous System

As Margie messaged me on Instagram, *"I'm autistic and anosmic* (total or partial lack of sense of smell) *and I love, love, love your content—for my actual child and my own inner child, your content has been beyond helpful! Thank you!"* You may be autistic or an "ADHDer," or experience differences around executive functioning, appetite signals, and more. Perhaps the content in this book can give you insight into your childhood and how you feel about food now, as well as help you understand and support your child.

See meal planning tips that support neurodivergent parents (Chapter 10), and more on interoception and external support later in this chapter, if you find that tuned-in eating is challenging or new. Increasingly, there are resources that support neurodivergent adults who want to work on their eating.

How We Think and Feel About Food Matters

Eating enjoyment is a "central aspect" of how and why children eat.[4] Goal one for many families is improving the atmosphere at mealtimes—finding and rediscovering joy and connection.

You've learned that stress can sabotage appetite. Think about the last time you were afraid or anxious. Perhaps you don't like flying. Are you hungry on a plane during turbulence? Hungry before a presentation at work?

A focus on felt safety and connection is another way of thinking about the atmosphere at the table.

Another piece of the puzzle is that those who restrict or diet tend to eat *more* in response to stress.[5,6,7] Some are soothed by eating certain foods, others aren't. Being responsive means you can handle it either way.

How We Think About Food Impacts Appetite, Physiology and More

Feeling good, or good enough about food, improves health and nutrition. This sampling of studies illustrates how our thinking affects how we relate to food, and even how nutrients are absorbed.

First, how I think of these terms (simplified definitions):

- Appetite: The desire to eat or drink, based on smell, how food looks and tastes, culture, past experiences, time of day, and so much more.
- Hunger: The physical need for food to sustain energy and bodily functions.
- Satiety or satisfaction: The feeling of being done, or satisfied after eating or drinking, usually after hunger and appetite have been met.

Consider the "Mind Over Milkshakes"[8] study. Participants were given *the same shake* and told on the first occasion that it was "sensible" and fat-free. Another time, they were told that it was rich, fatty, and "indulgent." Guess which time they thought *tasted* better? Answer: when they thought it was "indulgent." No surprise there. Interestingly, despite identical calories, fat, and nutrients, what the study participants *thought* about the shake affected the body's measured hormone response.

A mindset of "indulgence" meant lower hunger-hormone (ghrelin) levels after drinking the shake, and presumably, less hunger. A perception of "sensible" (might trigger a feeling of deprivation), meant that the "hungry-hormone" level did not fall as much.

When we have to use willpower to get through the day, many of us feel deprived, which triggers a sense of craving. How we *think* about food affects how much we enjoy it and how our bodies respond. The authors concluded, "Mindset meaningfully affects physiological responses to food."

Mindset also affects food choices. When one study's participants were told they were eating "low-fat" or "low-calorie" foods, even if they were the high-fat and calorie versions, they reliably ate *more* for the rest of the day, presumably to make up for those "lost" calories.[9] This is known as the "halo" effect (people think they are being good). Even the "organic" label makes people tend to eat more.

Another indication that our thinking brains might get in the way of our bodies' wisdom, is that nutrition knowledge doesn't translate into better nutrition. A study comparing citizens from France and the United States found that the Americans scored significantly higher on nutrient knowledge, but it didn't translate into eating in a more balanced way. The authors wrote, "Consumers might lose sight of the 'big picture' when it comes to nutritional information and become consumers of nutrients instead of food . . . the 'nutrient approach' might further confuse consumers. . ."[10]

Kids are susceptible too. A study titled "If it's Useful and You Know It, Do You Eat?"[11] is described in the Substack article from Laura Thomas PhD: "Why Teaching Kids That Food Is 'Healthy' Can Backfire." (Read the whole thing for more research and analysis.) She summarized the study with this, "The researchers concluded that **not only did telling kids that food was healthy stop them from eating the food in the moment, it signaled that they were less likely to want to eat it in the future."**[12]

These studies contribute to our understanding of why cognitive (thinking/mindset) control and external rules can be an obstacle to eating well.

Pleasure and Taste Affect How Food Is Used and Absorbed in the Body

Stress and a food's appeal play a role in absorption of nutrients. Take these often quoted studies: First, Swedish women were fed a meal of spicy Thai food; a group of women from Thailand were given the same meal. The Thai women, who presumably enjoyed the flavor more, absorbed more iron. Further, when the meals were pureed, presumably making for a less pleasurable way of taking in the same food, absorption of iron decreased across the board.[13]

Another study showed that minerals were absorbed less well when the participant was stressed, versus under calm circumstances.[14]

You learned in Chapter 2 that when we are stressed and dysregulated, our digestive system doesn't work as well, and there are impacts on our heart rate, blood pressure, thyroid, and insulin hormones. Stress also likely impacts how nutrients are absorbed and metabolized.

Understanding that stress and emotions play a role may help you stay focused on felt safety as a way to support nutrition and wellness.

How We Think About Health (Placebo and Nocebo) Matters

The previous examples show us that we can't separate the brain from the body. Our bodies have healing wisdom that we can try to help our children tap into (or at minimum not undermine). You've probably heard of the placebo effect. It's very powerful. For many conditions such as depression, anxiety, functional gut problems like irritable bowel syndrome, chronic pain, blood pressure, even Parkinson's dementia, the placebo effect may account for 15 to 60 percent of *improvement* in clinical trials. (Feeling better when given the "sugar pill" or placebo, and not the medication or treatment being tested.)[15]

There is even research showing that when people know they are taking a sugar pill (open-label placebo), they still feel better![16] Humans are amazing!

Just having a healthcare provider be kind and enthusiastic about a treatment can lead to improved outcomes.[17] We could think of the placebo effect as a positive health mindset.

The flip side of placebo is nocebo. Essentially, this is a negative health mindset where someone who believes they will have a symptom, poor outcome, or side effect is more likely to have that experience.[17] It helps explain why study participants experience unpleasant side effects even when they unknowingly take a sugar pill or receive an injection of inactive salt water instead of the vaccine in a clinical trial.

A study in the New York Times called "Mind May Trump DNA" showed that when adults were given fake DNA results suggesting (falsely) that they were prone to o*esity and also more likely to have poor exercise tolerance, their bodies responded accordingly. So after a meal for example, their measurable hormone levels associated with hunger and fullness changed (ghrelin again). They also had decreased measured oxygen efficiency and lung capacity on exercise testing.[18]

Especially for those in bigger bodies, weight-biased doctors repeatedly warn that they will likely die young, get diabetes and heart disease... (I was one of those doctors trying to scare my patients into losing weight. I'm sorry.) A weight-centered medical and feeding model effectively robs higher-weight patients of placebo healing and may harm them with an overdose of nocebo.

Maybe trying to take care of ourselves and our children from a place of fear interferes with the healing powers our bodies possess? The placebo/nocebo effects may deprive us of the healing of felt safety. (See page 176 on Gabi's son who seemed to do worse after visiting doctors.) This is why I try to focus on capabilities and what we can control, and reject the standard line that health and weight are the same, when it is far more complex (see Chapter 7). Assume your child will do well. Avoid scare tactics to try to motivate them to take care of themselves. It may make them *less* healthy. Help them learn to critically deal with these messages that will come from others, school, media etc.

"Moderation" Is Sneaky

While these days you're more likely to hear, "We don't diet," it may be followed with, "We just eat in moderation." However, trying to eat in "moderation" doesn't result in weight loss or improved nutrition for most people. Consider a study of teens, in which even "sensible" weight management tactics, such as trying to eat more fruits and veggies or drinking more water, resulted in heavier teens with more disordered behaviors.[19] How can this be, when moderation seems so, well, *moderate*? (See page 178 on subtle restriction.)

To most people, "moderation" in terms of food means eating less quantity or fewer of the foods you enjoy most. You never hear anyone say, "Eat broccoli in moderation." "Eat cookies in moderation" makes me want more, almost like that food-insecure child. If I tell myself, "Sit down with as many cookies as you want, with a glass of milk, and enjoy them," I'm usually satisfied with two. And if they're fresh out of the oven and taste amazing, I might eat three or four and be satisfied. Maybe at the next opportunity, I will have less of an appetite for cookies.

Ironically, responsive feeding and tuned-in eating results in less extreme patterns of intake. Moderation is the result, not the sneaky diet-culture code word for "eat less."

Food Is Not Addictive

One common objection to the idea of trusting ourselves and our kids with food is that processed foods are engineered to taste so delicious that they overwhelm our taste buds; brain reward-circuitry takes over, and we have no control. In effect, we *can't* eat in a tuned-in way because these foods are too powerful and *addictive* (see Chapter 7). Yes, these foods are designed to maximize sensory input, but in my experience (and others), it is mindset (again!) that matters most.

I've experienced people who beat their "junk food addiction" not with abstinence, but with *permission*. My own out-of-control drive for Doritos (really anything covered in orange nacho-cheese-flavored powder) went away with permission and banishing the shame. It's just another food.

Virginia Sole–Smith tackled this subject in "So, What About Processed Foods" in her Newsletter. She described how these foods are sometimes eaten, sometimes go stale at home with her two children. "I want to be clear: The victory here is not that my children turn down processed foods. The victory is that they don't feel out of control around these foods. They don't feel compelled to eat them just because they're there—which is what everyone assumes will happen when you have a mountain of processed foods on hand."[20] The power we give a food may matter more than the food itself. Sole–Smith writes, ". . . your emotional relationship to that food is much more about access and permission than it is about flavor."

Christy Harrison, MPH, RD, wrote in *Anti-Diet*, "Chronic dieters do eat more in the presence of highly palatable food. They're also more susceptible to food advertising, and we see more brain activity in response to sweet foods. But people who are not restrained eaters do not show the same response. Their pleasure centers still light up, but there isn't this immense reward in their brains, because they haven't experienced that immense deprivation."[21]

Lisa Du Breuil LCSW, a social worker who treats eating disorders at Massachusetts General Hospital and in private practice, also uses the phrase "Abundance + Permission=Discernment." I found this was the case for me. When I ate a Whopper for the first time with a total permission mindset, I realized I didn't like it very much (I prefer Big Macs). And sometimes Doritos hit the spot and I eat a lot, and other times bags go stale in my pantry.

Take a moment to consider a food that you tend to eat in an out-of-control way. Journal about your history with that food. Explore what giving yourself permission might feel like.

How Kids Think About "Healthy" and Veggies

Aside from the fact that vegetables tend to be more bitter and have complex textures, maybe part of the reason why kids don't seem to like veggies is that we oversell them, prepare them plain because it's "healthier," talk about nutrition, and bribe with dessert. They probably think that veggies are bad if we work so hard to convince them, or if they have to slog through veggies to get to the "good" stuff. Rather than teaching children to rely on the body's natural drive for variety and pleasure, these tactics mess with mindset and get in the way. And remember that even when we label foods they like, such as crackers, as "healthy," they choose them less often.

Ironically, the last sentence of the "Mind Over Milkshakes" study said: "Perhaps if we can begin to approach even the healthiest foods with a mindset of indulgence, we will experience the physiological satisfaction of having our cake and eating it too."[8] This still smacks of trying to manipulate messaging to *get* folks to eat "healthy." We aren't tricked that easily. Slapping an "indulgent" label on a carrot isn't the answer.

When we approach foods informed by internal drives of pleasure, curiosity, seeking variety, and eating with joy, a piece of cake may hit the spot one day, and a juicy mango, or yes, a crunchy salad, can also satisfy. Rejecting labels of "good," "bad," "healthy," or "unhealthy," frees the wisdom of our bodies from being spoiled by mindset.

Helping Kids Have a Healthy Relationship with Food

An alarming trend, worse since the first edition of this book, is increasingly common and harmful nutrition "education" for children—in schools, at home, on children's programs, and in social media. It's everywhere. Consider a kids' coloring activity at a local farmer's market, which asked: "What is the healthiest option (fewest calories)?" and had the children chose from:

- Fruit salad plain
- Fruit salad with 2 tablespoons of orange juice
- Fruit salad with ½ cup of low-fat yogurt

My daughter's recent high school health class suggested that losing 40 pounds was a simple matter of setting goals! (My eating disorder colleagues were as horrified as I was. We all know children and teens with serious eating disorders triggered by school assignments.) All too often, the information presented to children by untrained adults is simplistic and wrong; demonizes fat, sugar, calories, or food in general; and is not presented in age-appropriate ways.

Even other children get in on the action; my daughter reported one day that two of her kindergarten friends told her she would get fat because she drank 1% milk and it had "too much fat." Poorly conceived programs in schools have peers rewarding "healthy" eating, which invites bullying and shame (what if the child rewarded for eating a plain salad is in the throes of anorexia?). You may need to be proactive and learn about what your kids are taught in school, or messages they may get from billboards, TV, etc.

Nutrition Messaging Unfairly Burdens Children

Michele Gorman, RD, cares deeply about food messaging to children. She shares her story: "My father, a blue-collar man, raised his children with little help. He worked a lot and made sure we had food in the cupboard. My early recollections of food are simply that it was just part of life. We never heard messages about being too fat or too thin, we were simply told we were loved, and eating at the table was a requirement, even if it was pasta or cereal. Looking back now, I see what an accomplishment that was. I remember clearly learning about the food groups in second grade. Already feeling like an outsider since all of my schoolmates were raised with a mom, I panicked and intuitively felt that something else was wrong with my family—we didn't eat that way. We had cola, sugar cereals, and not many vegetables. **I felt a lot of shame, fear, and somehow responsibility beyond what a seven-year-old should feel. Looking back, I wish that I didn't take the burden of worry.**"

Teaching Nutrition

Instead of supporting healthy attitudes toward food, schools encourage six-year-olds to count calories and give extra credit for weight loss, and youth sports teams sponsor sugar-free challenges. Children are taught to fear sodium, fat, sugar, gluten, meat, or anything nonorganic. The focus on what they can't eat, the shame, and the extreme attention to body size, gets in the way of attuned eating and thriving.

Was it "irresponsible," as one mom accused me, to skip nutrition lectures with my preschooler? Remember, Americans already have a pretty good sense about "nutrition" while we struggle with actual eating, and healthy labels make foods less appealing to kids. Anna Lutz, RD, eating disorder specialist and cofounder of Sunnyside Up Nutrition, is working to reform harmful nutrition education. She shares, "We can teach children about nutrition without creating fear, shame, and guilt about food. As parents, it's important to protect our children from diet-filled and developmentally inappropriate information about food and bodies." Even correct nutrition concepts are abstract, and children are concrete thinkers until about middle school. This means they can misinterpret messages in harmful ways.

Our current cultural climate around food raises kids who do not trust (note I did not say, cannot trust) their bodies around food.

We don't really need to teach "nutrition" so much as help children learn about food and eating as one aspect of being human, most of which is learned through experience, rather than talking or lessons.

Positive, Age-Appropriate Ways to Teach About Food

- Young children, up through grade school, can learn that a banana grows on a tree, but don't need to know the word "carbohydrate."

- Teach children and teens about where food comes from and let them experience different foods in neutral, pressure-free ways.
- Teach about food in a fun, positive way, stressing taste, cultural significance, and cooking.
- Talk about foods (if at all) in neutral terms without linking to weight or judgment.
- For middle school and above, discuss modifiable behaviors, such as not skipping meals, or stress reduction, rather than factors kids have little control over, such as weight or what is served.[22]
- Respect, teach about, and celebrate body diversity.
- Promote self-esteem and healthy body image.
- Provide opportunities for fun physical activity.
- Model taking care of yourself by making time to nourish yourself with food.
- Focus on what bodies can do, rather than on how they look.
- Wait to teach the concepts of nutrition in regard to health until late middle school or high school, while still not teaching "good" and "bad" food concepts. (Even then, keep an eye on your child's curriculum. Much of the material out there is harmful.)
- Teach media literacy in age appropriate ways (identifying fat-bias in books and TV shows etc.).

Dietitians 4 Teachers is an online resource with age-specific lessons for schools and support for parents. Sunnyside Up Nutrition is another, with letters for teachers and more.

What Not to Do in Nutrition Education

- Condemn cultural food differences, such as, "white rice, fried plantains, or tortillas are unhealthy."
- Judge children around food, such as you're "good" if you eat this and "bad" if you don't.
- Incite shame or fear, as in, "If you don't eat (or avoid) ______ , you can get sick."
- It's not okay to pressure or make children eat any food. For example, a farm-to-school presenter I talked with required children to taste and swallow food out of "respect to the farmer." Even a sticker for tasting a food can pressure anxious eaters.
- Use stigmatizing language such as o*erweight or o*esity.
- Use "fat is bad" messaging, such as "fat people eat too much," or "fat people eat the 'wrong' foods."
- Teach children that weight gain is bad. It is a sign of health for children to gain and grow.

- Comment on what children are eating or not eating.
- Talk negatively about your own or others' bodies, or model dieting behaviors.

Poor body image, shame, and fear increase behaviors such as dieting and disordered eating, which contribute to eating disorders and weight dysregulation.[22,23]

Emotions, Internal Motivation, and Eating

This section introduces some of the elements where emotions and eating intersect, and how you can increase the odds that eating will be part of a healthy and joyful life for your child (or at a minimum, less negative). Since emotions and sensations such as hunger and fullness are experienced in the body, we will also explore interoception.

"Emotional" Eating

The advice to separate emotions from eating is impossible. Culturally, we eat together to celebrate holidays or share a meal on a date. Feeding a child is a loving act, which enhances emotional attachment not only by meeting their physical needs, but also by sharing in food preparation, perhaps the ritual and culture of a family meal, and the pleasant aromas and flavors. Think about how a particular dish or even smell might bring back a flood of wonderful memories of a treasured aunt.

And, eating a warm, delicious chocolate chip cookie can make us feel good, and that is okay. Eating two or three can make us feel good. Eating a dozen, while not being aware while we are doing it, is not an ideal way to enjoy cookies—or deal with emotions.

To try to make eating *just* about hunger, fullness, and nutrition is unrealistic and joyless, and probably makes us less healthy.

People of all shapes and sizes use food as a coping option. Problems can arise if eating is one of the only tools a person has to deal with, or avoid, difficult emotions. Secret eating or eating that feels shameful or out of control, is more troublesome. This can lead to the restrict and binge cycle: restriction leads to out-of-control-eating (binge) which leads to shame and restriction, back to another binge… and repeat.

Coping using food is resilient. Healing from coping behaviors that no longer serve us is possible.

Interoception Awareness and Gentle Support

Consistent and responsive feeding supports interoception (the body's experience of internal senses and signals such as hunger, appetite, and emotions as well). I do not recommend specific coaching around feeling full or hungry for the vast majority of children and even teens; it can confuse them and make matters worse. Especially for kids in bigger bodies, they may not want to "admit" they are hungry after hearing comments such as, "You can't still feel hungry after two pieces of pizza!?" (See page 198 for more on rating hunger.)

Supporting interoception awareness is about curiosity and discovery. If it is driven by an agenda to try to get a child or teen to eat more or less, it will feel like restriction or pressure, and it will backfire

And it's worth paying attention and getting curious. A change in behavior or energy level may be the child's signal of hunger rather than, say, a mild sense of gnawing in the stomach area. Skye Van Zetten of Mealtime Hostage reminds us, "*Feeling hunger is different for different people. When I was a teenager, I'd forget to eat for a day. The next morning I was dizzy; that's when I knew to think about eating.*" While Skye may have benefited frm some gentle external support (a flexible meal and snack routine for example), her experience illustrates that hunger and the body's need for fuel is expressed in different ways.

A qualified (non-diet) registered dietitian or therapist may help to gently explore hunger. But again, I believe over time, most children will learn what hungry and full feels like with responsive feeding at home, and that the more talk there is, the worse things get. However, some children and teens, especially if they have nervous system and sensory differences or other barriers to interoception, may do well with some gentle external appetite supports while they're learning. (Even so, the majority of neurodivergent children I've worked with did not need support beyond a responsive approach.)

Interoceptive Awareness

Julie Zivah, dietitian and parent coach/mentor, defines interoceptive awareness as sensitivity to stimulus inside the body and lists three benefits of supporting this awareness: 1) to learn to distinguish between emotional and physical needs, 2) to observe and attune to the body to recognize patterns and improve access to the "thinking brain" (witnessing a sensation, for example, can activate neural pathways to better access executive functioning or quiet mental chatter), 3) to grow self-compassion by fully experiencing physical signals.

There are resources that go into more detail on this complex topic. Trauma-informed helping professionals can be invaluable. Practicing interoceptive awareness during connected moments helps us better access our awareness during stressful times. You might provide your child with invitations (as they come up) to notice throughout the day, during play in particular, but don't let that tip into pressure and let it go if it feels like one more thing you have to stress about.

For younger children, after play or exercise, you can observe:

- "Wow, when I put my hand on my head, it feels hot!"
- "My hair is wet and I'm sweating, I wonder if your hair feels wet."

- "This grass is tickly on my feet!"
- "When I put my hand over my heart, I can feel it thumping." (If you have a pet, they can start by feeling the dog's heart, or the rapid heartbeat of a rabbit at the county fair.)
- "Would you like to feel my heart? Can you feel yours?" (Remember that direct questions can feel like a demand to some children. (See page 67 on declarative language.)
- "Ooh, the sand feels soft and hot, but my knees feel scratchy crawling on it."
- "When I spin around and stop, I feel like I might fall down!" (Older kids might like to learn about the little rocks in their inner ears in charge of balance.)
- "My skin has little bumps. I think that's amazing. When we get cold, tiny muscles pull on the hair in our skin and make it stand up! I wonder if your skin has little bumps too?"

For tweens or teens, you might practice interoceptive awareness in calm moments. Zivah suggests teaching older children how to take their pulse and feel their heartbeat, observing which nostril is "on," stretching sore muscles after exercise, experimenting with sensation by placing their hand in ice water to test for tolerance. These kinds of "somatic," or engaging-the-body exercises, can help expand interoceptive awareness, and help parents connect with their children (and their own bodies).

Remember Suzanne Stratford, OT from page 148? This is such an important point that I'm repeating it here: "Whether it is being held and read to at the beginning of the day, going for a walk, playing at the park, singing together, or snuggling before bedtime, moments of connection create a deep inner sense of security and trust that lay a strong foundation for the development of interoceptive awareness in the growing child. In these cases, it has consistently been my experience and observation, that a child's interoceptive sense, including that of appetite and hunger, emerges naturally."

Gentle External Support and Prompts

Some children and teens have a harder time with executive functioning, planning ahead, following complex instructions, and with their sense of time—in addition to having trouble accessing hunger and fullness. Gentle external prompts can help. For young children, these may come mostly from you; as they get older, visual calendars and technology may help.

Flexible structure with regular meals and snacks is an excellent way to offer gentle "external supports" for appetite.

Here are some other ideas to help:

- Apps or visual calendars and reminders.
- Keep instructions simple, and repeat.
- Visual cues.

- Working with an OT or RD specializing in supporting neurodivergent kids and families.

Hopefully this chapter has helped fill in some of the gaps of understanding so you can better support your children on this journey.

Chapter 9
Eating Disorders

"I'm scared to DEATH of passing on my eating disorder, and your easy intro to family meals has me feeling far more at ease. I've learned to quit freaking out when my child only eats meat and potatoes—she obviously needed it, because she shot up two inches the following few weeks and went back to normal eating after the growth spurt."

— Isobel, mother of Francine, age five years

While I'm not an eating disorder specialist, I hope to introduce you to eating disorders and disordered eating, some red flags, as well as how responsive feeding may lower the risk of more serious problems.

A simplified way to conceptualize disordered eating versus eating disorders (EDs) is to think of it as existing on a continuum. On one end is a functional relationship with food, moving along to disordered eating, and to the other end of the continuum being an eating disorder that may result in life-threatening malnutrition, and a brain and body impacted by starvation.

Dieting (considered by many as disordered eating) is dangerous. Even moderate dieting greatly increases the risk of developing an ED. **If your child's/teen's eating gets in the way of their physical, social, or emotional development, then it's a problem and they (and you) need help.**

Diagnostic categories for EDs evolve and don't give a full picture of the lived experience; and current research has major limitations. EDs are defined by the American Psychiatric Association with specific clinical criteria: examples include anorexia nervosa, bulimia, and binge eating disorder. They are complex illnesses with genetic and environmental contributing factors

Diagnostic codes also have limitations. For example, many EDs require body image disturbance to diagnose. The ED known as ARFID (see page 234) is not supposed to include body image issues such as a fear of gaining weight; yet many who otherwise qualify for ARFID do grapple with body image—a thinner teen may resist efforts to support appetite, and those in bigger bodies may wish to be thinner. The same child could qualify for a diagnosis of a pediatric feeding disorder and ARFID, which would lead to different treatment approaches in many scenarios. It is more complex than diagnostic codes (which one child psychiatrist described as a "checklist of symptoms"[1]) make it out to be.

Experts estimate that anorexia affects about one percent of Americans, with bulimia also at about one percent. The most common eating disorder, affecting between two and five percent of the population, is binge eating disorder (BED). (Actual numbers may be higher as many impacted by EDs, especially people of color, are likely underdiagnosed and undertreated.[2])

Most eating disorders exist along with other conditions such as anxiety, depression, substance use disorder, or obsessive-compulsive disorder. Eating disorders are more common in neurodivergent folks, gender-diverse individuals, and with a trauma history. Food insecurity is a risk factor as well.

It's also important to know that eating disorders come in bodies of all sizes and shapes. Fat people can have anorexia, with all the medical and psychological risks. It may be difficult to believe, but higher-weight individuals can be medically starving and need the same level of treatment as those who are very thin. (This is currently referred to as "atypical anorexia," though it is likely more common than anorexia in thinner bodies.) Regardless, many treatment centers are still weight-centric and may not offer comprehensive or appropriate care to people in bigger bodies.

Although anorexia in thin people gets the most attention, and has long been believed to be the most deadly of eating disorders, a 2009 study in the *Journal of Psychiatry* concluded, "Individuals with eating disorder not otherwise specified, which is sometimes viewed as a 'less severe' eating disorder, had elevated mortality risks, similar to those found in anorexia nervosa. This study also demonstrated an increased risk of suicide across eating disorder diagnoses."[3] These are serious illnesses, and research is ongoing.

Eating disorder diagnoses are on the rise in children and teens. A child or teen is many times more likely to be diagnosed with an eating disorder than Type II diabetes. Black and Hispanic teenagers are more likely to struggle with disordered eating and EDs, but less likely to access treatment. When they do, they are likely to experience treatment that is not culturally competent. Many ED treatment programs are also anti-fat.

The following is an incomplete list of behaviors that you should discuss with your child's healthcare provider as soon as possible. You and your child may need support from eating disorder professionals (therapists, and/or dietitians):

- The child continues with worrisome behavior, or it gets worse, after parents have stopped counterproductive feeding behaviors and begun a responsive approach.
- Their eating is impacting their physical, social, or emotional development.

- A significant anxiety, obsessive-compulsive disorder (OCD), or depression component exists.
- There is weight loss.
- The child who once enjoyed a variety of foods self-restricts her eating, calories, or types of foods.
- The child is preoccupied with body image or weight, or is newly hiding their body, wearing oversized clothing etc.
- The child is preoccupied with food (talking about it, watching cooking videos/ YouTube, or cooking) but not eating.
- The child has required medical intervention for not eating or drinking, such as a nine-year-old who has had emergency room visits for dehydration.
- Any indication of the child making themselves vomit, or using laxatives or diet pills.
- See page 95 for worrisome exercise behaviors.

And here is a sneaky one that children are often praised for early on... Many eating disorders start with a child or teen saying they want to "eat healthier." Changes in eating that exclude certain foods (sugar, fat, white rice, animal products...) need attention. Get curious. (More in Chapter 11.)

Children Who "Binge"

Parents sometimes ask if their child has binge eating disorder; but the observed behaviors are part of the food-preoccupied picture. (And almost always improve with feeding support, see Chapter 7. Though some youth may benefit from individual support.) These children come in all shapes and sizes. Some examples include:

- A slim six-year-old who sneaked into her neighbor's house, drank three juice boxes, and ate most of a box of Ritz crackers before she was discovered. Her parents don't keep "junk" at home.
- A seven-year-old whose weight is "normal" but increasing. She's been on "portion control" and no sweets or fried foods since she was four because she "can't stop herself." She's no longer invited on play dates because all she wants to do is eat.
- A larger-than-average nine-year-old girl whose mother found a frosting tub under the bed. The girl had pulled the half-used frosting out of the trash.
- A fat 12-year-old-boy whose mom, a nurse, has tried desperately to keep him on "green-light" foods and followed doctor's orders to not keep "junk" in the house: "You're the parent, act like it!" On his bike on his way home from school, this boy stops at the grocery store and eats a dozen donuts.

Here is a little of what we know about kids who binge, or as the studies say, "eat in the absence of hunger" (EAH):

- When "forbidden" foods are overly restricted, girls as young as age four report feeling guilt and shame and increased EAH.[4]
- Youth who have a history of dieting or restriction tend to binge or EAH with stress.[5]
- Parents who restrict and binge tend to raise kids who do the same.
- Studies in young girls show the more parents restrict, the more it correlates with increased weight gain and EAH.[6,7]

Whether or not the children above eat in out-of-control ways because they are seeking a "forbidden" food, they feel guilty, they are on an outright diet and are hungry, or a combination of factors—these kids are not "sugar addicts" and may not be particularly concerned with body image. While they may not qualify for "eating disorder" diagnoses, I worry that if they are not supported, they are at high risk for going on to have diagnosable binge eating disorder or other struggles.

The good news is that the earlier this is addressed, the easier it is to get children back on a better track with eating.

ARFID, the "New" Eating Disorder

A newer eating disorder diagnosis is avoidant restrictive food intake disorder (ARFID). These children and teens have always been here; they're now given a new label (see Chapter 6 for low appetite, sensory, and anxious/avoidant eating). Increasingly, children who "fail" pediatric feeding therapy end up in eating disorder treatment facilities.

I have reservations about categorizing avoidant and anxious eating as an eating disorder. Here are three reasons why: 1) If the child is diagnosed with an eating disorder, the focus is on treating the child, and the feeding relationship is often ignored, leaving significant opportunities for healing untouched; 2) While "eating disorders" are the most deadly of mental illnesses, ARFID overall doesn't seem as medically compromising as anorexia nervosa for example.[8,9] That means that individuals with ARFID don't experience medical problems or need higher level of care as often (especially the more common low appetite and selective subtypes); 3) Eating disorders are often described as life long, similar to how many view alcoholism. Parents may be told or have the impression that the child or teen will always struggle, when I've seen complete return to or achievement of typical eating, or eating in a way that allows the child to meet their nutritional needs and resolves anxiety, even if it isn't "typical." Viewing anxious and avoidant eating as an eating disorder may encourage setting the bar too low with treatment expectations.

Another major shortcoming of the ARIFD diagnostic code is that it covers a wide range of presentations: from an autistic preschooler with average weight, limited variety, sensory challenges and anxiety; to an acutely malnourished tween who was a typical eater until choking on a piece of chicken and then developed a phobia with rapid weight loss; to an adult who is low weight, selective, but overall doing well in life. Most research is conducted in intensive settings where individuals tend to be sicker and lower weight, and with the fear of choking/vomiting subtype. (This less common subtype, also known as emetophobia or phagophobia, is briefly discussed in the medical appendix.)

Because ARFID and anorexia are eating disorders with limited intake, many children with ARFID are treated with older teens diagnosed with anorexia. Treatment is often with standardized protocols, but it's hard to imagine one effective treatment for the many ways ARFID presents.

I've heard from, and of, kids and teens diagnosed with ARFID who've gotten worse in these facilities. Some approaches try to scare patients into eating better; children as young as 10 are told they can get cancer if they don't eat vegetables. With parents, kids, and teens usually already scared for their health, this doesn't support felt safety and can make matters worse.

While many diagnosed with ARFID are similarly low weight as with anorexia, clinically, many of us working with these children and teens find that they are less sick, and may not benefit from the same weight-gain goals as someone medically compromised with anorexia. They may function well with stable and low weight, rather than an anorexia picture with rapid weight loss and overall decline in function. But this is complicated, and a standard accepted treatment doesn't exist.

An anonymous autistic author with ARFID shared her ED treatment center experience: "Wiping my hands stopped them being sticky—a sensation I absolutely hate and dominates my brain . . . Small bites meant I could process each mouthful. Eating with my hands made the food safer . . . these were ways I had of coping with eating . . . However, they weren't deemed to be 'normal' and therefore couldn't be allowed."[10] Not considering her neurodivergence or letting her use her coping strategies made things worse.

Luckily, she found a therapist who listened, and helped her heal. There is a growing movement for more flexibility and understanding around neurodivergence in eating disorder treatment, but it's not yet universal. Considering the high rates of overlap with neurodivergence and EDs, this is critical.

I am deeply concerned for the children who tend to be small, or "problem" eaters who've been pressured to eat, even in therapy. When a mother called about her six-year-old ballet dancer who had gagged and vomited daily during therapy meals for years, I feared that the treatment may even increase her risk for bulimia. Treatments that reinforce anxiety, vomiting, or gagging may predispose children to more problems with eating.

I've seen children, teens, and even adults labeled with ARFID learn to eat with less anxiety and be able to meet their nutritional needs without intensive treatment (though not all). My colleagues and I have seen some children labeled with ARFID who "failed" pediatric feeding therapy see significant improvements, simply with parent support, in a matter of months.

Dealing with Feeding and Eating Struggles

The key is *each child and family* needs the best resources for their situation, whether it's the information in this book, or working with professionals to promote felt safety and connection and RF, working with the child on eating and anxiety issues, the child or teen working with professional support, or all of these.

Parent Support May Be Enough

If a child has feeding challenges but their weight (low or high) and health are stable and the child is not overly concerned about body image or worried about getting "fat," parent support is often enough. (See Max's story on pages 200-201 and Amari's story on pages 132-133 for examples.) In these cases, after parents are able to feed responsively, the child's eating usually improves. Here are some examples:

- The selective eater who branches out slowly in variety when the pressure is off.
- The twelve-year-old who stops sneaking forbidden foods, such as the half-used frosting container from the trash.
- The child who stops vomiting when pressure and force-feeding stop.

Parents Set the Tone

For a long time, the mother who was "too controlling or was always dieting" was considered *the cause* of eating disorders. Many children/teens diet and have mothers who diet, and few develop anorexia (though many will battle with disordered eating and yo-yo dieting).

Blaming mothers doesn't help and it's far more complex; **but don't underestimate the positive role parents play in shaping a child's attitudes and experiences around food.** (I write most about mothers, because mothers are primarily the ones sharing their eating histories with me and who are most involved with the child's eating. Much of the research also focuses on mothers.)

However, many adults (maybe some of you) *were* raised in less-than-supportive and even abusive situations around food, and I do not wish to diminish those experiences. If you experienced trauma, abuse, or neglect around food, were taken to your first Weight Watchers meeting at age eight or dieted as a teen like most of your friends, of course that plays a role in how you feel about food and your body and how you feed your family.

Those of us who work with families, from physicians to speech therapists and early childhood teachers, must do better to partner with parents and support them with feeding and parenting—in setting the stage at home for healing around food. I ache for the mothers who've called me crying, *"I know this isn't right, but everyone told me she would get used to normal portions,"* or, *"because everyone said, 'don't let her have treats.'"* These parents are doing what they are told, and are not neglectful, cruel, or heartless; they are scared and doing what they think (or have been advised) is best.

Responsive Feeding Likely Lowers the Risk of Eating Disorders

Based on the dramatic improvements I see in children with food preoccupation, bingeing, and selective eating, I have hope that supportive and responsive feeding can prevent some of the suffering associated with disordered eating and EDs. (Research on non-responsive feeding practices backs up this belief.)

You have a better chance of raising an individual who does well with eating and their experience in their body if you try for the best possible feeding relationship with your child. Some of the following is repetition from earlier chapters, but is worth summarizing some guiding principles:

- Trust your child with eating.
- Support him to trust his body to the best of his ability.
- Teach them to feed themselves filling and good-tasting foods at regular intervals. (Children who grow up eating with family eat more regularly into adulthood.)
- Support her in learning to be guided by internal cues of hunger and fullness.
- Teach your child (over months and years with responsive feeding) that she can trust her body to know how much to eat.

Be a good role model:

- Eat meals together when you can.
- Make your home a no-dieting zone. "In this family, we don't diet."
- Don't label food as "good" or "bad." A balanced and healthy diet has room for all foods.
- Limit time with adults who make frequent comments about weight, calories, etc. If your family makes comments in front of your child, ask them privately to stop, or chime in with, "All bodies are good bodies. How was the movie?" (More on "meddlers" in Chapter 10.)
- Look for ways to support and nourish yourself with food and consider working on your relationship to your body.

Support Body Kindness

It's harder to be kind to a body you're ashamed of. Fat individuals bear the brunt of shaming, bullying, and bias, but thin and small children suffer as well. **Body dissatisfaction is a prime motivator for disordered eating and plays a major role in EDs. Feeling supported and loved in the body they have will help your child take better care of their body.**

Support healthy body image for all children in these ways:

- Don't talk badly about your own body or anyone else's.
- You don't have to love your body, but try to learn to not hate it. (Courtesy of Michelle Allison at The Fat Nutritionist blog.) This idea of "body neutrality" has become more widespread. Our bodies in essence enable this experience of living on this planet.

- Focus on what bodies can do, not on how they look.
- No teasing or weight talk. "In this family we don't tease or talk about how people look."
- Normalize and celebrate body diversity, such as, "Daddy is bigger than Uncle Jim. People have different hair color, and maybe it's curly, their eyes and skin are different colors, and their bodies are different, too. I'm taller than my sister, and I'm fatter, too."
- Talk with your children, as is age appropriate, about "media literacy." That is, about how retouched images don't show how real bodies look. "You know, no one really looks like that." Thin or small children, as well as children in bigger bodies are harmed by the narrow range of celebrated bodies.
- Think about the media children have access to, from social media to cartoons and books. (A great example is the fat-shaming of the Dursleys in the Harry Potter series or how Peppa Pig's father is treated.) Once you look for it, it's everywhere.
- Delete social media accounts that make you feel bad; if your child/teen has access to social media, talk to them about doing the same.
- For teens in bigger bodies, share fat-positive social media accounts with them. (See caring for kids in bigger bodies in Chapter 7.)

Eating Together May Be Protective

As we've explored, family meals are linked with good outcomes for children, and for their relationship with food. Continuing to eat together throughout early and late adolescence may be protective. Even with busy lives, it's worth prioritizing if you can. Eating together can offer a "guardrail" and helps you observe how your child/teen is doing with food, and emotionally etc. I've heard about parents noticing early warning signs at mealtimes when a child suddenly started cutting out sugar, then carbs, fat, and so on.

Parents with a History of Eating Disorders

At least half the moms I work with share with me a history of an eating disorder or disordered eating. This isn't surprising, as most women wrestle with eating and body image to some degree. These moms describe an almost paralyzing fear of passing on their eating problems: *"I was scared to death I would make her crazy about food, but I also didn't want her to be fat. I didn't know what to do."* At one of my first ever workshops, the mother of a healthy nine-month-old (!) cried, *"Every time I feed my daughter, I feel like I'm on the knife-edge between anorexia and obesity."* It takes a lot of courage to be vulnerable and reach out for support.

Even mothers who have recovered can feel triggered (the return of thoughts or behaviors related to the eating disorder) or anxious if a child's weight is "too high," or "too low," or if a child eats a particularly large or small meal.

Be curious. I'm told time and again by clients that it was an "ah-ha moment" for them to see their child eat a larger meal and then less later in the day, save some of their favorite ice cream for later, or try a new food. (Seeing my daughter's capabilities emerge inspired me. If she can do it, maybe I can too!)

A Mother's Journey with Feeding and Her Own Eating Disorder

"Before I had children I was terrified that I'd pass on my disordered eating. It was soul-destroying. Before I got pregnant I did therapy (again!) to get a grip on my ED.

When my kids were toddlers, I thought I was doing everything 'right.' I made everything from scratch, offered healthy snacks, only milk or water to drink, etc. I used to get very frustrated at the biscuits (cookies) and squash (juice) they ate loads of when we were out (no warning bells at this point for me though!). Before long I was hearing, 'How many spoonfuls of this do I have to eat so I can have pudding?' and, 'I've eaten everything on my plate. Is that good?' Suddenly the warning lights came on in my head; my children were losing the ability to listen to their bodies and were eating to please me/to get pudding (dessert). All the things I'd sworn I didn't want my children to grow up with.

I had to find a better way for my children, though I was still struggling with my ED. For example, I was deep-down happy to have to restrict my own eating even further when my newborn had food allergies and I had to cut out dairy and wheat. I tried Baby-Led Weaning with my third, which led me to the Division of Responsibility. I give the term 'control freak' a whole new meaning, so this was my worst nightmare. Three meals and two snacks a day, and no commenting on what they eat, or whether they eat at all. It was all so difficult! My daughter didn't go near vegetables for a few weeks. I had to sit on my hands at times and clamp my mouth shut so I didn't comment or ask them to try something.

I had some great email support at this time, reassuring me that it was all normal (that was you, lovely Katja!). Now, all three children love trying new foods. Often new things are served a few times before everyone has tried them, but it's about familiarity and not feeling pressured to try anything they're not comfortable with. I leave it up to them.

I've finally started to deal with my own eating and am almost three months into recovering from the eating disorder that has been with me for nearly 30 years. I am starting to apply these principles to myself. Starting with three meals and three snacks a day. Trying to listen to my body and relearn hunger and satiety. I will have to keep working at it, but for the first time ever, I am convinced that I will get there."

– Mira

As a parent, the more you wrestle with your eating, the more difficult feeding will feel. If you are pretty close to tuned-in eating or on the journey, your kids can be powerful inspiration. If, on the other hand, you are mired in obsessive thoughts about your body or food, you may feel stuck, even set back, by the demands of feeding children.

Most children eat four to six times a day in a responsive model. If your own eating is causing significant anxiety and struggles, and is affecting your feeding relationship with your child, I hope you are able to access support, perhaps from a non-diet, ED professional. While you're working on your own eating, the following are a few thoughts to help guide you:

- Be open with your partner or close family/friends if you can; so they can better support you.
- Find resources and learn about tuned-in eating.
- If family meals or certain foods are too difficult, or right now you can't participate for some reason, ask your partner or a trusted adult to take over. One mom's partner completely took over meals with the kids while she was in treatment. He was able to eat with his stepdaughter and allow the girl to eat as much as she needed of all kinds of foods (including mom's trigger foods).

Exercise, High-Risk Sports, and Eating Disorders

People with eating disorders and poor body image frequently exercise excessively. If your child has a rocky time with eating or growth or is at risk for eating problems, carefully consider extracurriculars. It may be wise to steer clear of weight- or appearance-centered sports such as gymnastics, wrestling, or dance. (See page 95 for "bigorexia" and concerning exercise.)

If your child has a passion for a particular sport, you may need to be proactive. Consider having a frank, confidential discussion with coaches to ask what they are talking about in terms of weight and nutrition. For example, one mom was shocked when her daughter's track coach recommended a weight-loss tea. Some dance or gymnastics programs promote joy and body positivity and don't shame bigger bodies, but that isn't the norm. Pay attention, advocate as needed, and hopefully, enjoy!

What to Do if You Suspect Your Child Has an Eating Disorder

Eating disorders do not discriminate between adopted or biological children, race, size, gender expression, or social status. If you are concerned, do not wait, talk yourself out of seeing worrying signs, or let others dismiss your concerns without seeking an evaluation. (See pages 232-233 for a partial list of potential red flags.) **Early diagnosis and support/treatment improve outcomes.**

Have a list of your observations ready to talk to your child's healthcare provider and make sure that any referrals are to professionals specializing in eating disorders.

While serious eating disorders present more extreme challenges, the next chapter covers day-to-day feeding of families.

Chapter 10
Feeding Stages and Day-to-Day Feeding

This chapter looks at feeding stages, such as transitioning from liquid to solid foods, and the perfect storm of the toddler stage. Since children develop at different rates and may be "ahead" or "behind" in some areas, your child may benefit from approaches covered in ranges different than their age. The key is following the child's lead and centering felt safety. The chapter wraps up with topics such as eating out, bringing home a sibling, menu planning, outside influences, and more.

Feeding Infants

I'm not an infant feeding specialist or lactation consultant. However, I will touch briefly on responsive feeding principles before solids and then go more in detail again around navigating solids and beyond.

There are other comprehensive resources to support infants. Find local breastfeeding support groups or a lactation consultant if you're breastfeeding. If you're formula feeding or interested in combo feeding, The Formula Feeding Mom is good online resource to start with.

Moving on to feeding infants... sometimes it will be fairly clear what they are trying to communicate, and sometimes less so. They will learn to express their needs, and you will learn to read their cues over time by trial and error: trying to feed, diapering, or rocking; feeding in a quiet room; or perhaps offering a pacifier.

Unlike with older children, infants are ideally fed on demand, so they decide *when* to eat as often as possible. (Note: If they go longer than two to three hours without seeming to indicate they are hungry, it's worth offering the breast, a bottle, or some solid foods if they are eating solids.)

Loose feeding schedules in childcare settings are generally well tolerated. Allowing the child to decide how much is the most important.

The more you try to impose timetables, specific amounts, and how much weight she needs to gain, the more you fret, pressure, restrict, and override her cues, the higher the chance is that things won't go well.

It's okay to experiment and see if they're hungry or maybe need a cuddle. Offer a bottle or solids as appropriate and take "no" for an answer. Even if you are eager for your infant to eat and gain weight, avoid getting pushy with a bottle. You can always offer again in a little while. It will get easier.

Cues an Infant Might Be Hungry:

- Crying, fussing, or screaming.
- "Rooting" in the young infant—turning the head toward a touch on the cheek or face.
- Sucking on hands or other objects.
- Continuing to suck or eat eagerly, or with attention and interest, even if she finishes a bottle.
- Watching you eat with interest; reaching for food.
- More subtle cues: getting quiet or changing demeanor, losing interest in toys or play, looking at you more, getting flushed in the face, or becoming more easily distracted.

Cues an Infant Might Be Full or Not Interested in Eating Right Now:

- Stops sucking and looks away.
- Sucking has slowed or stopped; she seems distracted.
- She appears content when the feeding is over, doesn't open mouth for more.
- Turns head away.
- Pushes nipple out of the mouth.
- Gets upset with attempts to get her to eat: cries, arches her body, or bats at bottle.

Apparent discomfort or pain with eating may indicate something else is going on and should be discussed with your child's doctor. (See the medical issues appendix.)

They Decide How Much

Remember Fannah? Her doctor worried that she was "almost overweight" and recommended specific ounces at specific intervals—and no more. Mom cut off feedings, even though Fannah screamed at the end of every bottle and still seemed hungry. Unfortunately, ignoring her cues and not letting Fannah decide how much set this family up for struggles (see page 187).

Instead of interrupting bottle feeding, allow them to drink from a bottle until they pause or appear uncomfortable. You can try burping then, and after that you can check to see if they're still hungry by offering the bottle. Follow their cues. Stopping and checking how much they've had to eat or to see if they need burping, or because you are curious, may be so distracting and upsetting that your child eats less. Another good resource for infant feeding is Ellyn Satter's DVD, "Feeding with Love and Good Sense II."

As explored in Chapters 1, 5, 6, and 7, recognize that trying to get infants to take in more or less is likely to backfire.

Feeding Challenges

If you're struggling with feeding or interpreting cues, an infant feeding specialist can be a great resource. Lactation consultants should also be able to help with bottle feeding and help decipher the infant's cues. You may need to look for one who is supportive of bottle feeding.

"Paced" Feeding Is Rarely Necessary

Paced bottle feeding originated as a way to feed preemies in the NICU; it helps coordinate suck, swallow, and breathing and keeps oxygen levels in the healthy range. In the last few years, I've been seeing advice on paced bottle feeding for all infants, in theory to avoid nipple confusion (no data currently supports this).

Paced feeding is described in different ways, and includes sitting infants straight up, counting breaths and swallows, and interrupting the flow every few swallows by either taking the bottle out of the mouth, or tilting it back and forth. I've seen concerning quotes in online how-to videos about "making baby work for their milk," and using paced feeding to prevent overeating and "too much" weight gain.

You can bottle feed responsively. If the flow seems too fast, you can adjust to a slower-flow nipple. If an infant has trouble with frequent coughing, choking, or distress while bottle feeding, consult their doctor and hopefully, an infant feeding specialist. I do not broadly recommend paced feeding; Leslie Schilling, dietitian, eating disorder specialist, and co-author of *Born to Eat,* agrees: "It's not necessary and overcomplicates feeding for the average baby."

Formula

All infants 0–12 months of age should be on breast milk or commercially prepared formula. (There are case reports of parents making home-made formulas leading to severe malnutrition and hospitalization.) Ideally, if the formula your child is drinking is appropriate, nutritionally adequate, and well-tolerated, keep her on that formula. If you can't get the same brand, then over a period of days, start by mixing small amounts of the new formula into the former, gradually increasing as tolerated until you've switched to the new formula. (The Formula Feeding Mom has excellent resources developed during the 2022/23 formula shortage.) Most infants will accept a new formula, while others may be wary.

If your infant is not tolerating formula or appears to have problems, discuss options with their doctor. Try not to swap formulas frequently to "see if it helps," as this can confuse the picture.

If your infant appears ill, seems uncomfortable or in pain, have her evaluated. Signs of poorly tolerated formula are difficult to interpret, since other things may be going on. Some signs may be:

- Fussiness
- Crying or colicky behaviors

- Constipation
- Distended tummy and gas
- Poor weight gain

Any bloody or black stools (beyond the first few days of life when stools are dark in color) should be reported to the infant's doctor immediately.

Switching from Formula to Milk

After about 12 months of age, if your child is doing pretty well with solid foods, you can switch to whole cow's or goat's milk (I don't recommend raw milk) or a non-dairy alternative (talk to the child's health provider). *Do not use these milks before 12 months of age.*

If your child is having a slow start with solids, you may want to support nutrition with formula for a few more months. Talk with your doctor or a pediatric dietitian. Cana offers an example where using formula beyond 12 months was ideal. Cana was at the 10th percentile and growing steadily, but was only beginning to explore solids at 12 months. She had developmental differences and poor muscle tone, but was improving. Cana's mom served appropriate finger foods and purees, but Cana ate slowly and not as much as her brother did at the same age. Cana's mom was surprised when at Cana's 12-month visit, her doctor advised switching from formula to low-fat (!) milk.

Since we were already talking about Cana's feeding, and she still got most of her nutrition from liquids, I advised her mom to continue with the formula for a few months and see how things progressed. Cana benefited from the nutrition in formula while she learned to enjoy solids. Cana's mom discussed the plan with the pediatrician, who agreed. By 16 months of age, Cana was eating a variety of solid foods and was switched slowly to whole cow's milk. (See page 284 for why low fat was not the ideal choice.)

Transitioning to Solids Stage

Starting solids can be an enjoyable introduction to family foods, or it can set the stage for problems down the road. Typically, this six- to 12-month period (or so) is called the "transition," when a child goes from getting most of their nutrition from formula or breast milk to having most of their nutrition needs met by a variety of solid foods.

It can take children *many* non-pressured, neutral opportunities to learn to like solid foods. Children learn by watching you eat, by smelling, squishing, licking, mouthing, and spitting out. Ask your child's doctor about any allergy concerns before starting solids if there is a family history. Don't start before four months of age.

Guiding Principles for Transitioning to Solids

- Start when they show signs of readiness, usually around 5 to 6 months. (Check with the child's doctor as recommendations change, especially around introducing foods like peanuts.) Signs include:

- Watching you eat, leaning forward, reaching for food and pulling to mouth, able to sit upright (or with assistance if there are neuromuscular differences), tongue thrust reflex is gone (tongue pushes food out of the mouth automatically).

- Feed based on what your child can do, not age.
- Approach feeding with a calm demeanor, ideally in your own zone of felt safety.
- Have them eat with you or join in at family meals if you can, even if they have some different foods for now. Maybe start with one meal a day and see how it goes. By joining family eating times, your baby will gradually transition to more regular eating times, if not already.
- Trying to get an infant to eat more or less will not make them grow faster or slower. Pressure with feeding almost always backfires.
- Expect a mess. Allow them to touch and explore food with their hands.

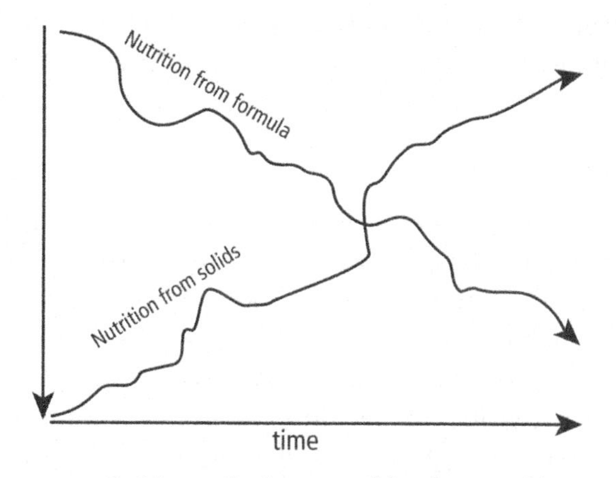

Figure 10.1: Schematic for transitioning to solids. As intake from solids increases, nutrition from bottle or breast decreases.

Be Responsive

- Observe and take cues from your child.
- Some babies intensely want to "do it myself!" and will reject the spoon. Help him with appropriate foods, load the spoon, and let him put it in his mouth.
- Don't trick, force, or play games. Help your child to feed herself if she's able.
- Let him eat as fast or as slow as he wants.
- You can follow the Baby-Led Weaning approach (described in the following pages) and skip spoon-feeding, or a combination of spoon-feeding and allowing your child to feed himself.

Some Specifics

- Be sure she is sitting upright, can open her mouth in anticipation of the spoon, and can close her mouth around the spoon.
- If she is unable to sit upright, work with an OT for safe positioning.
- Aim to feed about every two to three hours by the time she is around 12–16 months of age, or by the time she is self-feeding with some skill.
- Be aware of choking risks; have her eat upright, and stay close.
- Let him play with and explore appropriate utensils.
- Serve different tastes and textures often, and don't assume she "doesn't like it" if she doesn't try it or she spits it out.

The earliest weeks of solid foods are more about exploring and having a positive experience. It is not about getting in food. She may stop after one or two bites, and that's okay. (It's also fine if she consumes an entire jar or pouch of puree and wants more.) Beware of the popular idea that "food before one is just for fun." This is too simplistic and may falsely reassure parents where there may be feeding challenges. With typical development, exploring and advancing textures helps infants learn to manage and chew a variety of foods.

First Foods

There isn't one right or wrong way or food to feed first (as long as it respects baby's cues.) A few decades ago in France, my niece was introduced to foods based on color. In the United States, rice cereal was recommended when I trained as a doctor, and in the 1950s, strained lamb and rice were ideal first foods.

As dietitians and authors Schilling and Peterson wrote in *Born to Eat*, "From birth, babies around the globe are fed in a variety of manners, whether it be the breast, a bottle, pre-masticated food (pre-chewed and fed to baby), food from the hands of a caregiver, or using a spoon. Many cultures around the world feed their babies what the family is eating and in the same manner. There are also places in the world where families don't make or have access to baby foods, yet their children are still fed and grow."[1] You can use commercial baby food, make your own, or adapt the family foods.

Gagging and Choking

Gagging in infants and young toddlers is a reflex that protects their airway; it occurs as part of normal oral-motor development. Gagging moves food away from the airway to the front of the mouth. The infant's gag reflex is triggered closer to the front of the mouth, so they gag fairly regularly as they mouth toys, hands, spoons, and solids. Mouthing and gumming helps them learn to handle and chew foods, and even if a child gags herself with her hands or spoon, that's okay. Over time, the gag reflex weakens and moves farther back in the mouth.

Gagging is common as infants eat more texture. If your child gags frequently, offer fewer pieces at a time if he overstuffs, or check that the flow of liquids isn't too fast from the bottle or cup. Gagging more than a few times a meal may mean you are advancing textures too quickly: Try pureeing or mashing foods and move on with more texture again in a few days or weeks. Some infants like to take big bites (as my daughter did) and might not do well with teething biscuits or crackers or the more strict interpretation of baby-led weaning (where the child is supposed to self-feed *all* foods), while other children may do just fine.

If she gags or vomits repeatedly, is in distress or upset by the episodes, not gaining weight, or not advancing with textures, talk to her doctor.

Gagging can be scary to watch, but as much as possible, try to stay calm. If you jump up and hold a cloth under her or appear panicked every time she gags, she will feel scared, which may affect her eating. Many parents misinterpret gagging as choking, which can lead to not providing opportunities to advance textures, making eating challenges more likely.

A choking child is distressed, will not make sounds or progress in clearing the food, and may change color.

If your older child is gagging frequently with eating and/or you are engaged in feeding battles, find help. These are scary and negative experiences.

Get CPR trained so you can spot and know how to deal with choking.

Tips to Lower Choking Risk

- Prepare foods that are appropriate for her skill level.
- Avoid foods that are a choking hazard, including popcorn, grapes, peanuts, candy, and hot dogs. Ask the child's doctor for a list.
- Have the child sit upright (not in a car seat or carrier or on her back) to eat, where you can see her.
- Don't have him eat in the car or on the go.

Spoon or Self-Feeding ("Baby-Led")

The Baby-Led Weaning (BLW) approach has become mainstream over the last decade or so and is pushed by some as the *only* way to transition off the breast or bottle to solid foods. BLW grew popular after a book was published nearly two decades ago. The idea is that infants are to self-feed rather than be spoon-fed. It became widely promoted as a way to raise less picky children, to help them self-regulate, and to prevent o*esity.

I like a lot about this model, mostly because it promotes having baby join in mealtimes and supports the infant's autonomy. However, I have some concerns with the strict BLW approach:

- It may increase choking risk.
- Risk of low iron and other nutrients may be higher.

- It can take more time and create more mess and work for busy parents.
- Children with developmental differences, delays due to prematurity, neuromuscular or oral motor differences may need support, and are at higher risk of nutritional deficiencies.

More and more I hear from parents and see on social media a sense that BLW is *the best* way to start solids, and parents feel guilty if they don't do it "right." Rather than serving modified family foods, parents now have to specially prepare foods or make mini muffins packed with veggies. The guilt and extra work/products are not helpful. Be responsive to what works for you and your baby.

Responsive Feeding with BLW, Spoon, or Combination

The authors of the original *Baby-Led Weaning* book wrote, "Being spoon-fed by someone else means the baby is not in control of how much she eats."[2] It is easier to push a spoon-fed baby, but responsive parents let the baby decide how much—spoon-fed or not.

A combination of spoon and self-feeding may be best: One study noted that the "modified version of BLW was associated with a number of benefits including: a reduction in food fussiness compared to traditional spoon-feeding; higher iron and zinc intakes than have been reported for unmodified Baby-Led Weaning; and no evidence of an increased risk of iron deficiency, choking, or growth faltering."[3] If you want to learn more about BLW, I recommend the book *Born to Eat*.

And you and your family's needs matter. If you have more time you may want to let your child explore self-feeding, and some meals you can spoon feed, or use a combination; letting her explore foods and self-feed while you load the spoon for her, or let her take food from the spoon. By 12 months, most babies eat in similar ways, whether spoon fed, or started with BLW.

While many infants happily suck and gum biscuits or roasted veggie wedges, my daughter chomped huge bites and had trouble with the pieces. I spoon-fed, and as she was able, she palmed and scraped and fed herself mashed foods such as sweet potatoes, banana, and squash. She could chew and gum on toys, spoons, foods in the mesh feeder, and her hands. To support her interest in doing it herself, I would load the spoon, which she would grab and pull into her mouth, sucking and chewing on the spoon. She ate prepared baby foods, alongside what we ate, with minor adaptations, and advancing textures. She grew more confident and capable with her eating.

Ilene, a colleague, chuckled as she remembered feeding her three children, "*The first was spoon-fed all home-made purees, which was the fashion at the time; the second used a combination of purees and self-feeding; and the third just ate a version she could manage of what we were all eating. Her first meal she just palmed food off my plate. They are all now enthusiastic and varied eaters some years on.*"

Pediatric dietitian Hydee Becker summed it up: "Parents should do what they feel most comfortable with and do what works best for their child. **Some babies want to do it themselves. Others want to be, or need to be, spoon-fed. Either/or, or both, is just great as long as you are responsive to the child's cues."**

Toddler Stage: The "Perfect Storm"

When children become toddlers, their growth rate slows and their appetites may become less predictable. Many toddlers seem to eat less than they did as infants. Most toddlers go through a phase where even if they ate a good variety of foods previously, they now approach new foods with caution, or "neophobia," which means fear of the new. This common "picky" phase may mean:

- Your child won't want different foods touching.
- Her first, second, and usually third response to a new food will be "no."
- She may show a preference for simple carbs and sweet foods.
- She may try to get you to serve her favorites. She may tantrum and throw foods she doesn't like.
- Foods she used to love are suddenly rejected.
- She no longer explores much of what you put in front of her.

Tips for navigating the "perfect storm":

- Keep serving the foods, without comment, praise, or pressure. What they reject one day, or one minute, they may enjoy the next.
- Expect tantrums. Trying to feed with the goal of avoiding age-appropriate upsets will make your job harder in the long term.
- Stick with flexible structure when you can.
- Stay calm and try to be good company.
- Have realistic expectations. A toddler's appetite varies meal to meal. They may be done after five minutes. Consider having a tub of toys that she can play with nearby, or if you allow screen time, this may be the time for it. This is a rough stage when sitting down to meals and getting yourself fed too is difficult. It will get better.

Review Chapter 1 on how kids learn to like new foods, as well as Chapters 5 and 6 on typical and more extreme picky eating. This will help you not fall into counterproductive patterns during this frustrating phase.

For children with brain-based differences, experiment with more flexibility. A toddler tantrum is different than a dysregulated child having a 90-minute emotional release. A dysregulated child may do better with pouches, a cuddle, or eating in front of a screen with a familiar show. Focus on felt safety, and feed her as best you can.

Throwing Food

Early eaters throw food because: they're no longer hungry, they're learning about gravity, cause and effect, and how they can get you to do something! (They, as well as older children may throw food if they feel pressured to eat it or if they have trouble communicating preferences.) *Be prepared for a mess.* Here are ideas to minimize throwing:

- Put out small amounts of food. Too much can overwhelm.
- Don't give them more if it has turned into a game.
- If they're doing more throwing than eating, you can end the meal and try again in a few hours.
- Let them serve themselves or put food on their trays or plates. If you pre-plate something they don't want, they may fling it on the floor. They're less likely to throw a food that they put on their plate by themselves.

Eating with Older Children

While school-aged children may be able to sit longer than younger children, continue to have realistic expectations. If they can keep you company while you finish eating, that's great, but they may not be able to sit for 20–30 minutes if they finish eating after 10.

See what works for your family. With older children, you can work toward having them be able to play nearby, start on homework or art, or enjoy a show while you finish eating. "Momma and I are still enjoying dinner. Why don't you play with your Legos nearby? We'll be done soon."

Grade School/Middle School

If and when they're ready, your child can begin to take on more responsibility. If you've been at this for a while, they may already have reinforced skills with self-regulation and enjoy a variety of foods. For the most part, your job is still to provide, and they decide how much.

Continue to eat primarily at the table or a predictable place. Though he may seem like he doesn't need you, offer company at meals and snacks if you can. As he's ready, your child can take on more tasks, such as:

- Choose more often what he will have for snack, as well as timing. He can try to be done in time to support his appetite for dinner.
- Become more involved with menu planning, if he's interested. Keep it simple and consider food groups. Ask him to offer ideas for dishes or sides when you're making your shopping list.
- Help more with cooking and food prep. Remember, though, just because she can fix herself breakfast and scramble her own eggs for dinner, doesn't mean she should be left to get her own food and eat alone regularly.
- Decide more of the what when eating out. You might suggest food groups, etc.

High School

As your older adolescent is able, you are likely preparing her to live more independently. Your child does not have to be cooking entire meals at this point. Eating together and allowing her to see you plan and cook, reheat foods, and incorporate takeout is important. Try not to force an uninterested child to cook. Eat together when possible. We tend to think of teens as "too old" for family meals, or they think it's not cool or that they don't need their parents as much—but they do. Meals are a dependable time to connect.

- Allow the teen to get her own snack after school. Have a variety of options available. Convenience matters. You may want to have chilled water in the fridge or cut-up fruit and veggies, or yogurt if your teen seems to only choose quick, prepackaged snacks. It may seem like too much effort to peel an orange, but grabbing cut-up melon with chips and salsa might do the trick.
- If interested, the teen can perhaps take on some grocery shopping with a list that you've reviewed. Find fun ways to include them if you can.
- If interested, he can take on planning and cooking one meal a week (or more). Boiled pasta with a jar of marina sauce, baby carrots, and bread is a great start.

"Food isn't just food. My teen is exploring the experience of food. She might want to make sushi or have goji berries and make smoothies. Knowing about the importance of the feeding relationship makes me more purposeful around supporting that exploration. That's part of my job."

— Dawn, mom and therapist

Twenty-year-old Rose (who earlier described her memories of feeding therapy as a young child) made several excellent points relating to teens. Here are some of her observations.

"Cooking with my brother is a way we can connect. He's kind of an angsty teen otherwise, but when we cook we don't have to talk about much. There are steps to follow and we can connect and cooperate."

"I do like having the freedom to make some choices, and my mom supports me if I want her to get me something from the store."

"I started learning about cooking with really easy go-to family dinners. My mom would supervise. So it might be boiling spaghetti and serving with a jar of tomato sauce, and then maybe another time we try Alfredo sauce."

As you move through the stages with your child, some children will master skills before others. Some children will benefit from support into adulthood. At any stage, there will be challenges, big and small, and they will affect how you parent and feed. Dawn, from a few paragraphs back reminds us, "You don't need to raise a finished person at 18. There is still a lot of growth and discovery that will happen. We want it to happen."

Helpful Feeding Gear

The following is a rundown of some tools that can make feeding easier (most being useful in the early years or for children who need more support), and a few words about unnecessary gear. (I recognize that not everyone will be able to afford or have the space for these items.)

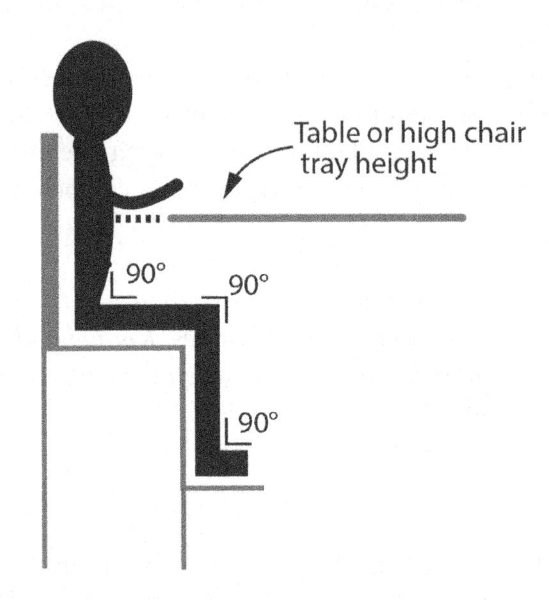

Figure 10.2: Correct highchair placement.

Highchair: Look for a highchair that's easy to clean and fits your space. IKEA has a simple, lower-cost model. If your child needs support while eating, ask their therapist for suggestions on adapting your seating. Rolled-up towels tucked in on both sides can give her stability. A hand-me-down highchair may be the best choice. Try pulling the highchair to the table during shared eating times.

- Placement: The child sits at a 90.90.90 sitting position if able—that is, 90 degrees at the hip, knees, and feet.
- Level of tray: Start with the tray or tabletop at about halfway between the nipple line and the belly button. If set too high, self-feeding is more challenging. See what your child prefers.

- Foot support: A footrest offers stability and a sense of security. You can make your own footrest with a plastic bin or cardboard box filled with heavy items. This is especially important for children with neuromuscular differences, sensory, or brain-based differences.

Look for an adjustable chair that can grow with your child such as the Tripp Trapp or OXO Tot Sprout. If you can spend the money or get one used, it may be worth it. (I spent almost as much on various disappointing boosters over the years.) These chairs have built-in, adjustable footrests.

Some children prefer kneeling, which is not ideal in terms of chair tipping, but can be okay against a wall or with a parent's foot on the chair for stability, or on a secure bench seat. Some children benefit from a weighted blanket across their lap.

Plates with compartments: You can go straight from putting food on the highchair tray or table to these. When children enter the naturally selective stage (typically about 15 to 18 months), it can help to separate the food. Made a stew? Put some chicken, carrots, and potatoes in separate sections if they don't like foods touching. Some older children and teens prefer to eat this way; you can find dishwasher-safe trays with compartments, like those used at cafeterias.

Silverware: Not having the right tools can be frustrating. I've seen capable older kids struggle with forks meant for beginning eaters. Find a spoon with a deeper bowl than many "baby" spoons. Use a dessert fork or similar small fork to help kids eat. If you're working with an OT, they can help you find adaptive gear. Offer options.

Knives: Various knives allow kids to safely help with food prep such as a plastic lettuce knife or a dull butter knife. Kids can quite easily cut things like mushrooms, muffins, bananas, peeled fruit, and lettuce. When at the appropriate level of challenge, the activity will help them feel competent, capable, and useful. Small dip spreaders are great for spreading nut butters, hummus, and even cutting soft foods.

A mesh bag or silicone teether/feeder: Mesh or silicone bags can be helpful if used properly. For example, this worked well when we ate out with our daughter when she was between ages six and 10 months. We would pop a piece of apple or other food from our plate into the bag, and she loved to work on it. It can be a way to introduce new textures and flavors and soothe teething pain (frozen fruit or ice cubes can help). Follow usage instructions.

Straw, spouted, and open cups: During the transition to solids, you can introduce cups. Try not to let children wander (or put them to sleep) with anything other than water. Milk and juice can sabotage appetite, and frequent sipping increases cavity risk.

Primer on Cups from Heidi Moreland, SLP

Most people have a favorite kind of cup. I prefer using a straw, while others like open cups. Many people drink coffee from one kind of cup and water from another. Children also usually develop preferences.

Open cup: Many children gravitate toward things they see "their grownups" doing, especially children who are cautious with food or experiences. They might prefer sips from your cup or a water bottle, even if they are messy. In fact, this is how all children learned to drink from cups until fairly recently!

Once they feel comfortable taking sips from your cup, try pouring it into a small open cup of their own. These cups allow them to see in so they know what they are drinking and can take small sips until they know what to expect. Make sure to fill it so they can slurp from it as they feel ready, and you don't need to pour it into their mouth. They won't be able to hold the cup themselves for some time. Small Solo or Dixie cups work well, although they will spill and are easily crushed. You can try the EZPZ tiny cup, a shot glass, or even the cap to their bottle. They will eventually become skilled enough to drink from it independently. Once they've had some success, they might be more open to trying low flow or no-flow top cups (such as the 360 brand) that would spill less.

Straw cup: Kids who like to sit up and control the situation often prefer a straw cup. Try using the straw as a dropper first–it can be easier if you cut the straw shorter. If you see them round their lips slightly around the straw, a straw cup might be a good choice. Let them learn with a preferred drink so they are motivated to keep trying. Straws with a valve may make the first drops easier.

Kids who continually bite on the straw (which stops the flow) may not be ready for the straw. If a cup is still important but the straw isn't working, that may be a case for trying the sippy. You may need to take the valve out or use a spout cup without a valve to help them understand that liquid can come out. Once they understand what they are working for, it can be easier to transition from bottle to sippy.

Sippy cup: A sippy cup is an extension of the bottle and may be a helpful transition for children who love bottles. It allows for the same sucking and swallowing motion. Most feeding therapists prefer for kids to skip these, as they don't help advance oral skills and may contribute to dental problems, especially if they walk around with them.

- Soft spouts may be preferred because they feel and function more like the bottle and have a little more "give" than hard spouts.
- Other children enjoy the firm feeling of the hard plastic spout; it gives more solid feedback and may even allow them to do some biting to stabilize it as they learn.
- The toys they prefer mouthing might give you some ideas on the cups to try first.

There's no magic cup! The most important thing is for your child to be comfortable and successful and for them to become efficient enough to meet their needs. This is a learned skill for all kids, so you may need to try a few to land on what works for your child and situation.

Step stools: We rotated three stools over the years, from the small stool/kneeling pad that came with the baby tub, to a sturdy mid-sized model, to a taller one from the hardware store. As children grow, they'll need different heights for different tasks. I would think we were done with one, only to pull it out for toothbrushing or reaching the kitchen counter. Rubber bottom features help them stay put. Activity/learning towers with guard rails that pull up to the counter are less prone to tip, but are pricey and bulky. See what works for you, and always supervise.

Water bubbler or playful spout: It can help your child access water herself. You can install cute spouts on a faucet and set up a step stool so your child can get her own water. Have cups nearby where she can reach them, or fill an insulated water bottle with a straw top in the morning, decorated with her favorite stickers. Good hydration can help with constipation.

Sprinkle shaker: Kids usually like sprinkling. Use an empty saltshaker or buy a shaker with bigger holes. Make your own mix of cinnamon and sugar; try it on applesauce, yogurt, buttered toast, and apples. You can use regular colorful sprinkles to help introduce new foods. Some children enjoy Furokake (a Japanese topping that has popped up even in our local grocery store), sesame seeds or colored sugar. Our family laughed when we heard the parmesan cheese in the green canister referred to as "spaghetti glitter." Sprinkles can bridge to new foods (see page 122).

Tea strainer: Use it to sprinkle! Add powdered sugar, cocoa powder or cinnamon, or a mix, and make "snow" on pancakes, waffles, or fruit.

Teething rings, Duo spoon, or other dippers: Offer teething rings and mouthing toys with various textures to help with mouthing and chewing skills (such as Tri-Chew or similar). This can help children get comfortable and used to more sensation, and gives them control. Allow infants/toddlers (or anyone if it helps) to dip the spoon or ring into purees, yogurt, or mashed foods and suck or lick the food off.

Cooking or Food Prep Gear

Getting meals together and served takes a lot of time, effort, and money. Below are recommendations for gear that can help make the process easier and more affordable.

Extra freezer: Buy and freeze meats on sale, other pricey items such as non-dairy milks, or convenience foods. You can also freeze batch-cooked meals or meals from friends, bulk items, frozen fruit for smoothies etc.

Slow cooker/steamer: Buy frozen, ready-made, slow-cooker meals and put them in the slow cooker on your way out the door in the morning. Or cook up a pork shoulder for pulled-pork BBQ sandwiches one day and pork tacos the next. Freeze servings for easy, quick meals. Young children tend to do well with softer, slow-cooked meats.

Air fryer: Air frying helps with that crisp and crunchy texture (which many selective eaters prefer). Also, it helps bring foods from freezer to table quicker; for example, in 20 minutes I can have cooked and somewhat crispy homemade fried potatoes on plates. ("Somewhat" crispy because I crowd the basket, no time for just one layer!) Frozen sweet potato fries can take less than 10 minutes. Cauliflower with olive oil and some cheese on top at the very end takes 12 minutes. Grilled cheese or crescent rolls in 6 minutes. And the tater tots! Yum! Some models have exposed heating coils in the lid, so use caution or opt for a different option. Air fryers can be safer and easier to use than a traditional oven. Instant Pot and Food Ninja make combos with slow cooker, rice cooker, steamer/air fryer all in one (these have the exposed coils).

Food grinder/processor: You can use a hand-turned or electric unit to grind veggies, meat (or other foods) that you're eating for dinner, right at the table. Add water, broth, or sauce as needed to make it moist enough for your child to handle. Spread ground-up meat on toast or crackers or put a blob on the table or tray for your little one to feed herself.

Frozen pop molds: Make your own pops to support nutrition/hydration while they progress with eating.

Gear and Products You Might Not Need

Sometimes gear is unnecessary or can get in the way.

Skip the plate, add a spoon: Babies don't *need* utensils or plates. You can use spoons if you're spoon-feeding. He may want to play with the spoon, or not. Sometimes using two or three spoons, so he can hang on to one while you load the other, helps. Put finger foods where he can reach it directly on the table or tray. Plates can distract. And sometimes shallow bowls and plates offer an edge for the child to push against to help pick up food.

Child-sized tables: While these may be ideal for crafts and occasional snacks, it's tempting to allow children to always eat at a child-sized table. Some dining tables are counter height, requiring extra-tall chairs and complicating eating with small children. Consider getting a standard table or shortening the legs of a taller table. When children eat separately, they miss out on the most critical "gear"—*you*.

Snack traps: It's easy to allow a child to carry around a snack trap of cereal or puffs, but this increases cavity risk and can undermine structure and appetite. Use for planned snacks or special occasions.

Mesh bag or silicone teether/feeder: I've seen these misused when a child is capable of eating without them, but a parent uses them almost exclusively because of a fear of choking. It's not a substitute for learning to deal with textures. Relying too heavily on mesh or silicone teether/feeders interferes with a child's learning and development with eating.

Puree pouches: Pouches are convenient, less messy, tend to be sweet, and can be used responsively. If feeding an infant, at least for some meals, pour the puree into a small bowl or compartment and use a spoon. Allow her to explore and lick the puree off fingers, spoon, or dipper. Offer other family foods, mashed or prepared as finger foods.

Some older toddlers and preschoolers can get stuck on pouches (getting almost all their calories from them) and have trouble transitioning to other foods. Yes, it's solid food, but delivered in a way that keeps the child sucking and not advancing textures. I tend to see this happen when parents worry about intake and growth, or fruits and vegetables, or with underlying challenges. A child may prefer controlling a pouch to being fed by an anxious parent pushing food.

If a child is only eating purees beyond 12 to 15 months or so and isn't progressing, talk to their doctor. (See page 147 on oral-motor concerns.)

> Some experts advise against pouches at all because of this potential reliance and the less-than-ideal oral-motor experience; but they can be enjoyed in a responsive way. Children who are unfamiliar with a variety of foods can use pouches to sample flavors. Pouches can offer a comfortable and familiar food children can control if they need to reinforce felt safety while eating. For a child only drinking from a bottle or cup who has more advanced skills, a pouch can be introduced while maintaining cuddle and connection time. Positive experiences build confidence for parents and children alike which supports internal drives to eat; pouches can be part of that process.

In general, pouches can round out a snack at the park, or be served with one or two eating times a day. Be careful if you're serving them at every meal or snack "just to get something in." The same goes for any food, whether it's a smoothie, frozen pop, or supplement. **If you're terrified when they don't eat it, it's time for support.**

Day-to-Day Feeding Situations and Challenges

Let's now look at some common challenges where anticipatory guidance can make a big difference.

Big Changes Impact Eating and the Idea of "Regression"

If things have been going relatively well with food and now have fallen apart, what else is going on in your child's life? Is a sibling joining the family? Is there anxiety over a move, a new school, or a big leap in development such as learning to walk, run, or read? Any of these may exhaust a child's reserves.

And events in your life can impact how you're able to be present and participate; perhaps you're grappling with a decision to return to school, had to pick up extra shifts, or all the talk about holiday weight gain is tugging you back into diet mindset.

Seven-year-old Gavin's story illustrates how life stressors can impact eating. In the fall of his kindergarten year, Gavin wanted to eat more bread and pasta. Carol, Gavin's mother, became concerned about weight gain (his growth was stable for years at the 75th percentile). Carol began limiting portions, asked Gavin to eat more veggies, and wait 20 minutes before having second servings. During this time, Gavin was getting used to full and overwhelming school days, peers, and new expectations.

Gavin's behavior at school and at home worsened dramatically; he constantly whined for food, and before long was sneaking food. His weight began accelerating rapidly. Interestingly, when I reviewed Gavin's growth, within a few months of his initial interest in more carbs, he grew about 2½ inches.

With behavioral and feeding challenges coinciding, life was miserable and meals were the worst. Mom (describing herself as naturally slim) encouraged Dad to diet, and she routinely "forgot to eat." It annoyed her that Gavin needed to eat so frequently. As happens occasionally, they did not follow up after the initial evaluation.

I suspect that Carol was too worried about Gavin's weight to let go of the sense of control. Gavin's story demonstrates the spiral of control and resistance, as well as how challenges intersect with feeding.

Perhaps if Gavin had been trusted with his eating, his increased energy needs and need for autonomy and felt safety at mealtimes may have been understood as preparation for a growth spurt or looking for comforting and familiar foods. Reducing stress at meals may have helped Gavin's food preoccupation and weight acceleration. Getting their feeding relationship back on track might not have addressed issues at school, but **family meals could have been a safe place to connect, rather than a flashpoint for more conflict.**

Another mom, Alana, shared that things with her three year-old, Lindsay, fell apart when her little brother was born. Lindsay ate a decent variety and enjoyed meals. When baby Ben came home, Lindsay had some challenges adjusting, and Alana began to worry that Lindsay wasn't eating enough. She "regressed" in other areas as well, such as toileting. They ended up stuck in counterproductive patterns:

- Alana only served foods Lindsay requested, gradually offering fewer options.
- Lindsay started withholding her poops and was back to diapers for BMs.
- Worried about constipation, Lindsay served pureed fruit and veggie pouches, letting Lindsay have them whenever she wanted.
- Lindsay would tantrum until she could eat on mom's lap or in front of a screen.
- Alana and her husband started eating after the kids were in bed.

- The routine fell apart (understandably) with a new infant in the home.
- Alana quit her job to stay home and lost her joy with cooking.

During times of stress, say a sibling joins the family, an illness, job stress, a pandemic, whatever it is—families understandably focus on getting through each day. Parents may lovingly turn to feeding strategies that seem to help in the short term, but then get stuck.

Knowing that things may get worse with a transition can help you hold steady, or get back on track, when it happens. Sue experienced difficulties when daughter Mary's half-brother came to live with them. *"Mary backtracked slightly around the time her brother came home (age 2½ for her), but we'd been prepared for regression as a possibility in a variety of areas when a sibling was added to the home. She got back on track in due time."*

Be kind with yourselves, know there may be times where you rely on convenience foods, takeout, or letting some things slide because you're dealing with bigger concerns. Getting "back on track" with how and what you want to feed will be easier with a responsive model, where the focus is on felt safety and connection first—not the guilt.

Alana and her partner focused on connection and getting back to a more predictable routine. Gradually, mealtimes became less chaotic, they served pouches along with other foods, and Lindsay even enjoyed her role as big sister and helping to eat with and feed Ben. Dad took over some meals and snacks. He had special time to connect with Lindsay, and fed Ben sometimes so that Alana and Lindsay could have one-on-one time. Once Ben was sleeping for a few more hours at a time, Alana felt ready to come back to cooking, which she missed.

One mom on social media shared how her autistic teenager struggled with going back to school after break. When stressed, this teen had decreased appetite and his sensory threshold was lower. During that time he ate mostly French fries in his room, but within a week or so of starting school, and with other supports, he was feeling less stressed and able to join the family again at meal times. They had learned from past experience that pushing him to join in meals and eat beyond his comfort foods upped the risk of burnout.

If we consider these three example through the lens of felt safety and connection, we realize that it isn't necessarily "regression" but what your child/teen can handle in the moment.

Sibling Stress

Under the best of circumstances, siblings can have epic battles. With neurodivergence and/or sensory differences, this can be amplified.

Therapist Eileen Devine works toward building empathy and connection between siblings. "If we use language that puts the situation into the neurobehavioral context, it will help siblings understand the brain-behavior connection, and help them have more empathy for their brother or sister who is struggling." Most of the following is excerpted with permission from Devine's blog post on The Resilience Room, "Supporting Siblings in a Chaotic Space":[4]

- Kids can begin to understand that "brains work differently," and can grow into a more sophisticated understanding as they get older. Try: "We're all in different places, everyone in our family has brains that work differently."
- There is no age that's too early to begin talking about this in relation to a brother or sister who struggles.
- This is a conversation to have regularly and consistently over time.
- Explain that fair does not necessarily mean equal.
- Make a point to tell a child that it's okay to have feelings of resentment and anger toward their brother or sister.
- Try not to unintentionally "parentify" siblings. It's easy to ask siblings to help in ways that ideally are the role of the parent. This can leave them feeling as though they are not allowed to be the child.
- One-on-one time for siblings is essential for them, for us, and for our relationship with them. It requires being present: Turning off phones and tuning in while on a walk, playing a card game, or talking during a drive to the store are all meaningful starts.
- Finally, the best thing we can do to support the siblings in our family unit is to take care of our own emotional, physical, and spiritual well-being. (More in Chapter 12).

Katherine Zavodni, RD, recommends using language of "different" versus more or less in terms of support needs, preferences, hunger etc. "You and Imani like different things. That's okay."

A parent shared an experience when her son was struggling during a meal, reached over and took his sister's cookie, and fed it to their dog. The girl, a tween at the time, sighed loudly and slumped her shoulders as if to say, "It's really hard having a brother like this sometimes."

Luckily, the parents had done a lot of preparation that helped their daughter cope with this situation. Her understanding of her brother's brain-based impulsivity helped keep things from erupting (this time) and helped her move away from the "I'm so mad at you!" response. Her cookie was replaced, and after the meal, he was able to apologize.

The good news with a responsive approach is that you can avoid many battles about fairness around food as children are fed the same way. You don't need to try to get more food into one child, or less into another, as they will eat based on internal cues. You can't control hunger. RF is *fair* and avoids those battles.

Eating Out

Many families regularly eat out. If you eat together, it's a family meal. If you're having fast food you usually eat in the car, go into the restaurant if you can, and enjoy the food and each other.

Waiting for food can be tough. Bring fidgets or activities, order ahead online, or plan for screen time. When my daughter was young, I looked for booths (so she could kneel) and a buffet. Our favorites were Ruby Tuesday and local Chinese and Indian buffets, which had mild options and a variety of fruits, veggies, proteins, sauces, and starches. Salad bars are a great way to introduce veggies, fruits, sauces, and more with little risk. Grab a plate or two, sample options such as cherry tomatoes, green beans, sunflower seeds, and pasta salad, add a few containers of different dressings for dipping, and put it in the middle of the table as "appetizers."

Kids might be bored or hungry and interested in something new while waiting for their entree—without pressure. You may need to get him his own plate, but the child who is healing from food preoccupation will see that there is plenty of food.

Ordering When Eating Out

How you will guide your child with ordering depends on how frequently you eat out, and on your child. If you eat out frequently, you may choose to be more involved. If you only eat out once or twice a week, you can probably let that go.

With young children, you're still in charge of what is offered. I find that in restaurants, it works well if you give choices from the menu: "So, you want fries; would you like chicken or a burger with that?" The following are some ideas if you eat out regularly:

- You might offer one fried choice; for example, chicken tenders with pasta.
- Consider letting them choose soda or dessert; or lemonade or dessert.
- Share a dessert or ask for a kids' option, showing the servers the size of ice-cream scoop you would like, for example. (A restaurant dessert might be three scoops of ice cream plus a brownie.)
- If there aren't many options—and frankly, many restaurant veggies are not very appealing (although Applebee's broccoli side is good)—aim for variety the rest of the day or week.
- Teens may need more leeway in choosing what to eat. (See Chapter 6 on anxious eaters, where fries may be a win.)
- For children (or you!) overwhelmed by choice in restaurants, look at menus online in advance so you can choose with fewer distractions.

Inviting Children to Cook with You

Children who participate in growing food, shopping, and cooking tend to explore more. But pressuring a child to cook with you (hello power struggle) may backfire.

As a child, I preferred climbing trees and watching TV to cooking. My father worried, as I was heading off to college, that I couldn't cook. My mother's attitude was: "I'm not worried. She likes to eat. She'll learn." As I moved into my first apartment, I called home for tips on teriyaki chicken or mashed potatoes, and cooked with my mom during visits home.

When my daughter was a preschooler, she too had little interest in helping in the kitchen. At age six, however, she seemed to enjoy pitching in, for a while, then not so much. Around age 12 she got into baking, and in high school enjoyed experimenting with stir-frying but less baking (boo!). Offer opportunities, take "no" for an answer, and try again. You never know when a child might come around. And social media can be a good thing here with enticing and even trendy recipes you can look at together and prepare.

Cooking and Accommodations

For children and teens who find following directions, managing time, and planning to be difficult—meal planning and cooking can feel defeating. (There is more later in this chapter on flexible menu and meal prep.)

Kitty described how at her home the boys rotated making meals. *"They had a hard time getting shopping lists together, or would forget to thaw the chicken in time. I learned to say, 'Hey, it's four and you wanted chicken parm tonight. Do you need me to do anything to get dinner started?' Versus, 'Dude, you're slacking!'"* Kitty came at it from a helping place, and accommodating their needs and skills.

Worksheets, visual cues, simplifying recipes and directions, using apps or timers, are some ways to support neurodivergent youth. If your child is still struggling, consider working with an occupational therapist to help break down tasks. Here are a few more ideas to help the process:

- Start with success: pre-measuring, helping dump ingredients, or stirring.
- Expect a mess.
- Share about times when your recipe attempts failed, or the flour flew all over the kitchen. Cooking is about making mistakes and learning.
- Have them thread cut-up fruit on skewers.
- Help them get baked cookies off the cooled cookie tray.
- Frost cookies or cupcakes with them.
- Count out blueberries for muffins together.
- Look for recipes online that also include video and printable instructions.
- Make "charcuterie board" meals with no cooking required. Cheese and crackers with some fruit, or bagels with different spread options, and a smoothie.

Friends, Family, and Community Influences

People and events outside your home influence how your child will eat and feel about their body. You won't be able to control all or even most of it, but you will can address some things to support your child. This next section will address: family and friends who may try to meddle, helping childcare providers get on board, and dealing with diet talk.

Dealing with Meddlers

Most people don't believe that children can be trusted with eating; they won't understand what you're doing, or make an effort to understand *why* you might be doing it. If you do things differently than your parents did, they may take it as a rejection of how they raised you. They may even actively undermine your feeding strategies. For example, my friend's son had a dairy-contact allergy (touching dairy caused a reaction), but her in-laws didn't believe in it, and sneaked him ice cream—with predictable results.

Family and friends who aren't following the same approach as you are may whisper, or even shout in your ear, "You're making her o*ese!" While another parent might hear, "Why can't you get him to eat?" It's easier to deal with those comments when you feel confident with you're approach, which is why this book offers so much background.

Dr. Lesley Williams, eating disorder expert, author, and mom commiserates, "It's difficult to overcome the guilt you feel and the silent (or not so silent) blame that others put on you when your child is larger (or smaller) than other children. People feel very comfortable offering you *or your child* advice, re: how to make their body smaller. It's important to safeguard them against this behavior from other adults."

Here are some experiences shared by parents:

"I know that some friends and family quietly questioned my methods and wondered if it was necessary."

— Sophie, mother of Quinn who has sensory differences

"I got the occasional, 'We're going to slip her an M&M when you aren't looking' comment. This felt hurtful because it undermined my parenting intentions to do what I knew was best for my child. And it proved my family just did not understand. I didn't offer M&Ms at 18 months because it was a choking hazard with her compromised swallowing ability."

— Leah, mother to Elise

Your feeding (and parenting) may feel questioned. Patricia shared how hurtful family comments can feel. *"My parents made subtle remarks implying that I was overreacting. My dad made comments that really bothered me—like I was causing the problem, and I should make her eat everything on her plate."*

Therapist and mom Dawn Friedman says tension dealing with family is a common source of second-guessing and pain. Friedman brings it back to core values: "Are you going to choose what will make your child feel good or what will make their grandparents feel good?" One mom echoed this advice, saying, "*Don't worry about hurting other people's feelings when it comes to doing the right thing for your child.*"

I'm not suggesting that you panic if Grandma offers double desserts or extra snacks. For the occasional visit, a more lax structure or more sweets is fine. It may be a way for family to connect with your child, and having that time at Grandma's where the rules don't always apply can be very special.

However, if extended family or others who care for your child routinely undermine your feeding and parenting, you can advocate. I know this issue was fraught for me as a parent of a child with a bigger appetite in a bigger body. Parenting, like nothing else, forces us to do our own work, to figure out boundaries for our children when doing it for ourselves maybe didn't feel doable.

Honoring Our Elders: Multigenerational Households and Caregiving

Parent coach and feeding specialist, Jule Zivah RDN (zivahcoaching.com)

According to the United States Census Bureau, the number of multigenerational households is on the rise. There are many reasons for this, including financial necessity, shared childcare, as well as a return to cultural norms.

Tensions can arise when elders approach feeding and eating differently than parents. So, where is the balance between honoring cultural roles of elders (which may include feeding children) and advocating for your child? The magic is in leading with love by "Calling in" rather than "Calling out." The idea is that rather than telling someone what they're doing wrong, we can instead invite them into conversation to find out why the practice is important to them and then use that meaning to invite them into our children's lives in a new way.

By taking a stance of reflection and curiosity, we build connections. For example, if Grandma is offering the toddler food to carry and eat throughout the house, but Mom is concerned about choking, we can call Grandma into conversation to find out what her reason might be (what's the why?). Let's say she's concerned the child will get hungry and doesn't yet know how to ask for food. There is an opportunity to ask for Grandma's help in looking for subtle hunger signals, rather than just lecturing her about choking. Addressing Grandma's worry will more likely change her behavior than would lecturing her about choking.

And, interactions with different adults enrich the child's experiences from which they will develop their own eating competence. Inviting elders to share their food positive memories, stories, and wisdom honors traditions that become woven into the fabric of the family. When physical and emotional safety are a concern, clear boundaries stated with loving kindness are appropriate.

Boundaries, and Knowing When to Intervene

If your childhood memories of eating in your family were traumatic—i.e., you were made to diet, forced to eat, weighed daily, or taunted—that's a pretty good clue to avoid leaving feeding up to your relatives if you have other options. This is especially tricky if you rely on them for childcare. Do the best you can. It isn't always clear when to speak up and when you can let things slide, but the following are a few scenarios in which I feel strongly that a child needs an ally:

- If your parents/relatives force your child to eat or taste foods.
- If they make your child eat something to the point of upset or vomiting, or if they make the child eat "gagged-up" foods.
- If they yell or are angry at meals about who is eating what or how much.
- If they try to get your child to lose weight, or talk about food or the child's body in harmful ways.
- If they try to get your child to gain weight by pushing or forcing food.
- If they won't follow your family's religious or cultural diet, and/or repeatedly talk about food, health, or weight in ways you think will harm your child.

Ragen Chastain, fat activist and athlete who writes the Weight and Healthcare newsletter, wrote on her website *Dances with Fat* on the topic of family interference around food: "First, I always suggest that you be prepared for boundary setting when you go into this type of situation. Think about what your boundaries are, and what consequences you are willing to enforce. So, think about what you would be willing to do—Leave the event? Stay at a hotel? Cease conversation until the person can treat you appropriately? Be sure that you know what you want and that you can follow through."[5]

When I learned that boundaries are not rules for what other people can or cannot say or do, but are about what I will accept, that was a game changer. Nedra Glover Tawwab's book *Set Boundaries, Find Peace,* and her Instagram page have lots of practical advice on healthy boundaries.

Tough stuff. If you have extended visits, it's reasonable to ask relatives to try their best to follow your lead. I regularly reminded my parents to be sure to let my daughter decide when she was done eating. I would say, "Even if she seems to eat a lot—or nothing—please let her eat until *she* is done."

How to Advocate

Ideally, before you leave your kids with relatives, share a few meals together and observe. Let the small stuff slide, but protect your kids—not from cookies, but from comments like, "Look at your tummy, you've obviously had enough," or "You have to eat all your food before you can go."

"There were eight of us for dinner at my parents', including my son and his girlfriend—both high school seniors. Mom sat next to poor Girlfriend, and announced

that Girlfriend wasn't eating anything green, and told her she needed more nutrition. Triggering my past issues, I responded, 'It's Thanksgiving, we all get to eat what we want.' Which seemed to resolve the issue."

— Tammy, a blog reader

Let's anticipate your next family holiday table. Maybe Grandma Eve raised six kids, and they're all "fine." Uncle Sam recently lost 30 pounds at his company's Biggest Loser contest (again), so he's eager to share. Betty force fed your three-year-old mashed potatoes last year (he threw up) because she's convinced he'd "love potatoes if he tried them."

Your family may intrude, saying or doing the opposite of what you're trying to accomplish. The following section offers ideas on how to handle well-meaning, but unhelpful and unsolicited, advice.

"Please, Follow My Lead"

The phrase I've found particularly useful with my own family and for clients is, "*Please follow my lead.*" Your family doesn't have to understand, agree with, or partake in your feeding philosophies, but you can ask them to "follow my lead." If you have a family with a pattern of trying to get your child to eat more or less, try foods, pressure, shame, or bully, step in with a polite but firm, "*Mom, please follow my lead with this.*" Try not to explain, draw attention, or argue during the meal.

Ideally, find a moment beforehand to talk with your family. "Mom, we're trying something with Maya's eating. We're allowing her to choose what foods, and how much to eat, from what's on offer. Please don't ask her to eat more, and also, don't make a fuss or praise if she does eat something new. I know it's not how you would handle it, but I hope you can *follow our lead*." Use those words in your preparatory explanation. A brief reminder when they slip up ought to be enough.

They *will* slip up, and that's not the end of the world. With repeated reminders, hopefully they will back off. This way of feeding may be different from anything your family members know. "Follow my lead" allows them to observe *you* and hopefully pick up on how responsive feeding works. And remember, what happens all the other days of the year in your home matters most. (And they may surprise you when they see things improving and ask to learn more and get on board.)

If family continues to push, you can change the topic and try to offer other ways they can help: "I appreciate your concern, but I can't talk about his eating or weight with you. It doesn't work like that for us. If you want to help, could you bring in our recycling bins? I usually have my hands full on Thursday nights and that would be a huge help."

The following are a few more examples of what you might say. Practice these phrases in advance or find words that work for you:

Grandpa: "If you take that piece of toast, you have to finish it."
You say: "Actually Dad, that's not how we do it. Please follow my lead. Billy, why don't you start with half a piece. If you're still hungry, you can have more."

Restaurant server: "You can't have dessert, sweetie, until you finish your broccoli!" (This really happens.)
You say: "No tip for you." (Just kidding.)
Try: "We're doing fine here. Please bring her dessert now, thanks."

Grandpa: "Let's hide his bottle. He's distracted. Haven't you heard that o*ese babies will be fat adults and get diabetes and..."
You say: "Grandpa, we let Téo decide when he's done. He'll let us know. May I have his bottle back, please?"

Uncle Bob: "You'll hurt Aunt Betty's feelings if you don't eat her dressing."
You say: "Oh, Bob! We love Aunt Betty, and thank her for making dinner, but we don't ask Sylvan to eat anything he doesn't want to. *I'd* like some dressing, though, please."

Your Sister, Jasmin: "We had to sit and keep quiet as kids. Can't you control him?"
You say: "Yeah, I remember we were always so happy when dinner was over. I'd like us all to enjoy eating together, and Mani's body feels best when he takes breaks."

You may also need to prepare your children for different expectations that you're okay with: "At Grandpa's, throwing away food makes him really upset, so we'll start with smaller amounts and take more when we're ready." Or, "Remember that they serve dessert after the meal in case you want to save some hungry."

If family and friends aren't able to adapt their words or behaviors, and it's negatively impacting your child, you may need to set a firm boundary, such as, "If you keep trying to make him eat, we won't be able to come over for meals anymore."

Dealing with Diet Talk

What to do when the talk turns to calories, fat, and weight loss, and impressionable ears are listening? Katherine Zavodni, RD, reminds us that, "The message that it is shameful and terrible to gain weight and get bigger is profoundly harmful for kids who are continuously gaining weight and getting bigger."

First approach may be to remove your child from the conversation, "Let's go see what your cousins are up to," or try changing the topic, "Hey, how was your camping trip? We're thinking about going next year!"

Look into the media they are consuming. Peppa Pig famously mocks the father for his tummy. I watched about five minutes of a Nickelodeon show popular with my daughter's second-grade classmates before a tween boy mocked a woman for her "cankles"! That show (and most Disney and Nickelodeon shows of that era) were avoided in our home. When your child does encounter diet talk or weight bias on TV and other media, depending on their age, you may need to help them unpack what they heard.

You might ask them what they think it means or if they have heard about diets before to get a sense of their understanding. I tend to keep things as simple as possible. I've said versions of the following over the years as it has come up:

- Dieting is when people try to eat less than they're hungry for or their body needs. It can also mean not eating foods they want to eat. Usually it's to try to make their body smaller.
- Oh, your teacher said cake is bad because she thinks she needs to lose weight? Yep. That's dieting. And diets are bad for you. They are especially bad for kids because you are still growing.
- Body size isn't the problem, sometimes when people diet they can make their bodies smaller for a while, but usually it feels really bad, and most times their bodies will get bigger again. It's not their fault.
- A lot of people don't know that diets are bad for you. Some people, like Aunt Lucy, think diets and losing weight is healthy. So you'll hear confusing things.
- In our family, we don't diet.
- What do you think the message of that Tik Tok is? Businesses make billions of dollars a year trying to convince people that they should be thin, and they try to sell books, pills, drinks, foods, clothes... using fear.
- You can trust your body.

Refer back to Chapter 7 for more ideas on how to talk about these tricky issues with your kids.

Avoid Commenting on Weight

You never know if someone is losing weight by dieting, over-exercising, purging, severe restriction, or due to a serious illness. Complimenting weight loss means you think high weight is bad. Because commenting on someone's appearance is so automatic, it took me a while to come up with something else. Skip the looks, clothes, and the weight. How about a sincere, "I'm so glad to see you!" or "I missed your smile!" and, "Tell me about school/soccer, what books are you reading/shows are you streaming..."

Daycare or Schools

The people who care for our children want what's best for them. Finding affordable, safe, convenient, nurturing childcare is difficult. Many parents feel conflicted if they disagree with feeding practices and policies. U.S. childcare providers usually feed the way most Americans do—they pressure, bribe, enforce two-bite rules, and don't support eating based on internal cues.[6] To be fair, many parents ask childcare staff to try to get their children to eat more, or certain kinds of foods, and centers generally also have to comply with government or licensing standards.

While researching childcare, ask how they manage snacks and meals. I toured one facility and saw a single pretzel stick with a Dixie cup of water for snack. When I asked what they would do if my child was still hungry, they assured me, "Don't worry, we won't let her have any more because we do our part against childhood o*esity." That well-respected center got crossed off my list.

Many childcare centers and schools have a policy that children eat "real" or "growing" food before any sweets, even if you pack the meal. This is not responsive. Children's lunches are commonly inspected in front of other children. One kindergartner's snack size candy bar (in packed lunch that included a sandwich and fruit) was held up in front of the class as an example of a "bad" food kids should not bring to school. Even fruit cups have been called "unhealthy" (for having too much sugar) and children shamed for enjoying them.

Here are some tips on how you can advocate for responsive feeding at your childcare or school:

- Copy, fill in, and laminate the "lunchbox card" on page 349 (also online at thefeedingdoctor.com). Place it in your child's lunchbox and tell him that if an adult asks him to eat certain foods, he could hand over or point to the card. This is a lot to ask a child to do, but it may work.
- Have a private meeting with the daycare director and/or teacher.
- Reassure staff that this means less work for them, not more. You are simply asking them to allow your child to eat from what you pack, in any order and amount.
- Thank the staff for their efforts, but inform them that you are working on the issue at home, and that pressure or restriction will slow the process. (Sunnyside Up Nutrition has letters on their website that you can share with teachers and camp counselors around these issues.)
- Ask them not to report on what or how much they ate, in front of your child. If you must know, ask for an email or text (see pages 78 and 112 on how attention to their eating can feel like pressure).

If the staff simply won't do as you ask, consider asking to have the child transferred to a different group or class, or look for an alternative.

During the Q and A after a workshop for early-childhood teachers, an attendee told a story. She had actually been one of my daughter's teachers at a pre-K summer camp a few years earlier. I remember vividly going in on that first day with my daughter's lunch and her lunchbox card, and making my request about letting her decide what and how much to eat. I was always nervous doing this, but knew it helped to do it from the start. I didn't hear much about meals that summer from my daughter or the staff, and had forgotten about it until this teacher shared that her class now has an "open lunch bag" policy.

She reassured the skeptical audience: "It works! You wouldn't think it does, but they eat more variety and behave better. The staff likes it too since we don't have to pressure and manage the kids." I was especially touched when she came up afterward and said, "After we had your daughter in our class and saw how you did things and how well it worked, we instituted the policy. Not all the teachers do it, though. One teacher makes the kids eat their 'real' food before they can go to recess, and a little boy was gagging and upset every lunch. He changed to our room and that stopped from day one."

Getting Meals on the Table

There is little recognition for how hard feeding families is day to day! And while I can't fix work schedules, lack of childcare and family support, cost of food, transportation, and other barriers you may face, I hope this section may make this task a little easier.

Menu Planning

I've tried websites, printouts, and menu planning apps; none worked for me. Until we found a system, I didn't enjoy menu planning. I'd skip it and find myself many afternoons with no idea of what was for dinner. We ate out and threw more food away than we wanted to.

It all changed when we lived in an RV for a year, working and "road-schooling" across the United States. It forced us to menu plan in detail, as we had limited pantry space and spotty access to shopping. We enjoyed canned fruits and more beans, and adapted to a different way of cooking. We have largely stayed with this way of planning (which also decreased our food costs).

We plan together, with our daughter chiming in as she got older. We generally plan for four to five days at a time. Early in the Covid-19 pandemic, we went as long as 12 days with planned meals, eating fresher foods in the first days, and frozen and shelf-stable toward the end.

How you plan to get food on the table will change with your circumstances. Be kind with yourself. If you've had a tough day, or a late-running therapy appointment, take-out on the way home may be the best solution (or breakfast-for-dinner, frozen meals, or delivery). Here are some advantages to planning flexible menus:

- One person can shop and the other can cook. (With no plan, the person cooking usually ends up doing the shopping.)
- Helps you stick to a list and budget.
- Many parents enjoy the process and the predictability that kids need.
- Decreases food waste.
- Can help you plan and provide a variety of foods.
- Online and smartphone apps organize menus and shopping lists.

- Reduces last-minute trips to the store.
- Helpful if you use a grocery delivery service or curbside pickup.
- Helps get food on the table after a long day.
- If you're new to cooking or family meals, it can help keep you on track and avoid last-minute delivery because you couldn't think of an alternative.
- Can reduce decision fatigue and end-of-the-day planning burnout.

A meal-prep delivery service can kickstart planning. One new mom and reluctant cook got three months of meal kits delivered and found that it introduced ingredients and techniques that helped her confidence and skills. When the service ran out, she felt better able to plan, cook, and explore recipes, and she didn't dread the task (most days) as much.

Currently, our system looks like this: We have a small notebook that lives on the counter. During the week if something runs out, we add it to the shopping list. The back of the page lists the days and meals: usually a meat or alternative, a veggie and a starch, or stews, soups, etc. As we come up with the menu, we add to the list what we need to buy. We usually do this after dinner the night before a shopping day, using the family recipe binder for inspiration. We check if we have items in the pantry. We consider things such as chips, snacks, lunch packing, and breakfast. Planning for four to six days usually takes about ten minutes. With the menu on the back, it's easier to make substitutions if the store is out of, say, green beans.

We organize the shopping list based on where things are in the store: non-perishables (chips, cans, pasta, etc.) first, then on to eggs and dairy, meats, and fresh and frozen last.

If you're new to planning meals, start with what you eat now, serve it family style, and sit down and eat together. Next try to plan—maybe before you leave for work in the morning—what you will eat that night for dinner. Then plan a few days in a row. Don't try to force a method to work, give it a try when you have the energy.

If you're trying to stick to a list and budget, consider shopping after a meal. When I shop hungry I toss lots of items in my cart that aren't on the list. It all looks appealing on an empty stomach!

Go slow and see what works for you. If meal plans spoil the experience, and you feel guilty that you couldn't or didn't do it or stick to it, take a break or try something else. Have convenience foods in the freezer/pantry you can rely on and a few quick recipes. It takes time to build a repertoire. For every four new recipes I try, maybe one is worthy of regular rotation (it tastes good enough and isn't too much trouble). My recipe book is a three-ring binder with plastic sleeves and tabs. Most new recipes are printed from websites and can be easily added.

While our system works for us right now (and you may be happy with what you've worked out), another approach might work better down the road. But just like with eating, don't let the "shoulds" spoil the process.

Leslie Jordan Garcia MBA, MPH, CEDRS, an anti-diet eating disorder recovery and wellness practitioner (Leslie Jordan Wellness) talked about Feeding a Family with Diverse Needs (this is the title of the episode and it's worth a listen) on the Sunnyside Up Nutrition Podcast. She suggests that overwhelmed parents who want to work towards less chaos in the kitchen might start with theme days; maybe Meatless Monday, Taco Tuesday, Whip-it-up Wednesday, or Leftover Saturday. She advised to make it as simple as possible, and if a week is too big, start with three days.

Planning and Cooking When You Are Neurodivergent

"I have ADHD and I'm on my own with the kids, so this is really hard. I try to menu plan when I'm really fresh, and keep it simple. I have phone alerts to remind me in the morning in case I need to take something out of the freezer to thaw. I do my best, and honestly, sometimes I lose track of time and we have sandwiches or frozen meals, but we all get fed. Some weeks are better than others. As the kids get older, they're more helpful. It's a work in progress."

— Social media comment

You may have family members with different sensory needs in terms of food—some preferring smooth, others enjoying more crunch. With chronic pain, executive functioning differences, or burnout from work, making a meal can give parents demand anxiety! There are more and more resources directed towards ND parents to help with feeding families that you can access, and here are a few more ideas.

- Let go of the idea of meal-specific foods. Leftover takeout for breakfast or waffles for dinner are awesome.
- Have simple "meals" for days when you don't have the capacity or interest to do more. The "charcuterie board" trend can inspire you, but it doesn't have to look fancy: some crackers, cheese, and a handful of berries makes a great meal.
- Air-fried frozen tater tots and ketchup are a meal. Not every meal has to be "balanced." Add when you can.
- Review "Ideas on What and How to Serve" on page 120. Serve deconstructed meals from paper plates: baked potato with toppings, pizza bagels with choices of toppings, make rice bowls with pre-cooked rice, leftover rotisserie chicken and whatever else you can find.
- To deal with decision fatigue and overwhelm, and help with shopping, the idea of having days for certain meals, like Leslie Jordan explained above, can be very helpful.

Menu Planning Stories from Parents

Over the years, readers of my *Feeding Doctor* blog shared how planning worked for their families:

"I enjoy making a weekly meal plan; it gives me a sense of calm in a chaotic week. I do it on a whiteboard so if I want to switch Tuesday's green beans with Wednesday's broccoli, one swipe of the finger does it. The kids, I think, like being able to see our week laid out. Dinner is such an extraordinarily important part of their day. Meal planning also helps me clear out the fridge and freezer. Most importantly, planning helps balance our meals. I can see that, okay, I've got one beef meal, one chicken meal, one bean meal, one starchy meal, etc."

"I go once a week to Target for nonperishables, and every few days I walk to the co-op with my son and we shop for fresh items. We enjoy the outings, and I can cook what appeals to me that day. When I go back to work fulltime, this won't work, and I'll miss it."

"I make a menu and buy from recipes, but I also have some staples always on my list to make last-minute things if something on my menu doesn't work. I've found that being in school has really messed up my menu planning/grocery list because my schedule is unpredictable and time-pressed. I used to soak beans and make bread, but we're eating canned beans and buying bread these days. Sometimes it's homemade soup and sometimes it's take-out, but at least we're having good family time eating together, so that's all good. I'll go back to cooking when time allows."

"I have about 12 entree recipes—some with meat and some without. My kids and husband don't care if we have quiche every week. We rotate in sloppy joes, homemade calzones, black bean burritos or quesadillas, split pea soup, roasted chicken, scrambled eggs, and baked pasta. Things that don't include protein/vegetable/starch are rounded out with bread, frozen or fresh vegetables, noodles, or rice. The freezer means I can buy meat and frozen vegetables, and I 'shop' in the freezer in weeks when money is tight or I don't have any big ideas."

"My husband and I plan together as part of our Sunday mornings: a leisurely breakfast followed by meal planning over coffee. ***We also look at our schedules for the week and know who's picking up our son. That tells us how many meals need to be super quick to prepare, and how many we can take more time preparing.*** *We don't eat meat, so I like to look at meals over the week to see that we have a variety of protein sources. I try to balance meals that may be challenging for our son with meals that are a sure hit. And we try to get at least one meal that provides leftovers. All of us go to the store together. We make a list of meals, but we don't plan it out that Monday is X, and Tuesday is Y, so there is flexibility. We always have staples for quick meals (scrambled eggs, spaghetti and jarred sauce, or bean burritos) for nights we just don't feel like cooking. Now that my son can read and reach a lot of things at the store, shopping together is becoming fun."*

Keeping Kids Busy While You Cook: Ideas from Parents

Another obstacle you may face is keeping kids busy while you prep/cook. Here are a few ideas from my social media platforms:

"A bag of pom-poms (the bigger 1½–2 inch ones) provides hours of fun for toddlers. They can put them into boxes and bottles, take them out, sort them, shoot them through paper towel tubes, etc."

"This is such a hard time that I save screen time so I can get dinner going. We've had a chance to connect after school, and the screens wind the kids down and get us all ready for dinner."

"We have a counter with barstools in the kitchen near an 'art supplies' cabinet with paper, crayons, colored pencils, paint, Play-Doh, stickers, and activity books. Also, refrigerator magnets—we have letters, numbers, dinosaurs, and now poetry magnets."

"I filled a lower cabinet with plastic bowls, containers, and other unbreakable items. They loved taking them all out, stacking, and sorting while sitting on the floor."

"I let my kids roll their cars through my legs while I cook, let them play with Tupperware and, most of all, let them 'help' me cook with their stools pulled up to the counter."

"Sometimes my daughter (age 2½) is fine sitting on a chair out of the way. If she's content, I talk about what I'm cooking and what's going into the pot/pan (which she loves to recount when it comes time to eat). I let her participate as much as possible (helping me count as I measure, dumping things into a mixing bowl, bringing eating dishes to the table, etc.). She's in a really independent phase right now. Other times, she plays with Dad or sits at the table with crayons."

Make sure items aren't choking risks and supervise based on your child's age and capabilities. The online world is full of ideas, such as sensory bins and tips from occupational therapists. Also see page 61 for getting regulated before eating and the mealtime environment.

Ebbs and Flows

And your capacity and support for menu planning, shopping and cooking will ebb and flow over the years. Get back on your track, when and if you feel ready. Jacqueline stayed focused on eating together when they could, no matter what was on the table, or what else was going on in their lives, *"I've been amazed when we go around the table and share our favorite part of the day, how often they say, 'Dinner is the best part of my day,' or they reference our meals and eating in their writing at school. It is clearly such an important part of their lives."*

Throughout the stages and challenges described in this chapter, it's invaluable to have a philosophy to help guide your responses and help your child develop with her eating. Observing and focusing on felt safety, and flexibly working toward goals will help your child to feel better about food and her body and help you feel better about feeding and mealtimes.

Chapter 11
Nutrition Worries and What to Serve

"I wish someone had told me not to worry about trying so hard to only offer the 'healthiest' foods. It made it all so much more stressful with our picky eater."
— Lori, mother of Stan, age four

In this chapter, I'll touch on nutrition worries, including protein, sugar, salt, and a discussion about iron and dairy. You'll read about unique situations, such as when your child can't eat what others eat because of allergies, they decide to become a vegetarian, or you want to see if they feel better by cutting out dairy.

Common Nutrition Worries

Nutrition worries are one of the main reasons parents pressure. Here are some of the most common nutrition concerns that get in the way of feeding well. The main goal of this section is to reassure you that most of the time, you don't need to worry. (This is not a comprehensive nutrition guide.)

Protein

Protein (just beating out veggies) is the main nutrition worry many parents get stuck on. As Laura Thomas, RD, PhD and eating disorder specialist wrote, "YOU DON'T HAVE TO WORRY ABOUT HOW MUCH PROTEIN YOUR KID EATS." Yes, she used all caps. She continued, "They don't need protein bars, or high protein snacks, or, protein powder that tastes like sweets marketed at kids . . . You don't have to worry about 'combining' protein sources in a single meal, even if you're vegetarian or vegan. And you don't need to make protein bars for your toddler!"[1]

Most parents greatly overestimate how much protein their child needs. One mother gave a perfect example. After a workshop, she asked about her 15-month-old: *"I give my son chicken nuggets every night because I know he'll eat them and he doesn't eat enough protein."* After asking her a few questions, it was clear that she overestimated how much he needed; he ate several foods high in protein, and had no other difficulties. Only offering his favorites, out of a misguided protein worry, made it more likely that he would refuse other protein sources and demand chicken nuggets.

Almost universally, when I see an intake analysis for even a selective or "underweight" child, the child eats more than the minimum recommended amount of protein. For example, a toddler drinking a cup or two of milk over a day, part of an egg, and a slice or two of deli meat gets *more* than enough protein. When parents understand how relatively easy it is to get enough protein, they can relax and not pressure. Offering different sources of protein—even if he doesn't reliably eat them—will help. Opportunity is a key factor in how children learn to enjoy a variety.

Laura Thomas from above wrote more: ". . . you don't need to calculate anything. Here's why: Having enough protein is a function of our energy intake. If we are eating enough calories, then we are more than likely to be getting enough protein. If your child is growing as expected, and is over time getting some food from most food groups, then we can be assured that they're likely getting enough protein. Even kids who don't really like traditional 'protein foods' like dairy, meat, beans and nuts are probably doing better than you think."[1]

And while you don't *need* calculations (and if you're not worried, skip to the next section), I am offering the following general formulas for daily protein needs in case that helps you worry less. Talk to your child's doctor if you have concerns:

- One- to three-year-olds need about .55 grams of protein per pound of body weight. A 29-lb. child would need roughly 16 grams of protein, or about the amount in two cups of milk.
- Four- to six-year-olds need about .5 grams per pound of body weight.
- Seven- to 14-year-olds need about .45 grams/pound of body weight.
- 15- to 18-year-olds need about .4 grams/pound of body weight.
- Adolescents who have likely reached their adult height need about .36 grams/pound of body weight.

Non-meat protein sources (amounts given to show how it adds up):

- Milk: 1 cup = 8 grams
- Cheese: 1 ounce = 6–8 grams
- Yogurt: 1 cup = 8 grams
- Greek style yogurt: 1 cup = up to 18 grams (check labels; protein varies)
- Nuts or nut butters: 2 tablespoons = 7 grams
- Eggs: 1 egg = 7 grams
- Fish and shellfish, such as shrimp: 1 ounce = 7 grams
- Beans and lentils: ½ cup cooked = 7–10 grams
- Edamame soybeans: ½ cup = 14 grams (children can shell these for a fun snack)
- Tofu: ½ cup = 20 grams
- Veggies: ½ cup cooked = 1–3 grams
- Grains: ½ cup cooked pasta, 1 slice of bread, or ½ cup oats = 2–4 grams

The Canadian Food Guide includes dairy in the protein category along with beans and meats.

Meat is high in protein and is often well liked. Here are a few examples:

- Chicken: ¼ cup cooked = 10 grams
- Deli turkey: 1 slice = 4-6 grams
- Ground beef: 1 small, cooked burger patty = 12 grams

What About Too Much Protein?

A mom emailed: *"I want to serve meat lasagna tonight, but I heard too much protein is bad for kidneys."* If a child is otherwise healthy, it would take multiple pans of meat lasagna to affect their kidneys. This question is another case where an unfounded worry interfered with joyful feeding.

In my medical practice I saw one healthy young person get into trouble with protein and kidneys when he took protein powder supplements (to "bulk up") and severely dehydrated himself on purpose (to make his weight category) for an all-day wrestling tournament. The combination of excessive protein load, dehydration, and extreme exertion led to temporary kidney problems—avoidable with common sense (notoriously lacking in teens).

Be on the lookout for and consider talking to your child/teen's doctor if they are using protein supplements or bulking powders/foods (which have exploded in popularity). The risk of too much protein is higher in young people who exercise excessively or with disordered eating. Unfortunately, this is more common with the pressure on boys, in particular to have unrealistic, hyper-muscular physiques.

Salt

One mother of a girl being evaluated for low weight fought at every meal with her daughter about salt. Mom cooked balanced, from-scratch meals most nights, but wouldn't let her 10-year-old add salt. Mom worried about sodium—one *more* thing to worry about. Or maybe not?[2]

Research suggests you don't need to worry. Especially if it helps your child enjoy foods—pass the salt! Consider adding flavor with fats such as nut butters or olive oil, spices, acids such as lemon juice, hot sauce, other sauces, or toppings. The health claims about following a low-sodium diet are not conclusive, especially in children, and are not a compelling reason to battle. A review of research[3] on salt found no difference in health outcomes with low-salt diets (largely in white male adults as they were most commonly studied), and a Danish study showed that folks with the highest urine sodium (correlating with intake) had the *lowest mortality and health problems*.[4]

Unless your child has known kidney or heart problems where they have difficulty managing fluids or salt, it is difficult to overdo it, particularly if much of the food is cooked from scratch. Processed foods tend to be high in salt, and even that doesn't worry me much. Focus on supporting joy and flavor, and lean into the relief that this is a battle you don't have to fight. In addition, when you stop trying to limit or control salt, your child may become less interested in it.

Salt and Infants

Before 12 months of age, an infant's kidneys are less able to manage salt, and in very rare cases can result in salt toxicity. Salt toxicity doesn't come from some salted sweet potato wedges or the occasional processed salty food. (Once during my medical training we did labs to rule out salt toxicity in a 9 month old drinking Gatorade and teething on beef jerky.) If your infant/toddler is eating the foods you eat, save the salt (gravies, sauces) while cooking and let others add salt to taste. Try not to frequently serve highly salted foods such as cured meats (jerky), olives, pickles, soy sauces, etc.

Nitrites

Nitrites are a kind of salt added to preserve meats and stop bacteria growth. There is a small association between increased cancer risk and regular consumption of large amounts of nitrite-cured meats. If you serve hot dogs or lunchmeats more than a few times a week, choosing "nitrite/nitrate-free" options may lower the risk. Otherwise, if cured meats aren't served every day, I don't worry about it.

Sugar

With our current sugar panic, it can feel difficult to know what to believe and how to manage sweet foods and drinks. (See sweets discussion in Chapter 4.) Let's unpack sugar a bit.

One of my favorite studies looks at children's versus adults' preference for sweet taste, and when the shift to adult tastes happens. At various ages, study participants were asked to add sugar to a drink until it got "too sweet." (Note, this study was with American participants. We know that the foods people are raised with impact preferences. When we had two Japanese college students staying with us, they found that most of the U.S. desserts or candies were "too sweet." I'm curious what their preferences would have been as children. But I digress...)

For the children in the study, there was pretty much *no such thing* as too sweet. They added sugar until it no longer dissolved. Adults stopped at about the sweetness of soda, finding more "too sweet." Interestingly, the point at which the shift occurred was not determined by age or what children learned in school. The shift to a more "adult" preference tended to occur after the growth plates in the long bones fused,[5] meaning the child had reached close to adult height.

This suggests a biological drive behind that preference for sweet. Children are growing, and it makes sense that they would be attracted to sweeter/higher energy, foods to fuel growth. I marveled when my 15-year-old one day declared that orange soda—the same soda she had previously enjoyed—was "too sweet" after a four-inch growth spurt and reaching 5 feet 10 inches.

Think back to your own childhood. I loved, and ate large amounts, of sugar-sweetened cereals at hotels or sleepovers (banned in our home). Now as an adult, the thought of that pink oversweet milk, marshmallows, and cereal is off-putting. Have you experienced similar? Children's tastes tend to evolve, and they will do so more readily if we don't interfere.

Sugar Is Not Addictive

Another myth is that sugar is "more addictive than heroin." You've probably heard that the pleasure centers involved with addiction light up when we eat sugar, but they also light up with sex, a hug, donating money,[6] and listening to music. Anything that promotes survival, including food and human connection, will tie in to those reward pathways. A review published in the *American Journal of Clinical Nutrition* concluded, "There is no support from the human literature for the hypothesis that sucrose may be physically addictive or that addiction to sugar plays a role in eating disorders."[7]

What convinced me most that sugar is not addictive is that *permission* to eat sugar greatly reduces or eliminates obsessive behaviors and out-of-control consumption. When the food-preoccupied child is allowed matter-of-fact access to sugar within a framework of supportive feeding, they learn to handle sweets. They might pester you for them like any other child, but they are no longer *obsessed* and, on their own, might even leave Halloween candy after three or four pieces.

I highly advise against using an addiction model for food or sugar with children or teens (or adults). I saw a phone app for o*ese teens using the addiction model. How sad. These young people are told they have a disease they will have to manage, like alcoholism, for the rest of their lives.

The "addict" label can harm. This tells the child he is incapable and damaged, and can never learn to have a healthy relationship with food. Words matter. If thinking of sugar as an addiction has helped you with your eating, that is one thing, but I would caution against using addiction language with children and teens, both as you model your own eating, and talk about theirs. Examples of addiction language are: "I can't control myself around bread!" or "I can't stop until I eat the whole bag; I have no self-control," or, "You're having a sugar craving, let's count to ten and bring that craving intensity down."

Sugar Does Not Cause "Hyperactivity"

Over a dozen large studies show that sugar does not cause hyperactivity. (Parents rated children's behavior worse when they believed the child had consumed sugar, when the child had *not.*) Our beliefs (see mindset in Chapter 8), and talking to kids about how sugar makes them lose control, can be self-fulfilling. At our daughter's sugar-free preschool, the teacher prepped the kids for the special "sugar day" all week, warning them they'd better behave, and how she was preparing herself for their antics. The kids were frenzied before the treats were even served; then, she repeatedly and loudly lamented, "You're all totally crazy on sugar day!"

Sugar blowouts tend to happen when many kids are around, during celebrations, or there has been a lot of anticipation. (Caffeine in sodas may impact behavior and mood.)

Low Blood Sugar May Influence Behavior

I suspect it's more common to see poor behavior with *low* blood sugar. If your child only consumes sugar or simple carbs in a short period of time, as in the party with candy and juice, there is a rapid blood sugar peak, followed by a rapid fall. The *drop* in blood sugar, rather than the peak, likely contributes to the behavior. Here are some ideas to limit blood sugar crashes:

- If offering high-sugar foods, also serve protein, fat, and foods with fiber. Pour a glass of milk or add some crackers, cheese, and fruit to the spread.
- Consider sweets with fat and protein, such as Snickers with nuts, cake or cookies, or granola bars.
- Kids will learn that if they only eat candy, they won't feel so good afterward. Those "mistakes" are how they learn to listen to their bodies. It's more useful for them to learn how it feels than to hear lectures about it.

Some parents who avoid food dyes have observed that their child's behavior issues improve. This begs the question: Perhaps the child is reacting to the food dye in candy and sweet foods, rather than the sugar? I also don't think this is common, but something to consider, especially with increasing options for natural dyes. Belief can be self-fulfilling. One boy said he was allergic to red food dyes, but enjoyed bright red Swedish Fish and Skittles with no ill effects.

Natural or Artificial Sugar Alternatives

The current quick fix for o*esity is to ban sweet drinks including fruit juice, with some recommending diet drinks. Are artificial or other sweeteners better? Are they safe?

An article on artificial sweeteners from the U.S. FDA website says, ". . . numerous research studies confirm that artificial sweeteners are generally safe in limited quantities, even for pregnant women."[8] There are over 100 studies on the safety of aspartame alone. They are among the most widely tested ingredients.

While the research is reassuring in terms of safety, I consider artificial sweeteners as "preferred" for reasons such as to help manage blood sugar for those with diabetes, or taste preference. (Consult your nutrition team with metabolic disorders or genetic syndromes or mutations.)

Diet drinks aren't associated with weight loss at the population level and don't lead to weight loss for most individuals. In 2023, the World Health Organization warned against using artificial sweeteners for weight loss since they don't achieve that goal (I agree with the data here). The WHO also categorized aspartame as a "possible carcinogen," a list that includes aloe vera and pickled vegetables.[9] I choose not to worry about the artificial sweeteners my daughter and husband enjoy most dinners in their drinks. If you serve diet drinks, try to do so with meals and snacks (the sweet taste in diet drinks releases a small amount of insulin).

Within a responsive approach, children can enjoy refined sugar, honey (after 12 months), maple syrup, or foods sweetened with fruit juices or high-fructose corn syrup. A study supported by the National Honey Board showed that honey, agave nectar, table sugar, coconut sugar, brown sugar, and maple syrup metabolize pretty much the same in the body.[10] In fact, agave nectar has *more* fructose than high-fructose corn syrup. This may help you relax about high fructose corn syrup as well (it did for me).

Juice Doesn't Make Kids Fat

For many years now, juice has been blamed for problematic weight gain. Here is an example of research that adds to this belief. The study in a nutrition journal was titled, "Risk factors for obesity at age three in Alaskan children, including the role of beverage consumption."[11] It implies that an extra ½ cup of apple juice caused higher weight, but the paper found that witnessing domestic violence and rates of food insecurity were more closely associated. French fries were also not consistently linked with higher weight. I bring up this study because public health and media tend to focus on "easy" solutions, instead of more complex issues such as food insecurity. It's easier to scold parents, but it leads to fearing foods.

A 2022 review of 31 studies showed no link between juice and o*esity in kids.[12] (Neither did a 2016 review of 22 studies.[13]) But you've probably heard that juice is bad for your child. You don't need to serve juice, but you also don't have to fear it. Especially if you have feeding challenges, juice can help.

Potential benefits of juice:

- Kids who drank 100% fruit juice had higher intake of fiber, vitamin C, magnesium, and potassium.[13]
- Juice tastes good! Positive experiences with food or drinks can help children who are anxious with eating.
- Can help with constipation and hydration in hot weather or if a child doesn't prefer other drinks.
- Can use juice to introduce new flavors, which may be especially helpful for anxious or avoidant eaters.

How to:

- No juice before age 6 months without talking to your child's doctor or feeding team.
- After 6 months formula, breast milk and water are still preferred.
- After 12 months you can offer juice (consider diluting) with meals and snacks (also offer water and milks).
- You can water juice down, especially for toddlers who maybe aren't used to very sweet things; this can also stretch a food budget.
- Juice can be used to mix with other foods or make smoothies or refreshing frozen popsicles.
- Avoid sipping outside of meal or snack time as prolonged exposure can increase cavities.
- If appetites are low, or for young children, filling up on juice can decrease intake.

Some days they may drink more juice, some days less. Served within a supportive feeding relationship with meals and snacks, I don't believe that juice contributes to problematic weight gain. (I feel the same way about other sweetened drinks such as lemonade.) I do think that young children should not regularly drink soda, and that between eating times, water is the beverage to consider first. Too much water can be dangerous for infants. Check with your child's doctor.

Some Thoughts on Dairy

I get asked a lot about dairy. Low fat? Organic? None? Cow's (or goat's milk), yogurt, and cheese are easy, delicious choices to help you offer your child balanced nutrition. (I don't recommend raw dairy products.) Regular, reduced, and low-fat dairy provide carbohydrates and protein, and variable fat. Ultra pasteurized milk boxes (don't need to be refrigerated) in both chocolate and white (one and two percent fat), can support nutrition on-the-go. Cheeses provide protein and fat. Dairy products are a great source for calcium, vitamin D, and potassium, important nutrients the U.S. Dietary Guidelines identifies as lacking in the American diet.

Dairy foods are a convenient way to get essential nutrients, including magnesium, zinc, phosphorus, and riboflavin. An "essential nutrient" is something you need to take in for healthy body functioning, as your body can't make it in sufficient quantities.

Official Recommendations on Dairy

The Dietary Guidelines for Americans (DGA) encourage all Americans to increase intake of low-fat or fat-free milk and milk products to the equivalent recommended daily amounts: 2 cups for children two to three years of age, 2½ cups for children four to eight years of age, and 3 cups for those nine years of age and older. Dairy is an easy way to meet nutrition needs, and there are other ways to cover your nutrition bases.

Reassurance alert! Nutrition is not an exact science. For example, U.S. calcium recommendations for children are almost twice as high as in the UK. So even if you're not quite meeting U.S. recommendations, it is likely not as worrisome as it seems. Some days we eat less, some days more of various nutrients.

The following are some thoughts on serving dairy:

- Aim for an average of not more than two to three servings of dairy or alternative per day.
- Avoid reduced-fat dairy before age two. No study shows that fat-free dairy lowers BMI in children, and it may contribute to some young children not getting enough fat.[14] Infants and toddlers need 30 to 40 percent of their calories from fat. Another paper showed that kids who drank whole milk had the lowest BMI of the children studied.[15]
- After age two, children need about 25 to 30 percent of their calories from fat. You could switch to low-fat milk if you wanted to. But if the taste of whole-fat dairy is preferred, that's perfectly fine.

Low Fat and Fat Free

For years, a "low fat" or "fat free" diet was recommended. We weren't supposed to eat eggs, red meat, coconut oil, or cheese—and it didn't make Americans weigh less. In place of fat, food manufacturers increased sugar and simple carbohydrates. But there is controversy about how much saturated fat (from sources like meat or dairy) is "ideal." Many health concerns around saturated fat are now understood to be largely attributed to those highly processed trans fats, which have been phased out by the FDA since 2015 due to safety concerns.

Diets too low in fat can result in deficiencies in vitamins A, D, E, and K, which need fat to be absorbed by the body. Some fat sources come from meat, fish, dairy, and eggs, while others come from plants such as avocadoes, vegetable oils, olive oils, nuts, and nut butters. Fat improves taste (for most people), mouthfeel, helps us feel satisfied, evens out blood sugar levels, and last until the next meal or snack.

Trends with eating come and go. Fat was avoided when I was a child, and sugar is the most feared at the time of writing this edition. Maybe someday we'll realize that demonizing foods hasn't made us healthier or happier.

He Won't Drink Milk

Avoid pressure, even over nutrient-dense foods. You can meet nutritional needs without dairy foods, though it may take a little more planning. One of my most popular blog series was about my daughter not drinking milk for almost a year.

When she refused milk, I looked for ways to add calcium from other sources such as cooking with evaporated milk or having sesame seeds to sprinkle. (See calcium below.)

This was also a time when I got to experiment and observe. I reached out to colleagues, and one suggested I serve milk to everyone and calmly say, "We're all having milk." That resulted in a battle. Lesson learned. I knew she felt that approach as pressuring because of how she reacted, so in the spirit of responsive feeding, I backed off and let her come back to milk on her own time, which she did off and on over the years. This is a process that parents and kids figure out together.

Milk Can Sabotage Appetite

Milk is food and fills kids up. Some toddlers take in a lot of milk (more than 16 to 24 ounces a day), and it interferes with appetite and can contribute to iron deficiency. When I see this, other things are usually going on. These kids tend to drink milk throughout the day and carry it around. Or, the child is "picky" and pressured to eat. Similar to puree pouches (where the child has more control), drinking the energy in milk is easier than stressful mealtimes. (If there are other concerning signs around sensory-motor challenges, high milk intake can be a sign that a child is struggling with solid foods.) The following are some options to manage milk:

- Offer milk with meals and snacks.
- Try to offer only water in between.
- Stop pressuring with feeding, if you have been.
- Change to serving milk in an open cup if she is able to drink from it (usually between 12 and 18 months of age).
- If your older child still has a bottle or straw cup of milk before breakfast, move the milk to breakfast time.
- See tips on page 289 on making water more enticing.

Flavored Milk (Dairy or Alternative)

While my daughter shunned milk, I offered her chocolate and strawberry milk, even syrups she could mix in herself (none of which appealed but was worth a try). When I get asked about flavored milk, it's usually over a concern about calories, sugar, or corn syrup. I would rather a child drink and enjoy chocolate milk versus no milk. (There is no conclusive evidence that flavored milk causes higher weight in children.)

Some brands have been reformulated with less sugar or high-fructose corn syrup, if that worries you. Many of my RD colleagues are happy to see their children enjoying chocolate milk. As always, you choose what to offer, but this is another area where I feel the worry is exaggerated. If flavored milk is offered in the context of responsive feeding, I think it's a fine option. And it can be particularly helpful with children if there is concern over low appetite or slow weight gain.

Hormones and Organic

Many moms I talk to want to buy organic but can't afford it and feel guilty. One content creator, also an RD, admitted she feels fine buying conventional milk, but is self-conscious.

Let go of that guilt. Standard milk in the United States is highly regulated. Dairy cows are not routinely treated with antibiotics, like some chickens, hogs, and farmed fish are. If a cow is sick, perhaps with mastitis (an infection of the milk-producing glands), she is treated with antibiotics, and her milk is not put into the milk supply. Milk is tested at the farm and again at processing centers for traces of antibiotics. If antibiotics are found, the farmer pays a large penalty, so they have an interest in keeping the milk antibiotics-free.

Do you need to buy milk from cows not treated with rBST (artificial bovine somatotropin) to be safe? Milk from cows treated with rBST (increases production) and untreated cows is identical on testing.[16] Milk does contain hormones made naturally by the cow (as does human milk), but rBST and dairy in general has not been proven to affect hormones in children or early puberty, if that's your concern. Bottom line: I believe you can feel safe about conventional milk.

Worried About Calcium?

Many foods have calcium added, such as cereal, bread products or juices; check the labels. Here's some other calcium-rich foods:

- Fortified soy, almond and rice milk, or orange juice (many have similar calcium as cow's milk).
- Tofu with calcium sulfate.
- Turnip, collard greens, and kale.
- Garbanzo (chickpeas), kidney, navy, and canned baked beans.
- Almond butter.
- Cooked broccoli, edamame, and acorn squash.
- Dried apricots, figs, dates, and prunes (stewed, added to muffins or smoothies, or plain prepared in safe ways for their eating skills).
- Hummus with tahini or sesame seeds.
- Molasses (baking and cooking).
- Canned salmon and sardines with bones—who knows!?! Just watch the bones.

Lactose Intolerance

Lactose intolerance is higher in children of African, Asian, and Central American descent versus those of northern European descent. Universally, infants are born able to digest lactose, the sugar found in human or animal milk, so infants should be able to digest lactose even if they lose that ability as young children.

Why can some people eat lactose comfortably and others can't? About ten thousand years ago, a genetic mutation allowed some individuals to continue to produce the lactase enzyme and benefit from nutrients and energy in animal milks, which were otherwise scarce. These individuals survived at higher rates and passed that mutation on until more than 90 percent of northern Europeans now have that gene. China, in contrast, didn't domesticate milk-producing animals until relatively recently, so there was no survival advantage to lactose digestion; therefore, we see higher rates of lactose intolerance in those of Chinese descent.

Lactose intolerance is usually characterized by:

- Abdominal discomfort or pain.
- Bloating and gas.
- Decreased appetite.
- Loose stools.

Lactose intolerance does not necessarily mean that your child can't tolerate all dairy, and it is not an *allergy*, in which case you would want to carefully avoid milk products. (An allergy is an immune response, often to small amounts of the trigger food, with symptoms including hives, mouth and throat tingling, and swelling.)

Many lactose-intolerant adults can comfortably consume the amount of lactose in one cup (eight ounces) of milk, or two cups divided over the day, with food.

If your child has digestive problems, it is reasonable to reduce dairy or attempt a dairy-free trial. (See therapeutic diets on pages 299-303 for more.) Stomach upset or loose stools are a tricky thing to figure out, particularly if: 1) there is a communication challenge; 2) infections or parasites have been present; or 3) the child has received antibiotics, in which case you may also want to supplement with probiotics and a fish- or flax-oil supplement.

Consider these options:

- Chocolate milk is better tolerated by some with lactose intolerance.
- Aged cheeses like cheddar, Swiss, parmesan, and Colby are lower in lactose and tend to be better tolerated.
- Yogurts with live, active cultures can be comfortably consumed by some.
- Lactose-free milk.
- Lactaid helps digest the lactose and reduce symptoms.
- Non-dairy options such as oat drinks or coconut-based ice creams.

Non-Dairy Alternatives

In addition to allergy and intolerance, there are valid reasons why people choose not to consume dairy products, including concerns over sustainability, carbon footprint, and animal welfare. The number of fortified milk alternatives has increased over the last decade, with many offering similar nutrition to cow's milk, including some brands of soy, oat, pea, almond and cashew beverages (they tend to cost more than dairy).

It's worth some time to compare nutrition labels. (Nut-based drinks are not appropriate for persons with nut/tree nut allergies.) Finding one that your child enjoys drinking may be a challenge or an adventure. Many are sweet, so your child might like them better.

Remember, if any food groups are off limits, consider consulting with a pediatric RD. This is particularly important if your child already has a limited variety of foods or there are growth concerns.

Go Slow with Changes Such as Switching Milks

If you're switching to non-dairy milk or other major dietary changes, consider going slowly. Reports of discomfort or not tolerating non-dairy milks are not uncommon. For example, when a friend switched to oat milk, she experienced bloating, cramps and gas. She backed off and slowly increased the amount of oat milk to completely transition over about a month and it helped. Introducing small amounts with any dietary changes and gradually increasing as tolerated is something many experts advise. It may be a case of intestinal bacteria populations getting used to different food sources. (Gut bacteria produce gas as a by-product.)

"He Barely Drinks Anything!"

The child who refuses to drink to the point of dehydration is extremely rare, but it happens, more so with brain-based differences and challenges with interoception. If you're battling over liquids, it can interfere with his tuning in to thirst. (Urinary tract infections or dark urine need to be evaluated by your child's doctor.) Some children do fine with less liquids than others.

One client used to bribe with a favored food to try to get her son to drink, with the predictable results of him engaging in battles and drinking less. The following are some ideas to boost fluid intake without battles:

- Try a fancy cup, straw, or a water bottle with her favorite cartoon character. One mom said, *"It's amazing what she'll drink if I just put a straw in it."*
- Add ice if she likes it cold, or try room temperature.
- Have a tea party at snack time, with teacups and caffeine-free fruit tea. Let her add some sugar or honey (if she's more than a year old). When we got the play tea set out at snack time, my then four-year-old daughter loved pouring tea into her tiny cup so much that she drank two pots. This can also work with (diluted or not) lemonade, water, or milk.
- Let them pour when possible. Use a small pitcher and give them some control. Expect spills.
- Enjoy hot chocolate together. Pretend not to notice if he doesn't drink much. Float a few marshmallows on top if he likes them.
- Find a way for your child to be able to help himself to water.
- Serve fruits, veggies, or other foods with high water content. There's a sur-

prising amount of water in many foods; fruits such as melons or strawberries may be accepted.
- Try cherry tomatoes (cut in half if you have a young child) or cucumbers with or without dip. Serve fruit frozen occasionally or pack fruit with snacks, such as little cups of diced peaches.
- Serve soups, Jell-O, pudding, smoothies or shakes. Consider Popsicles; you can make your own.
- Consider getting a Soda Stream to carbonate water. Some kids really like pushing the button, choosing how fizzy to make it, and adding flavors. Sensory seekers (see page 140) may especially like the input.
- Offer juice, diluted or not. If you haven't tried it, juice is an option with meals and snacks.

For children who may benefit from external prompts with interoception challenges, and while they learn to tune in to cues, consider gentle verbal or visual reminders, prompts on phones, or an app. Or check out the water bottles that show how much to drink by certain times of the day (I don't recommend these unless there is a compelling reason). A special consideration is medical: Diane's son was high risk for another stroke, and dehydration was dangerous. In this case, liquids were treated as medicine, and he was encouraged with the above, as well as having certain amounts he needed to drink each day, and even rewards. They figured out together how to make it work.

Nutrients That Deserve More Attention

I hope the last section reassured you. This next section covers a few nutrients that in general could use more attention with meal planning or thinking about supplements.

Iron

Many parents forget about iron. With a vegetarian/vegan diet, iron is more challenging than protein to get in adequate amounts. If your child is not eating meat, it's important to offer iron-rich foods. This may be a question for your RD or doctor in terms of supplement needs.

Children who experience catch-up growth, or a growth spurt with puberty, have a higher risk of iron deficiency, and may also need supplements. Food insecurity, particularly for infants and toddlers, increases the risk as does eating very limited variety or excessive milk intake. Menstruation, especially if it is heavy (not always easy conversations to have), also increases risk. (See page 334 for more on iron deficiency anemia.) Pica, eating non-food items, or chewing ice/oral seeking may indicate low iron levels and needs to be considered.

Iron deficiency has serious consequences, from affecting IQ to energy. **It is important to recheck iron levels after supplementation to be sure your child is getting enough and that it is absorbed.** Hydee Becker, RD, suggests giving iron to young children during bath time, since the drops can stain clothing. The bath also helps distract from the taste. You may notice a temporary staining of teeth. Iron supplements can be harsh on tummies and make constipation more likely, so work with your doctor to find a way to supplement that works for your child.

Here are some good iron sources:

- Meats, such as red meat and pork.
- Poultry, such as chicken and turkey.
- Egg yolks.
- Dark leafy greens (spinach, collards).
- Dried fruit (prunes, raisins).
- Iron-enriched cereals and grains (check label).
- Beans, lentils, chickpeas, and soybeans.
- Artichokes. Surprisingly, many children like artichokes, peeling the leaves and dipping them in sauces like balsamic vinegar and olive oil, or butter. Don't underestimate what children will like. I vividly remember eating my first artichoke at a neighbor's when I was 10 years old, and I loved it.
- Cook in cast-iron pans, especially acidic foods such as sauces with tomatoes.

Iron is reported to be absorbed better when taken in with vitamin C; this might include orange juice, tomato sauce, or a vitamin C supplement. Taking iron supplements with dairy blocks the absorption, so try to not take it with dairy foods or milk.

Vitamin D

Moderate vitamin D deficiencies are common in Northern zones, especially in winter (sun is necessary for our bodies to make Vitamin D). People with darker skin more commonly have low levels and it might play a role in bone health. And it's complicated! For example, older white folks are at much higher risk of fractures from osteoporosis, and supplementation may be more effective for Black children.[17] But we don't have good research on doses and outcomes. Ask your child's doctor.

Fiber

Most U.S. children take in less than the recommended amounts of fiber. Fiber is an undigestible form of carbohydrate—but it has other important functions in the body. Fiber helps keep us feeling satisfied, helps even out blood sugar, and can help with bowel movements and gut health. In adults it is linked with better blood pressure, lower cholesterol, and lower diabetes risk. While it's a good thing, increasing fiber in your child's diet is not an emergency and not worth battling over. See Chapters 5 and 6 on working toward greater variety.

Some good sources of fiber are pears, apples, prunes and prune juice, berries, avocado, popcorn, nuts, oatmeal, carrots, sweet potatoes, chia seeds, nuts, legumes, fiber-fortified foods or drinks, and versions of whole grain breads, cereals, crackers, and pastas. Prepare foods like seeds, nuts, and popcorn in ways that your child can safely manage as they are a choking risk. Increase fiber slowly to avoid bloating or cramps.

And, when it comes to fiber, *you can have too much of a good thing!* I've seen children referred to gastroenterology doctors for low weight, diarrhea, excessive gas, bloating, and stomach pain who were eating many times more fiber than recommended (and often not enough fat). I usually see this in parents who follow "clean" eating and avoid white flour/processed grains, or vegan diets. Too much fiber, especially for young children, can fill up tummies and not leave room for fat, protein, and digestible carbs. This can contribute to kids not getting enough fuel, which can slow weight gain. Gut symptoms usually improve slowly as the amount of fiber is decreased.

The aim is not too little and not too much fiber. If lunch is a quinoa/veggie bowl with fruit smoothie and chia seeds, that one meal may have more fiber than a child needs for the whole day. In this case, serving more refined carbs, such as swapping white rice for the quinoa—or a flour tortilla, bread or regular pasta—can help. Talk to your child's doctor or a dietitian if you're not sure.

Considerations Around Vegetarianism and Veganism

Vegetarianism and veganism (avoiding all animal products) are ever more common. You can raise healthy, happy kids on a variety of diets. As you and your children consider things like climate impact and animal welfare, taste preferences, satisfaction, budget and feeding history, this section can help you navigate how different ways of eating may impact your family.

For context, my family members like the taste and texture of meat and feel it generally leaves us more satisfied than meals with no animal products. And, we have been decreasing the amount of meat and cooking more meat-free options, and staying open and curious. We are careful to stay tuned to whether it stirs up feelings of scarcity. How we eat down the road may or may not look different.

If you're interested in reducing animal products, here are some thoughts. If animal welfare concerns are at play, look for humane and welfare certifications on the packaging, grass-fed/pasture-raised eggs, dairy, and meat. There are delivery subscription services that certify more humane practices. These are more expensive than conventional, so families may choose to eat these products less often or in smaller portions. Some cuts of meat may be more affordable, such as chicken thighs or ground meats. Options are also impacted by location. Our big city co-op had more options than the shops in the small town we moved to. Local/regional farmers (many have websites, post on Craigslist or appear at local farmer's markets) may have cheaper products than chain stores. If the environment is a main concern, you can try to eat fewer/less animal products, or try meat-analogs such as vegetarian breakfast sausage, or learn new ways to prepare tofu and legumes.

When You, the Parents, Are Vegetarians

If you choose not to eat meat or fish (lacto-ovo vegetarian), offering dairy, egg products, and beans and lentils will round out nutrients. Become educated about nutrition basics, take a bit of extra care, and enjoy eating together. Reputable cookbooks, websites, and social media accounts can help plan meals and snacks and cover your nutrition bases. Avoid resources that use scare tactics, sell supplements, or promote weight loss.

Some vegetarian parents have children who sneak "forbidden foods," and eat them in large quantities with access. (Like the five-year-old at a picnic who ate about a half pound of deli meat in the few minutes her parent's back was turned.) If this is the case, some vegetarian parents allow their children to choose meat away from home. Some will prepare meat for their children, if asked, or allow a teen to prepare meat. Some families prefer meat analogs, such as soy hot dogs, while others do not.

If you choose a vegan diet (no dairy, meat, fish, or eggs), especially for children, I recommend researching the topic and considering working at least initially with a registered dietitian (RD) familiar with vegan nutrition as it can be particularly challenging to get enough calcium, vitamin B12, iron, and even iodine.

If You Eat Meat

The next sections address if *you* enjoy animal products, but the topic is coming up around meat or children/teens express interest in vegetarianism or veganism.

The Younger Child with Questions About Meat

I've talked with several moms who fretted about telling their young kids about meat. A typical scenario is the four- or five-year-old who has recently put together where meat comes from and has questions.

My thoughts on this come from personal experience and from helping clients. My daughter was almost three years old when she started eating the typical dinner-type meats like chicken or beef. (I'm guessing having molars helped, and we never pushed it.) At around age four, she asked, "Mom, where does chicken come from?" I answered, "This is chicken that lived on a farm, and now we're lucky to enjoy it for dinner. Isn't it yummy?" I said this in a matter-of-fact way and changed the subject while enjoying the meal. She asked a few questions about the chicken dying—"it was quick." She asked, "Is that blood?" My reply, "Yes it is. Some people like to eat that part." (We were eating a roasted chicken with a red spot near the bone.)

The topic came up on occasion to establish that pork was from pigs—"we are thankful to the farmers and the pigs for this delicious meal"—and that there were no eyes in our chicken or on the fish because her parents didn't grow up eating that part.

In addition, young children may look up to someone who talks about being a "vegetarian." My daughter's interest came up in second grade when one of her teachers often talked about it. When our daughter casually said she wanted to be a vegetarian like her teacher, I asked why. She wasn't able to give a reason, so I replied, "Our family enjoys meat." She sat at the table and helped herself to a variety of foods, including the meat. Your child will let you know if she is asking, or ready, for more information.

If "we eat meat," doesn't satisfy your child, learn about their concerns and support their convictions/preferences. (Many children don't enjoy the texture, taste, or idea of meat, and that's okay.) Meanwhile, regularly serve choices that include protein and iron, such as beans, legumes, or nut butters, and leave the door open for your child to return to meat. Don't push her to eat it or fight over it.

When Your Older Child Explores Vegetarian/Veganism

When a 13-year-old asks to be a vegetarian, it's different question than the four-year-old's. Telling a teen, "We eat meat," will sound like you don't respect her decision-making skills or acknowledge her growing independence. Ask her to explain her interest.

If she talks about weight loss or calories, or you notice signs associated with disordered eating or an eating disorder (see Chapter 9), pursue an evaluation. **Any change that excludes foods or food groups needs attention.** If they are being consistent with their actions, such as not wearing animal products (versus only focused on restricting food), that is reassuring.

Here's a typical example: My then-sixth grader informed me that she wanted to be a vegetarian. A vegan nutritionist (not an RD) spoke to her gym class, and the kiddos came away with the message that they would get cancer if they ate meat, and since cows get all they need from grass, humans can too. We talked through the misinformation. We also decided, based on environmental and animal welfare concerns, to look for some satisfying meat-free or less-meat meals. And, I sent an email to the gym teacher and principal with my concerns. (Dietitians 4 Teachers is a great resource in this kind of situation.)

Even a desire to "get healthy" invites curiosity. What does "healthy" mean to them? Many eating disorder colleagues say that this is sometimes a sign of an early eating disorder.

Assuming you sense no cause for worry, look at this as an opportunity. (See the previous page for ideas on reducing animal products.) If your teen wants to follow a vegetarian diet, he can help take responsibility as he is able. You can help by purchasing a cookbook or researching websites and keeping an eye out for overall variety. If your child wants to be a vegan, look for non-diet vegan information. A visit with a dietitian may help (see the following section on dietitians), particularly if they are an athlete or heading into a puberty growth spurt. Your involvement will vary depending on your child's age and need for support.

Dairy products and eggs are easy (and often affordable) ways to round out nutrition. If your child chooses to only have fruit and pasta for several dinners each week, but eats protein and iron sources at other times, he'll likely cover his nutritional bases. If you're concerned, you can work with a dietitian to see if a few additional offerings or supplements will help.

Many young people are anxious about climate change and the impact on our planet and their futures. For some, taking action such as recycling, buying thrifted clothes, and reducing animal products can help them have a sense of control and purpose. It can be a positive choice, with the right support.

Laura Thomas PhD wrote about Gentle Nutrition For Vegan Kids in her Substack newsletter.[18] Here are some takeaways.

Supplementation: Vegan kids need supplements including vitamin B12 and vitamin D in winter (October to April in Northern hemisphere). It could also be helpful to add iodine, zinc, selenium, and DHA, and if your child doesn't like fortified dairy alternatives, then possibly calcium. If they don't eat fortified cereals or breads, then maybe iron too. "The best bet is a good multivitamin."

Foods fortified with essential nutrients fill in gaps. "Don't get hung up on portions. Find things your kid likes and offer them regularly as part of meals and snacks. Offer dairy alternatives for calcium: vegan cheese, milk alternatives, yoghurts, yoghurt drinks, and pouches. It doesn't mean EVERYTHING has to be fortified but it's something to be mindful of. Offer fortified grains for iron."

When Only Your Child Is a Vegetarian/Vegan

How do you plan family meals when one child is a vegetarian/vegan? If your vegetarian child is allowed to eat peanut butter and jelly every meal, you can imagine hearing, "Why does Sam get to eat peanut butter, and I have to eat casserole? It's not *fair*!" Consider nutrition, rotate in a few vegetarian dishes, serve "deconstructed" meals like a taco or pasta bar with meat and meat-free options, and be mindful about including vegetarian choices and sides such as beans with lunch or peanut butter toast at breakfast.

Try to create a respectful environment. That means no teasing the vegetarian, and the vegetarian doesn't get to make mooing noises if others are enjoying meat.

"Healthy" Eating Pitfalls

Some parents choose to avoid many foods, such as anything with artificial coloring, "processed" or "white" foods, including sugar, flour, and rice.

Most families I've encountered have a difficult time managing this successfully. Those who do, likely talk about and engage with food in positive ways. (I don't hear from many families managing this successfully so I can't be sure.) For example, while shopping, I watched children help their mother pick out fruit. The children were sniffing the fruit and marveling at the pretty colors. If you chose to feed this way, and your child is thriving, then feel free to skip to the end of this section.

Nutrition talk focused on forbidden foods and their perceived health risks can set up shame and conflict. As mom Lori said, *"For us, 'perfect' became the enemy of the good."* I see this challenge more commonly in "clean" eating families. For some children, avoidance leads to intense interest. If you have one child who does well with your food choices, and another who is preoccupied with what she can't have, realize that temperament and history play a role.

Not infrequently, when parents find me because of a child's selective eating or sweets "obsession," there is also a history of disordered eating or an ED for the parent. One mother was unable to keep breads, pastas, or cereals in the house because she was convinced they were dangerous, and they triggered her binges. Her daughter panicked in situations where she might not find a food she liked. This mother, on further reflection, had carried many of her disordered behaviors from her battle with anorexia into a more acceptable way of restricting foods—sometimes known as "orthorexia."

While orthorexia is not an official eating disorder, it is characterized by an unhealthy obsession with "healthy" eating, resulting in intake that cuts out whole groups and types of foods, which can lead to inadequate energy and nutrient intake.

Many children with anxiety or a genetic susceptibility to eating disorders find this kind of eating, with the negative food talk, particularly stressful. When feeding comes from a place of anxiety and avoidance, children pick up on that.

"The seed of 'felt safety' gets lost when the focus shifts solely to what is 'healthy.'"
— Kitty

One client's four-year-old son rejected fruits and vegetables not labeled organic because they were "poison." Another child raved about his grandmother's chicken soup, "All organic and no chemicals!" His mother sighed when I shared how much he loved the soup. "Campbells from a can," she said. These messages confuse children and don't help them do well with eating. One mom summed it up: *"Don't focus so much on 'healthy.' My intense focus on 'healthy' eating caused so many battles and didn't make him eat any better."*

It comes down to Ellyn Satter's well known statement, "When the joy goes out of eating, nutrition suffers." Whatever foods you provide, keep the focus on felt safety and joy.

Considering Food Allergies

A food allergy occurs when the body's immune system reacts to a certain food. The immune system actors (antibodies), most commonly IgE, react with the food and trigger the release of chemical messengers, including histamine, can lead to symptoms such as itching, tingling and swelling in the lips, mouth, and throat; and hives. More rarely, food allergies can result in difficulty breathing; vomiting and diarrhea; a drop in blood pressure (child looks pale and clammy, is lightheaded or faints); and very rarely, death (from anaphylaxis).

Food allergies seem to be on the rise, and parents also overestimate how common they are. In one study, parents overestimated by two-fold the presence of food allergies in their children.[19] And it *is* confusing. Part of the issue is that many reactions that may be the result of skin sensitivities or intolerances (or merely a coincidence) are interpreted as allergies. For example:

- Citrus and other acidic foods can cause redness around the mouth and bottom, particularly if the child is still in diapers.
- Some kids have looser stools in response to fiber. Parents tell me they limit the child's fruit intake due to loose stools, and that the child is "allergic." This is not an allergy and, other than the mess, is not necessarily problematic.
- Lactose intolerance can have unpleasant symptoms, but is not an allergy. (See page 287).

Things To Think About, Including When to Introduce Allergenic Foods

Check with your child's doctor for the latest recommendations on when to introduce common allergenic foods, or if there is evidence of or a family history of allergies, asthma, or eczema (atopic signs).

- Introduce solids when your child is ready; for typically developing children, this is usually at around six months but not before four months. For children with developmental differences, follow their cues and talk to your doctor or dietitian about supporting intake. (See Chapter 10 in feeding stages.)
- A 2020 American Academy of Allergy, Asthma, and Immunology statement says, "To prevent peanut and/or egg allergy, both peanut and egg should be introduced around 6 months of life, but not before 4 months." And, "There may be potential harm in delaying the introduction of these foods based on past observational studies." Even with eczema or other allergies, you may want to introduce peanuts at around 6 months, but "Parents must talk to their doctor as it may be safer to introduce peanuts following a specific protocol."[20]
- It is generally no longer felt necessary to introduce one new food at a time and wait three days to watch for a reaction.
- Do not pressure her to eat. Sometimes even young children know when a food has made them feel poorly, and they will choose not to eat it.
- Eosinophilic esophagitis (EoE), an uncommon inflammation of the esophagus (swallowing tube), is associated with food allergies. Symptoms can mimic reflux. (See page 331.)

Before Eliminating Foods or Food Groups

Eliminating food groups unnecessarily complicates feeding and can make allergies worse. I've seen parents omit foods even with mild eczema (harsh dry winters, or chlorinated pools can cause a flare). Eczema is generally not enough of a reason to cut out food groups, particularly if you can manage a mild case—and if you are already dealing with selective eating or nutrition concerns. (See the medical issues appendix for more on eczema.)

Colleagues who work in allergy and GI clinics explain a typical scenario: a fussy child, or a child with mild eczema, gets the nonspecific blood test (RAST) for possible allergies from the primary doctor (or a home test). The test shows potential problems with one or even several foods. The parents are told to eliminate the foods, typically with little further guidance.

Parents scramble to find foods the child can eat, then see the allergist a year later for follow-up. The child has had no exposure to the targeted foods, and the fussiness and eczema may or may not be better. Then, when even small amounts of these foods are reintroduced, the child has a severe reaction. In addition, the worry has introduced a counterproductive dynamic into feeding.

Many children do outgrow mild food allergies, which means children like those above may be robbed of that natural process. It is important to pursue a thorough evaluation, and have expert support (pediatric allergist or pediatric RD if possible), before eliminating foods. Note: Blood tests vary in accuracy with the child's age and other factors. This is part of why seeing a specialist is helpful.

I recommend against home "food sensitivity" testing, which is heavily advertised online. The Food Allergy Canada advocacy organization agrees: ". . . the presence of IgG antibodies indicate exposure and possibly tolerance to a food, not allergy. Due to a lack of evidence supporting their use, IgG tests are not recommended for diagnosing a food allergy, or even a food intolerance or sensitivity."[21] Because these tests are not specific/accurate, overdiagnosis occurs. **Unnecessary restriction can trigger conflict, anxiety, and food seeking, increase the risk of malnutrition, and make mild reactions worse.**

If Your Child Has Food Allergies

If it is confirmed that your child has a food allergy, decide if they have the temperament to not eat the same foods as the rest of the family, or if you will *all* follow the restrictions. Perry has one child with severe tree nut and peanut allergies as well as milder dairy and gluten allergies. Avoiding nuts is a safety issue, and it was important for her to cook one meal for the family and not have her daughter feel singled out. Though Perry doesn't like cooking, she found cookbooks and websites for dairy-free cooking and baking. Perry's consistent efforts have preserved the joy around food for her family. Here is what helps Perry:

- Focus on what your child can eat, rather than on what she can't.
- When your child goes to parties, bring a treat. Perry has learned to send along gluten-free, casein-free (GFCF) cupcakes for her child. She bakes and freezes them for special occasions. Purchase GFCF baked goods if you prefer not to bake.
- Find support groups and online forums for more information.

- Learn about reading labels. For example, milk products may appear on labels under "whey, rennet, quark, nougat, lactic yeast, ghee..."
- Multiple resources, such as printable cards, and support groups are available. The National Institute of Allergy and Infectious Diseases (NIAID.nih.gov) is a reputable resource.

Finding a Dietitian

Like any professional, you may need to do a little digging to find someone who fits your needs. RDs have standardized training, specializing through practicums and work experience, such as with a feeding clinic or a diabetes practice. (However, most are still trained in a weight-centered/ biased model.) Work with a pediatric RD if you can. Trust your gut, ask questions, and get recommendations from other parents or a trusted member of your healthcare team. **Questions to ask your RD:**

- Are you "anti-diet?" Is your practice weight-neutral?
- Do you recommend calorie or portion restriction or other ideas such as the stoplight system to get a child to eat less?
- Do you work on weight loss?
- Do you think my child needs to be taught portion control?
- Do you believe that pushing my child to eat more will make him grow better?
- Will you talk about any foods being "bad," or about "red-light foods?"
- Will you talk to my child about his weight? What do you plan to say?
- Can you help our family support my child's nutrition following a vegetarian diet while not being negative about animal products (especially if others in the family enjoy them)?
- Do you belong to a pediatric practice group or a vegetarian nutrition practice group?

On professional websites and social media, words like "responsive feeding," "Division of Responsibility," "Health at Every Size®," "weight neutral," "anti-diet," and "intuitive eating" can help you get a sense of a practitioner's approach. "Weight loss" or "weight management" are red flags.

"Therapeutic" Diets Such as Gluten and Casein Free (GFCF)

"We changed to gluten free/casein free (GFCF) as a family. I don't know how you could do it otherwise. It's incredibly hard to have one set of rules for one child and another for the adopted child. These kids are often already so different, with meds, school IEPs, and therapy. I just said, 'This has to be all of us.'"

— Lara, mother of Brian

"We were so desperate to help his outbursts and read glowing testimonials about elimination diets. We tried the GCFC diet and avoided food dye. It was so hard and expensive, and it didn't seem to make a difference."
— Jemma, mom of three-year-old Will, who has FASD

It's natural to look to food when there is suffering, especially gut symptoms. Online experts and influencers are quick to list foods to avoid for pretty much every issue. A few years ago, out of the blue, I developed severe heartburn. Over about six months I cut out beloved foods and drinks such as coffee, tea, chocolate, tomatoes, garlic, gluten... Nothing helped. I figured if I hurt anyway, I'd go back to eating what I liked. About a month after going back to my previous foods, my heartburn disappeared. I'm grateful that my heartburn didn't resolve while I was off that long list of foods! I may have been convinced it helped, and then stayed on a very restrictive diet. I would have been sad to miss out on my favorites (especially if I didn't need to).

When a child is struggling with stomach upset, constipation, rages, or learning difficulties, parents want to do everything possible so the child can be healthy and happy. Increasingly, more attention is paid to how nutrition affects children, including not only physical needs, but also their cognitive processes. In addition to traditional therapies and medications, many parents consider dietary interventions for children with cognitive differences, or other behavioral challenges. Some online sources even claim to "cure" autism with dietary interventions, which doesn't work and can cause harm, not to mention reinforce stigma.

A lot of the research on this topic is poor quality and inconclusive. A meta-analysis did indicate that some children with ADHD (the most studied) may see improvements with diet and suggests that "an elimination diet should be considered a possible treatment for ADHD, but one that will work partially or fully, and only in a potentially small subset of children."[22]

Elimination diets are difficult, risk nutrient deficiency, and tend to target the child's preferred foods. As always, you know your child best, so if a therapeutic diet helps, great. If you are curious to try it, it's reasonable. If you contemplate an elimination diet, don't do it lightly. Talk with your child's doctor or RD before proceeding.

I know families who feel that eliminating some foods and ingredients has helped their children feel better, and other families for whom the trial did not help. Some parents observed that going "dye-free" helped a child's attention and behavior, while others saw no benefit. There are no clear answers.

If you choose to pursue an elimination diet, having a positive feeding relationship will be key to the success of the trial. Remember that neurodivergent folks have far higher rates of eating disorders. Extra care needs to be taken to protect a positive relationship with food.

Therapeutic Diets and Responsive Feeding

Therapeutic or elimination diets require learning new ways of cooking and meal planning. Be kind with yourself through the process, and ask for support when you can.

Two of Lara's three children have brain-based differences. Her adopted son, Brian, had frightening rages. Lara explains, *"Brian acted out, and our daughter, Hailey, acted in."* Hailey, meanwhile, had a family history of celiac disease (allergy to gluten), and was on a stool softener and an acid blocker. Lara recalls seeing information about GFCF years ago. *"I had been seeing posts in parent support forums for years, and I would delete them. I wasn't ready. I will try not to beat myself up over that. I think our son was ready sooner, but our daughter has more severe trust and attachment issues, so I don't think she would have been ready earlier."*

In an effort to help her children focus on what they could eat, Lara loaded the countertops with clear containers of things like cashews, dried fruit, and rice, and made homemade potato chips on the first day.

Any intervention trial should be followed consistently, to see if it helps. How long depends on why the food is being eliminated. You may know as quickly as a week if your child is lactose intolerant, while a trial to see if avoiding dairy impacts behavior may need three to six months. Here are some responsive tips for pursuing a specialized diet:

- When removing food groups from a child's intake, check in with an RD or your doctor.
- Approach it with a positive attitude. When we feel sorry for our children, we tend to give in and allow guilt to take over. For example, we think, "He can't have so many things, so I'll let him have sweets whenever he asks to make up for it."
- Try to adapt familiar recipes while also adding new options.
- If possible, the whole family would follow the diet, but find what works for your family. Are others feeling deprived? Can you consider the child with dietary restrictions, while meeting the needs of others? (For example, Lara's older son enjoys cheese pizza when out with friends.)
- Be matter-of-fact about what she can or can't eat. Lara calls it a "plan." She laid out the new eating plan for the family.
- Try to link it back to how the child feels: "Milk from cows makes your tummy feel bad, and we want you to feel good. Let's try this milk today."
- Stick with flexible structure and allow mostly water between meals and snacks.
- Eat together. Serving your child's special foods at the kitchen island while you graze on other foods means missed opportunities.

Lara and I share a reluctance to talk about dietary interventions because we know that so many parents can't take on another *should*. Sit with the decision for a time, focus on building your relationship, learn what you can and, when and if you feel ready, consider giving it a try.

The good news is that there has been an explosion of resources and products that avoid certain items such as gluten. Experiment with recipes. Have a potluck/recipe-sharing picnic, or host a taste-test party where everyone can buy one or two items; you can try 10–20 new things and not break the bank. If your kids are old enough and interested, invite them along.

If you are laughing at this section because your son only eats mac-n-cheese and French toast fingers, first treat him like any other selective eater. Begin with structure and eat together if you can. Serve his mac-n-cheese and French toast fingers along with the foods you are eating so he can get familiar with them (see Chapters 5 and 6). Introduce GFCF versions of his favorites.

"I am hesitant to talk about the success we've had, because I know there are families who will try this and not see significant improvement. I don't want to give false hope that this is a magic bullet. Our son's sensory experiences have improved greatly in the last year since we've been doing GFCF. Ironically, we initially did it more for our daughter, but Brian has seen the most dramatic improvement."

— Lara, mother of biological and adopted children. Lara's daughter Hailey was able to stop her GI medications.

When elimination diets result in positive changes, I wonder if the success is due to the actual removal of certain foods or sometimes that these ways of eating tend to give more attention to making sure the child is eating regularly, overall balance, preparing meals, and eating together. Time is also passing where the child may be spending more time in felt safety. **I've had many families see significant improvement in behavior and other areas just with the switch to responsive feeding.** You'll know it's helping if your child is happier and healthier—so trust your instincts.

Reintroducing Food or Drinks After an Elimination Trial

If you tried taking your child off dairy and didn't notice improvement, take some care reintroducing it. Natalie had been off all gluten and dairy for almost a year to see if it would improve her low energy and loose stools. Unfortunately, her symptoms did not improve. Mom felt that reintroducing dairy would help her meet Natalie's nutritional needs and make snacks and meals easier.

She started serving small amounts of hard cheeses a few times a week. With no observed change in her daughter's behavior, stools, or activity, Mom gradually increased the amounts of cheese and introduced yogurt. Natalie had not yet chosen to drink milk, which may have meant she didn't like it at the time, or that it could have made her uncomfortable. While rehabilitating the feeding relationship after years of food battles, Natalie's energy and activity began to improve.

If your child has been stable and on a restricted diet for some time (not due to allergy), if you would like to see if you can serve those foods again, it may be worth trying to reintroduce them to see if they are tolerated.

Complementary Therapies and Supplements

If you decide to pursue complementary therapies, including dietary interventions or supplements, look for a physician or provider who is familiar with them. Increasingly, medical centers have integrative medicine departments, and more doctors are trained in or have a special interest in integrative or complementary modalities, including dietary interventions.

Be wary of companies and practitioners who amplify worries and sell pricey and questionable supplements. **Supplements, unlike prescription drugs, are not regulated.** That means they don't have to prove their claims, and more worrisome are studies revealing they may not contain what they say they do. In one study, hundreds of independently tested samples were tainted with prescription medications not listed on the label (such as steroids).[23] Even "natural" supplements can have side effects and interact with other medications. Let your child's doctor know if you use supplements. Look for reputable, independently tested brands.

Vitamin and supplement patches are in the early stages of research. While tempting so as to avoid pills and liquids, patches are unregulated and absorption can differ. Ask your doctor or a pediatric dietitian.

While things like essential oils may be soothing and a tool in the coping toolkit, they do not cure illness and should not be ingested. Smelling peppermint oil can help with nausea, and lavender may have a calming effect, but they don't cure ear infections.

Dangerous Elimination Diets

One diet I never recommend is keto or no- or low-carb. The brain has to run on carbs. Keto is not appropriate for children or teens (or, in my opinion, for adults) unless there is a specific medical reason, such as a rare form of epilepsy that responds to a low-carb diet. A 2023 article in the American College of Cardiology reported that adults who followed a keto-like diet of low carbs and high fat (for more than a decade) had *more* worrisome cholesterol profiles and almost twice as many cardiac events than those who did not limit carbs.[24] Talk to your doctor or dietitian.

Promoting Gut Health

Tips to promote gut health that won't hurt:

- Consider a probiotic supplement (good bacteria that support a healthy gut system).
- Use a probiotic supplement during and after any antibiotics or with diarrheal illness.

- Offer yogurt or kefir drinks with live active cultures as choices in the meal and snack rotation. Kombucha or similar fermented drinks contain probiotics as well as tiny amounts of alcohol as a product of fermentation. To ensure safety for children, buy store-bought varieties that regulate alcohol levels, introduce them slowly, and limit to 3 to 4 ounces for young children and 8 ounces for older children.
- Look for foods (even milk) or supplements fortified with DHA and omega fatty acids. Some fish oil supplements are chewy and don't taste too bad. Flax oil has almost no flavor and can be mixed into smoothies or oatmeal. You can also add whole or ground flax seed to baked goods.

Religious Considerations

If you follow a religious way of eating, ideally the whole family would eat that way. It is easier if you also have a community that shares your practices. Religious eating requirements can present challenges, such as menu planning or meeting nutritional needs while keeping kosher.

Fasting can be particularly dysregulating and can trigger disordered behaviors for those who have experienced food insecurity or restriction, are repeat dieters, or grapple/have grappled with an eating disorder. And most people, children especially, tend to feel best with predictable eating and more stable blood sugar levels.

Explore concerns with your religious leaders and with your conscience. Seek support and understanding from others in your religious tradition who will consider your situation.

Clinical social worker Shira Rosenbluth (@theshirarose) wrote this on Instagram: "If you need to eat this Yom Kippur because you're in eating disorder recovery, please know that eating is not just permissible, but a MITZVAH (a precept or commandment or a good deed done from religious duty). Of course, you should consult with your Rabbi if that makes you feel more comfortable, but your connection and spirituality happens through eating, not restricting. You don't need to be harming yourself in the name of religion. I want to clarify that this is referring to ALL eating disorders. Not just anorexia. Your mental health and recovery is a priority whether you grapple with restricting, bingeing, purging, or any other eating disorder behaviors. This should go without saying, but your weight is IRRELEVANT. If you're struggling (or in recovery), I want you to know that you don't have to be on death's door to need to eat on Yom Kippur. Your recovery first, always."

The following ideas can help incorporate religious guidelines into your feeding routines:

- Focus on what you can eat. Your child can eat pizza, maybe with cheese or meat.
- Celebrate cultural and family connections.

- Celebrate and explore the reasons behind the food rules. For example, talk about how it makes you feel closer to God and that it is important for your family traditions.

These are deeply personal issues, but it is valid to consider: If restrictive and proscriptive eating rules have the potential to do more harm than good, what are the lessons or values being instilled?

What You Serve Is Up to You

What you serve is not unimportant, and it is up to you, the parent. I purposely steer clear of recommending certain foods because every family I interact with is doing the best they can to feed their families, and has different resources, core values, and cultural traditions. If it is important to you, learn more about your food choices and do what you feel is best. The above information was mostly intended to help decrease some of the worry and anxiety around these choices.

Chapter 12
Your Role and Wrapping Things Up

Let's check in on how things are going. The issue I've witnessed parents wrestle with most is transitioning away from trying to get kids to eat more, less or different foods. Are you ready to jump in, or do you feel held back by your fears, your child's needs, and/or advice from family and friends? Maybe you've started with structure and stopped praise. Are you arguing with your partner? Remembering your own childhood meals? Falling into old patterns?

Responsive feeding means observing how your child responds to what you're doing with food and mealtimes. Is he pushing back? If so, against what? Is he in felt safety more of the time? Are you feeling more connected and calm at the table?

You might have to fake the confidence at first, and you will stumble as you learn. With time, you will get more comfortable as you and your child gain skills.

Responsive feeding supports, nurtures, and rehabilitates your child's ability to tune in to cues of hunger and fullness.

What Parents Bring to the Table

To understand your role in feeding, as with all aspects of parenting, you may need to explore your past. Many adults have a difficult relationship with food, and this makes feeding more complicated.

One dad shared that he didn't like family meals growing up because they were "formal," and he wanted eating to be fun for his kids. He recalled as a child not being allowed to talk at the table, and lots of pressure to eat. Exploring his feelings about his childhood meals helped him find the balance between structure and autonomy: having the ketchup bottle on the table, or serving from takeout containers while connecting during meals.

Another mom says she hated being forced to eat veggies growing up and remembers being the center of attention as the picky eater. She didn't want her kids to feel the same way, but her husband wanted them to eat veggies. She needed reassurance that no, she wasn't overreacting by not wanting Dad to pressure, and that as long as she provided them with pleasant opportunities, she was feeding well and giving her kids the best chance to learn to like veggies. She and her husband needed to have

Your Feeding Legacy

The following is from psychologist and feeding expert Jo Cormack, PhD, to help you consider how your history with food impacts feeding.

Our feeding legacy is the sum of influences over how we feel about food and feeding. This may go back several generations and is not always in our conscious awareness. So many factors impact the person we are when we arrive at parenting: our cultural heritage; our health; our feelings about our bodies; how we were parented; whether money was scarce in childhood... This list is endless. Take some time to get a better understanding of your feeding legacy (and your partner's if you have one) because this will help you help your child with their eating.

For single parents: Consider asking a close friend or family member if you can spend some time together talking through your feeding legacy (as described for couples below). You can focus on yourself or your friend can share their answers too, if that feels more reciprocal. Having someone act as a sounding board can help you gain clarity. On the other hand, you may prefer to write down your answers and reflect on them by yourself. There is no right or wrong–choose whichever approach feels comfortable.

For couples: Take some time to go through these questions separately, writing down your own answers without looking at your partner's. Dedicate an evening (or as long as you can spare!) to talking this through. Listen without judgment or interruption to one another's answers, question by question. (You can refer to the list of feeding practices after the Legacy questions to jog your memory.) Ask for more details... How did it feel? What is it like to talk about? Ask if they have said everything they need to say, before moving on. Try summarizing your partner's answers, checking to see that you have understood them. Next, swap roles, so that you have both shared your answers.

Some people like to do this question by question, others like to go through all the questions then switch. It's up to you. At the end of the exercise, chat about what you have learned about one another that is new. Did anything surprise you? Does anything that confused you before, make sense now? Or did you know all about each other's feeding legacies already? What can you take from this conversation, into how you parent in relation to food?

Questions:

1. What is your happiest memory about food from your childhood?
2. What is your worst memory about food from your childhood?
3. What were the rules about food and mealtimes when you were growing up?
4. How is your answer to question 3 different from the rules in your family now that you are a parent?
5. Pick three words to describe mealtimes when you were younger.
6. Which aspects of your upbringing (in relation to food) would you *like* your child to experience?
7. Which aspects of your upbringing (in relation to food) would you *not* want your child to experience?
8. If you had grandparents in your life, describe their attitude to eating and their relationship with food. You may need to ask other family members (if available) for information about this.
9. Describe your parents' or caregivers' main beliefs and feelings about food.
10. Where do you think these beliefs came from?
11. Can you see any traces of your answers to questions 8 and 9 in your own beliefs, feelings, behaviors, and thoughts about food and eating?

some long talks and learn about nutrition and growth as they reconciled their different approaches. They agreed that what they were doing wasn't working and were willing to change.

Some parents find the table triggers memories of childhood trauma. Mika would feel her body tense and her heart race when sitting with her kids at the table. She resisted family meals, and frequently hopped up to get things and felt agitated, making excuses to avoid shared meals. With her therapist, she explored her own childhood dinner table; a place of dreaded silence and unpredictable behavior from her alcoholic father, with frequent verbal abuse and smacks. These memories carried over to mealtimes with her children. Working through the trauma and grief, as well as ways to signal safety to her body, helped Mika be more present for her children. She started with less-threatening snack time, moving eventually to connected dinners.

For more specifics or to jog your memory, check any of the following non-responsive tactics used with you during your childhood:

☐ Bargaining

☐ Bribing (a sticker, toy car, extra TV time if you ate a certain food)

☐ Rewarding or controlling your behavior with food

☐ Promising a special food, such as sweets, for eating something or trying a food

☐ Persuading you to eat ("Come on, you want to grow up to be healthy and strong, don't you?")

☐ Playing a game to get you to eat

☐ Forcing you to eat

☐ Withholding food as punishment

☐ Taking over/feeding if you refused to eat (i.e., spoon-feeding even when you were capable)

☐ Threatening punishment for not eating

☐ Making you clean your plate

☐ Praise

☐ Limiting portions or asking you to wait for seconds

☐ Mentioning your weight or calories while eating

☐ Talking to you about nutrition or health benefits of food

☐ Feeding you differently than siblings

☐ Letting others (siblings for example) eat more or different food than you were served

If you experienced any of these tactics, do you think they hurt or helped *your* eating? How did it make you feel?

____

Now look at the list above, but this time think about how you are feeding *your child.* Do you use any of these tactics? If so, which ones?

____

How long have you been using them?___________________________________

Do you find you have to constantly "up the ante," as in negotiate longer, give better bribes, etc.?

____

If you are trying to get your child to eat more, less, or different foods, are these tactics *successful*? If yes, how? (Remember, most tactics work a little, at least for a while.)

____

In which areas do you define "success" with feeding? (Check any that apply):

☐ How much your child eats

☐ Your child's behavior

☐ What he eats

☐ How he is growing/weight patterns

Reflecting on what you've read, can you think of other ways to define "success" moving forward?

____

Consider Personality

Often, when families feel stuck, there is a mismatch in how the adults and children approach food. The following is a quick refresher of the basic categories of temperaments or personalities around learning to like new foods:

- Outgoing (or easygoing) and curious: Generally likes to try new foods; a "no thank-you-bite" rule may be fine with this child. "Hey, I do like this!"
- Cautious and sensitive: The initial response is almost always rejection, and it may take a while before this child learns to expand his tastes.
- Somewhere in between: May not try a food the first few times, or like it when they do, but over the years learns to like the family's foods.

Think back to your personality, childhood, and family of origin.

- Which type describes you as a child? ______________________________

  - Did it change? Were you "picky" as a child but branched out in high school, for example? ______________________
  - Which one do you think describes your child? ______________________
- Does understanding your child's food "personality" help you feel more calm and patient with the process? ______________________

You may need to grieve if you are a foodie who gets pleasure from food and mealtimes, and your child isn't and doesn't. Continue to journal to help you understand a child whose experience is so different from yours.

Caring for the Caregivers

You may be dealing with financial burdens, navigating school IEP plans, sibling adjustment, or therapy appointments, not to mention perhaps your own health issues, work, or relationship turmoil. Parents can find themselves chronically dysregulated, in fight, flight, or freeze—and that takes a toll. When friends, family, and doctors pile on and imply that you aren't doing enough, you're doing it wrong, you aren't "compliant" with a diet, or your child is "failing to thrive," it feels awful.

Sometimes struggling for years, clients have cried during sessions, sharing feelings of hopelessness, anger, regret, and an overwhelming sense of failure and guilt. A 2011 *Infant, Child, & Adolescent Nutrition Journal* devoted to pediatric feeding problems acknowledged, "Many families have developed a negative pattern of feeding that is so pervasive it can result in clinically significant mental health symptoms for parents. Anxiety and depression are very common and can leave parents feeling hopeless, afraid, and unable to make changes in the mealtime patterns."[1]

On our third call, Maxine, mother of Asiah, cried, *"I've just been dealing with this for so long, I feel like I am at the bottom of a dark pit."* I highly suspected that she was to the point of being clinically depressed, and urged her to seek counseling and support.

It's hard to take care of your kids if you are falling apart. It's hard to be available for co-regulation and connection when you aren't in felt safety.

Maxine and Asiah had made progress with responsive feeding, but were still struggling. Mom's assessment was, *"Nothing is better; she is still so obsessed with food, and I feel like there is no hope that she will ever get this."* I gently pointed out that in the same call, Maxine had shared at least five anecdotes where they had made major strides, such as the successful transition of the morning bottle to breakfast time, and that her daughter had on a few occasions left food on her plate and left the table without fussing—things she had never done in the years since she had joined the family.

From her "dark pit," Maxine couldn't see the light. She had trouble noticing and acting on the positive changes, and was sliding back to counterproductive practices (pulling a screaming Asiah out of her highchair to end a meal) because she thought, "nothing was working."

Grow Your Resilience

To best help your child, you have to help yourself. I'm not going to lecture about self-care or recommend a spa day or regular date night. If you had the time and resources for that, you'd probably already be doing it. As Eileen Devine, social worker and founder of the Resilience Room online community, wrote in a blog post, "It's kind of like, 'time for self-care? In my life? Are you kidding me?' I've found that calling it 'nervous system health' and focusing on *building resilience* is key." Here are some ideas:

- Spend an extra minute or two in the shower. Pay attention while you're there. Focus on the feel of the water, relax into the heat.
- Lean on your religious community and faith, if that is part of your life.
- Sing or find some music you can play during the day. Make playlists for different moods: booming bass when you need to get pumped up, sad songs when you need the release of a cry, soothing or upbeat for in between.
- Look at favorite family photos, and put a few on the fridge or the mirror in the bathroom.
- Find a soothing mantra that you can say to yourself when things are difficult.
- Find a soothing aromatherapy oil, perhaps lavender or lemon.
- Laugh—at anything you can find. A video on your phone, a book of jokes, your favorite silly movie, even the absurdity of life.
- Keep a gratitude journal. Aim for three things each day that went well or that you appreciated. "The sun was shining. Lisa smiled at dinner. I enjoyed a hot shower without interruption. I didn't burn the pancakes . . ." Or snap a quick picture during the day of that warm mug of tea, or a sunset, and store it in an album on your phone.
- Access soothing food rituals for yourself. Virginia Sole–Smith wrote about "car sushi" in the *New York Times*.[2] This isn't about secretive binging; it's enjoying the pleasure of food, by yourself. When she picked up groceries, she would eat takeout sushi alone, with whatever she wanted to play on the radio in her car.
- Brew a cup of tea or enjoy a cup of coffee with some chocolate.
- Add your ideas: ____

Eileen offers this advice: "I have parents start with self-compassion and find some movement. Just start." I've included more of her tips here:

- Identify emotions, even the shameful, guilty, grieving ones that feel bad, that we don't want to feel.
- Gently acknowledge those emotions. Those feeling are appropriate.
- Recognize: "This is grief; I can feel it and it didn't take me under."

- When you have those "awful thoughts," sit with it and try, "Man, this is as hard as I think it is," versus, "I'm a terrible person."
- Have a cry and say, "Thank you, nervous system, I needed that reset."
- "Invite movement" doesn't mean hitting the gym. Start with small movements, which may be clenching and unclenching your fists a few times, noting that tension and release. Maybe increase to more muscle groups, or a quick walk, jumping jacks, or a silly dance, or thump your chest to a song with a strong bass beat.
- Who in your support network have you thought of asking for help, but never have? What is stopping you? Many times, people want to help, but just need to know how. Be specific: dropping a child off after dance class, taking a child to school, picking up a grocery cart delivery?
- Delegate where you can.
- Don't volunteer unless it fills your cup. There will be a time in your life when you can come back to the neighborhood committee.
- Consider letting go of toxic relationships.
- Explore time wasters such as social media apps. Be honest about how you feel after scrolling and delete some or set a time limit.
- Find more resources and support, such as Kristen Neff's The Mindful Self-Compassion Workbook or parent support online. Being seen and heard, knowing you are not alone, that your experience matters—is healing.
- Know it won't always be this way. When things are tough, there is a tendency to think it will always be this way. It won't.

Devine adds another piece of advice that was a recurring theme from the therapists and parents I interviewed: "Let go of expectations, for now, knowing that you can come back to them down the road." This is common in religious traditions, particularly Buddhism, and is central to Neff's self-compassion work. Suffering is the gap between expectation and reality. Let go of those expectations.

And because experts with lived experience have so much wisdom to share, I'm including one more from Dr. Casey Ehrlich. She wrote this at the end of a Tik Tok video on At Peace Parents: "I would say that the majority of the progress and the catalyst for your child's progress is this:

- Transforming yourself.
- Letting go of control.
- Non-reactivity.
- Radical acceptance of what you cannot change and finding agency within that.
- Working on shifting from compliance to connection.
- Working on your own healing and nervous system regulation.
- Being able to witness your child without trying to change them.
- Seeing moments of pain and suffering as part of the human experience.

- Non-attachment.
- Allowing emotions and your own nervous system activation without avoiding or attaching to it as part of your identity or who you are (unless you want to).

". . .entire spiritual traditions over millennia teach this. Nobody 'accomplishes' this and then it is done. It is a lifetime of practice that you commit to a more peaceful life with a PDA child/teen. Simple, right?"

Talk About Feeding with Your Support People

It can feel vulnerable to share, or even cry in front of other parents, but also incredibly healing when you realize you are not the only parent who dreads dinner or serves chicken nuggets most nights, and that things can improve, little by little.

If you have a formal or informal support group, consider using this book to guide a discussion. Go over some of the questions in this chapter. Tell stories about how you were fed and how it backfired, share your successes, and be open to sharing your "mistakes," or as I prefer to call them, "learning opportunities."

Other parents may have ideas to help with meal prep, keeping kids busy while cooking, or allergy-friendly snacks; but be aware that other parents may not feed in responsive ways. If others demonize sugar or recommend restriction or other non-responsive practices (which are, as you recall, the cultural norm), you may need to bow out of those discussions.

Feeding with a Partner

If you are one of two or more adults who are the primary feeding partners, that can help immensely to share the work, and can also introduce conflict around beliefs about feeding, weight, and more. This section explores feeding with partners.

Lean on Your Partner or Support Person

Hold hands under the table or grab the chair during those transition meals when you want to jump in with old patterns. Check in with each other about a situation that seems difficult. Celebrate your successes together. Anneliese shared that when her selective eater took a piece of chicken, she could tell her husband was about to praise him. She grabbed her husband's hand and shook her head. They shared their joy over their son's progress after the kids were in bed.

Feeding with Different Parenting Styles

These struggles can wear at your bond with your partner. (If another person such as *your* parent is your feeding partner, conflict can be difficult to navigate.) It is known that in general, marital satisfaction plummets when young children enter the picture. One mother, stuck in an incredibly difficult feeding relationship for more than two years, says that the feeding and weight worries were *"ripping our family apart."*

I've observed that the person doing most of the feeding and meals is more consumed with this topic, while the partner who comes home for dinner (or breakfast after a night shift) doesn't seem to understand "all the fuss." This has mostly meant mothers in this feeding grind, and they've shared that they feel incredibly isolated.

I'm not dumping on partners who are less worried. In general, fathers seem to worry less (they also seem to resist letting go of trying to get kids to comply with eating), and let's face it, most have traditionally had an easier history with food and body image than women.

The good news is that different parenting approaches to food can be an asset if one parent is stuck in that worry. Maxine shared, *"My wife is way more relaxed about all this than I am. I'm letting her take the lead on this feeding stuff, and it seems to be helping."* If you're not the one staying home or dealing with "I'm hungry!" or "I'm not eating!" for hours on end, your partner is bearing the brunt of the judgment—from what feels like *everyone.* Try to be supportive and compassionate, and help your partner get their needs met. If you can't be that sounding board, find a way to reach someone who can: parent support forums, friends, family support specialists, or a therapist.

Many parents have shared that just having someone listen helps the most. As Meredith says about her trusted listener, *"Being able to cry and be honest with one person about what a failure I felt like was so important. And for that trusted person to just listen and say, yes, this was absolutely difficult. No solutions, no judgments, no fairy-tale view making me think I was crazy. Just accepting how I was feeling."*

Support Your Partner

If your partner is primarily the one planning and serving meals, there are ways you can help. As early as possible, participate in feedings, sit close when your partner gives bottles, and give some too, as your child permits. Serve and join in meals and snacks as often as you can. Share menu-planning or shopping tasks, thank your partner for cooking and shopping, and clean up after meals.

If they ask you to be involved in feeding therapy appointments, make every attempt to go along, at least initially. Read the books together or at least be willing to discuss what your partner is reading, and support the efforts of the person taking the lead. I encourage primary caregivers to cut your partners some slack, too. Let the little things slide, and support all efforts to be involved. Assume everyone is doing their best.

If You and Your Partner Don't Agree About Feeding

Feeding children is made more difficult when the adults involved don't agree on the approach. Here are some strategies that can help you get on the same page:

- Examine where you are now. What have you tried so far; is it helping? What is going well, what isn't? Identify strengths and build on those. If snacks are going well, how do they differ from meals? Your journal can help.

- Figure out where you're both coming from and why. (Do the Feeding Legacy exercise a few pages back.) How are your decisions a reaction to your own childhood experiences? ("I turned out ok!")
- Refine goals and learn about appropriate expectations. Think of short- and long-term goals. Using the example of extreme picky eating, short-term goals might include:
    - Focusing on felt safety and connection.
    - Working on making time for meals together.
    - Serving meals family-style.
    - Not bribing with dessert.

As the short-term goals of improved mood and decreased anxiety are met, the long-term goals come next: Children's skills around eating based on internal cues of hunger and fullness emerge and variety improves.

- Start eating together on a weekend, or agree to try family-style meals. Maybe Dad handles weekend snacks while Mom is out.
- What are you worried about? Deep down, is one of you still scared your child is too small, or not getting good nutrition? Do you feel judged? Don't want a "spoiled" child? You want to "win?" Try to be specific.
- Track progress, keep a journal, and share the little victories that build faith in the process.

Dawn Friedman, family therapist and adoptive mom advises to agree on values, goals, and absolutes.

Agree on the main values: "If Mom is saying, 'Let's stop battling over food' and Dad is saying, 'No, she needs to eat her vegetables,' talking about values can help them realize that they both want the same thing—healthy kids. Getting to the values piece helps direct the conversation to be supportive of both parents' goals instead of arguing about something else entirely, like trying to convince Dad about dessert when that's really not what his concern is at all."

Agree on goals: "Mom may be trying to build independence in eating so a new approach makes more sense to her, but Dad is thinking more about obedience, so not enforcing bite rules looks like 'giving in.' If that's the case, we talk about other ways to support Dad in his parenting goals, like focusing on what the family feels is polite behavior."

Agree on absolutes: Maybe that means no force feeding, no bribes, and stopping whatever is happening that may be behind a child gagging, vomiting, or dysregulating out of felt safety.

If you just can't agree, agree to disagree. Find a feeding therapist, dietitian, or family therapist to help with the discussions. Read a book together or listen to some podcasts. Sometimes, families find success when they allow one parent to take the lead for six months and then re-evaluate. I've had many a skeptical parent won over within a few weeks after witnessing improvement.

Trusting the Process

A very human response to change is to choose what feels comfortable and resist what doesn't. If you're wary about parts of this approach, this section addresses trusting this process, starting with celebrating success and moving on to examining your worries and motivation.

Celebrate Success

When you are alone or with your support person (not in front of your child), pat yourself on the back for getting dinner on the table, for not pestering him to eat, or for letting her eat until *she* is done. Celebrate changes in your child: they are happier at mealtimes, perhaps they put broccoli on their plate or tolerated a dish sitting next to them, asked for more chicken, or asked for seconds and stopped after one or two more bites. (See pages 129 and 196 for a reminder of what to look for.)

Early successes will be yours: getting the kitchen table cleared off for family meals, getting dinner on the table, or bringing a snack to the park.

How's That Journal Going?

It's easy to forget how far you've come. Progress can feel painfully slow. Most selective eaters will not suddenly devour roasted peppers. In the meantime, **looking back to where you have been helps you see progress more clearly.** Write down your victories:

- You had a more peaceful meal tonight.
- Your child calmly passed a bowl of a food that used to trigger meltdowns and gagging.
- Your child served himself some pizza, even if he only ate the crust this time.
- Your teenager is coming out of their room for mealtimes, even though they still aren't saying much.

One parent, frustrated with how few new foods their child tried in six weeks, read their journal and realized with relief that they had made progress: Their child no longer needed to eat sitting on their lap, she was eating yogurt from a bowl when for years she had only eaten it from a tube, everyone was less emotional and more connected at mealtimes, and she *had* tried three new foods.

Let Go of Guilt

More than one mom has asked how to deal with the guilt of realizing that some of their feeding practices made matters worse. I've been there. I get it. I've made feeding "mistakes." But for myself and my clients, and pretty much every parent, Fred Rogers sums it up: "Of course, there were times in our parenting that we wish we'd done something differently, but we've tried not to feel too guilty about that. One thing's sure is that we always cared and we always tried our best."[3]

Most of my clients tried for months and years to do as they were told, knowing all along that something wasn't right and that things were not getting better, but they didn't have the right support or information. So, find a way to move forward. Take that emotion and use it to energize the effort to feed with structure and not fall into old patterns. You would probably not harshly judge another parent who did her best with what they knew at the time. Extend that kindness to yourself. Cry, talk to a friend, pray, or even write a letter to your child that you may, or may not, ever share with her. Every day is a chance to try again.

Lingering Worries and Resistance

Success builds confidence and whittles down doubts—and you begin to believe that your child can do better and feel better around food. But waiting for those early signs isn't easy. What if you're not sure if RF is helping, or you're still mired in conflict? Usually when parents feel stuck, there is still some form of pressure or restriction—for example, they still withhold dessert until the child has eaten at least something else, or can't give up on making them take one bite of a vegetable.

You are not giving up control, but the illusion of control, temporary control, and—potentially—compliance at a cost. The good news about feeling stuck is that it usually means there are still opportunities for healing.

I've helped parents hang in there, cheering and pointing out successes along the way, but I also challenged parents to dig deeper. I hope this book, and the advice and successes parents have shared, will help you hang in there while you wait for signs of progress. The following exercises help to examine what's behind any resistance.

Ask Yourself:

What am I currently doing to try to get my child to:

- Eat more? ____________________
- Eat less? ____________________
- Eat different foods? ____________________
- Other: ____________________

  ____

If I am still trying to get my child to eat more or less:

What am I worried about? ____________________

Is it a valid worry that I need to look into? ____________________

Am I falling into old patterns? ____________________

Do *I* ever look forward to meals and snacks, or would I rather be poked with sharp sticks?

____

How do mealtimes feel? ____________________

____

Is there progress? (See pages 129 and 196 for signs of early progress.)

____

If yes (even with pressure), in what ways do you see progress? For example, does bribing with dessert get in a few more bites?

____

____

____

Which of the following statements makes you uncomfortable?

- ☐ I can serve dessert *with* the meal.
- ☐ I trust that my child has the ability to learn to know how much to eat.
- ☐ Serving family style and letting my child serve herself will help her.
- ☐ If my child is offered a variety of foods within the context of structured, pleasant eating opportunities, she is likely over time to increase variety.
- ☐ It is not so much about *what* my child eats at one meal, but how the meal *feels*.
- ☐ Even though milk (or protein or vegetables) is important to me, I will not encourage or pressure her to drink/eat more.
- ☐ Tactics such as bribing with dessert, or a "no thank-you bite," are not helping him learn to like new foods.
- ☐ I am okay with parenting a child in a bigger body, and that my child may never be slim.

The items where you sense resistance may indicate where you need to read and learn more, where you might slip up, or where there are unaddressed worries.

Start with a deep breath as you consider the following:

- Am I focusing on felt safety and connection, pleasant meals, and reducing conflict?

- Am I doing my job of providing and letting my child decide how much from what is served?
- Do I have enough information to deal with my worries?

Early on, you might overcompensate; maybe you say nothing about food or never offer to pass a bowl. No, it's not pressure if you ask your son if he wants you to pass the potatoes; however, it is pressure if you ask him 10 times. It's not restriction if you ask them to share the cupcakes; it won't help if you ask him to eat his peas first. Your motivation matters. Your child will feel the difference. If you say, "No, you can't have any more shrimp, that's enough, you should be full," it's not the same as, "That's your share of shrimp. It's a little expensive, but if you're still hungry, you can have more bread and milk." Feel the difference? Your child will.

Ask yourself, how would I feed my child if I wasn't worried about nutrition or their size? If she was thinner, or weighed more, how would I respond? That will usually offer some insight when you feel stuck.

Consider Your Child's Perspective

Earlier in the book, 16-year-old Yiseth advised parents to try to see things from *"the kid's point of view."* This exercise might help. If you have a partner, consider putting on a little play, or act it out with someone who is supportive.

"Pudding" on a Play

Props: two cups of pudding. You can even stir something into the pudding that might be unexpected, such as walnuts or chocolate chips, but don't tell your partner what it is—be kind, no anchovies or hot sauce.

Ask the audience (or yourself) to focus on how it feels to be the child. Before the exercise, read these questions and ask the audience to pay attention to them as you role-play:

- How does each scenario feel? Comfortable or stressful? Pay attention to how your body feels: clenched muscles, tight gut?
- What made me want to try the food?
- What turned me off or made me not want to try the food?
- Can you guess which of the scenes represents responsive feeding? (If you get this wrong, you may want to re-read this book from the beginning.)

Scene 1

Parent: Standing, holding the phone, hands the cup to the child and says, "Here's your snack."

Child: "I don't want that, it's gross."

Parent: "It's not gross, you like it, and it's good for you. It's has calcium for your bones and protein for your muscles."

Child: "But I don't want it. I've never had that kind before. I want graham crackers."

Parent: "You'll like it!" (Phone rings, parent answers the phone: "Ok, just a minute, I'll call you right back, I'm giving Max his snack. I know! He's so picky!") To the child: "If you eat half, I'll give you a graham cracker. I have to grab this call, and when I get back, you better have eaten half of this pudding."

Child: "I won't! It's slimy!"

Parent: "It's not slimy, it's good. If you don't eat it, I'll tell Dad, and he'll be really upset when he gets home. Think about all the kids who don't have enough food." Parent leaves the room.

End scene

Scene 2

Parent: Holds two pudding cups, spoons, and napkins. Sits across from the child. "Thanks for washing your hands." (Phone rings and Mom silences the ringer.)

Child: "What is that? I don't think I had it before. It looks gross."

Parent: "It's called rice pudding. I used to love this with frozen blueberries when I was little. It's got a vanilla flavor, like the pudding you like, but it has a little chewiness to it."

Child: "I don't want any."

Parent: Tries a bite and says, "OK, you don't have to eat anything you don't want to. There's a napkin if you don't like it, you can spit it out.* And there's graham crackers."

Child: Takes bite of graham cracker.

Parent: Dips corner of graham cracker in rice pudding. "I forgot to get a drink, would you like milk or water?"

Child: "Milk, please."

Parent: Gets milk, sits down. "Did you like the new clay project at school?" Takes a few more bites.

Child: Pokes corner of graham cracker into pudding and smells it.

End scene

*You don't have to tell her every time she can spit food out or explain that she doesn't have to eat what she doesn't want. That might be too much talking and can feel like pressure.

Review the questions posed before the two scenes. The following is usually how parents answer during workshops. See if your answers match up.

What made me not want to try the pudding?

- Being argued with, "It's not slimy" or "You'll like it."
- Being called "picky" made me mad.
- Nutrition talk. If it's "healthy," I figure it won't taste good.
- The pressure.
- The threat felt scary.
- Being left alone with the food.
- Not having something I wanted to eat.

What made me want to try the pudding?

- Mom sitting with me and eating the food.
- Flavor context and relating it to an accepted food.
- Knowing I could spit it out.
- Seeing Mom dip the graham cracker.
- Relaxed atmosphere.

The Foreign Country

If you're not an actor at heart, simply imagine the following scenario. You are in a country where you don't speak the language.

Scenario 1: You are alone at a restaurant. The owner comes and tells you, "This is the house special. However, it is VERY rude in my country to spit out food. This is very good for you, it will make you very strong, and it is cheap, too." He sets down a large bowl of lumpy gray food and walks away.

Scenario 2: Same country, same food. A friend gave you a recommendation of a well-respected chef and restaurant. The chef sits with you briefly (an honor!) with a bowl of the same lumpy gray food in the middle of the table and a serving spoon. He says, "I am happy to share the table with you. I made pudding that is a little sweet, with vanilla and dried grapes. I hope you might enjoy this pudding." He sits, serves himself a small portion, and clearly savors his first bite. You have a paper napkin that you can spit your food into discreetly if you need to.

In Scenario 1, you may have felt nervous, alone, and suspicious, with no context of whether it would be spicy or sweet, or what was in it—whether those lumps were meat or fruit. You had very little control.

Scenario 2 had:

- Pleasant company
- Modeling
- Trust in the chef, by way of recommendation and his demeanor
- Enjoyment

- Context of flavor
- Permission to take a small portion and try at your own pace, knowing what to expect

Which scenario *felt safer* and helped you imagine taking a bite and enjoying it? This is what feeding feels like for small children who don't have a context, have a communication barrier or other challenges. Try to put yourself in your child's shoes.

Consider these statements and how a child might feel:

- "Do you really need another pork chop?"
- "No more bread, but you can eat as much celery as you want."
- "Your body has to catch up. It doesn't know if you're full yet; wait 20 minutes, then you can have fruit if you're still hungry."
- "You can't be full; you only ate two bites."

Notes: ____

____

____

____

____

Can You Spot Opportunities, Using the Child's Perspective?

"He was prone to tantrums at every meal. If he didn't like what he saw on his plate, he'd scream and cry. If he finished the cheese on his plate and ate nothing else, he'd signal that he wanted more cheese. If we told him he needed to finish his other food and then he could have more cheese, he would spiral into a tantrum with no ability to rebound. Meals were extremely stressful."

— Sue, of Marcus' mealtime tantrums

Can you spot a few opportunities to avoid the power struggles in this scenario? Think for a minute about Marcus' experience and write down your answers.

____

____

____

If you noticed the phrase, ". . . he didn't like what he saw on his plate," good for you! This family pre-plated, starting with conflict before the meal begins. For whatever reason, whether it's anxiety or feeling pressured and sensitive around autonomy, the request to finish what was on his plate dysregulated Marcus. The motivation was to help Marcus eat in a more balanced way, but it made things worse.

Rather than setting down a pre-plated dish, serve family style. Put all the choices in bowls on the table and let him choose and serve himself as he is able.

Marcus gets to choose how much from what is on the table, and he can be allowed to eat as much cheese as he wants without having to eat or earn other foods (assuming there is enough for everyone, and he's not lactose intolerant). Sue can let him have more cheese. Eventually, he will tire of cheese, probably sooner if he's not restricted. Sue can promote felt safety by supporting Marcus's autonomy. He learns to trust his mother, and when he is calm and his curious brain is able to participate, he will be more apt to learn to like other foods.

From Your Child's Perspective, Worse Behavior Can Signal Good Things

Sometimes behavior initially *worsens* when a responsive approach is introduced (see page 199 for more on the freedom to play). It can be reassuring to think of it in terms of the child's growing comfort; as the conflict around food fades, the child feels safe to experiment with limit-setting in other ways. This child who felt anxious, trapped, and locked in a battle over food is now relaxing and experimenting with more typical behaviors, like throwing food.

Annaliese recalls that only days into the transition, she found her two-year-old son, Adan, had dumped all the shampoo out on the floor. *"I was actually happy. This is normal two-year-old stuff, which when he was food obsessed and clinging to me, he never seemed to have the energy or interest to explore. Yesterday, he was standing on the table pretending to swordfight with his brother and I clapped—I was so happy I couldn't help it, though of course I got them down. I can't believe how he has blossomed with just addressing his food worries."*

Many parents worry so much about keeping the table pleasant that they second-guess themselves relative to behavior at the table. Help a dysregulated child, and deal with behavior that sabotages connection, such as teasing siblings or physical aggression. However, avoid punishing and praising based on what or how much your child is eating. The amazing thing is, once they don't *have* to push back against efforts to try to get them to eat more, less, or different foods, meals can be more about connection, and even a lot more fun. For some families, that transformation happens quickly. Remember, attitudes improve first. Enjoy it.

If You Need More Help

Some of you will read this book, perhaps watch a webinar, listen to some podcasts, or follow a newsletter or two. Armed with information, you'll make changes that help establish more supportive feeding. You will be better able to observe your child's responses and adjust. You will enjoy (more) pleasant meals and, with time, a child who is more capable with self-regulation and enjoys a wider variety of foods.

Some of you will read this book and feel confident that this is the right approach but need more support. This is where a dietitian or feeding therapist who works in a responsive, non-diet approach can help. There may be lingering questions, doubts, or scenarios not covered in this book. Many parents I've worked with needed help seeing progress and receiving encouragement and reassurance that their experiences in the transition weren't unusual.

And some families will need even more help. If you think back to the Worry Cycle from Chapter 1, families who are deep into the cycle of pressure/restriction and resistance may need support turning things around. I see this most when:

- Problems have become more entrenched over years, perhaps with different therapeutic approaches.
- Parents resist letting children eat foods with sugar, fat, processed foods etc. and restrict to only "clean" or limited options.
- Parents continue to focus on weight loss.
- Serious concerns about weight or nutrition continue.
- The parent is frequently dysregulated and not accessing felt safety. This may include dealing with depression, anxiety, substance use, or an eating disorder.
- The child has more severe brain-based, behavioral, medical, nutritional, oral-motor, or sensory challenges.
- Brain-based differences or neurodivergence impacts interoception or executive functioning for the parent or child.

I have been thrilled that some families who have suffered for years, even failing multiple interventions, have turned things around with just my books. Other families, even with seemingly less severe concerns, struggle and continue to engage in regular conflict.

If you think you may need more support, try to find professionals who work in a responsive and nervous system-informed approach. You may already be working with a pediatric RD, therapist, couples counselor or family therapist, pediatric psychiatrist, or social worker. Your child may need support, and you, the parent, may also need help.

Wrapping It Up

It's not always easy, but many parents feel immense relief when they finally feel they are on the right track.

"It is amazing that already he seems happy again. He has come running to me saying, 'I am so happy, I love you Mommy!' And even, 'I am full Mommy!' followed by a full belly laugh. I know that it may seem impossible to see his happiness return already,

but it has. A week into this and our 'food-obsessed' son is breaking free from his food anxieties, and our picky eater actually helped himself to some chicken the other night with no prompting. All of this is beyond our expectations."

— Annaliese, mom of two boys, one biological, one adopted at 11 months

When I read Anneliese's words, I shed a joyful tear or two. It's been deeply satisfying to accompany parents on this journey of bringing peace to mealtimes and helping to raise kids who are happier and healthier. Adan and Annaliese are on their way. My hope is that this book will positively impact others and prevent suffering—and to make room for more "belly laughs."

This book simply can't include every scenario or combination of challenges you might encounter. The day after it heads to the printer, I'll find new studies, or work with parents who come up with a solution that works for them that they want to share, or new ways of thinking about how this all fits together. But I want this information out there to help families, and the professionals who help them, to raise children who feel better about food and about (and the experience of living in) their bodies.

With a focus on felt safety and connection, you'll learn to observe and flexibly respond to day-to-day questions that come up as you feed and parent the children in your care.

This is a process, a journey you get to take with your family. Some things will improve quickly, others won't. Some days you will see progress, and other days you might feel frustrated and stuck. Observe your child, compare him only to himself, and remain open and curious while you enjoy their company.

I'll end with one mom's final words of advice for other parents: *"It really will get better... one meal at a time."*

Acknowledgements

Thank you to the parents who shared your highs and lows. I have learned from your strength, passion, and dedication to helping your children and families thrive. Thank you also to the adult adoptees, the teens, and the family support professionals for sharing your wisdom and insights. To my blog and social media followers over the years: Your stories teach and inspire me.

Thank you to my thoughtful and generous mentors and colleagues, to the authors and content creators from whom I have learned so much.

Thank you, dear husband, for your unwavering support and patience. A big thank you to my daughter for being a delightful dinner companion, and a kind, smart, steadfast, and funny person whom I get to share my life with. You are my greatest teacher.

Thank you to my generous and brilliant colleagues; for the discussions, debates, shared meals, and emails over the years, and to those who read drafts of this edition and offered feedback that made the book better.

Appendix

Medical Issues That Can Affect Feeding

This is an overview of some of the more common medical issues that may affect eating (and a few uncommon ones you might want to know about). **Remember, if there are changes or concerning symptoms, it's safest to check with your child's doctor.**

Also keep in mind that short and long term stress is associated with the following: headaches, skin rashes, chronic pain, fatigue, constipation, diarrhea, muscle tension, diabetes, heart disease, attention and executive function differences, aggression, communication differences, bed wetting and soiling, sleep disturbance, elevated stress hormones, hormone impacts, high blood pressure, autoimmune diseases, anxiety, and asthma. Felt safety focus can only help. (See page 33 for the Brain-Body Connection diagram.)

Anal Fissures

Painful, small tears on the sensitive anal tissue associated with firm stool, withholding, and constipation. Treatment is the same as for constipation; some prescription creams may help. In addition to painful bowel movements (BMs), you may see small amounts of bright red blood when wiping. Pain makes the child want to avoid BMs even more; a vicious cycle.

Anatomical Abnormalities

Such as cleft palate, cleft lip, and malformations of the breathing and swallowing tubes make the mechanics of feeding more difficult. Rarely, bowel and even rectal developmental anomalies (megacolon) are ruled out with gut or bowel problems.

Anemia

Not enough oxygen-carrying capacity in the blood. Most commonly due to iron deficiency, the risk is increased with catch-up growth or growth spurts (my teen daughter grew over four inches in a year, and though she eats a diet rich in iron, she had symptomatic anemia). Anemia can be due to a blood disorder, such as with sickle cell disease. Symptoms are similar to iron deficiency anemia (see Iron Deficiency Anemia in this appendix).

Dental Health

If a child is having problems chewing or eating, a dental evaluation is in order. A critical factor in developing tooth decay is the *frequency* of snacking or drinking. Structured meals and snacks with mostly water in between, regular dental care, and proper hygiene, promote dental health.

Diabetes

Diabetes occurs when there is a problem with the production or function of the hormone insulin. Insulin moves energy (glucose) into the cells where it can fuel the body or be stored. Type I diabetes occurs when the pancreas does not make enough insulin. It is rare, but should be considered if there is weight loss, decreased energy, increased thirst and urination, extreme hunger, and sometimes bedwetting. It's diagnosed most frequently in children and used to be called "juvenile" diabetes. If a child has Type I diabetes, that complicates feeding as there is a risk of blood sugar being too high or too low, and attention must be paid to how much and what the child is eating in order to dose insulin. Children and teens with Type I diabetes also have increased risk of eating disorders.

Type II diabetes occurs when the body isn't able to use insulin effectively, and is rare in children. It is many, many times more likely (estimates are over 200 times) that a child will suffer with an eating disorder.

Type II diabetes is correlated with weight acceleration and higher weight, if there is a family history, or they are in a high-risk population. It is often without symptoms. Doctors can screen for this. (See Dr. Williams' advice in the next paragraph for a weight-neutral approach.)

Rates of both Type I and II diabetes in young people are still low, but increasing.

Pre-diabetes

Pre-diabetes is a newer category developed to help determine when someone is at increased risk of developing Type II diabetes; defined by lab tests. Dr. Lesley Williams believes, "Monitoring trends over time is more valuable than one value. I have seen several patients stay in the prediabetes zone for years." Dr. Williams sees diagnoses such as pre-diabetes or fatty liver as an opportunity to guide care. **"Most often I see a blanket recommendation from physicians of 'eat less and exercise more.' Dieting supports the idea of avoiding or restricting certain foods/calories to achieve short term weigh loss. This approach is rarely helpful or successful.** I have found that speaking privately to close family and friends who spend a lot of time around your children is helpful. Also, letting new caregivers know the type of conversation and terminology that is appropriate."

Dr. Williams works closely with patients and their families. "For children with evidence of insulin resistance I recommend helping them find physical activity they enjoy. I also like to review their food choices and make sure they have access to and interest in a wide variety of foods. It's not, 'you can't eat mac-n-cheese', it's looking for ways to find other things they might enjoy, let's do some food exploring, they might find some things they like."

Pre-diabetes is a controversial diagnosis, with most adults who get that label not going on to develop diabetes and even returning to normal blood sugar levels.

Eczema

Eczema can start in infancy. It presents with dry, bumpy, red (or darker than usual), sometimes itchy patches. It is associated with asthma and other allergic conditions, including food allergies. It is often triggered by dry or cold air, or swimming or frequent bathing. Topical (applied to the skin) medications can help. Keep your child's fingernails short to minimize scratching. A dermatologist can help manage more severe cases.

Skin Care with Eczema

Breakdown of the skin's protective barrier may play a role in allergic illnesses and food allergies. To keep skin healthy, the following might help.

- Avoid using soaps often. Medically, there is no need to bathe a child daily or wash hair unless they have been playing in the mud or had a leaky diaper.
- Black children are more prone to eczema. Consider: quick showers versus baths that can strip the skin of oils, lotion a few times per day, appropriate scalp and hair cleaning and moisturizing. There are resources online.
- Try oils in bathwater or for massage, like grapeseed or olive oil. Massaging an infant or small child with all-natural oils can soothe skin, and be a nice bedtime ritual.
- Vanicream soaps and creams are free from unnecessary additives and perfumes. If you see red or rough spots, moisturize twice daily. Many "baby" products contain irritating ingredients.
- Wash clothes in detergents made for sensitive skin. Avoid fabric softeners.
- Double-rinse clothing in the wash cycle to remove excess irritants.

Emetophobia (Fear of Vomiting) and Phagophobia (Fear of Choking)

A fear of vomiting or choking usually develops after a frightful episode and responds best to early evaluation and support; requiring urgent attention with weight loss. Children may progressively limit intake to liquids; and social and emotional development is impacted, which may present as refusing to eat at school or to socialize around food. While categorized as a subtype of ARFID, some experts feel it is more of a true phobia. A qualified mental health professional with experience in cognitive behavioral approaches should be consulted.

Eosinophilic Esophagitis

Eosinophilic esophagitis (EoE) is an inflammation of the esophagus, or swallowing tube, associated with food allergies and more common in children with an atopic (including eczema) or allergy history. It is associated with reflux, and appears to be increasing with about 5/100,000 people impacted. EoE may present with distress and avoidance with eating, poor weight gain, weight loss, unusual vomiting or gagging, or foods getting stuck.

A GI doctor will need to be involved as the diagnosis currently is via biopsy with a scope. Treatment is usually acid blocking medication, sometimes steroids, and therapeutic diets avoiding allergenic foods. There is ongoing research to try to find less invasive ways to diagnose and treat. Care with GI and potentially a pediatric dietitian is important. Responsive feeding is supportive.

Fetal Alcohol Spectrum Disorder

Fetal alcohol spectrum disorder (FASD) is the umbrella term encompassing: FAS (fetal alcohol syndrome), PFAS (partial fetal alcohol syndrome), ARND (alcohol related neurodevelopmental disorder), and ARBD (alcohol related birth defects). FASD impacts the brain and the body, occurring when alcohol was used during pregnancy, particularly early on when many individuals don't know they're pregnant. Many times more children are impacted by alcohol exposure who do not have facial features associated with FAS.

Children with FASD are often shorter than average and weigh less than peers (and are more likely to have a smaller head circumference). This can impact interpretation of growth, and ultimately feeding, since there is often pressure put on parents of smaller children to get them to eat more. Children with FASD may have sleep and sucking problems as babies, and higher rates of sensory integration issues, impulse control, and executive functioning.

FASD is thought to effect roughly 1 in 20 children in the United States and Canada. There is no blood test to confirm diagnosis, and there is overlap (in terms of observed characteristics) with ADHD, autism, certain learning differences, and the effects of complex trauma. Pediatric developmental specialists and psychologists can help with diagnosis and support. There are increasing efforts to reduce stigma and support impacted individuals.

Gut Disorders

Bowel and gut problems are common challenges; many are "functional," meaning no underlying disease process is discovered. Symptoms can overlap, so ruling out organic disease such as celiac (true gluten allergy) or Crohn's disease is important. Below are some common (lower) GI issues. (Upper GI issues of the swallowing tube, such as reflux are described separately.) Chronic stress impacts gut motility and can lead to constipation, diarrhea, and sometimes both. I do not recommend IgG food sensitivity testing (see page 298) or stool microbiome tests; we don't have enough data to know what to do with that information. Consult with your child's doctor.

Constipation

Sometimes a painful diaper rash or other issue can set up the cycle of withholding stool that the child can simply "out-clench," in spite of a diet full of fruits and fiber. Other times, low fiber or fluid intake contributes. Some children with food intolerances (such as lactose) experience constipation. And sometimes, interoceptive challenges (not being aware of the urge to empty the bowels) and muscle discoordination such as pelvic floor dysfunction (where the body can't figure out how to empty the rectum) play a role.

I (and the colleagues I've asked) often see constipation and later toilet training in children who are also selective eaters where there are significant feeding battles. I don't understand the connection, but I have theories: A medical issue or pain from constipation decreases the child's appetite; interoceptive issues with sensory challenges; or the need for autonomy may play a role.

If your child has more than occasional firm stool or straining/pain with pooping, this can also lead to decreased appetite and, at times, cramping and rarely, vomiting. Large BMs can hurt, and muscle dysfunction can lead to anal fissures, which make matters worse (see Anal Fissures). Some children have a BM most days and still have significant constipation. If your child has unexplained abdominal pain, soiling of the underpants (encopresis, which happens when stool leaks around a firm ball of stool), or a distended abdomen, then impaction and constipation need to be ruled out.

A simple X-ray can be diagnostic if the history isn't clear-cut. Very rarely, there are anatomical reasons for chronic constipation, but almost always it is a "functional" problem improved without surgery. Your child's doctor may want to do a rectal exam, where a gloved finger is put in the child's bottom. Ask that this is discussed with you in advance. Often, a trial of treatment can be done without the need for a rectal exam.

Once a child is significantly constipated for weeks or months, the colon stretches, and this becomes a "chronic" condition. The colon is made of smooth muscle, and like any other muscle, it can get out of shape.

Many families will try medication (such as a stool softener) for a few days or even a week, see a few softer BMs and stop treatment only to have the problem resume almost immediately. There is no quick fix. It takes up to six months for a dilated colon to return to proper function. If a child has had significant constipation or pain, the body's natural reflex is to hold the BM in. Over time, it can be hard for them to understand and pick up on what their bodies are telling them. As frantic parents stand over the sweating, purple-faced withholder encouraging, "Let it out of your body, you will feel better!" the child simply can't.

In general, **optimize intake of liquids, fruits, and vegetables** (search the index for "hydration"). However, chances are if you are reading this book, this is already a challenge! So, when that fails in the short term, talk to your child's doctor about **stool softeners or a laxative.** The goal is to help your child have a daily, soft, pain-free BM for *months*. It can take *a long time.* You basically need to overpower the child's ability to hold in the BM.

Stay home when you start and expect soiling and accidents initially, but every few months wean the dose down and see what happens. Hopefully by then your child will have learned to respond to their body's cues. Oh, and don't forget to relax yourself, don't pressure, stay in *your* felt safety, and don't stop too soon. It may be that an occupational or pelvic floor therapists who specialize in this issue can help.

Some "functional" bowel disorders can cause constipation alternating with diarrhea. You learned in the introduction how chronic stress can alter how the gut moves and the gut/ brain connection. "Gut-directed hypnotherapy" may help, with a qualified practitioner (CDs at home may be as effective as in-person therapy for children with irritable bowel symptoms), cognitive behavioral therapy,[1] or a physical therapist to help with pelvic floor dysfunction. A "squatty potty" or stool where they can get their feet up a bit, can help with body positioning. Sometimes even a *low* fiber diet is called for, and prebiotics or live active culture foods may help.

New-onset constipation with other concerning signs indicates that sexual abuse needs to be considered. Older children may also regress with toileting in times of upheaval.

Diarrhea

Diarrhea can be complex to diagnose. There may be infectious causes such as parasites, bacteria, or viruses, or associated with antibiotics. Loose stools may result from excess fiber, such as when a child consumes large amounts of fruit, and may not be problematic (see page 291 for more on fiber). Food intolerance or allergies should be considered. Changes in stool or concerns over stool pattern or consistency, or with other symptoms like fever or pain, should be discussed with your doctor. Bright red blood, dark or black stools (which may indicate blood from higher in the digestive tract) must be looked into immediately.

Inflammatory Bowel Disease

These include Crohn's, celiac disease and ulcerative colitis. There is often a genetic component. Less common than "functional" bowel challenges. Any blood in the stool, fevers, weight loss, should be discussed with the doctor.

Hemorrhoids

Hemorrhoids are painful or itchy swollen tissue in the rectal area, which sometimes protrude from the anus. These are usually associated with constipation, so treatment of constipation is key, although some prescription creams, wipes, or suppositories may help. Good hygiene is critical. Discuss this with the child's doctor.

Iron Deficiency Anemia

Iron deficiency (ID) can occur with a limited diet, particularly of iron-rich foods. It can also occur after periods of rapid growth or with heavy menstrual cycles. It is more common in infants and young toddlers experiencing food insecurity. (See Anemia, above.) ID anemia is characterized by (from more common to less common symptoms and findings):

- Fatigue and weakness.
- Shortness of breath, especially with activity.
- Rapid pulse, especially with activity.
- Headache.
- Lightheadedness, especially on standing after lying down (head rush).
- Cold hands and feet.
- Unusual cravings for non-nutritive substances, such as ice or dirt (a condition known as "pica").
- Difficulty sleeping.
- Poor appetite (especially in infants and children).
- Irritability.
- Difficulty concentrating.
- Hair loss.
- Inflammation or soreness of tongue.
- Brittle or spoon-shaped nails.

Iron deficiency must be treated with iron supplementation. Talk to your provider for the dose and follow-up testing to be sure the iron is being absorbed.

Lead Poisoning

Talk to your child's care provider about screening. High lead levels often have no clear symptoms, but can present with irritability, GI symptoms, loss of appetite, decreased energy, weight loss, and learning difficulties—which may be irreversible. Exposure is primarily from environmental sources like paint, toys with lead, contaminated dirt and dust, and sometimes water (think of the ongoing Flint water crisis). Treatment is to first remove sources of exposure, and medication that binds with and excretes the lead may be indicated. (See Centers for Disease Control and Prevention at cdc.gov for information.)

Mouth Breathing and Eating with Mouth Open

There are medical reasons why a child might chew with his mouth open or mouth-breathe (it's not just "bad manners"). Snoring is another clue. Some kids have nasal allergies or inflammation from infection that can make it hard to breathe through the nose. Think about a time when you had a cold and were stuffed up.

Another possibility is enlarged adenoids and/or tonsils. This can cause difficulty with nose breathing. I'm not saying you have to have adenoids removed, but be aware that there may be a reason why your child chews with his mouth open; including sensory-motor differences (see Chapter 6).

PANS/PANDAS

Rare at any age, but especially after age 12, pediatric autoimmune neuropsychiatric disorders associated with streptococcal infections (PANDAS) is a neuropsychiatric (brain and behavior) reaction to strep infections. There is often sudden onset or worsening of symptoms of obsessive-compulsive disorder (OCD) and a combination of other associated symptoms that start around the same time. PANDAS might be more common with FASD. Some common accompanying symptoms can be:

- Severe separation anxiety.
- Generalized anxiety, which may become outright panic.
- Hyperactivity, abnormal movements, and restlessness.
- New sensory experiences, including hypersensitivity to light or sounds, distortions of visual perceptions, and occasionally, visual or auditory hallucinations.
- Concentration difficulties and loss of academic abilities, particularly in math and visual-spatial areas.
- Increased urinary frequency and new-onset bedwetting.
- Irritability (sometimes with aggression) and mood swings. Abrupt onset of depression can also occur, with thoughts about suicide.
- Developmental regression, including temper tantrums, "baby talk," and handwriting deterioration (also related to motor symptoms).

Think of a seven-year-old, who has been happily bumping along, when suddenly she stops eating and develops severe anxiety and mood swings, rapidly losing weight with no other explanation. There may or may not be a recent history of a sore throat, but PANS must be on the differential diagnosis.

PANDAS is a subcategory of the recently described PANS (pediatric acute-onset neuropsychiatric syndrome), which is similar but is not proven to be related to a strep infection. (Visit the National Institutes of Mental Health website at nimh.nih.gov for more.)

Pica

Pica is eating nonfood items. The condition may be behavioral, offer stimulation or regulation, or be linked with nutritional deficiencies such as iron and zinc deficiency. Also consider testing for lead.

See Rumination Syndrome for ideas for addressing pica. The few children I've worked with dealing with pica were adopted and had developmental trauma and brain-based differences. Behaviors naturally lessened as the child felt safer and more regulated over time. It can be associated with rumination syndrome, and rarely, with ARFID. These are more recently defined as eating disorders, and treatment research is ongoing. Avoid shame, praise the child's resilience, and continue to support felt safety and connection.

Premature Puberty

When signs of puberty (pubic hair, and breast buds in girls) appear before age eight in girls and age nine in boys, it is worth discussing with the child's doctor. An American

Society for Reproductive Medicine fact sheet states, "the first signs of normal puberty in girls can start as early as age 7. African-American girls may have normal puberty signs as early as age 6."[2] Based on one large study, the average age of breast development is around 8.8 years old for Black girls, 9.3 for Hispanic girls, and 9.7 for both white and Asian girls.[3] A history of growth delay then catch-up growth, may trigger hormones that bring on early puberty. (Malnutrition can delay puberty.)

Early puberty can result in premature closure of growth plates and a lower adult height than the genetic potential (not necessarily problematic). In general, if true puberty is occurring early, an evaluation with a pediatric endocrinologist who has experience with premature puberty is in order. There is the option to treat the child with hormones to delay puberty.

Girls entering puberty earlier are at risk of being sexualized and adultified (also more commonly experienced by Black girls), and studies are mixed as to a relationship with depression and anxiety. This is a complex decision process regarding potential medications. Find a knowledgeable doctor who will listen to your concerns.

Reflux

Reflux is a condition where the stomach contents slip up into the esophagus or swallowing tube. The muscle between the stomach and the esophagus is relatively underdeveloped in infants, which is part of why they spit up so easily. Infants spit up often, and if they are not bothered by it and are gaining weight, it is almost always nothing to worry about. Clinical reflux is when the acidic stomach contents irritate and erode the esophagus lining, causing pain and impacting eating. (Humans avoid things that hurt!) Reflux is associated with distress and decreased appetite, perhaps to the point of affecting weight gain and growth. The baby may arch or scream with feeding. Coughing or lung infections can occur with aspiration if the stomach contents make it into the lungs.

Most infants outgrow spitting up and mild reflux. More serious reflux should be addressed with your doctor and may warrant a trial of treatment.

Treatment trial should use the lowest effective dose and the infant should be weaned as soon as possible. If medication isn't helping observed symptoms, find feeding support, and rule out other potential causes.

Reflux Is Confusing

Over dinner with my new parent's group back in the day, it come up that five of the seven infants were on a proton-pump inhibitor (PPI) that lowers acid for reflux. That struck me as a high number. Similarly, when polling staff at a center for baby classes where I gave workshops, the staff remarked on the large proportion of infants on PPIs.

During my clinical work 20 years earlier, infants were not routinely treated with PPIs. Diagnoses of colic, irritability, and a hug and a "hang in there" were common; PPIs were not. Were some cases of reflux missed initially? Probably, but I fear the medication is overprescribed. In fact, several studies ". . . of PPIs have shown a consistent lack of efficacy in relieving 'distressed' GORD behaviours thought to be indicative of painful stimuli, suggesting they may have other underlying causes."[4] There are also questions about the long-term safety in infants.

How Is Reflux Diagnosed?

Mostly, clinicians diagnose reflux based on history and symptoms: Does the baby scream with feeding, or arch his back and appear to be in pain? That is often enough for a diagnosis and prescription.

Let me tell you about a baby with the diagnosis: Mom was scared from day one that her little boy was not eating enough. A nurse stressed that he was "small" and encouraged feeding certain amounts every few hours, waking him to do so. Soon he didn't seem to want the breast or pumped milk from a bottle. He was diagnosed with reflux and started on a PPI. However, no one asked *how* feeding was going. It turned out that in her attempts to get him to eat the recommended amounts, Mom tried to force him to finish each bottle, and he resisted. It's easy to imagine that an infant coughing, sputtering and protecting their airway—might cry, arch his back, and turn his head.

When medication didn't improve things, the baby was hospitalized for a pH probe test (a small probe placed through the nose into the esophagus for 24 hours to detect acid levels) which found no reflux and the medication was stopped. The baby probably never had reflux as his feeding and intake improved almost immediately with responsive feeding support.

Doctors need to ask more questions and provide more support. I am concerned that this medication is overprescribed. Do some infants have reflux and pain and might benefit from meds? Absolutely. But a thorough history and exam, along with feeding support, would help clarify who might benefit from treatment with PPIs, and where other support or wait-and-see with follow-up is more appropriate.

Rumination Syndrome

Rumination syndrome is when a person brings swallowed food back up from the stomach and then chews or mouths the food and then swallows again or spits it out. It is usually during or shortly after meals, but I've heard from parents whose children regurgitate food many times an hour throughout the day. It is characterized as both an eating and feeding disorder, and a functional gut disorder. It is quite rare. I've encountered it mostly with severe early neglect or with neurological involvement, such as severe cerebral palsy.

Rumination is a confusing and challenging problem. My interpretation is that the behavior seems to offer some soothing or comfort to the individual, perhaps helping them self-regulate. It's not usually in the child's thinking brain control. Additionally, RD has been linked with "emotional and conduct problems" in adolescents.[5,6] It is also seen more commonly with pica (see above).

Rumination causes bad breath, can erode tooth enamel, and those around the child find it "gross." Few studies guide treatment, and researchers can't agree on a definition. When I've referred a few families, the key is that the individual wants the ruminating to stop. Without motivation to stop, treatment is less successful.

So far the main treatment I've seen is training in "diaphragmatic breathing," often at scheduled times. There is also cognitive behavioral therapy (CBT) using diaphragmatic breathing and other strategies. Another option is biofeedback. However, as you know, adding one more therapy and trying to "get" your child to do it may be challenging. If you notice the behavior improving and happening less frequently, making your doctor aware and watching and waiting may be appropriate. If/while you pursue a workup or treatment, here are a few thoughts:

- Check with a physician, they may want to test for micronutrient deficiency, rule out reflux, and consider a GI referral.
- Keep track of potential triggers: certain foods, situations, beverages, or stressors?
- See if you can decrease the time the child is able to ruminate:
    - Do they like to sing? Enroll them in choir. If they need to play an instrument at school, consider a wind instrument.
    - Allow them to chew gum or consider other tools such as Chewelry or chewable pencil toppers if they are looking for oral input.
- Address and get the child help for any trauma history; consider embodied therapies.
- Consider working with a skilled therapist in anxiety who may be able to help with some breathing training as well.
- See a dentist for potential preventive treatment.
- Medications are being studied.

Avoid shaming the child. Framing the child as resourceful and resilient, that the behavior may have offered them self-soothing and regulation may help. Continue to prioritize felt safety and connection.

Sickle Cell Disease

Sickle cell disease is an inherited blood disorder impacting roughly 1/360 people of African descent. (It is less common in folks with Central and South American, Middle Eastern, and Mediterranean ancestry.) It is a lifelong chronic condition requiring specialty care. It can impact growth and delay puberty onset. It also leads to anemia, pain crises, infections, and swelling of hands and feet.

Thyroid Abnormalities

Thyroid hormones help regulate metabolism, energy, and growth and weight. If your child has either high or low weight, or there are concerns about energy or listlessness, a thyroid test is reasonable to rule out hypo- or hyperthyroid (under- or overactive thyroid), especially with a family history. I've not seen hyperthyroidism as the cause of rapid weight gain without other clear symptoms.

Urinary Tract Infection

A urinary tract infection (UTI) happens when the otherwise sterile bladder gets infected. The bacteria irritate the bladder, leading to pain, urgency (the need to urinate that comes on fast), new onset bed-wetting, and frequency of urination. Unexplained fevers in infants and pre- and non-verbal children can indicate a UTI. Children with severe constipation may also be more prone to UTIs with incomplete bladder emptying if there is stool impaction. UTIs are more common in girls. Depending on the age of onset and the number of infections, more testing to look at the urinary tract, ureters (tubes to the kidneys), and kidneys may be in order. Teach children proper wiping, avoid bubble baths, take off swimsuits after swimming, and use the skin care advice under the eczema section above in terms of soaps and detergents. If there are other symptoms or any concerns, sexual abuse may need to be considered.

Tips for Navigating the Medical System

Most families dealing with feeding and weight worries or a child with health or developmental issues will have ongoing care with multiple providers. The reality is, you are your child's "care coordinator." Keep copies of medical records. Danny's mother Beverly shared that she often picked up on things, including a potential drug interaction, before the doctors did. Here are some tips for navigating the healthcare system, which can be a major burden of its own.

Find Your Partners in Care

- Ask other families for recommendations, try a local online forum.
- Try to find a provider who will listen. Some research indicates that women providers take more time with patients and have better outcomes. Find someone you and your child are comfortable with.
- Consider an "allied" health professional, like a nurse practitioner or a physician's assistant. Mom Camille found her best partner in a nurse practitioner, who listened, researched, and advocated. They may also schedule for longer appointments.
- Ask for a point person at the doctor's office if your child has complex needs. Someone should be familiar with your child if you have questions and your doctor is unavailable.

Stay Organized

- If you have a friend or a family member who is in healthcare, ask him or her to review and explain any medications or conditions if you still have questions.
- Keep an updated medical history with current medications, conditions, surgeries, etc. Keep a printout in a known place in case you or a sitter has to make an urgent-care or E.R. visit. There are also smartphone apps for this.
- Start binders and folders now. Document every phone call, time, date, and who you spoke with if you are dealing with insurance or billing issues.
- Write letters or emails and keep copies.

Make the Most of Your Visit

- If your child is being sedated for any reason, call the other doctors involved in your child's care to ask if there are any other necessary procedures that can be done at the same time to avoid additional sedation.
- Take your partner or another family member with you to critical appointments. Have one person take notes.

- Follow up and give medications as instructed.
- Have growth data and plot it yourself if you have to, including Z-scores.
- If your child has concerning symptoms, write down:
  - When did it start?
  - Was it related to an event, travel, food, or medications?
  - How has this impacted your child? Is it interrupting sleep, appetite, any other details like bowel changes, mood or behavior, rashes, etc.?
  - What have you already tried?
  - What are you worried it might be? (Bring in your internet search if you have to. You need to have your questions answered; even if your suspicions aren't the answer, you won't worry about it anymore.) "I'm hoping you can reassure me that we're not dealing with X."

If it is safe* for you to do so, ask for the reasoning behind invasive testing and what the plan is for follow-up. Doing this helped Sue postpone, and eventually avoid, a swallow study while her daughter progressed (page 158). Avoiding *necessary* tests is not the goal, but it is helpful to be clear about what you want to learn from a test, if it is safe to wait and see, and if there are other options.

This final tip seems out of place in the 21st century: If you are a woman and experiencing difficulties with a child's care, take a male partner, friend, or relative along to appointments. I have heard from too many mothers who felt their concerns were dismissed. Take Rebecca's example: "*The first two doctors kept blowing me off, and only wanted to talk about Adina's weight. I have two other children; I knew something was wrong. I'm not unreasonable, but I needed an explanation for what I was observing. When I sought out a third doctor, he was rolling his eyes as he entered the room . . .*" She added, "*I should have brought my husband. I could tell the doctor had no patience for me. He told me Adina was fine before he even examined her or asked a single question.*"

It turns out Adina, who you may remember from Chapter 7, had blood in her stool and was not progressing with physical therapy as expected. While the doctors focused on her higher-than-average weight, several red flags were ignored and indicated tests were not done—including basic blood work to rule out anemia, which she had risk factors for. Rebecca felt that she was written off as "hysterical." (This is yet another example of medical weight bias.) I've personally experienced how differently I was treated with a complex medical issue when I brought my husband with me—and I'm a physician! Three-minute visits with antibiotics and a boot out the door became a thoughtful, 20-minute discussion of treatment options. My husband didn't say a word. He just sat in the room. Go figure.

Too many mothers get labeled as irrational or hysterical when they are desperately scared (in some cases, this can even result in a child welfare report). Becky Henry, author of *Just Tell Her to Stop: Family Stories of Eating Disorders*, explains that this is a common scenario for parents seeking help. *"When we've been fighting for our child's life and getting nowhere and show up crying, it is assumed we are controlling and hysterical so we're not taken seriously. I wish I'd said, 'I'm crying because my child is seriously ill and I feel helpless but I still need to be treated respectfully.'"*

Another mom explained that her daughter was quickly dismissed as having "psychological" problems, when a GI evaluation had not yet been pursued for new and rapidly increasing vomiting episodes.

Finding a healthcare provider who will listen to and address your concerns makes a huge difference. Enlisting support, note-takers, and witnesses may help.

*Navigating the Medical System When It Doesn't Feel Safe

First, I want to acknowledge that it may be confusing to read "check with your child's doctor" after reading about the many ways that some doctors don't know how to help with challenges described in the book. I share your frustration. But there are circumstances and medical complications that I can't be aware of as an author and that hopefully your child's medical provider would help to keep your child safe. It's also why I'm passionate about educating healthcare professionals.

The second issue I want to acknowledge is that in some scenarios, I've encouraged you to seek a second opinion. For example, if a provider wants to put your child on severe calorie restriction with the goal of weight loss, I believe this is harmful. Or for a child with a low appetite if they're encouraging you to pressure or force bites, I also believe this is not helpful.

I recognize it may not be safe to appear to challenge or question your child's medical team. Looking for second or third opinions could result in the label, "unable to comply with medical orders," or "noncompliance," and can at times lead to a referral to child protective services.

Medical professionals have power over patients in many ways, from access to referrals and treatment, to impacting custody. (I once asked a provider to consider removing an offensive and weight-biased poster in the exam room. My heart was pounding even though the stakes were low, and I am a white woman and a doctor!) It will be harder to challenge or question care if you are someone living in a body that already experiences medical bias (such as fat, Black, and disabled patients). It's hard, and you are not making it up. Here are a few thoughts that may help:

- Try to get grounded before visits. Take deep and calming breaths. It's not fair, but if you're crying and/or angry, medical professionals may get defensive or dismissive, and treatment may suffer.
- Come in with organized notes if you can. Take notes during the visit.
- Bring a friend who can help you remain calm, and step in if needed. "I'm here to help take notes and with communication. As you can imagine, worrying about this is quite stressful for my friend."

- If a test you or another care team member has requested is denied, politely ask the provider to document the reason why in the chart. (This is when having another person in the room might help.)
- If they are refusing care or treatment until a weight loss goal is met, ask, "What would you recommend if my child were in a thin body?" Or mirror the doctor's language, "What would you recommend if my child weren't overweight?" and, "Can we do that while we work on his eating and activity?"
- Before firing off an angry email or voicemail: Write out a script or draft; sleep on it for 24 hours; have a friend read it over before you send it (if you do at all).
- Consider asking childcare providers or others to offer their insights, or a note, or accompanying on a visit to back up your observations.
- Look online for resources. Ragen Chastain and others, for example offer webinars on advocating for care in higher-weight patients.

Rachel's medical professionals insisted she force her son to eat: *"After a few sessions of verbal dueling, I came up with my own 'coping' mechanisms to get through the appointments without reverting to pressure. A few days before appointments, I practiced my 'ignore and smile' motif. I thought through a bulky outfit so our son's weight would be on the higher end of the scale. And then I just suffered through the session, not getting real help and hoping it did not harm—because it is hard—very, very hard to withstand the pressure of doctors, psychologists, nutritionists—and my husband, who is often swayed during these appointments. In the end, what helps, though, is that I KNOW nothing else works. Any pressure at all backfires. The only time our son does well with eating and weight is when I trust him and leave him alone to do what he is supposed to do: decide what to eat and how much."*

These are difficult issues to navigate. Ideally you would find healthcare providers who listened and considered all factors.

Snack and Meal Ideas

Try for most snacks and meals to include a carb, protein, and fat, even if children don't eat from each category. Many foods cover more than one group. If it's easier, think in terms of food groups. Look for a starch or grain, protein source (meat, beans, dairy, nuts, legumes, soy), add a fruit and/or veggie, some fat, and you should be covered. It takes planning, but almost all kids can learn to enjoy a variety of foods if given the opportunity, without pressure. Prepare foods based on your child's ability to chew and swallow. Address allergy concerns with your child's healthcare provider. I hope this list will give you ideas as you stare into your fridge and cupboards. There is a mix of convenience and from-scratch items. Plan for sit-down eating opportunities about every 2 to 3 hours for younger children, and every 3 to 4 hours for older children.

In General for Snacks

Aim for two to three items from various groups:

Grains (carbohydrates): pita bread, bread, rice, cereal, graham crackers, whole-wheat crackers, pasta, tortillas, bagels, English muffins, popcorn, rice cakes, crackers, njera, corn bread, jollof rice, cereal, or granola bars.

Fruits (fresh, frozen, dried, or canned): banana, apple, pineapple, pear, melons, applesauce, grapes cut in half, mangos, kiwis, strawberries, berries, dried fruits like prunes (cut up,) raisins, Craisins, fruit leather, and smoothies.

Veggies: carrots, peas, corn, peppers, cucumbers, pickled veggies, cherry tomatoes, beets, squash, edamame, sweet potato, potato, lettuce, olives, pickles, avocado, celery, hummus, salsa, falafel, and beans.

Protein and meats: peanut or other nut butters, lunch meats, chicken, lentils, pork, beef, turkey, hummus (chickpea dip), baked beans, refried beans, milk, cheese (slices, sticks, shredded, melted), yogurt, soy products like edamame or tofu, shrimp, and fish. (Try ground meats or prepare them in the slow cooker. Add sauces and gravies to make them easier to chew.)

Dairy: milk, cheese, yogurt, cottage cheese, puddings, and smoothies.

Fats: often included with dairy (butter, milk, yogurt, cheese, and cream cheese), meats, and some crackers. Potato chips and similar. Sauces and dips (ranch, thousand island, etc.) oils, avocados, olives, homemade dressings, nuts and nut butters, ice cream, cookies, fried foods.

Sample Snacks

Serve with milk (dairy or alternative), water, or juice (see page 283).

- Baked beans, crackers
- Small muffin(s) with butter they can spread, carrot sticks
- Scrambled egg with grated cheese, apple slices
- Leftover pizza, cherry tomatoes cut in half
- Ham sandwich or wrap (whole-wheat or white bread, or tortilla, ham, cheese, or mayo) leftover veggie like carrots and peas, cut-up pineapple
- Injera with lentils, yogurt, canned peaches
- Leftover mac-n-cheese with tuna, pickles (spears or rounds)
- English muffin with flavored cream cheese, sliced red peppers
- Leftover spaghetti with marinara or meat sauce, yogurt, clementine
- Rolled-up lunch meat with cream cheese or Miracle Whip/mayo, applesauce
- Whole-wheat bread with turkey and hummus, cut-up grapes
- Soft mini-bagel with cream cheese, sliced strawberries
- Cooked shrimp with cocktail sauce, whole-grain or regular crackers, cucumbers
- Whole-grain crackers, cheese stick(s)
- Apples with nut butter, dry cereal
- Oatmeal and raisin cookies
- Ants on a log (celery with peanut butter or cream cheese with raisins)
- Tortilla chips with melted cheese (and salsa), canned mandarin oranges
- Baked pita chips with hummus, baby carrots
- Quesadilla (tortilla with refried beans and melted cheese), pickles
- Tuna salad (tuna with Miracle Whip or mayo and sweet pickle relish), crackers
- Cut-up grapes, fig cookies
- Cucumber strips, ranch dip or hummus, pita bread
- Banana smoothie with yogurt and berries, graham crackers
- Cinnamon-raisin toast with butter/spread, fruit yogurt
- Toaster waffles with syrup or jam, applesauce
- Frozen mixed veggies (some kids like it frozen!), crackers
- Cottage cheese, berries, chicken nuggets
- A few slices of shredded lunch meat (or rolled with cream cheese), toast, pineapple
- Carrots and ranch dressing, leftover beans and rice
- Rice Krispies treats, banana
- Tortilla rolled with cream cheese or butter, apple slices
- Tortilla with melted cheese, orange slices
- Popcorn with butter and a sprinkling of salt and/or sugar, dried fruit

Feeding and Intake Journal

"We did a food diary before. How is this different?" Standard nutrition intakes usually ask for the WHAT and ignore the HOW. The Feeding and Intake Journal on the following page asks for more detail, including when and where you are offering foods. What are you offering, how is the interaction going? How does it feel? What is the context? This is a great starting point and is a valuable tool to see patterns with structure, what you are offering, and interactions. If you are working with one, it can also give your registered dietician (RD) or feeding therapist a good overall picture.

Instructions

Record what your child has had to eat or drink immediately after meals and snacks and in between if they are eating then. List each food on a separate line. When possible, list the brand name, type of milk (whole, 2%, 1% or skim), and whether the food was fresh, frozen, or canned. Specify amounts roughly in cups, tablespoons, teaspoons, and dimensions of a piece of pizza or serving of lasagna as best you can (you don't need to measure it, but try to get close). Include everything, even liquids, condiments, and candy. Include at least two weekdays and one weekend day. In the notes you may wish to write where or how your child was fed or anything else you feel may be helpful for the provider to know. (See pages 184-185 for examples of filled-in intake journals.)

FEEDING AND INTAKE JOURNAL

Name:________________ Date of Birth:__________ Ht:_____ Wt:_____ Day 1 Day & Date:______________

Meal/Snack	Time of day	Food(s) and/or beverage(s) offered	Amount(s) consumed	Notes

Lunchbox Card

Chose the one you prefer, copy, fill in, and laminate a "lunchbox card" (also available online at The Feeding Doctor under "Resources"). Place it in your child's lunchbox and tell them that if an adult asks them to eat certain foods or amounts or in a specific order, they should hand over the card, or point to it. This is hard to ask a child to do, but it may work for some. Please see my website: thefeedingdoctor.com for a list of additional resources.

Choose the version that's right for you

Hello!

Please allow__________________to decide how much to eat, and in what order, from what I have packed. Even if that means all they eat for lunch is "dessert," or if they start with dessert.
I trust that__________________ can rely on hunger and fullness signals to know how much to eat. If they need help opening containers, I thank you for that help. Otherwise,__________________ should be good to go.

Please call my cell_________________________
if you have any questions.

Thank you for all you do for our children.

Hello!

Please allow__________________to decide how much to eat, and in what order, from what I have packed. Even if that means all they eat for lunch is "dessert," or if they start with dessert.
I trust that__________________ can rely on hunger and fullness signals to know how much to eat. Otherwise,__________________ should be good to go.

Please call my cell_________________________
if you have any questions.

Thank you for all you do for our children.

Hello!

Please allow__________________to decide how much to eat, and in what order, from what I have packed. Even if that means all they eat for lunch is "dessert," or if they start with dessert.
If __________________needs help opening containers, I thank you for that help. Otherwise, they should be good to go.

Please call my cell_________________________
if you have any questions.

Thank you for all you do for our children.

Hello!

Please allow__________________to decide how much to eat, and in what order, from what I have packed. Even if that means all they eat for lunch is "dessert," or if they start with dessert.

Please call my cell_________________________
if you have any questions.

Thank you for all you do for our children.

Food Preference List

When filling out this list, be as specific as possible: include brands, restaurants, specific flavors, preparation details such as "crust off," etc. For example:

- McDonald's fries
- Regular Triscuit
- Grilled cheese sandwich with one American cheese slice, crust cut off

Consider using pencil so you can come back and move food entries from one box to another. If you want to print out a copy, this form is also available under Conquer Picky Eating resources at: extremepickyeating.com/teenadultresources.

The categories and lists in the left "food categories" column are meant to jog your memory and provide new foods to consider. To add any food you don't see on the list, use the blank spaces at the bottom or write them into a similar category. We know a few of you don't "enjoy" any foods you eat. If there are foods you can tolerate, put those in the first group, "eat now and enjoy." Do your best to make this table work for you.

The following is an example:

food categories	eat now and enjoy	eat now but don't enjoy	used to eat but do not eat now	interested in trying	can't imagine eating
fast foods: pizza, burgers, fries, chicken nuggets/ tenders	plain cheese Domino's®, room temp		plain cheese Little Caesars®	plain cheese Little Caesars®	mushroom pizza

Name:________________________________ Date:__________________

Circle any condiments/dips/sauces/toppings you eat:

butter
margarine
ketchup
hot sauce
ranch dressing
barbecue sauce
yellow mustard
Dijon mustard
pickle relish
Sriracha
wasabi paste
mayonnaise
Miracle Whip
rainbow sprinkles
cinnamon sugar
frosting
Nutella
hummus
caramel sauce
peanut butter
melted chocolate
melted cheese sauce
Parmesan cheese from Kraft can

Others ____

____

____

____

food categories	eat now and enjoy	eat now but don't enjoy	used to eat but do not eat now	interested in trying	can't imagine eating
bread: pita, whole wheat, white, brand names, toasted, no crust					
breakfast breads: waffles, French toast, pancakes, from scratch or frozen, muffins					

food categories	eat now and enjoy	eat now but don't enjoy	used to eat but do not eat now	interested in trying	can't imagine eating
bagels, English muffins					
sandwiches: tortilla/wraps					
sandwiches: grilled, on soft white roll, plain, no crust, subs					
pasta: ramen, noodles, macaroni and cheese, elbow macaroni, shells, buttered spaghetti, with sauce, pasta salad, plain					
rice: brown, white					

food categories	eat now and enjoy	eat now but don't enjoy	used to eat but do not eat now	interested in trying	can't imagine eating
cereal: cold, dry or with milk; brand; warm cereals, including oatmeal, Cream of Wheat, and any toppings					
crackers: Ritz, Goldfish, Graham, Club, other brands					
food bars: granola, cereal bar, energy or fiber bar such as Clif bar					
crunchy snacks: potato chips kettle-cooked, Ruffles, Pringles, Cheetos, pretzels, cheese puffs					
desserts: cookies, cake, pie, cupcake, homemade, store-bought					
ice-cream or frozen treat flavors, brands					

food categories	eat now and enjoy	eat now but don't enjoy	used to eat but do not eat now	interested in trying	can't imagine eating
candy: chocolates, red licorice, bars, hard candies					
red meat: steak, ground beef, burger, beef hot dog, lamb chops					
pork: pork chops, ham (thin or thick slices), brats, hot dogs, bacon					
poultry: chicken, turkey, fried, roasted, nuggets, in soups					
deli meats: roast beef, bologna, turkey, salami					
seafood: breaded, fish sticks, shrimp, scallops, crab, tuna salad, plain tuna, baked or grilled					

food categories	eat now and enjoy	eat now but don't enjoy	used to eat but do not eat now	interested in trying	can't imagine eating
mixed entrees: stews or casseroles, lasagna, soup					
beans: bean soup, navy, black bean, refried, bean salsa					
tofu or other soy: edamame (soybeans), in the shell or without					
dips and salsas: Hummus, egg-plant dip, yogurt dip, onion dip, tomato/corn/fruit salsa					
protein or supplement drinks					
egg whites: scrambled, boiled, fried					

food categories	eat now and enjoy	eat now but don't enjoy	used to eat but do not eat now	interested in trying	can't imagine eating
whole eggs: scrambled, fried, boiled, salad					
nut or seed butters: peanut, cashew or sunflower butter, crunchy, creamy					
nuts: plain, roasted, honey-coated					
milk: lactose-free, flavored, whole milk or skim, in hot cocoa, Chai, or coffee drinks					
non-dairy milk: soy, almond, cashew, coconut, hemp					
yogurt: from cup, fruit-on-the-bottom, drinks, tubes, kefir yogurt drink					

food categories	eat now and enjoy	eat now but don't enjoy	used to eat but do not eat now	interested in trying	can't imagine eating
soft cheeses: cottage cheese, sour cream, cream cheese					
hard cheeses: cheddar, Swiss, melted, plain, grated, on chips					
smoothies: milk shakes, home-made, brands					
fruits (fresh or frozen): citrus, melon, berries, apples (with peel, without), bananas, pears					
fruits (dried, chewy): raisins, prunes, fruit leather					
fruits (freeze-dried crunchy): strawberries, blueberries					

food categories	eat now and enjoy	eat now but don't enjoy	used to eat but do not eat now	interested in trying	can't imagine eating
fruits (canned): cocktail, mandarin oranges in syrup, half peaches, pineapple rings, chilled					
vegetables (cooked): plain, with sauces, frozen (eat frozen or cooked), corn, mixed veggies, broccoli					
vegetables (raw or freeze-dried): plain, with dips, carrot sticks, grated carrot, jicama slices					
vegetables (canned): black olives, beans, peas, corn					
fast foods: pizza, burgers, fries, chicken nuggets/tenders					
other:					

food categories	eat now and enjoy	eat now but don't enjoy	used to eat but do not eat now	interested in trying	can't imagine eating
other:					
other:					
other:					
other:					
other:					
other:					

References

Websites listed were accessed in 2023.
Note that many citations use stigmatizing language and perpetuate weight bias.

Disclaimers and Terms of Use

1. Chastain, R. (February 5, 2015). "Health and the Usual Disclaimers." Dances With Fat blog. www.danceswithfat.org

Introduction

1. Engle PL, et al. 2011. Responsive feeding: implications for policy and program implementation. J Nutr. Mar;141(3):508-11.
2. American Academy of Pediatrics. 2017. "Is your baby hungry or full? Responsive feeding explained."
3. Black MM, et al. 2011. Responsive feeding is embedded in a theoretical framework of responsive parenting. J Nutr. Mar;141(3):490-4.
4. Rowell K, et al. 2023. "White Paper on Responsive Feeding Therapy: Values and Practice." Version 2. Responsive Feeding Pro. www.responsivefeedingpro.com.
5. Rosen H. 2014. Is obesity a disease or a behavior abnormality? Did the AMA get it right? Mo Med. Mar-Apr;111(2):104-108.
6. Cormack J, et al. 2020. Self-determination theory as a theoretical framework for a responsive approach to child feeding. J Nutr Educ Behav. Jun;52(6):646-651.

Chapter 1

1. Manikam R, et al. 2000. Pediatric feeding disorders. J Clin Gastroenterol. Jan;30(1):34-46.
2. Crawford PB, et al. 1991. How obesity develops: a new look at nature and nurture. Obesity & Health. 1991;(5):40-41.
3. Nicholls DE, et al. 2011. Childhood eating disorders: British national surveillance study. Br J Psychiatry. Apr;198(4):295-301.
4. Mascola AJ, et al. 2010. Picky eating during childhood: a longitudinal study to age 11 years. Eat Behav. Dec;11(4):253-7.
5. Orrell-Valente JK, et al. 2007. "Just three more bites": an observational analysis of parents' socialization of children's eating at mealtime. Appetite. Jan;48(1):37-45.
6. Stanek K, et al. 1990. Diet quality and the eating environment of preschool children. J Am Diet Assoc. Nov;90(11):1582-4.

7. Ventura AK, et al. 2010. Feeding practices and styles used by a diverse sample of low-income parents of preschool-age children. J Nutr Educ Behav. Jul-Aug;42(4):242-9.
8. Pelchat ML, et al. 1986. Antecedents and correlates of feeding problems in young children. J Nutr Educ Behav. 1986;18:23-8.
9. Pinhas L, et al. 2011. Incidence and age-specific presentation of restrictive eating disorders in children: a Canadian Paediatric Surveillance Program study. Arch Pediatr Adolesc Med. Oct;165(10):895-9.
10. Zhao Y, et al. 2009. Hospitalizations for Eating Disorders From 1999-2006, Statistical Brief #70. The Healthcare Cost and Utilization Project. April.
11. Harvard School of Public Health. 2021. "Eating Disorders in Teens Skyrocketing During Pandemic."
12. Stallings VA. 2016. Feeding Infants and Toddlers Study (FITS): Findings and Thoughts on the Third Data Cycle. J Nutr. 2018 Sep 1;148(suppl_3):1513S-1515S.
13. Neumark-Sztainer D, et al. 2004. Weight-control behaviors among adolescent girls and boys: implications for dietary intake. J Am Diet Assoc. Jun;104(6):913-20.
14. Gustafson-Larson AM, et al. 1992. Weight-related behaviors and concerns of fourth-grade children. J Am Diet Assoc. Jul;92(7):818-22.
15. Leung KC, et al. and the Canadian Pediatric Society Nutrition and Gastroenterology Committee. 2012. The 'picky eater': The toddler or preschooler who does not eat. Pediatric Child Health. 17(8): 455-57.
16. Jo Cormack PhD 2022 published PhD thesis.
17. Aldridge V, et al. 2009. The role of familiarity in dietary development. *Developmental Review*, *29*(1), 32-44.
18. Forestell CA, et al. 2007. Early determinants of fruit and vegetable acceptance. Pediatrics. Dec;120(6):1247-54.
19. Haines J, et al. 2006. Prevention of obesity and eating disorders: a consideration of shared risk factors. Health Educ Res. Dec;21(6):770-82.
20. Scaglioni S, et al. 2008. Influence of parental attitudes in the development of children eating behaviour. Br J Nutr. Feb;99 Suppl 1:S22-5.
21. Neumark-Sztainer D, et al. 2004. Are family meal patterns associated with disordered eating behaviors among adolescents? J Adolesc Health. Nov; 35(5):350-9.
22. von Kries R, et al. 2002. Reduced risk for overweight and obesity in 5- and 6-y-old children by duration of sleep-a cross-sectional study. Int J Obes Relat Metab Disord. May;26(5):710-6.
23. Hasler G, et al. 2004. The association between short sleep duration and obesity in young adults: a 13-year prospective study. Sleep. Jun 15;27(4):661-6.
24. Grummer-Strawn LM, et al. 2010. Use of World Health Organization and CDC Growth Charts for Children Aged 0-59 Months in the United States. www.cdc.gov.

25. Madsen KA, et al. 2021. Effect of School-Based Body Mass Index Reporting in California Public Schools: A Randomized Clinical Trial. JAMA Pediatr. Mar 1;175(3):251-259.
26. Legler JD, et al. 1998. Assessment of Abnormal Growth Curves. American Family Physician. 1998;58:158-68.
27. Mei Z, et al. 2004. Shifts in percentiles of growth during early childhood: analysis of longitudinal data from the California Child Health and Development Study. Pediatrics. Jun;113(6):e617-27.
28. Bennett WE Jr, et al. 2014. The natural history of weight percentile changes in the first year of life. JAMA Pediatr. Jul;168(7):681-2.
29. Sole-Smith V. (June 15, 2021). "Ask Virginia: Is My Child's Body Size My Fault?" Burnt Toast Substack. www.virginiasolesmith.substack.com.
30. Orrell-Valente JK, et al. 2007. "Just three more bites": an observational analysis of parents' socialization of children's eating at mealtime. Appetite. Jan;48(1):37-45.
31. Kerzner B, et al. 2015. A practical approach to classifying and managing feeding difficulties. Pediatrics. Feb;135(2):344-53.
32. Wolstenholme H, et al. 2022. 'Fussy eating' and feeding dynamics: School children's perceptions, experiences, and strategies. 2022 173(1).
33. Lamenzo, J. (July 8, 2015) "All Eyes on Me." www.lemonhousepublishing.com.
34. Hurley KM, et al. 2011. A systematic review of responsive feeding and child obesity in high-income countries. J Nutr. Mar;141(3):495-501.
35. Jo Cormack PhD 2022 unpublished PhD thesis.
36. Black MM, et al. 2011. Responsive feeding is embedded in a theoretical framework of responsive parenting. J Nutr. Mar;141(3):490-4.

Chapter 2

1. Delahooke, M. *Beyond behaviors: using brain science and compassion to understand and solve children's behavioral challenges.* PESI Publishing & Media, 2019.
2. Purvis, K. *The Connected Child: Bring Hope and Healing to Your Adoptive Family.* McGraw Hill LLC 2007.
3. Porges, S. *The pocket guide to the polyvagal theory: The transformative power of feeling safe.* W W Norton & Co, 2017.
4. Perry BD. "Effects of Traumatic Events on Children." Child Trauma Academy. http://www.fa-sett.no/filer/perry-handout-effects-of-trauma.pdf
5. Devine E. https://www.eileendevine.com/brain-first-parenting
6. Holt-Lunstad J, et al. 2010. Social relationships and mortality risk: a meta-analytic review. PLoS Med. 2010 Jul 27;7(7).
7. Bradley P. (July 30, 2020). "I'm All In." No Kid Hungry blog. www.nokidhungry.org

8. Sole-Smith V. (May 7, 2020). "I Know You're Angry with Me Right Now Because You're Hungry." New York Times.
9. Hazzard VM, et al. 2020. Food Insecurity and Eating Disorders: a Review of Emerging Evidence. Curr Psychiatry Rep. Oct 30;22(12):74.
10. St. Pierre C, et al. 2022. Food Insecurity and Childhood Obesity: A Systematic Review. Pediatrics. July; 150 (1).
11. Jones SJ, et al. 2003. Lower risk of overweight in school-aged food insecure girls who participate in food assistance: results from the panel study of income dynamics child development supplement. Arch Pediatr Adolesc Med. Aug;157(8):780-4.
12. Sole-Smith V. (May 7, 2020). "I Know You're Angry with Me Right Now Because You're Hungry." New York Times.
13. Deci EL, Ryan RM. *Handbook of Self-Determination Research*. Rochester, NY: University of Rochester Press; 2004.
14. Leclère C, et al. 2014. Why synchrony matters during mother-child interactions: a systematic review. PLoS One. 2014 Dec 3;9(12).
15. Rogers, F. *The Mister Rogers Parenting Book: Helping To Understand Your Young Child*. Philadelphia, PA: Running Press, 2002.
16. Nummenmaa L, et al. 2014. Bodily maps of emotions. Proc Natl Acad Sci USA. Jan 14;111(2):646-51.
17. Perry B. "Bonding, Attachment and the Maltreated Child." Child Trauma Academy. www.ChildTraumaAcademy.org
18. Pepino YM, et al. 2005. Sucrose-induced analgesia is related to sweet preferences in children but not adults. Pain. Dec 15;119(1-3):210-218.

Chapter 3

1. Black MM, et al. 2011. Responsive feeding is embedded in a theoretical framework of responsive parenting. J Nutr. Mar;141(3):490-4.
2. Jo Cormack PhD 2022 published PhD thesis.
3. Rowell K, et al. 2021. "White Paper on Responsive Feeding Therapy: Values and Practice" www.responsivefeedingpro.com
4. Cicchetti, D. *Developmental Psychopathology: Theory and Method* New Jersey, United States: Wiley, 2016. (page 811).
5. Rogers, F. *You Are Special: Neighborly Wit And Wisdom From Mister Rogers*. Penguin Publishing Group, 1995.
6. Rogers, F. *The Mister Rogers Parenting Book: Helping To Understand Your Young Child*. Running Press, 2002.
7. CASA: The National Center on Addiction & Substance Abuse at Columbia University. 2007. "The Importance of Family Dinners IV."
8. Slaughter, C. *Hungry for Love: Creating a Mealtime Environment That Builds Connection, Life Skills, and Eating Capabilities*. CreateSpace Independent Publishing Platform, 2014.

Chapter 4

1. Rogers, F. *The Mister Rogers Parenting Book: Helping To Understand Your Young Child*. Philadelphia, PA: Running Press, 2002.
2. Newman J, et al. 1992. Effect of a means-end contingency on young children's food preferences. J Exp Child Psychol. Apr;53(2):200-16.
3. Wardle J, et al. 2003. Modifying children's food preferences: the effects of exposure and reward on acceptance of an unfamiliar vegetable. Eur J Clin Nutr. Feb;57(2):341-8.
4. Thomas, L. (June 9, 2022). "What Mealtimes Can Be When We Take the Pressure Off." Don't Salt My Game podcast episode.
5. Simpson CC, et al. 2017. Calorie counting and fitness tracking technology: Associations with eating disorder symptomatology. Eat Behav. Aug;26:89-92.
6. Rose HE, et al. 1968. Activity, calorie intake, fat storage, and the energy balance of infants. Pediatrics. 1968;41:18-29.
7. Epstein LH, et al. 1997. Effects of decreasing sedentary behaviors on activity choice in obese children. Health Psychol. Mar;16(2):107-13.
8. Annesi JJ. 2005. Correlations of depression and total mood disturbance with physical activity and self-concept in preadolescents enrolled in an after-school exercise program. Psychol Rep. Jun;96(3 Pt 2):891-8.
9. Norris R, et al. 1992. The effects of physical activity and exercise training on psychological stress and well-being in an adolescent population. J Psychosom Res. Jan;36(1):55-65.
10. Fedewa MV, et al. 2014. Exercise and insulin resistance in youth: a meta-analysis. Pediatrics. Jan;133(1):e163-74.
11. Segal I, et al. 2014. Role reversal method for treatment of food refusal associated with infantile feeding disorders. J Pediatr Gastroenterol Nutr. 2014 Jun;58(6):739-42.

Chapter 5

1. Forestell CA, et al. 2007. Early determinants of fruit and vegetable acceptance. Pediatrics. Dec;120(6):1247-54.
2. Moding KJ, et al. 2018. Does Temperament Underlie Infant Novel Food Responses?: Continuity of Approach-Withdrawal From 6 to 18 Months. Child Dev. Jul;89(4):e444-e458.
3. Mascola AJ, et al. 2010. Picky eating during childhood: a longitudinal study to age 11 years. Eat Behav. Dec;11(4):253-7.
4. Legler JD, et al. 1998. Assessment of Abnormal Growth Curves. American Family Physician. 1998;58:158-68.
5. Bennett, WE. 2014. The Natural History of Weight Percentile Changes in the First Year of Life. JAMA Pediatrics, Volume 168, (7).

6. World Health Organization. "Child Growth Standards: Weight-for-Age." https://www.who.int/tools/child-growth-standards/standards/weight-for-age.
7. Grummer-Strawn L, et al. Use of World Health Organization and CDC Growth Charts for Children Aged 0–59 Months in the United States. MMWR (CDC). 2010;59:RR-9.
8. Homan GJ. 2016. Failure to Thrive: A Practical Guide. Am Fam Physician. Aug 15;94(4):295-9.
9. Taylor CM, et al. 2016. Macro- and micronutrient intakes in picky eaters: a cause for concern? Am J Clin Nutr. Dec;104(6):1647-1656.
10. Black MM, et al. 2011. Responsive feeding is embedded in a theoretical framework of responsive parenting. J Nutr. Mar;141(3):490-4.
11. Mascola AJ, et al. 2010. Picky eating during childhood: a longitudinal study to age 11 years. Eat Behav. Dec;11(4):253-7.
12. Jo Cormack PhD 2022 published PhD thesis.
13. Batsell WR Jr, et al. 2002. "You will eat all of that!": a retrospective analysis of forced consumption episodes. Appetite. Jun;38(3):211-9.
14. Jansen P, et al. 2017. Bi-directional associations between child fussy eating and parents' pressure to eat: Who influences whom? Physiology & Behavior, 176, 101–106.
15. Michal M, et al. 2014. If It's Useful and You Know It, Do You Eat? Preschoolers Refrain from Instrumental Food. Journal of Consumer Research. Oct;42(3):642–55.
16. Rhodes-Courter A. *Three little words: a memoir.* Atheneum, 2008.
17. Scaglioni S, et al. 2008. Influence of parental attitudes in the development of children eating behaviour. Br J Nutr. Feb;99 Suppl 1:S22-5.
18. Fisher JO, et al. 2002. Parental influences on young girls' fruit and vegetable, micronutrient, and fat intakes. J Am Diet Assoc. Jan;102(1):58-64.
19. Pliner P, et al. 2000. "Pass the ketchup, please:" familiar flavors increase children's willingness to taste novel foods. Appetite. 2000;34:95-103.
20. Havermans RC, et al. 2007. Increasing children's liking of vegetables through flavour-learning. Appetite. 2007;48:259-62.
21. DeJesus JM, et al. 2019. Children eat more food when they prepare it themselves. Appetite. Feb 1;133:305-312.

Chapter 6

1. Cardona Cano S, et al. 2015. Trajectories of picky eating during childhood: A general population study. Int J Eat Disord. Sep;48(6):570-9.
2. Fernandez C, et al. 2020. Trajectories of Picky Eating in Low-Income US Children. Pediatrics. Jun;145(6):e20192018.
3. Zimmer M, et al. 2012. Policy Statement: Sensory Integration Therapies for Children with Developmental and Behavioral Disorders. Pediatrics. 2012; 129:1186-8.

4. Delahooke, M. *Beyond behaviors: using brain science and compassion to understand and solve children's behavioral challenges.* PESI Publishing & Media, 2019. (page 69)
5. Segal I, et al. 2014. Role reversal method for treatment of food refusal associated with infantile feeding disorders. J Pediatr Gastroenterol Nutr. Jun;58(6):739-42.
6. Bartoshuk LM, et al. 1994. PTC/PROP tasting: anatomy, psychophysics, and sex effects. Physiol Behav. Dec;56(6):1165-71.
7. Kupferstein H. 2018. Evidence of increased PTSD symptoms in autistics exposed to applied behavior analysis. Advances in Autism. 2018;4(1):19-29.

Chapter 7

1. Centers for Disease Control. "About BMI For Children and Teens." https://www.cdc.gov/healthyweight/assessing/bmi/childrens_bmi/about_childrens_bmi.html.
2. Wright CM, et al. 2022. Body composition data show that high BMI centiles overdiagnose obesity in children aged under 6 years. Am J Clin Nutr. Jul 6;116(1):122-131.
3. Pan, L, et al. 2013. Incidence of obesity among young U.S. children living in low-income families, 2008-2011. Pediatrics. Dec;132(6):1006-13.
4. Simmonds M, et al. 2016. Predicting adult obesity from childhood obesity: a systematic review and meta-analysis. Obes Rev. Feb;17(2):95-107.
5. Bacon L, et al. 2011. Weight science: evaluating the evidence for a paradigm shift. Nutr J. Jan 24;10:9.
6. Brann LS. 2008. Classifying preadolescent boys based on their weight status and percent body fat produces different groups. J Am Diet Assoc. Jun; 108(6):1018-22.
7. Wilkes M et al. Relationship of BMI z score to fat percent and fat mass in multiethnic prepubertal children. Pediatr Obes. 2019 Jan;14(1).
8. McCormick DP, et al. 1991. Spinal bone mineral density in 335 normal and obese children and adolescents: evidence for ethnic and sex differences. J Bone Miner Res. May;6(5):507-13.
9. Charbonneau-Roberts G, et al. 2005. Body mass index may overestimate the prevalence of overweight and obesity among the Inuit. Int J Circumpolar Health. Apr;64(2):163-9.
10. Ryan A, et al. 1990. Median skinfold thickness distributions and fat-wave patterns in Mexican American children form the Hispanic health and nutrition examination survey (HHANES 1982-84.) The American Journal of Clinical Nutrition.1990;51:925S-35S.
11. Eisenmann JC, et al. 2000. Growth and overweight of Navajo youth: secular changes from 1955 to 1997. Int J Obes Relat Metab Disord. Feb;24(2):211-8.

12. Weber DR, et al. 2013. Fat and lean BMI reference curves in children and adolescents and their utility in identifying excess adiposity compared with BMI and percentage body fat. Am J Clin Nutr. Jul;98(1):49-56.
13. Serdula MK, et al. 1993. Do obese children become obese adults? A review of the literature. Prev Med. 1993 Mar;22(2):167-77.
14. Whitlock EP, et al. 2005. Screening and interventions for childhood overweight: a summary of evidence for the US Preventive Services Task Force. Pediatrics. Jul;116(1):e125-44.
15. Madsen KA, et al. 2021. Effect of school-based body mass index reporting in California public schools: a randomized clinical trial. JAMA Pediatr. Mar 1;175(3):251-259.
16. Davison KK, et al. 2001. Weight status, parent reaction, and self-concept in five-year-old girls. Pediatrics. Jan;107(1):46-53.
17. Haines J, et al. 2006. Prevention of obesity and eating disorders: a consideration of shared risk factors. Health Educ Res. Dec;21(6):770-82.
18. Neumark-Sztainer D, et al. 2008. Accurate parental classification of overweight adolescents' weight status: does it matter? Pediatrics. Jun; 121(6):e1495-502.
19. Rollins BY, et al. 2016. Alternatives to restrictive feeding practices to promote self-regulation in childhood: a developmental perspective. Pediatr Obes. Oct; 11(5):326-32.
20. Hamer M, et al. 2012. Metabolically healthy obesity and risk of all-cause and cardiovascular disease mortality. J Clin Endocrinol Metab. Jul;97(7):2482-8.
21. Wei M, et al. 1999. Relationship between low cardiorespiratory fitness and mortality in normal-weight, overweight, and obese men. JAMA. Oct 27;282(16):1547-53.
22. Bacon L, et al. 2011. Weight science: evaluating the evidence for a paradigm shift. Nutr J. Jan 24;10:9.
23. Koolhaas CM, et al. 2017. Impact of physical activity on the association of overweight and obesity with cardiovascular disease: The Rotterdam Study. Eur J Prev Cardiol. Jun;24(9):934-941.
24. Barry VW, et al. 2014. Fitness vs. fatness on all-cause mortality: a meta-analysis. Prog Cardiovasc Dis. Jan-Feb;56(4):382-90.
25. Matheson EM, King DE, Everett CJ. Healthy lifestyle habits and mortality in overweight and obese individuals. J Am Board Fam Med. 2012 Jan-Feb;25(1):9-15.
26. Flegal KM, et al. 2005. Excess deaths associated with underweight, overweight, and obesity. JAMA. 2005;293:1861-7.
27. Allen DB, et al. 2007. Fitness is a stronger predictor of fasting insulin levels than fatness in overweight male middle-school children. J Pediatr. Apr;150(4):383-7.

28. Gruberg L, et al. 2005. Arterial revascularization therapies study investigators. Impact of body mass index on the outcome of patients with multivessel disease randomized to either coronary artery bypass grafting or stenting in the ARTS trial: The obesity paradox II? Am J Cardiol. Feb 15;95(4):439-44.
29. Howard BV, et al. 2006. Low-fat dietary pattern and weight change over 7 years: the Women's Health Initiative Dietary Modification Trial. JAMA. Jan 4;295(1):39-49.
30. Bjørge T, et al. 2008. Body mass index in adolescence in relation to cause-specific mortality: a follow-up of 230,000 Norwegian adolescents. Am J Epidemiol. Jul 1;168(1):30-7.
31. Fernandes MM. The effect of soft drink availability in elementary schools on consumption. J Am Diet Assoc. 2008 Sep;108(9):1445-52.
32. Shapiro LR, et al. 1984. Obesity prognosis: a longitudinal study of children from the age of 6 months to 9 years. Am J Public Health. Sep;74(9):968-72.
33. Rocandio AM, et al. 2001. Comparison of dietary intake among overweight and non-overweight schoolchildren. Int J Obes Relat Metab Disord. Nov;25(11):1651-5.
34. Rolland-Cachera MF, et al. 1986. No correlation between adiposity and food intake: why are working class children fatter? Am J Clin Nutr. Dec;44(6):779-87.
35. Günther AL, et al. 2011. Association of dietary energy density in childhood with age and body fatness at the onset of the pubertal growth spurt. Br J Nutr. Aug;106(3):345-9.
36. Rosenbaum M, et al. 2008. Long-term persistence of adaptive thermogenesis in subjects who have maintained a reduced body weight. Am J Clin Nutr. Oct;88(4):906-12.
37. Sumithran P, et al. 2011. Long-term persistence of hormonal adaptations to weight loss. N Engl J Med. Oct 27;365(17):1597-604.
38. Greenway FL. Physiological adaptations to weight loss and factors favouring weight regain. Int J Obes. 2015 Aug;39(8):1188-96.
39. Sole-Smith, V. (January 10, 2021). "How Fatphobia Is Leading to Poor Care in the Pandemic." Elemental.
40. Chastain R. (June, 2015). "Does it Matter That Dieting Can Lead to Weight Gain?" Weight and Healthcare Substack. www.weightandhealthcare.substack.com.
41. Yr Fat Friend. (January 12, 2020). "The Biggest Loser' Is One of the Most Harmful Reality Shows on Television." Medium.
42. Andreyeva T, et al. 2008. Changes in perceived weight discrimination among Americans, 1995-1996 through 2004-2006. Obesity (Silver Spring). May;16(5):1129-34.
43. Association for Psychological Science. (January 7, 2019). "Implicit Attitudes Can Change Over the Long Term." www.psychologicalscience.org.

44. O'Hara L, et al. 2021. Evaluating the impact of a brief Health at Every Size®-informed health promotion activity on body positivity and internalized weight-based oppression. Body Image. Jun;37:225-237.
45. McCormack LA, et al. 2011. Weight-related teasing in a racially diverse sample of sixth-grade children. J Am Diet Assoc. Mar;111(3):431-6.
46. Libbey HP, et al. 2008. Teasing, disordered eating behaviors, and psychological morbidities among overweight adolescents. Obesity (Silver Spring). Nov;16 Suppl 2:S24-9.
47. Gaesser GA, et al. 2021. Obesity treatment: Weight loss versus increasing fitness and physical activity for reducing health risks. iScience. Sep 20;24(10):102995.
48. Hampl SE, et al. 2023. Clinical Practice Guidelines for the Evaluation and Treatment of Children and Adolescents With Obesity. Pediatrics. Feb 1;151(2).
49. Golden NH, et al. 2016. Committee on Nutrition; Committee on Adolescence; Section on Obesity. Preventing Obesity and Eating Disorders in Adolescents. Pediatrics. Sep;138(3).
50. Van Hare, H. (October 5, 2017). "'Small Plates Help You Eat Less' and Other Nutrition Lies Were Based on Bogus Research." The Daily Meal.
51. Ueland O, et al. 2009. Effect of portion size information on food intake. JADA. 2009;109:124-27.
52. Rolls B, et al, 2007. Using a smaller plate did not reduce energy intake at meals. Appetite. 2007;49:652-60.
53. Westwater ML, et al. 2016. Sugar addiction: the state of the science. Eur J Nutr. Nov;55(Suppl 2):55-69.
54. Kirkpatrick M, Kinavey H, Sturtevant D. (March 8, 2019). "Rethinking Food Addiction." Center for Body Trust. www.centerforbodytrust.com.
55. Friedman, D. (2009). "The Night My World Caved In." Story Bleed. http://storybleed.com/2009/07/the-night-my-world-caved-in
56. Intuitive Eating Studies. The Original Intuitive Eating Pros. www.intuitiveeating.org.
57. Satter, E. (March 14, 2022). "ecSatter is Correlated with Superior Wellness Indicators." Ellyn Satter Institute. www.ellynsatterinstitute.org.
58. Nagoski, E and Nagoski, A. *Burnout: The Secret to Unlocking the Stress Cycle*. New York: Ballantine Books, 2019.
59. Sole-Smith V. (June 15, 2021). "Ask Virginia: Is My Child's Body Size My Fault?" Burnt Toast Substack. www.virginiasolesmith.substack.com.
60. Brooks, S and Severson, A. *How to Raise An Intuitive Eater: Raising The Next Generation With Food And Body Confidence*. New York: St. Martin's Press, 2022. Page 306.
61. Brooks, S and Severson, A. *How to Raise An Intuitive Eater: Raising The Next Generation With Food And Body Confidence*. New York: St. Martin's Press, 2022. Page 305.

Chapter 8

1. Lohse B, et al. 2010. PREDIMED Study Investigators. Eating competence of elderly Spanish adults is associated with a healthy diet and a favorable cardiovascular disease risk profile. J Nutr. Jul;140(7):1322-7.
2. Lohse B, et al. 2007. Measuring eating competence: psychometric properties and validity of the ecSatter Inventory. J Nutr Educ Behav. Sep-Oct;39 (5 Suppl):S154-66.
3. Intuitive Eating Studies. The Original Intuitive Eating Pros. https://www.intuitiveeating.org/resources/studies.
4. Van der Horst K. 2012. Overcoming picky eating: eating enjoyment as a central aspect of children's eating behaviors. Appetite. 2012;58:576-74.
5. Zellner DA, et al. 2006. Food selection changes under stress. Physiol Behav. Apr 15;87(4):789-93.
6. Herman CP, et al. 1987. The illusion of counter-regulation. Appetite. 1987;9:161-169.
7. Roemmich JN, et al. 2002. Dietary restraint and stress-induced snacking in youth. Obes Res. Nov;10(11):1120-6.
8. Crum AJ, et al. 2011. Mind over milkshakes: mindsets, not just nutrients, determine ghrelin response. Health Psychol. Jul;30(4):424-9.
9. Besson T, et al. 2019. The calories underestimation of "organic" food: Exploring the impact of implicit evaluations. Appetite. Jun 1;137:134-144.
10. Saulais L, et al. 2012. "Consumer Knowledge About Dietary Fats: Another French Paradox?" British Food Journal. Jan;114(1):108-20.
11. Michal Maimaran, Ayelet Fishbach, If It's Useful and You Know It, Do You Eat? Preschoolers Refrain from Instrumental Food, Journal of Consumer Research, Volume 41, Issue 3, 1 October 2014, Pages 642–655.
12. Thomas, L. (Feb 2023). "Fundamentals: Why Teaching Kids That Food is 'Healthy' Can Backfire." Can I Have Another Snack Substack.
13. Hallberg L, et al. 1977. Iron absorption from Southeast Asian diets. II. Role of various factors that might explain low absorption. Am J Clin Nutr. Apr;30(4):539-48.
14. Barclay GR, et al. 1987. Effect of psychological stress on salt and water transport in the human jejunum. Gastroenterology. Jul;93(1):91-7.
15. Newman, T. (September 7, 2017). "Is the Placebo Effect Real?" Medical News Today.
16. Lembo A, Kelley JM, Nee J, Ballou S, Iturrino J, Cheng V, Rangan V, Katon J, Hirsch W, Kirsch I, Hall K, Davis RB, Kaptchuk TJ. Open-label placebo vs double-blind placebo for irritable bowel syndrome: a randomized clinical trial. Pain. 2021 Sep 1;162(9):2428-2435.
17. Vance, E. *Suggestible You: The Curious Science of Your Brain's Ability to Deceive, Transform, and Heal.* Washington DC: National Geographic, 2016.

18. Reynolds, G. (January 9, 2019). "Mind May Trump DNA." New York Times.
19. Neumark-Sztainer D, et al. 2006. Obesity, disordered eating, and eating disorders in a longitudinal study of adolescents: how do dieters fare 5 years later? J Am Diet Assoc. Apr;106(4):559-68.
20. Sole-Smith, V. (July 20, 2021). "So What About Processed Foods?" Burnt Toast Substack.
21. Harrison, C. *Anti-Diet: Reclaim Your Time, Money, Well-Being, and Happiness Through Intuitive Eating*. New York, NY: Little Brown 2019.
22. O'Dea, J. 2000. School-based interventions to prevent eating problems: First do no harm. Eating Disorders: The Journal of Treatment & Prevention, 2000;8(2), 123–130.
23. Neumark-Sztainer D. 2009. Preventing obesity and eating disorders in adolescents: what can health care providers do? J Adolesc Health. Mar;44(3): 206-13.

Chapter 9

1. Delahooke, M. *Beyond behaviors: using brain science and compassion to understand and solve children's behavioral challenges*. Eau Claire, WI: PESI Publishing & Media, 2019.
2. Gordon KH, et al. 2006. The impact of client race on clinician detection of eating disorders. Behav Ther. Dec;37(4):319-25.
3. Crow SJ, et al. 2009. Increased mortality in bulimia nervosa and other eating disorders. Am J Psychiatry. Dec;166(12):1342-6.
4. Fisher JO, et al. 2000. Parents' restrictive feeding practices are associated with young girls' negative self-evaluation of eating. J Am Diet Assoc. Nov;100(11):1341-6.
5. Roemmich JN, et al. 2002. Dietary restraint and stress-induced snacking in youth. Obesity Research. 2002;10:1120-6.
6. Fisher JO, et al. 1995. Fat preferences and fat consumption of 3- to 5-year-old children are related to parental adiposity. J Am Diet Assoc. Jul;95(7):759-64.
7. Fisher JO, et al. 2002. Eating in the absence of hunger and overweight in girls from 5 to 7 y of age. Am J Clin Nutr. Jul;76(1):226-31.
8. Norris ML, et al. 2014. Exploring avoidant/restrictive food intake disorder in eating disordered patients: a descriptive study. Int J Eat Disord. Jul;47(5):495-9.
9. Strandjord SE, et al. 2015. Avoidant/Restrictive Food Intake Disorder: Illness and Hospital Course in Patients Hospitalized for Nutritional Insufficiency. J Adolesc Health. 2015 Dec;57(6):673-8.
10. Anonymous author. (June 1, 2018). "Autism and Controlled Eating." National Autistic Society. www.autism.org.uk.

Chapter 10

1. Schilling, L and Peterson, WJ. *Born to Eat: Raising Happy, Healthy Eaters on Real, Whole Foods.* New York, NY: Skyhorse Publishing, 2017.
2. Rapley, G and Murkett, T. *Baby Led Weaning: The Essential Guide to Introducing Solid Foods and Helping Your Baby to Grow Up a Happy and Confident Eater.* New York: The Experiment, 2010.
3. Williams EL, et al. 2018. Impact of a modified version of baby-led weaning on infant food and nutrient intakes: the bliss randomized controlled trial. Nutrients. Jun 7;10(6):740.
4. Devine, E. (December 16, 2019). "Supporting Siblings in a Chaotic Space." www.eileendevine.com.
5. Chastain, R. (November 24, 2014). "Dealing With Family and Friends Food Police." Dances with Fat blog. www.danceswithfat.org.
6. Ramsay SA, et al. 2010. "Are you done?" Child care providers' verbal communication at mealtimes that reinforce or hinder children's internal cues of hunger and satiation. J Nutr Educ Behav. Jul-Aug;42(4):265-70.

Chapter 11

1. Thomas, L. (May, 2023). "No, Your Toddler Doesn't Need Protein Bars...." Can I Have Another Snack Substack.
2. Taubes, G. (June 2, 2012). "Salt, We Misjudged You." The New York Times.
3. Hooper L, et al. (January 2004). "The Long Term Effects of Advice to Cut Down on Salt in Food on Deaths, Cardiovascular Disease and Blood Pressure in Adults." Cochrane Review.
4. Stolarz-Skrzypek K, et al. 2011. Fatal and Nonfatal Outcomes, Incidence of Hypertension, and Blood Pressure Changes in Relation to Urinary Sodium Excretion. JAMA. 2011;305:1777-85.
5. Coldwell SE, et al. 2010. Biological drive for sugar as marker of growth differs between adolescents with high versus low sugar preference. Clin Nutr. 2010;29:288–303.
6. Harbaugh WT, et al. 2007. Neural responses to taxation and voluntary giving reveal motives for charitable donations. Science. Jun 15;316(5831): 1622-5.
7. Benton D. 2010. The plausibility of sugar addiction and its role in obesity and eating disorders. Clin Nutr. Jun;29(3):288-303.
8. US FDA. "Additional Information About High-Intensity Sweeteners Permitted for Use in Food in the United States." www.fda.gov
9. Gorvet, Z. 2023. "Aspartame: What else is 'possibly carcinogenic'?" BBC.com.
10. Raatz SK, et al. 2015. Consumption of honey, sucrose, and high-fructose corn syrup produces similar metabolic effects in glucose-tolerant and -intolerant individuals. J Nutr. Oct;145(10):2265-72.

11. Wojcicki JM, et al. 2009. Risk factors for obesity at age 3 in Alaskan children, including the role of beverage consumption: results from Alaska PRAMS 2005-2006 and its three-year follow-up survey, CUBS, 2008-2009. PLoS One. 2015 Mar 20;10(3).
12. Sakaki JR, et al. 2022. Fruit juice and childhood obesity: a review of epidemiologic studies. Crit Rev Food Sci Nutr. Feb 28:1-15.
13. Crowe-White K, et al. 2016. Impact of 100% Fruit juice consumption on diet and weight status of children: an evidence-based review. Crit Rev Food Sci Nutr. 2016;56(5):871-84.
14. Satter E. 2000. A moderate view on fat restriction for young children. J Am Diet Assoc. Jan;100(1):32-6.
15. Huh SY, et al. 2010. Prospective association between milk intake and adiposity in preschool-aged children. J Am Diet Assoc. Apr;110(4):563-70.
16. Vicini J, et al. 2008. Survey of retail milk composition as affected by label claims regarding farm-management practices. J Am Diet Assoc. Jul;108(7):1198-203.
17. Rajakumar K, et al. 2015. Effect of vitamin D3 supplementation in black and in white children: a randomized, placebo-controlled trial. J Clin Endocrinol Metab. 2015;100(8):3183-3192.
18. Thomas, L. (June, 2023). "Gentle Nutrition for Vegan Kids." Can I Have Another Snack Substack.
19. Venter C, et al. 2008. Prevalence and cumulative incidence of food hypersensitivity in the first 3 years of life. Allergy. 2008;63:354-9.
20. Fleischer DM, et al. 2021. A consensus approach to the primary prevention of food allergy through nutrition: guidance from the American Academy of Allergy, Asthma, and Immunology; American College Of Allergy, Asthma, and Immunology; and The Canadian Society for Allergy and Clinical Immunology. J Allergy Clin Immunol Pract. 2021 Jan;9(1):22-43.
21. Upton, J. Food Allergy Canada. (February 25, 2020). "Mythbuster – Are food sensitivity tests (IgG tests) helpful for diagnosing a food allergy?" www.foodallergycanada.ca.
22. Pelsser LM, et al. 2017. Diet and ADHD, reviewing the evidence: a systematic review of meta-analyses of double-blind placebo-controlled trials evaluating the efficacy of diet interventions on the behavior of children with ADHD. PLoS One. Jan 25;12(1).
23. Rettner, R. (October 12, 2018). "Hundreds of Dietary Supplements Are Tainted with Prescription Drugs." Scientific American.
24. Low-Carbohydrate High-Fat "Keto-Like" Diet Associated With Increased Risk of CVDMar 05, 2023American College of Cardiology https://www.acc.org/latest-in-cardiology/articles/2023/03/01/22/45/sun-1215pm-kctogenic-acc-2023.

Chapter 12

1. Bentley B, et al. 2011. Practice roundtable, eosinophilic sophagitis in young children: a comprehensive approach. Infant, Child and Adolescent Nutrition. 2011;3(6):332-35.
2. Sole-Smith, V. (Dec 15, 2020). "The Restorative Power of Secret Food Rituals." New York Times. https://www.nytimes.com/2020/12/15/parenting/pandemic-comfort-eating.html.
3. Rogers, F. *The Mister Rogers Parenting Book: Helping To Understand Your Young Child.* Running Press, 2002.

Medical Appendix

1. Gordon M, et al. 2022. Psychosocial interventions for the treatment of functional abdominal pain disorders in children: a systematic review and meta-analysis. JAMA Pediatr. Jun 1;176(6):560-568.
2. The Patient Education Website of the American Society for Reproductive Medicine. (2014). "Normal and abnormal puberty in girls." www.reproductivefacts.org.
3. Biro FM, et al. 2013. Onset of breast development in a longitudinal cohort. Pediatrics. Dec;132(6):1019-27.
4. Safe M, et al. 2016. Widespread use of gastric acid inhibitors in infants: Are they needed? Are they safe? World J Gastrointest Pharmacol Ther. Nov 6;7(4):531-539.
5. Murray HB, et al. 2018. Prevalence in primary school youth of pica and rumination behavior: The understudied feeding disorders. Int J Eat Disord. Aug;51(8):994-998.
6. Murray HB, et al. 2019. Diagnosis and treatment of rumination syndrome: a critical review. Am J Gastroenterol. Apr;114(4):562-578.

Index

A

E

G

J

K

L

M

N

O

P

R

Made in United States
Orlando, FL
04 October 2024